Who Was
Franklin Roosevelt?

Who Was
Franklin Roosevelt?

by Margaret Frith
illustrated by John O'Brien

Grosset & Dunlap
An Imprint of Penguin Random House

For my American Mother—MF

For Terase—JO

GROSSET & DUNLAP
Penguin Young Readers Group
An Imprint of Penguin Random House LLC

Text copyright © 2010 by Margaret Frith. Illustrations copyright © 2010 by John O'Brien. Cover illustration copyright © 2010 by Penguin Random House LLC. All rights reserved. Published by Grosset & Dunlap, an imprint of Penguin Random House LLC, 345 Hudson Street, New York, New York 10014. Who HQ™ and all related logos are trademarks owned by Penguin Random House LLC. GROSSET & DUNLAP is a trademark of Penguin Random House LLC. Printed in the USA.

Library of Congress Control Number: 2009023143

ISBN 978-0-448-45346-0

20 19

Contents

Contents

Who Was
Franklin Delano Roosevelt?

When Franklin Delano Roosevelt died in 1945, a young soldier stood in front of the White House remembering his president. "I felt as if I knew him. I felt as if he knew me—and I felt as if he liked me." He was saying what so many Americans were feeling.

FDR, as he was called, had been president since 1933. He was elected four times, serving for twelve years. This was longer than any other president before or since.

When Franklin took office, there were lots of problems waiting for him. Banks were failing. People were out of work. Many had lost their homes. This was the Great Depression.

Franklin wasn't a man to sit around and wonder what to do. In the first hundred days, he signed fifteen major laws bringing help. No president had ever gotten so much done so fast.

Franklin not only dealt with the Depression, he led the country through the dark days of World War II.

What made him such a strong leader? Perhaps his strength came in part from a personal crisis. It happened when he was thirty-nine years old. He was on summer vacation with his family. Overnight he was struck with a disease called *polio.* Franklin never walked again. But he fought hard to stay strong and healthy. He never gave up. He ran the country with the same spirit and optimism.

Not everyone liked Franklin's ideas. But most of the country loved him. Millions wept as if he were part of their family when they learned of his sudden death. Many could not imagine the United States without FDR as president.

Chapter 1
Growing Up in Hyde Park

SPRINGWOOD

In a big house called Springwood, high above the Hudson River in Hyde Park, New York, a baby boy was born on January 30, 1882.

"At a quarter to nine my Sallie had a splendid large baby boy. He weighs ten pounds without clothes," his father, James Roosevelt, wrote. The baby's mother, Sara Delano Roosevelt, said that he was "pink, plump and nice." She named him Franklin after her favorite uncle.

When they met, Sara was twenty-five and James was fifty-one, a widower with a grown son. James fell in love with Sara at a dinner party. The hostess remembered that James couldn't keep his eyes off Sara. They were married in 1880.

Sara and James came from old, wealthy families in the Hudson Valley. They grew up in lovely homes with lots of help—cooks, butlers, maids, and gardeners. James was a gentleman farmer and hired workers to do the farming.

Franklin was an only child. He was the apple of his mother's eye and Franklin loved her very much, even when she was bossy.

Franklin grew up around adults. He did not go to school. He was taught at home by tutors until he was thirteen. Yet, even with no other

children around, Franklin found life at Springwood fun. In the winter, he went on sleigh rides or sledded full speed down snowy hills. He was happy exploring the woods and fields. Franklin loved horseback riding with Popsy. That's what he called his father.

From an early age, Franklin began collecting stamps. This was a hobby he enjoyed all his life. His greatest love, however, was the sea. He played with model boats. He sailed in the summer. And when he was older, he went iceboating on the Hudson River in the bitter cold. (An iceboat was like a sled with sails and went very fast.)

When Franklin was nine, Popsy bought a
yacht called the *Half Moon*. Franklin was excited
to go sailing on it at Campobello.

Campobello is an island off the east coast of Canada. The Roosevelts spent summers there in a cottage they had built. The strong winds and high tides made sailing around the island tricky. But Franklin loved the challenge and became a fine sailor. At sixteen, he had his own sailboat, *New Moon*.

Another family on Campobello told the Roosevelts about the Groton School. It was a boarding school north of Boston, Massachusetts. Franklin's parents decided to send him there.

Most of the boys started at Groton when they were twelve. But Franklin didn't go until he was fourteen. His mother couldn't bear to let him go earlier. Not surprisingly, he was homesick at first.

Life at Groton was very different from Springwood. It was modeled after an English boarding school with no frills and a harsh lifestyle. Franklin lived in a room with other boys. Once, during the night, snow blew in through an open transom of the dorm. Franklin and the boys woke up nearly freezing. Still, that didn't excuse them from the cold shower they had to take every morning.

Sports were important at Groton, and to Franklin. He loved playing football. He was slight and not very fast. Still, he fought hard and had the scrapes and bumps to prove it.

His parents were more interested in his studies. It pleased them that he was fourth in his class of nineteen boys.

HARVARD YARD

In the spring of 1900, Franklin graduated from Groton. That fall, he entered Harvard. For the past few years, his father's health had been failing. Soon after Thanksgiving, Franklin got word that Popsy was very ill. He died of heart failure on December 8.

Now Sara was a widow. Rather than spend the winter in Hyde Park alone, she moved to Boston to be near Franklin. Already close, mother and son grew even closer.

At Harvard, Franklin became a great success on the *Crimson*, the college newspaper. He was a natural writer with a knack for good interviews. His senior year, he was president of the *Crimson*. But the most significant thing that happened during his Harvard years was his friendship with his distant cousin Eleanor Roosevelt.

Chapter 2
Meeting Eleanor

Unlike Franklin, Eleanor had an unhappy childhood. Her father was the younger brother of Theodore Roosevelt, who became president in 1901. Elliott was handsome and engaging.

Eleanor adored him and he adored his little
daughter. But he had a bad drinking problem.
Her mother, Anna Hall Roosevelt, was a cold
and distant mother. She called Eleanor "Granny"
because she was such a serious child. Eleanor
felt like an awkward ugly duckling next to her
beautiful mother.

Both of Eleanor's parents and her younger brother had all died by the time she was ten. So she and her six-year-old brother, Hall, were sent to live with their grandparents. The Halls found it a burden to have two young children come to live with them.

Often lonely, Eleanor would escape into dreams of happy times with her father. One bright spot was Christmastime when she would see her Roosevelt cousins at parties.

Franklin was at one of these parties. He asked her to dance. She accepted even though she didn't know how. It didn't seem to matter to Franklin.

After that, they didn't see each other again for several years. Eleanor went off to boarding school in England. (She said later that these were "the happiest years of her life.")

At eighteen, she returned to America. As a young girl from a famous family, it was time for her to take her place in New York society. She said she was in "utter agony."

But she saw Franklin again at the parties. When he invited her to his twenty-first birthday party at Springwood, she went. Gradually they began seeing more of each other. He was fun and he made her laugh.

Franklin's mother didn't want her son to get serious about any girl. She wanted him to finish college and start a career. Yet Franklin grew fonder and fonder of Eleanor. She was smart and more interesting than other girls. She had lived and traveled in Europe. She spoke French even better than he did. And with her tall, slim figure, gold hair that fell below her waist, and lovely blue eyes, she was not an "ugly duckling." Not in his eyes.

Franklin asked Eleanor to marry him and she said yes. Sara was not at all pleased with the news. But she stayed calm and asked them not to rush into marriage. They were too young. So Franklin and Eleanor agreed to wait. Sara whisked her son off on a six-week cruise to the Caribbean. Secretly she hoped he might forget Eleanor. Instead, the trip made him long to get back to her.

Finally, in the fall of 1904, Sara gave in and they announced their engagement. Franklin and Eleanor were married in New York City on March 17, 1905. Eleanor's uncle Ted, the president, gave away the bride.

After a three-month honeymoon, the couple returned to New York City. Sara had taken care of everything, leaving Eleanor with nothing to do. They moved into a home completely furnished and only three blocks from where Sara lived in New York. (A few years later, Sara would build two buildings next to each other with connecting doors on different floors that were never locked. It was almost like living together.)

The couple's first child, Anna Eleanor, was born in 1906. James was born a year later. Sadly, their third child, Franklin, would die of the flu

when he was only eight months old. They would have three more children—Elliott, Franklin Jr., and John.

Franklin studied at Columbia Law School just as Eleanor's uncle Ted had. Then he joined a well-known law firm on Wall Street. However, the job never really excited him. And, although he loved Hyde Park, Franklin did not want to spend his life as a gentleman farmer like his father.

What did appeal to him? Politics! So, in 1910, Franklin ran for office. He was twenty-eight years old.

Chapter 3
Running for Office

Important Democrats in the Hyde Park area asked Franklin to run for the New York Senate.

If he won, he would work in Albany, the state capital. With a famous last name and the money to pay for his own campaign, Franklin seemed like a good candidate, even though most of the voters in the district were Republicans.

But he knew that the Roosevelt name wasn't enough. He needed voters to get to know him.

So he hired a large, flashy, red automobile and asked a popular congressman to travel with him. Off they went in high spirits, flags flying, the wind in their faces.

People enjoyed meeting this friendly young man who talked about honest government. On election day, he defeated his opponent by 1,440 votes. He spent three years in the state senate and became known for being independent. He was not someone who did what the party bosses

LOUIS HOWE

told him. It was also during this time that he met a newspaperman named Louis Howe. Howe became a lifelong friend and aide.

In 1912, Franklin attended the Democratic Convention in Baltimore, Maryland. He was backing Governor Woodrow Wilson from New Jersey for president. Wilson won the nomination and went on to win the election in November.

Franklin had supported Wilson not only because of his ideas, but also because he hoped to land a job in Washington. That happened

WOODROW WILSON

almost right way! Franklin was asked if he would like to become Assistant Secretary of the Navy.

"How would I like it? I'd like it bully well," he answered.

With his love of the sea and sailing, the navy was just the right place for Franklin. He wanted to learn all he could about the navy. He talked to everyone from admirals to sailors to builders in the yards. He visited naval stations around the

country. It was not unusual to see him climbing up the rigging of a ship as it plowed through the waves. Even top admirals came to respect this young man who had never been in the navy himself.

In 1914, World War I broke out in Europe. In 1917, the United States joined forces against Germany.

Franklin urged the navy to build powerful battleships.

It was a proud day when he hammered the first bolt into a brand-new battleship in the Brooklyn Navy Yard. It was named the USS *Arizona*.

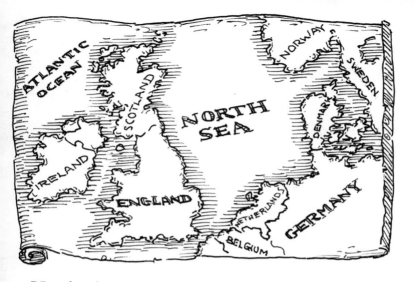

He also had a sharp understanding of warfare. Franklin convinced the navy to lay a belt of underwater mines in the North Sea. German submarines had to pass through this area to get to the Atlantic Ocean in order to attack British and American ships. It was late in the war, but by blowing up German subs, the mines kept the ships safer.

The war ended on November 11, 1918, with Germany's defeat. Franklin was sent to Paris to attend the peace treaty conference.

With the war over, Franklin was ready to return to private life. It was 1920—a presidential election year. To Franklin's surprise, the Democratic candidate for president—James Cox—asked him to run as vice president.

Franklin threw himself into the campaign. He visited twenty states by train, traveling eight thousand miles. He spoke to farmers, factory workers, city workers, businessmen, and women who were voting for the first time.

Franklin and Cox weren't expected to win and they didn't. In fact, they lost badly. But Franklin loved the race. All across the country, people got to know this sunny, optimistic man from New York who seemed to have a great future ahead of him.

Chapter 4
Facing a Crisis

In 1921, Franklin was back in New York working as a lawyer. That August, he joined Eleanor and the children at their cottage on Campobello.

One morning, when the family was out sailing they saw smoke rising from a small island. They sailed over and found a brushfire out of control. Franklin cut evergreen branches and they beat at the flames for hours. Finally, they got the fire out.

Back on Campobello, Franklin and his sons went for a swim. Then Franklin sat around in his wet bathing suit looking at the mail. He felt cold and his back ached, so he went to bed early. The next day, he woke up and could hardly stand.

Eleanor called a doctor. He thought Franklin had a cold. But as the days went by, Franklin grew worse. He couldn't get out of bed. His whole body ached. He was in terrible pain.

Another doctor came. He said the same thing. Franklin had a bad cold. Finally, Eleanor had a doctor from Boston come down and examine Franklin.

He knew immediately what was wrong. Franklin had polio. Polio was a virus that caused high fevers and often left people unable to walk.

Eleanor took Franklin home to New York. If he felt scared or worried, he didn't let on. Right away, he started exercising at home. He was determined to walk again.

In February, Franklin got steel braces for his legs. They were attached to leather belts around his hips and chest. When the hinges at his knees were locked, he was able to stand but not walk. (Later, when he was president, he had his braces painted black. He wore them with black shoes and socks so they wouldn't be noticed.)

Sara convinced Franklin that he would be more comfortable at Springwood. So the family moved to Hyde Park. It was hard for Eleanor. Once again, her mother-in-law was in charge.

The bedrooms at Springwood were on the second floor. There was no way Franklin could use the stairs. Luckily the house had a "trunk lift" for luggage. It was the size of an elevator, so Franklin could fit in it in his wheelchair. It was hauled up and down with ropes and pulleys.

Franklin tried anything he heard about that might help his legs— sunlamps, electric belts, massages, and pulleys.

Once, he even tried hanging from the ceiling by a
harness. Nothing worked. He couldn't walk and
he was no nearer walking with crutches.

Still, he made a wonderful discovery.
Swimming. He could float without any help.
He was sure it was helping his legs.

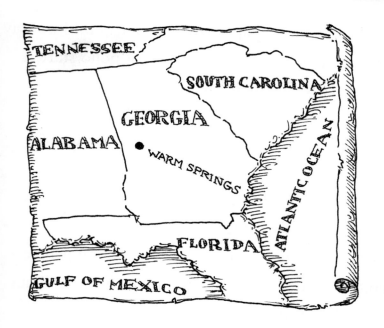

In 1924, Franklin heard about a place with "miracle waters." It was called Warm Springs and it was in the backwoods of Georgia. He and Eleanor needed a vacation so they went.

There was an old hotel, twelve run-down cottages, and a swimming pool. The minute Franklin got in, he beamed. The water was ninety degrees. "How marvelous it feels," he said. "I don't think I'll ever get out."

When a newspaper wrote about Franklin's stay at Warm Springs, other victims of polio started going there. Many of them were children.

Two years later, Franklin bought the resort and restored it. He kept one of the cottages for himself. He visited whenever he could.

Franklin had found a second home. Here he could be himself. He didn't have to pretend everything was all right. He was among people going through what he was going through. They loved Franklin. To them, he was "Rosy."

He had wonderful, boisterous times with the children. Loud laughter and splashing meant that Franklin and the children were playing water games in the pool.

In 1927, Franklin started the Georgia Warm Springs Foundation. It treated victims of polio and became a center for studying the disease.

As for Franklin, he was learning to live fully despite his crippled legs. His car was adapted so

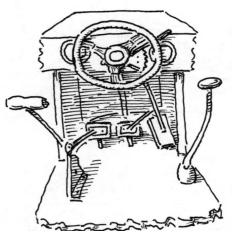

VIEW OF HAND CONTROLS
THIS MADE DRIVING POSSIBLE
WITHOUT USING FEET.

that he could drive using only his hands. He still loved to drive fast. He flew down the roads, stopping to talk to anyone along the way.

It was on these trips around Georgia that Franklin became aware of what it meant to be poor and struggling—to live without electricity or go to a rundown school. He never forgot what he saw.

POLIO

SOME VICTIMS OF POLIO RECOVERED WITH LITTLE OR NO DAMAGE. BUT MANY, LIKE FRANKLIN, WERE NOT SO LUCKY.

MOST POLIO OUTBREAKS OCCURRED IN THE SUMMER. IN THE EPIDEMIC OF 1916, SIX THOUSAND PEOPLE DIED. THE WORST YEAR WAS IN 1952 WHEN THERE WERE OVER FIFTY-SEVEN THOUSAND CASES.

IN 1938, PRESIDENT ROOSEVELT FOUNDED THE MARCH OF DIMES FOR POLIO RESEARCH. EVERYONE WAS ASKED TO SEND IN A DIME.

IN 1955, DR. JONAS SALK CAME UP WITH THE FIRST VACCINE TO PREVENT POLIO. SINCE THAT TIME, POLIO HAS BEEN ELIMINATED IN MOST OF THE WORLD. IT IS TOO BAD FRANKLIN DID NOT LIVE TO SEE A POLIO VACCINE.

AFTER HIS DEATH, HIS PORTRAIT WAS PUT ON THE DIME. HIS PORTRAIT STILL APPEARS ON IT, IN MEMORY OF HIS WORK FOR THE MARCH OF DIMES.

Chapter 5
Struggling to Walk

Franklin was determined to run for office again one day. But he wanted to walk first. It was important for the Democratic Party to remember him. So he kept in touch through letters and phone calls.

Eleanor was determined to keep Franklin's name alive. "I don't want him forgotten," she said. "I want him to have a voice." Louis Howe convinced her to attend political meetings. He coached her on how to speak in public. She began to enjoy a political life of her own. Women's causes were important to her.

Although Franklin worked as hard as he could, he still couldn't walk. But he came up with a way of standing and moving forward, swinging one leg, then the other. He would hold tightly to the arm of a person on one side and use a crutch on the other. Eventually he could lean on a cane instead of a crutch. It wasn't walking, but he made it look like walking.

In 1924, the Democratic Party asked Franklin to nominate Al Smith, the Governor of New York, to run for president. The convention was held in Madison Square Garden in New York City.

AL SMITH

Franklin wanted to appear strong and confident. He got to the podium with the help of a crutch and his son James. It was a great struggle, but Franklin made it with sweat pouring down his face. He gripped the podium and stood straight and tall. His face lit up with a big smile and the crowd went wild.

By now, he must have known that he would never walk again. But a life in politics was certainly possible. And when the time came to campaign, he would face the American people, standing tall.

Four years later, in 1928, Roosevelt was elected governor of New York. He won by only twenty-five thousand votes out of more than four million cast. Still, he won.

Republicans were in charge of the state government. At his opening address, Franklin was charming and cheerful. He spoke of new laws to protect workers and unions. But the Republicans were not interested in hearing about these issues.

Then, in October 1929, the unexpected happened. The stock market on Wall Street crashed and the country turned upside down. People lost their money. Then they lost their jobs.

This was the beginning of the Great Depression.

By 1932, at least twelve million men and
women were out of work. They lined up at soup

kitchens for free food. Many lost their homes and
had nowhere to live. With only the clothes on

their backs, they gathered in "squatter camps"—
sometimes called *Hoovervilles* after the president
Herbert Hoover.

Franklin was convinced that now was the time
to run for president. He campaigned across the
country on the "Roosevelt Special." At every stop,

this tall, attractive, confident man stood and promised to get people back to work. He offered them a future.

HERBERT HOOVER

Americans listened and saw a leader they could count on.

Franklin beat his opponent, President Herbert Hoover, by a landslide. Out of forty-eight states, he lost only six.

The Roosevelt era had begun.

Chapter 6
Becoming President

Franklin's campaign song had been "Happy Days Are Here Again." After he was sworn in as the thirty-second president of the United States,

Franklin spoke to the nation. He promised them: "Action and action now." He was going to start new programs to help them. He said, "The only thing we have to fear is fear itself."

People were certainly afraid. They no longer trusted banks to keep their money safe. So they lined up to take out their savings. Without money, banks were collapsing all over the country.

Immediately, Franklin declared a four-day bank holiday. No one could take out money because banks were closed. Franklin hoped this "time-out" would calm people down. The holiday worked, but Franklin had no way of knowing that beforehand.

All his life, Franklin was willing to experiment. If he tried something and it didn't work, he would try something else. He wanted to hear ideas and opinions from lots of people. "Above all, try something."

Franklin gave his first "fireside chat" on the radio. He wanted everyone to understand what he was doing to fix the banks. "It is safer for you to keep your money in a reopened bank than to keep it under the mattress," he told them.

The White House received thousands of letters and telegrams. The fireside chat was a huge success. The president had spoken to people as a friend. They felt he cared about their problems.

FIRESIDE CHATS ON THE RADIO

IN THE YEARS THAT FRANKLIN WAS PRESIDENT, HE HELD THIRTY-ONE OF HIS FAMOUS "FIRESIDE CHATS." THEY ALLOWED FRANKLIN TO EXPLAIN WHAT THE GOVERNMENT WAS DOING AND WHY. HE WANTED TO REACH AS MANY PEOPLE AS POSSIBLE. HIS TALKS WERE USUALLY BROADCAST ON SUNDAY EVENINGS AT NINE O'CLOCK WHEN MOST AMERICANS LISTENED TO THE RADIO.

FDR WOULD BEGIN BY SAYING, ". . . I WANT TO TALK FOR A FEW MINUTES WITH THE PEOPLE OF THE UNITED STATES . . ."

HE WORKED HARD ON WHAT HE SAID AND HOW HE WOULD SAY IT. "I'LL JUST THINK OUT LOUD," HE WOULD TELL HIS SECRETARY, "AND YOU WRITE IT DOWN." DURING A FIRESIDE CHAT, FRANKLIN HAD PEOPLE SITTING IN THE ROOM WITH HIM. HE COULD LOOK AT THEM AND IMAGINE AMERICANS ALL ACROSS THE COUNTRY LISTENING TO HIM ON THE RADIO. AND, INDEED, THEY FELT AS IF FRANKLIN WAS RIGHT IN THEIR HOMES TALKING DIRECTLY TO THEM, AS A FRIEND.

ONE TIME HE HEARD A WHISTLING SOUND COMING THROUGH A GAP BETWEEN HIS FRONT TEETH. HE DIDN'T LIKE IT, SO HE HAD A SPECIAL BRIDGE MADE JUST FOR HIS "FIRESIDE CHATS."

In the first hundred days, Congress passed fifteen major laws to help people get back to work. The programs Franklin had promised were getting underway. They became known across the country as the "New Deal."

He started many new agencies to get working on solutions.

The CCC sent young, out-of-work men to national parks and forests to plant trees, build fire stations, and put out fires.

The AAA helped farmers unable to sell their crops or pay their rent or mortgages.

The WPA built roads, hospitals, schools, and other public buildings. Artists, writers, and musicians were asked to paint murals in public buildings, write books, and perform in concerts around the country.

The NRA drew

up rules to help businesses and workers get along. Rules for prices, wages, and hours of work were set and workers could join unions to bargain with companies.

The TVA brought electricity and other improvements to rural areas in seven southern states. Franklin hadn't forgotten all those people in Georgia living without electricity.

More programs were added later. An important one that still exists today is the SSA created in 1935. The government mailed checks to retired people over sixty-five, the disabled, the unemployed, and needy children. The government got the money from workers' payroll taxes and company taxes.

These new programs cost the government a lot of money. Some people said too much money.

And they didn't like the government running things that they thought should be done by private companies. They didn't like paying higher taxes, either. But these were unusual times. Franklin was sure he was doing the right thing. And the voters thought so, too.

In 1936, Franklin ran again. He won in an even bigger landslide. This time he only lost two states, Maine and Vermont.

TURN ON THE LIGHTS!

THE TENNESSEE VALLEY AUTHORITY (TVA) IMPROVED THE LIVES OF POOR FAMILIES IN THE SOUTH IN MANY WAYS. IT HELPED FARMERS GROW BETTER CROPS. IT BUILT FACTORIES THAT CREATED THOUSANDS OF JOBS. IT BROUGHT ELECTRICITY INTO THE HOMES OF PEOPLE WHO, UNTIL THEN, HAD TO DEPEND ON CANDLELIGHT OR GASLIGHT. THIS WAS MADE POSSIBLE BY GIANT DAMS THAT PROVIDED HYDROELECTRIC POWER TO SEVEN TVA STATES—MOST OF TENNESSEE, PART OF ALABAMA, KENTUCKY AND MISSISSIPPI, AND A SMALL BIT OF GEORGIA, NORTH CAROLINA, AND VIRGINIA.

THE TVA STILL OPERATES TODAY.

Although voters and Congress approved of the New Deal, Franklin faced a big stumbling block with the Supreme Court. If a law passed by Congress goes against the Constitution, it is the Supreme Court's job to strike it down. It did just that with some of the "alphabet" programs, especially the AAA and the NRA. The court said the government did not have the right to start them or pay for them.

Franklin was furious. He had not appointed any of these judges to the Court. They were all conservative judges who believed in as little government as possible. Franklin wanted liberal judges who believed that it was the government's job to be involved. Besides, seven out of the nine judges were over seventy years old and appointed for life. He claimed they weren't getting enough work done fast enough. Franklin decided to pack the Court by appointing an additional judge for every judge over seventy.

To Franklin's surprise, Congress didn't like this idea at all. And neither did the people. Thousands of letters of protest came in. It was not often that Franklin lost a battle. But this time he did.

Over time he did get to choose seven judges. But his power had been checked.

Chapter 7
Living in the White House

"How do you like being president?" a reporter once asked Franklin.

"I love it!" he answered in a great, booming voice.

Franklin also liked living in the White House.

Eleanor wasn't so sure. She once told a friend, "I never wanted to be a president's wife." The First Lady had to host dinners for foreign visitors and parties for members of Congress and other people in government. She would stand for hours shaking hands.

Sometimes, however, Eleanor found being the First Lady fun. When the famous pilot Amelia Earhart came to town, she took

Eleanor flying. "It was like being on top of the world," Eleanor said.

Eleanor also traveled around the country for Franklin. He needed someone he could trust to see how his New Deal was working. He said that she was "his eyes and ears."

In West Virginia, she went down into a coal mine to talk to the miners.

When Sara heard about this, she wrote to Franklin. "I see she has emerged from the mine . . . That is something to be thankful for."

Traveling gave Eleanor a chance to speak about her own causes. She was a champion of the rights of African Americans and women. She urged Franklin to appoint more African Americans and women to government jobs—and he did.

Eleanor constantly wrote memos to Franklin about things she wanted him to do. They were put in a basket in his room each night. He'd read them before bed. The pile got so high that he told her she could only give him three memos a night.

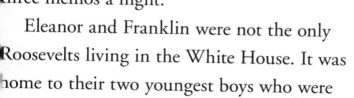

Eleanor and Franklin were not the only Roosevelts living in the White House. It was home to their two youngest boys who were students at Groton. Their daughter, Anna, moved in with her children. So did their son James.

Louis Howe had the Lincoln bedroom. Missy LeHand, who had been Franklin's loyal secretary for thirteen years, also came.

Franklin's Scottie, Fala, was there, too, roaming the White House by day and sleeping in his bedroom at night.

Franklin's bedroom was on the second floor along with his private study where no one went without being asked. He kept his stamp collection on a desk near the door. Being president had its advantages. He asked the State Department to send him stamps on letters from other countrie Every Saturday, a package arrived at the White House.

Franklin woke around eight every morning.
He ate his breakfast and read the newspapers in
bed. Only his grandchildren were allowed in. He
didn't mind at all if they jumped on his bed. He
enjoyed it. Then he dressed and went over his

schedule with Louis Howe. At ten o'clock, he went down to his office. Each visitor was only supposed to stay around fifteen minutes. But Franklin loved to talk and he loved to listen. That's how he learned a lot. So he hardly ever kept to the schedule.

He had lunch around one. Depending on the day, he met with his cabinet or advisors. In the late afternoon he took care of letters and paperwork before going for a swim in the pool.

Then it was cocktail hour. He loved relaxing with family and friends. After dinner, he often worked on his stamp collection or watched a movie.

Franklin enjoyed meetings with reporters. On Wednesday mornings, he talked to reporters from the morning papers and, on Fridays afternoons, the reporters from the evening papers.

Reporters liked Franklin. He sat at his desk and they all crowded around filling up the Oval

Office. Sometimes a reporter would fall right onto his desk from all the pushing to get to the front. Unlike other presidents, he didn't ask to see questions beforehand. They could ask whatever they wanted. Sometimes he didn't want to answer. But he knew how to charm them so they didn't hold it against him.

MARIAN ANDERSON SINGS

IN 1939, MARIAN ANDERSON, A FAMOUS AFRICAN-AMERICAN SINGER, WAS TO GIVE A CONCERT IN CONSTITUTION HALL IN WASHINGTON, D.C. THE HALL WAS OWNED BY A WOMEN'S GROUP CALLED THE DAUGHTERS OF THE AMERICAN REVOLUTION (DAR). THEY REFUSED TO LET AN AFRICAN AMERICAN PERFORM THERE. ELEANOR HAD BEEN A MEMBER OF THE DAR. BUT NOW NOT ONLY DID SHE RESIGN, SHE ALSO FOUND ANOTHER PLACE FOR MARIAN ANDERSON'S CONCERT—THE LINCOLN MEMORIAL.

ON EASTER SUNDAY AFTERNOON, SEVENTY-FIVE THOUSAND BLACKS AND WHITES CROWDED ALONG THE EDGE OF THE REFLECTION POOL TO HEAR MARIAN ANDERSON. MILLIONS MORE LISTENED FROM HOME ON THEIR RADIOS. MARIAN ANDERSON OPENED THE CONCERT WITH "AMERICA."

His life as president was exciting. Still, from the moment he took office, his goal had been to get people back to work. By the mid-1930s, times were getting better, but the country was not out of the Depression.

Then another problem—a big one—loomed across the Atlantic Ocean.

Chapter 8
Going to War

ADOLF HITLER

In 1933, Adolf Hitler had become chancellor of Germany. This was the same year that Franklin became president.

Hitler built up a mighty army. His aim was to conquer countries all over Europe. Germany would be the most powerful nation on earth.

In 1938, the German army rolled into Austria. During the next two years, Czechoslovakia, Poland, Norway, Denmark, the Netherlands, Belgium, Luxembourg, and finally France, fell to Germany. The people of Britain knew they could be next.

COUNTRIES UNDER GERMAN CONTROL BY 1940

America had sent troops to Europe to fight in World War I. Over 116,000 US soldiers had died. Americans didn't want to fight another war in Europe. In fact, Congress had passed laws to make sure America stayed out of wars between other countries. The US couldn't help any side; it couldn't even sell weapons. Still, Franklin knew that the US would probably become involved in the war one day. Germany might not attack America soon, but if it controlled all of Europe, it might.

Hitler was an enemy to be feared. Not only did he want to control the world, he wanted to get rid of what he considered inferior races, like Gypsies and Jews. Nazi death camps were set up in countries Hitler had invaded. Before the war ended, more than six million Jews were killed in these camps. As the war went on, other countries, including America, became aware of what was happening. But few acted. (It wasn't until 1944 that Franklin did anything to help rescue refugees

In 1940, Franklin's second term as president was coming to an end. No president had ever run for a third term. No one expected Franklin to. But with the war in Europe, he felt he had to again. So he did. He didn't win by a landslide, but he won.

In July, Germany began bombing Britain. Every night fires raged all over London. Every day military bases were hit hard. Young British pilots fought bravely, even though they were outnumbered. The prime minister, Winston Churchill, begged Franklin for help. Churchill understood that America could not enter the war. But Churchill badly needed destroyers.

"Mr. President," he pleaded, "with great respect, I must tell you that in the long history of the world, this is the thing to do now."

Franklin wanted to send destroyers. But ...ain couldn't pay for them. So Franklin's hand were tied. Then, together, he and Churchill came up with a plan.

America would loan Britain fifty destroyers. In return, Britain would allow America to have some military bases on British territory near the United States for ninety-nine years. This led to Congress approving the Lend-Lease Act. Finally, America could send badly needed war supplies to Britain. Convoys of ships went back and forth, often under attack from German subs.

Franklin not only had to worry about Germany, but he had to worry about her allies, Italy and, especially, Japan.

Japan had a strong military. The Japanese had been fighting in China for years. Now they had their eye on other countries in Asia such as Indochina and the Philippines.

Franklin was sure that one day Japan would attack the United States. But where and when it happened came as a horrible surprise.

On Sunday, December 7, 1941, Japanese warplanes attacked Pearl Harbor in the US territory of Hawaii. In fifteen minutes, the Japanese bombed the airfields and smashed battleships. Over thirty-five hundred Americans were killed or wounded. Two hundred and sixty-five planes were destroyed. Nine ships were damaged or sunk. Among them was the USS *Arizona*, the battleship Franklin had watched being built in Brooklyn during World War I.

The next day, Americans gathered around their radios to hear the president speak about the attack. He said that December 7, 1941, was "a date which will live in infamy." The United States declared war on Japan that same day. Three days later, Germany and Italy declared war on America. The United States was now part of World War II.

Men over eighteen joined the army and navy. Almost overnight, factories that had been building items like toys and cars were turning out weapons, trucks, tanks, and planes. Women worked

alongside men. Pictures of "Rosie the Riveter" became the symbol of women helping the war effort. No one was out of work now.

"It will not only be a long war, it will be a hard war," Franklin told the country.

But he added, "We are going to win the war and we are going to win the peace that follows."

The war was raging on three fronts—in Europe, North Africa, and the Pacific.

FRANKLIN AND WINSTON

ON AUGUST 9, 1941, IN THE WATERS OFF
NEWFOUNDLAND IN CANADA, WINSTON CHURCHILL
AND FRANKLIN ROOSEVELT MET FOR THE FIRST
TIME. THAT SUNDAY, BEFORE GOING HOME, THE
TWO LEADERS TOOK PART IN A MOVING SERVICE
ABOARD *THE PRINCE OF WALES*, A BRITISH
BATTLESHIP. SAILORS AND MARINES FROM
AMERICA AND BRITAIN STOOD SIDE BY SIDE
SINGING HYMNS AS THE PRESIDENT AND THE
PRIME MINISTER SAT TOGETHER.

IT WAS THE BEGINNING OF A WONDERFUL
FRIENDSHIP BETWEEN TWO GIANTS OF THEIR
GENERATION. DURING THE WAR, THEY WOULD
MEET ELEVEN MORE TIMES, IN EUROPE AND IN
NORTH AMERICA.

A breakthrough came in the Pacific on June 4, 1942, at the Battle of Midway. The Americans had broken the Japanese's secret codes, so they knew about the attack and were ready. The battle went on for four days. When it was over, the Americans had sunk all four Japanese carriers.

Finally, the US Navy had a victory. Japan never took control of the seas again. Still, a long struggle to victory lay ahead as brave soldiers fought fierce battles on Okinawa, Iwo Jima, and other Japanese islands.

JAPANESE CAMPS

AFTER PEARL HARBOR, FEAR SPREAD THAT THE JAPANESE MIGHT ATTACK THE MAINLAND. THAT NEVER HAPPENED, BUT PEOPLE WERE PANICKED. MOST OF THE JAPANESE AMERICANS IN THE UNITED STATES LIVED ON THE WEST COAST. WHAT IF SOME OF THEM WERE SPIES?

IN FEBRUARY 1942, FRANKLIN SIGNED AN ORDER WHICH FORCED JAPANESE AMERICANS ON THE WEST COAST TO SPEND THE WAR IN ARMED CAMPS SURROUNDED BY BARBED WIRE. ABOUT ONE HUNDRED AND TEN THOUSAND PEOPLE HAD TO LEAVE THEIR HOMES AND TAKE WITH THEM ONLY WHAT THEY COULD CARRY. MEN, WOMEN, CHILDREN,

AND ELDERLY PEOPLE ALL HAD TO GO. IT WAS A TERRIBLE THING TO DO.

NONE WERE CONVICTED AS SPIES AND ABOUT TWENTY THOUSAND JAPANESE-AMERICAN YOUNG MEN JOINED THE US ARMY AND FOUGHT BRAVELY IN NORTH AFRICA AND EUROPE.

WHEN THE WAR WAS OVER, PEOPLE WERE LET GO WITH $25 AND A TRAIN TICKET. MOST HAD LOST THEIR HOMES, THEIR FARMS, AND THEIR BUSINESSES. FINALLY, AFTER MANY YEARS, EACH DETAINEE OR THEIR HEIR WAS GIVEN $20,000 BY THE GOVERNMENT.

The invasion of Europe took place on June 6, 1944. It became known as D-day. Nearly five thousand ships ferried over one hundred thousand men across the English Channel to the beaches at Normandy in France. They met heavy fire from the Germans and Allied losses were staggering. But they held their beachhead and, within two weeks, close to six hundred thousand soldiers and equipment had landed at Normandy. It was an unbelievable accomplishment.

Eleven months later, on May 7, 1945, Germany would surrender.

Chapter 9
Saying Good-Bye

At home in 1944, it was time for a presidential election. Not only was Franklin running the war as Commander-in-Chief, now he was running for a fourth term as president. Senator Harry S. Truman from Missouri was his running mate.

HARRY S. TRUMAN

Franklin was tired. Still, he campaigned with the same confidence, charm, and good humor. He told crowds that his opponents now were attacking his little dog, Fala. With a straight face, he said, "Well, of course, I don't resent attacks, and my family doesn't resent attacks, but Fala does resent attacks." Everyone burst out laughing.

It came as no surprise when Franklin won

again. After all, America was in a war and many people felt that it was no time to change presidents.

In January 1945, Franklin traveled to Yalta on the Black Sea to meet with Churchill and Joseph Stalin, the Russian leader. Franklin's goal was to get a promise from Stalin that Russia would help fight Japan. And he wanted Stalin to agree that Russia would be part of a world peace organization after the war. It would become the United Nations.

Franklin returned home with Stalin's promises, looking tired and drawn. He had dark circles under his eyes and he had lost weight. Eleanor was worried about him.

He told Congress about the trip to Yalta. For the first time, he did not stand when he spoke. "I hope you will pardon me for . . . sitting down . . .

but I know that you will realize that it makes it a lot easier for me in not having to carry about ten pounds of steel around on the bottom of my legs, and also because of the fact that I have just completed a fourteen-thousand-mile trip."

Soon after, Franklin went to Warm Springs for a much needed rest. Eleanor stayed in Washington, but friends traveled down with him. After the first week, he looked better and was enjoying the company.

On April 12, he woke up with a headache and a stiff neck. He ate breakfast, dressed, and joined friends. His cousin remembered him looking particularly handsome in a gray suit and crimson tie.

Just before lunch, he was sitting at a table going over the mail. Suddenly he said he had a terrific headache and slumped down.

A doctor was called, but it was too late. A little before 3:30 PM, Franklin Roosevelt died of a burst blood vessel in his brain. He was sixty-three years old. Not just the country, but the whole world was stunned by the news.

Eleanor came down from Washington to take her husband home. The railroad station at Warm Springs was packed with friends and neighbors who had come to say good-bye to their old friend.

As the train wound its way to Washington, crowds of people stood along the tracks, weeping. A reporter wrote, "They came from the fields and the farms, from hamlets and crossroads and in the cities they thronged by the thousands to stare with humble reverence and awe."

In the morning, the train arrived in Washington, D.C. A caisson, drawn by six white horses, carried Franklin's coffin to the White House. There was a funeral in the East Room that afternoon. In the evening, the train continued up along the Hudson River to Hyde

ark where Franklin was buried at home at

pringwood the next day.

"The funeral was very beautiful," a friend

rote. "The day was gloriously snappy, very

unny and blue, white lilacs were in bloom . . .

nd the birds were singing."

Harry S. Truman was now president. Less than a month later, on May 7, 1945, Germany surrendered. In August, Truman gave orders to drop atomic bombs on two cities in Japan— Hiroshima and Nagasaki. (Scientists had been secretly working on the atomic bomb since 1941.) Japan surrendered on September 2, 1945.

World War II was finally over.

Soon after Franklin's death, a young soldier said what so many Americans felt about him. "I can remember the president ever since I was a little kid . . . America will seem a strange empty place without his voice talking to the people whenever great events occur . . . I can hardly believe he is gone."

Many terrible events occurred while Franklin was in office. Yet, with him, Americans felt as if they always had a friend helping them through the hard times.

TIMELINE OF
FRANKLIN ROOSEVELT'S LIFE

1882 —— Born in Hyde Park, New York, on January 30

1900 —— Graduates from Groton School, a boarding school in Massachusetts

1903 —— Graduates from Harvard with a B.A. in History

1905 —— Marries his distant cousin Eleanor Roosevelt on March 17; Anna Eleanor, the first of their six children, is born

1910 —— Runs for the New York State Senate and wins

1913 —— Becomes Assistant Secretary of the Navy

1919 —— Attends peace conference in France, formally ending World War I

1920 —— Runs for vice president on a ticket with James Cox

1921 —— Contracts polio

1924 —— Visits Warm Springs, Georgia, for the first time

1928 —— Elected governor of New York

1932 —— Elected president of the United States

1933 —— Gives first "fireside chat" on the radio

1936 —— Reelected president for second term

1940 —— Reelected president for third term

1941 —— Asks Congress to declare war on Japan

1944 —— Reelected president for fourth term

1945 —— Dies in Warm Springs, Georgia, on April 12

TIMELINE OF
THE WORLD

omas Edision brings electric light to one square mile in — **1882**
New York City

First Klondike Gold Rush begins in Yukon, Canada — **1896**

First World Series is played between Boston and — **1903**
Pittsburgh

Henry Ford's Model T car popularizes automobiles — **1908**

itanic sinks on its maiden voyage between Great Britain — **1912**
and America on April 14

World War I — **1914–1918**

Russian Revolution begins — **1917**

eteenth Amendment gives US women the right to vote — **1920**

Adolph Hitler becomes the leader of the Nazi Party in — **1921**
Germany

ormone insulin is discovered and used to treat diabetes — **1922**

rles Lindbergh flies the first nonstop, solo, transatlantic — **1927**
flight between America and France

Stock market on Wall Street crashes — **1929**

frican-American Jesse Owens wins four gold medals at — **1936**
the Summer Olympics in Berlin, Germany

melia Earhart's plane disappears over the Pacific Ocean — **1937**

tion Comics publishes the first Superman comic book — **1938**

Germany invades Poland and World War II begins — **1939**

Japan bombs Pearl Harbor, Hawaii — **1941**
United States enters World War II

Largest concentration camp in Auschwitz, Germany, is — **1945**
liberated by the Soviet Army

BIBLIOGRAPHY

The starred books are for young readers.

Brands. H. W. **Traitor to His Class: The Privileged Life and Radical Presidency of Franklin Delano Roosevelt**. Doubleday, New York, 2008.

*Freedman, Russell. **Franklin Delano Roosevelt** Clarion Books, New York, 1990.

Goodwin, Doris Kearns. **No Ordinary Time: Franklin & Eleanor: The Home Front in World War II**. Simon & Schuster, New York. 1995.

*Sullivan, Wilson. **American Heritage Junior Library: Franklin Delano Roosevelt**. American Heritage Publishing Co., Inc., 1970

*Thompson, Gare. **Who Was Eleanor Roosevelt?**
Grosset & Dunlap, New York. 2004.

*Waxman, Laura Hamilton. **Franklin D.
Roosevelt**. Barnes & Noble, New York. 2004.

Y0-AGO-288

MANAGEMENT
SERVICES
HANDBOOK

Management Services Handbook

The Accountant's Contribution to Planning, Systems, and Controls

Edited by Henry De Vos, M.B.A.
Loris Battin, M.S., Editorial Assistant

PUBLISHED BY THE AMERICAN INSTITUTE OF CPAS, INC.

This book represents the individual views of many authors. Its publication by the American Institute of CPAs does not constitute official endorsement or approval of the opinions expressed.

Table of Contents

Preface

THE INCREASED ATTENTION on behalf of businessmen to a more effective utilization of economic goods has generated much discussion and a profusion of articles concerning management assistance within the broad discipline of accounting. Although many of these articles have already appeared in print, several have probably escaped the busy practitioner, who recently has been swept up in the trend of equipping himself to provide additional services for his clients. This book was therefore conceived for the purpose of collecting in a single volume some of the many valuable suggestions and pertinent ideas relating to the practice of management services.

Since the inferred scope of management services is so broad and because technology is expanding at such a rapid rate, it becomes almost impossible to cover all of the functional areas and sub-areas comprised in the term "management services." It was obvious from the start that no individual practitioner could perform *all* of the various services that are considered to fall within the scope of management services today. The size of the practice, the nature of the clientele, and even the matter of location will determine the kind of service the CPA can offer; and, of course, attitudes and interests differ widely. Therefore, the selections included in this volume relate primarily to services which in the opinion of the editor could be performed by the average CPA.

The material for this book was drawn largely from publications of the American Institute of CPAs. These included articles from *The Journal of Accountancy* and *Management Services*, selections from the bulletins on *Management Services by CPAs*, and excerpts from unpublished committee reports. Other valuable sources were the publications of various certified public accounting firms and state society accounting journals, as noted throughout this volume. Space limitations naturally dictated the omission of a great many articles. Some overlapping was inevitable because several topics are interrelated.

A number of special credits must be extended. I am particularly grateful to Peter Southway of the Bank of Passaic and Clifton, Felix Kaufman of Lybrand, Ross Bros. & Montgomery, and Gordon L. Murray of Haskins & Sells for their many suggestions. In addition, I would be remiss if I did not acknowledge my indebtedness to Richard C. Lytle, director of the Institute's technical services division, and his staff for their valuable assistance. I also wish to thank Louis W. Matusiak of the Institute's professional development division, and Charles E. Noyes, Loris Battin, Barbara Shildneck, and Ann O'Rourke of the Institute's publications division for their assistance, suggestions, and patient follow-through.

Contributing Authors

Larry Allen

Edgar L. Andlauer

Milton B. Basson

Ralph H. Bearden, Jr.

Kenneth H. Bergstrom

George R. Catlett

Maurice B. T. Davies

Robert D. Elhart

Alan J. Fredian

William W. Gerecke

Oliver J. Greenway

Henry Gunders

John Hockman

Walter R. Hyman

Grandjean G. Jewett

Felix Kaufman

I. Wayne Keller

H. D. Kennedy, Jr.

William N. Kinnard, Jr.

John E. Kolesar

Paul W. Kuske

Thomas W. Leland

Harry E. Littler

Gordon L. Murray

R. J. Oravec

Manfred E. Philip

Raymond A. Rich

John B. Robinson

Robert E. Schlosser

Donald A. Schwartz

Clark Sloat

Robert M. Smith

Linden C. Speers

George E. Staininger

Arthur B. Toan, Jr.

Vance A. Wadhams

L. J. Walsh

Duane E. Watts

Glenn A. Welsch

William J. Wiley

Edwin D. Wolf

Robert G. Wright

Review of Management Controls

Introduction

THIS CHAPTER highlights the way in which review of management controls of a business may become a logical and continuous extension of the CPA's regular work. It is intended to provide CPAs with ideas as to how they may get started in management services work by uncovering control deficiencies in a business, thereby creating additional opportunities for service to management and increasing the profitability of their clients.

Particular emphasis is placed on how the review of management controls may best be conducted, and specific examples are provided of how control deficiencies may be located through the organized use of resources readily available to every CPA.

A review of management controls by CPAs can be defined simply as an extension of the CPA's regular work for the purpose of examining and assessing the adequacy of management policies, directives, and procedures, which together constitute the system of management controls, to determine that they produce optimum operational efficiency—the logical result of which is maximization of profit. It is not assumed that "regular work" necessarily means a financial audit leading to an opinion. Regular work, as used here, means only the *usual work of the CPA*, whether it be the annual opinion audit of his largest client or the monthly writeup for his smallest.

Where Are Reviews of Management Controls Most Needed?

A business without depth in numbers of management personnel is logically the most vulnerable to breakdowns in management controls, if indeed control exists at all. The independent CPA's inspection of the existent controls and resulting practices may be the only test these controls will receive in a small business.

A review of the management controls of a larger business more often serves to appraise and evaluate controls which management has already adopted and is continually inspecting. In a smaller business, review will often lead to the establishment of controls which management had not previously deemed necessary. The review can be of great value to any client. However, it is likely to prove most valuable to the smaller business client—one without a controller, internal audit staff, or other specialists.

How Does Management Benefit From the CPA's Review?

The primary objective of management is to make profit. It is sometimes questioned whether the annual financial audit (or the monthly write-up) contributes to management's profit objective, or whether it merely informs them about the job they have already done. The value to management of a review of management controls, performed as a supplement to the regular work, is illustrated by a practicing CPA.

"I will always recall one supervisor to whom I was often assigned as a junior. On every audit, he would quickly delegate the audit tasks and disappear into the president's office where he would spend several hours. Curiosity ultimately impelled me to mind my supervisor's business and ask him what he talked about for such long periods."

"I talk about their management problems, young man," he said. "Don't you know that every president likes to talk about his problems, and particularly to someone who is familiar with them, understands them, and can exchange ideas?"

This simple story not only helps to define what is meant by a review of management controls, but points up briefly its over-all value to management—that of the independent CPA identifying himself with management operations and controls which clearly affect profits. The certified public accountant's regular work, in itself, can rarely contribute to future profitability—unless it is used as a vehicle for uncovering profit potentials.

A survey has disclosed that many CPAs are now formally aiding management in most of the operational or administrative functions of the business, many of which are performed in areas distinctly detached from those in which the CPA has customarily been engaged. Profitability has been enhanced in these cases as the result of a certified public accountant *locating a problem, reporting it to management,* and then *assisting in its correction.*

2

How Does the CPA Benefit?

Much write-up work is performed by CPAs for small business clients because there is simply no one else to do it. As such, the writeup is most often only a minor phase of what could be a more complete service. If write-up work were extended to a review of management controls, it could become the conduit by which the CPA might discover and perform additional services which would command higher rates because of their greater contribution to profitability. The CPA's training and education can be demonstrated to his write-up client through the review of management controls and resultant management services. The CPA may enhance the growth of his practice by evaluating whether his present offerings provide as full a measure of service as he is capable of rendering.

There is evidence that practitioners who are already reviewing management controls have experienced the following benefits:

1. Improved image and acceptance of the CPA in the eyes of his client and of the entire business community. It is often not difficult to destroy a profit-minded president's image of his CPA if the president is subjected only to conferences wherein the out-of-balance condition of his subsidiary ledgers is discussed. Or if his annual management letter discusses only such issues as unendorsed checks or unperforated vouchers, a busy manager is most likely to pass it along to the bookkeeper. As a result, the CPA will not only have lost an excellent opportunity to identify himself with the profit function of management, but may also have unknowingly contributed to the destruction of the manager's image of the CPA.

2. A rise in the level of a CPA's practice as well as its profitability. A review of management controls is a challenging undertaking for a CPA, and its contributions to clients will be gratifying rewards for this extended service. The profitability to a CPA's practice will increase either directly or indirectly. If a specific management service engagement is obtained as a result of the review, a separate fee will result. If the effect of the review initially results only in the opportunity to provide counsel to management, the good will engendered will often find its way to higher fees for the regular work.

Need for a special engagement

However, CPAs should attempt to serve management on a separate basis. It is the experience of others that management services are best rendered on that basis—where the commingling of attentions to various problems is avoided. In contrast, there is distinct evidence that superficial observation in management services work, while better than nothing for both management and the CPA, can leave much to be desired by both. For example, what real value accrues to the small business client who asks his CPA to spend five minutes in evaluating the adequacy of a new organization chart?

Management, generally, will not obtain the full potential of a CPA's advice if the advice is provided only on the basis of superficial examination—and then too often forgotten—when dispensed by the CPA as a mere adjunct to the audit comments. The same advice, rendered on the basis of a special engagement, cannot help but extend to all facets of the problem and provide the best coverage of its solution.

Extent of the CPA's Work

It is not the intention of the first portion of this chapter to create the impression that a CPA must uncover deeply obscured deficiencies in order to render a valuable service to management through reviewing its management controls. To the contrary, the purpose is to encourage an examination of those areas into which the CPA's regular work normally extends and into *those areas with which a CPA is familiar, or with which he may quickly become familiar.* It is therefore impossible to provide an all-inclusive review for all CPAs. More correctly, it should be stated that the extent of the review cannot be defined, as the competence of each individual CPA in the various areas of specialized practice and business experience will dictate a different focal point.

Importance of experience

The factor of experience must be underscored. A CPA with practical experience in selling, for example, is more likely to intensify his review of the management controls in that area of the business and, because of his limitations, restrict the scope of his review of the personnel function. But as the CPA acquires more experience by (1) continually examining clients' personnel practices and (2) further studying the subject, he can equip himself to render a more valuable service to business in this or, for that matter, any other area in which he undertakes to gain experience and technical competence.

Resources Available to the CPA

A CPA should be encouraged to utilize those resources which will result in a more formal approach to, as well as a more thorough, review. The resources available are: the staff, review programs, and questionnaires.

There are a few basic resources without which the CPA could not undertake a review. These will be mentioned briefly.

The informal extension of the regular work, whereby the right *state of mind* is coupled with the expenditure of a little *time* to ponder why things are not done in other ways, will occasionally produce a profit-making idea for business management. The utilization of these resources alone, however, generally results in what might be called an unorganized review of management controls. It may, nevertheless, amount to more than some CPAs are now offering their clients. Such an informal approach could have a potential value for management, but experience shows that it constitutes a poor form of management service. It allows the CPA to exercise none of the formal tools by means of which he can expand the scope of his review and conduct it on a more organized basis.

The more formal resources available to the CPA are:

1. The staff
2. Management letters
3. Management control audit programs
4. Management control questionnaires
5. Industrial and trade statistics

The Staff

It is here that the factor of maturity is important. Experience has rightly been called the best teacher: whereas a partner or practitioner with many years of experience can draw upon his experience in reviewing management controls, the less experienced staff man cannot. This obviously creates a problem, for in typical engagements it is the staff man who is generally closer to the operational areas because of the part he plays in the audit of cash, accounts receivable, inventories, and so forth. Consequently, most firms are making formal efforts to orient their audit staffs in management controls review techniques.

State of mind and technical ability are the factors that will determine how valuably a staff member will perform, and the key to both lies in training. The experience of others points to four proven methods of staff training: self-improvement, specific staff training programs, special courses, and on-the-job training.

Self-improvement should be encouraged principally through the use of library resources and study of reference material. As in any other area of practice, appropriate reference material is a must for a firm expecting to practice management services.

Staff training programs should be developed within the firm, conducted by a principal or other person who has the appropriate qualifications for organizing and leading a specific educational program. Experience indicates that "informal" sessions too often will generate less than satisfactory results.

Such sessions should be well organized and specific as to coverage. They should also be geared to the level and capacity of the individual staff members. Few firms have met success in attempting to make management services specialists of their audit staffs solely from this type of training. For example, there seems nothing to be gained by concentrating a four-hour, semi-senior staff training session on how to install a wage incentive system in a plant. Rather, it is preferable to make a group of this level conscious of the types of wage incentive systems, so that the acquired consciousness can result in the automatic appraisal of a client's system when payrolls are audited. As a "semi" advances to senior and then to supervisor, this early staff training, supplemented continuously on each staff level as he progresses, logically results in the development of a man far better qualified to review management controls than he would otherwise have been.

Audit staff men who are particularly receptive to this type of training and interested in this kind of work can ultimately become the firm's management services specialists. For many years, the larger CPA firms with well-organized, separate management services departments almost always recruited the consulting talent they required from the outside. More recently, however, these firms have recruited many additions to their management services staffs from their own audit staffs, wherever staff men have demonstrated both potential and interest. There is definite evidence that the audit staff is becoming an increasing source of talent, which leads to the conclusion that management services training programs are paying off.

The written policy of a large CPA firm describing the qualifications desired of their management services staff man is reproduced below.

Qualifications of a
management services staff man

CPA firms might valuably test the basic qualifications of their audit staffs by referring to the following policy. Emphasis on the development of those staff men found to be basically qualified will logically result in a firm's ability to build the staff gradually from within. This in turn will result in a wider scope of management services which can be offered to clients in the future.

Furthermore, for the benefit of the CPA who believes that a management services man must have extremely specialized talents, certain statements have been emphasized in order to illustrate that *high degrees of specialization are not the basic factors of qualification*. It is ventured that many practitioners and small firms can point to men on their audit staffs who are admirably endowed with the basic qualifications and who, if provided with further training, could become competent management services staff men.

SEMPIER, NEST, AND CO., CPAs
QUALIFICATION POLICY
MANAGEMENT ADVISORY SERVICE PERSONNEL

Education. Degree from accredited college or university is required. Major study concentration, preferably in accounting. Graduates with major study in management or engineering must have some courses in, or knowledge of, accounting. Postgraduate courses or study in fields such as management, business machines, electronics, and systems and procedures are considered favorable.

Experience. Management consulting or methods and procedures experience is desirable but not required. A good depth of business experience and understanding is called for.

Experience which has involved contact with administrative and executive personnel, and which has required personal initiative rather than closely directed effort, is preferred. Evidence of having developed programs and written statements of proposals, and of having participated in the implementation and installation of such programs, is considered advantageous.

Personal attributes. A consultant must be able to work and communicate harmoniously and in a competent and businesslike manner with personnel at all organizational levels. He must be personable and diplomatic, yet have an inquiring approach and be an aggressive and diligent worker. He should have a high degree of intelligence, be imaginative, and have the capacity to proceed without close direction. He must be able to develop sound ideas clearly and logically, both orally and in writing, and have the power to persuade.

Work on assignments usually breaks down into five phases. A man qualified within the area of his specialization should have the capacity to perform the following:

1. Obtain the facts pertinent to the problem or situation
2. Analyze the facts
3. Prepare a program of recommendations for correction or improvement
4. Review the recommended program with management
5. Assist in or perform the installation after the program is accepted

General areas and nature of work

Assignments involve analyzing and developing solutions for a wide range of business problems which arise in client organizations. Many clients are industrial companies for which the firm has performed accounting and financial services for a number of years.

Obviously, all staff members cannot be highly proficient in all areas in which management services work is performed. For this reason, a staff member will usually have developed special abilities in one or more specific areas; he will have the background of education and experience necessary to enable him to recognize problems in other areas and broaden his abilities with added training and experience. Examples of specific areas of knowledge, training, and/or experience considered to be advantageous are listed below:

Organization and Management Controls

General Accounting Methods and Procedures

Information Processing Methods

Office equipment and methods (accounting machines, forms design, etc.)

Tabulating and electronic computer equipment and methods

Costs and Budgets

Clerical Work Measurement

The CPA firm that would like to initiate staff training programs with a view to assisting in the eventual development of some of its audit staff to management services specialists should design its own training program so that the desirable qualifications just outlined (page 6) can be imparted to each staff man. Reference to them may also help a firm decide whether to step up or reduce the training of specific audit staff men.

One method of developing a staff man into a better management services man involves special courses. Firm-sponsored attendance at study courses or seminars dealing with management services subjects will not only help the staff man to develop a management state of mind, but will also generally provide more instruction in specific techniques of management services practice. Examples of valuable course offerings are those of the American Institute's Professional Development Division, the American Management Association, and formal graduate course offerings.

Some CPAs believe that on-the-job training is the most valuable method of inculcating the idea of reviewing management controls among staff men and training them for it. Some firms practice it as a regular function. Others have experimented with it and have found it valuable, although somewhat time-consuming. In the medium and large-sized firms, it has generally involved sending a management services specialist to the client's office near the end of the engagement to review in more detail the management control deficiencies apparently uncovered by everyone on the job from the junior up to the partner in charge of the engagement. The specialist reviews the internal control questionnaires, the management services questionnaires, and the results of any management control audit programs that may have been used. He assists the staff in evaluating the severity of the deficiencies they think they have uncovered—he challenges those that the staff may have thought insignificant to make sure they are not worthy of management attention. He helps to draft portions of the management letter. But more important perhaps, he provides on-the-job training to the audit staff. As he challenges, aids, expands, and explains, the staff men learn and carry this experience to their next assignments.

Giving the client a clear picture. In some cases, the time spent by the specialist is charged and billed as audit time. A client rarely objects if it is understood that this is a normal review of basic internal and administrative controls which form a part of the regular work. However, the client should not derive the impression that his entire operation is being surveyed. If a deficiency is later found, either in a subsequent audit or by management itself, it may be difficult to explain why the "expert" failed to discover it. Caution should therefore be exercised so that the client does not misunderstand the true nature of the review and the benefits that can normally accrue to him.

Another type of on-the-job training in management services work involves taking a few of the best men (generally semi-seniors) from the audit staff and assigning them as assistants in the management services department for periods of three or four consecutive months in order to provide concentrated training. This is currently being practiced by both large and small CPA firms that have established management services departments. They have not found this to be a dead loss in salary cost. On the contrary, it has been a profitable move, for in every case they have successfully found more than enough chargeable time on management services engagements for these assistants. A corollary advantage has resulted: it has permitted the firms with few specialists to broaden their activities by turning over much of the detail to the assistants. After their training period, the men go back to the audit staff, but return again for a similar stint the following year if they have demonstrated interest and potential for management services work. After trainees have satisfied the experience requirements for the CPA exam, they are transferred as permanent additions to the management services staff.

Importance of thorough and intelligent training. A firm now experiencing excellent results with this type of program had abandoned a similar one a few years ago. Using hindsight, they can point to several reasons why the original program was a failure. Among the more significant were the following:

They did not really concentrate on training the men. This was the original intention, but they immersed the trainees in detail on engagements. They did not program their work carefully or provide close supervision. In short, they made the mistake of utilizing the trainees like experienced management services men in all respects except level of work. As a result, the trainees learned little, lost interest, and said they preferred to remain on the audit staff when asked if they were interested in returning to the management services staff for additional training.

Another mistake was that the firm's selection of the audit staff generally occurred only at times when help was badly needed. This precluded a concentration of training for an extended period and, more particularly, a concentration of training in one area, such as cost accounting. Furthermore, recruiting men from the "bullpen" resulted more often than not in a selection of staff men who were either not interested or who lacked the best qualifications for management services work.

This firm has corrected its own controls over its on-the-job management services training program and is now getting excellent results.

The staff can be the key to the extension of the regular work to the review of management controls. Training requires a certain investment of time and money, but based on the experience of others, it is worth while for any firm that wishes to render this service to management and expand its own practice.

The Management Letter

A vital step in the review of management controls is the report to management of the deficiencies noted. Much business management counseling in the form of informal conferences does take place, but it is apt to be unsatisfactory. Management often is less inclined to seriously consider deficiencies or take action on recommendations advanced on an informal basis. Conferences may be so lengthy that the results of the review of management controls are obscured in favor of the financial audit or other regular work.

Advantages

It is well, however, to at least briefly inform management during the usual informal conferences of what is intended to be submitted in writing. Consider the following advantages of the supplemental management letter, once the control deficiencies have been mentioned and acknowledged by management as worthy of attention:

1. It provides the CPA with another opportunity to give independent thought to management control problems and thereby render a judicious and complete presentation. It makes it possible for him to call attention to

deficiencies noted in previous letters. Management may not take action following the CPA's first notification, but it will often do so after the second or third.

2. It provides management with an opportunity to review the deficiencies independently of other matters. Experience indicates that an informal conversation, in which a business owner-manager heartily agrees that he should and will take action on the CPA's proposal that a budget system be introduced, is often forgotten. The same proposal formally set down in writing is more likely to result in action and can be called to the attention of others in the organization either by enclosing additional copies for distribution or by sending copies directly to other interested executives. The letter may thus constitute the basis of a formal discussion at the next executive or board meeting.

3. Reporting deficiencies in writing places the initial emphasis on the *problem*, rather than on the answer. Proper solutions are rarely found until the true nature of the problem and all the facts surrounding it are thoroughly investigated. Informal reporting of deficiencies often generates an impulse to seek quick remedies which may ultimately prove to be improper. A carefully programmed study of the problem and a separate solution will be more valuable to the client. From the CPA's viewpoint, initial concentration on the problem permits separate concentration on a proposal to management for its correction. *The difficulty that some CPAs have in submitting a specific work program stems from the fact that the problem itself has not been adequately researched and defined, and agreement was not reached with management as to what is specifically needed to solve it.*

4. By reporting separately and in writing on management problems, the CPA can appeal to the profit motive and thus enhance his image. A president or owner will interpret the letter as evidence of the fact that the CPA has identified himself with management's objective of profitability. The separate report may also afford an opportunity for client contact at a date following completion of the regular work, with resultant good will.

5. An important benefit to the CPA of the management letter lies in the separation of regular work and management services work. Personnel staffing is respected, and the assistance of client personnel generally tied up during the course of regular work may be enlisted. The solution to a problem is often the result of the joint or pooled effort of several of the client's personnel, the CPA and his staff, and perhaps other outside consultants. The smaller firms or practitioners in particular, with the pressure of many calendar year closings and attendant tax deadlines, will therefore find the separation of services especially advantageous. This will also permit separation of time for billing purposes.

6. It formally provides the CPA with a defense if a client suddenly discovers the need for improvement.

Illustration of a management letter

A sample management letter written to a business client by a small CPA firm is presented below by way of illustration. This particular letter reports on management control deficiencies in nine different areas. Some practitioners believe that several letters, each covering only a few areas, are more effective. Management letters do not lend themselves to standardization. Each engagement has its own problems; it is up to the CPA firm to determine the form and contents of a specific letter.

In practice, it is not likely that the management letter would include as many weaknesses as are revealed in the following example. The many items in this letter may suggest to the reader a possible extension of the review of management controls to other matters.

January 30, 19___

Mr. W. A. Kuehn, President
Foley Company
Floral Park, No State

Dear Mr. Kuehn:

Following the preliminary examination of the accounts of the Foley Company, which we performed in October in connection with our first annual audit of your records as of December 31, you will recall that we wrote you concerning certain deficiencies we noted during the course of our review of the internal controls. We are pleased to report that action has been taken on most of our recommendations for strengthening these financial internal controls.

We now take this opportunity to bring to your attention certain observations and suggestions for improvement of the company's management controls. These controls are also internal but constitute that portion of the over-all system of internal control which deals mainly with promotion of operational efficiency and adherence to the management policies of Foley Company.

Accounting system. The reliance on accounting data necessary for decision making in any business creates the need for a high degree of confidence in figures and for more effective analysis of facts and processes relating to them. The Foley Company accounting system does not wholly contribute to these ends, for the following reasons:

1. We observed that your *chart of accounts* is basically the same as it was many years ago. As the company has grown, different types of operations have been undertaken, but additions have not been made to the general ledger chart of accounts to provide information we believe would be helpful to management. We believe that a new chart should

be developed so that the data required for internal operating reports will be readily available. Examples of such data are profit figures by product groups and separate overhead rates for the different operations. This matter has been discussed with your controller, who agrees that the chart of accounts should be completely revised.

2. We recommend the installation of a standard cost system, controlled by the general ledger, which will provide more informative monthly operating statements. Estimated gross profit percentages are now used to arrive at cost of sales figures for the monthly operating statements. Under this method, material misstatements have resulted which were not detected until the year-end when the complete physical inventory was taken. Good internal and operating controls presuppose an adequate system for determination of the cost of goods produced. It follows then that the cost system should be tied in with the general books. It is therefore suggested that management consider the installation of a standard cost system, which appears to have many advantages in this case.

3. We note that the company now makes payroll payments by check. The time involved in maintaining payroll records could be considerably reduced if a pegboard system were employed whereby the check, payroll, employee pay slip, and employee earnings record are all prepared in one operation. Additional time could also be saved by opening a separate payroll bank account and placing the payroll on a biweekly basis.

4. We believe that many of the operations relating to cash disbursements, cash receipts, sales and sales statistics, billing, and the inventory operation might be performed more efficiently—at a lower cost to the company—by the use of bookkeeping machines instead of the present hand-process methods. For example, the installation of a machine bookkeeping system will save many hours of work now spent locating trial balance differences. The controller has informed us that the company's one bookkeeping machine is used exclusively for posting accounts receivable ledger cards, and that machine time is not presently available for other work. We suggest in this connection that consideration be given to eliminating the posting of customers' ledger cards in favor of an open invoice file for accounts receivable. The adoption of such a system would save considerable clerical time in the accounting department without loss of accounting control. Furthermore, it would greatly enhance the efficiency of the credit and collection system, which is presently handicapped because of failure to promptly post customers' charges to the receivable cards.

In view of the improved methods and applications of machine accounting in recent years, we suggest that the company survey its present accounting methods to determine whether any of the newer accounting equipment would prove beneficial. Our management controls department is experienced in this type of work and will be glad to assist you in making the survey.

Sales. Basing ourselves on a comparison of the relative cost of your sales effort with the operations of similarly situated companies in your industry, it is our opinion that reductions in costs could be realized through more effective control of your sales activity. The sales effort costs more than $470,000 annually. Of the present annual sales of $4.5 million, we note that no more than $2.5 million are sold through the field force activity. A comparison of your sales to sales-cost relationship with operating ratios attained by similarly placed members of your industry indicates that Foley's sales costs are either excessive or not effectively employed. We suggest that management immediately initiate a review of the sales/sales-cost relationship and establish the goal of besting the industry average in terms of this cost relationship.

We are not including in the foregoing certain laboratory costs insofar as they relate to technical service support for the sales department. The cost of servicing requests by the sales department is considerable. We note, however, that no time or expense controls are provided over this function. Further, it appears that the sales department makes indiscriminate requests of the laboratory. Your laboratory chief estimates that 25 per cent of the cost of this activity is wasted. We estimate that technical customer service activity represents an annual cost of about $60,000 or more, and we therefore recommend a re-examination of the policies governing this activity. It could yield substantial benefits to the company.

We noted further that the sales department is incurring significant sample-making and sample-shipping costs. In our opinion, the greater part of this cost is incurred on behalf of people and companies which do not appear to warrant the effort. Approximately 80 per cent of the cost of this activity last year was expended on behalf of customers accounting for only 15 per cent of Foley's sales. The cost of this activity approximated $74,000 during the last annual period; we believe the company might get more sales value for less expenditure. We suggest that management reappraise its sample program and its controls over this activity to determine if savings can be effected. It would be unrealistic and improper for us to assert categorically that some definite dollar figure represents a safely predictable figure of increased profit resulting from a revised policy. However, our appraisal of the foregoing indicates that informed and reformed managerial effort and control could successfully extract some profit. You and your management associates will necessarily be the ultimate judges.

Financial management. We note that it is an approved policy of the company to defer payment on most purchases to such an extent that cash discounts are seldom taken. The aggregate amount of cash discounts missed represents a substantial loss to the company each year and appears to be considerably greater than the amount of interest which would be incurred in the financial arrangements necessary to make payments within various discount periods. We recognize that the company's financial structure is under continuing study by the management, but it is our opinion that the present financial position of the organization merits more favorable consideration by lending agencies which could produce the necessary funds to enable the company to take advantage of profitable discounts.

Fixed assets. There is no formal policy in effect with respect to the authorization of expenditures for property, plant, and equipment. Policies with respect to the establishment of depreciation rates do not appear to be uniform, and the rates of depreciation being used are not consistent within the company. We suggest that management review the entire policy with respect to the authorization of expenditures for property, plant, and equipment and relative depreciation policies.

In our letter of October 19, we made certain recommendations in regard to initiating the use of a fixed asset ledger so as to safeguard these assets more effectively. The accounting department subsequently prepared a statement of fixed assets at December 31, which we were unable to verify because of the lack of supporting records. Owing to the company's very large investment in such assets and the effect they have upon the financial position of the company as a whole, we again recommend that complete and accurate fixed asset records be installed. This could be accomplished by an inventory or appraisal performed by independent appraisers or by a selected group of Foley Company employees working under close supervision.

Personnel. In connection with our examination, we observed that the responsibilities of the various supervisory employees are not precisely defined and that the assumption of duties and responsibilities by supervisors has been determined by custom and practice. This appears to result from deficiencies in the organizational structure and past failure to prepare and utilize an effective organization chart and procedure manuals, as mentioned later in this letter. We recommend the adoption of an organization plan which will delineate the authority and responsibilities of the various supervisory employees of your organization.

We further observe that periodic reappraisals of clerical operations and functions are not being made to determine that each clerical employee is fully employed on useful operations. An unusual degree of idle and nonproductive time was observed by our representatives during their assignment in your office. We recommend that the study of organizational structure be extended to the lower levels in order to recoup what appears to be wasted cost.

Budgeting and forecasting. We have noted that the company has not adopted regular procedures for forecasting and budgeting future operations. It is understood that the nature of the company's operations makes predictions of the future difficult and subject to frequent change. However, this very circumstance tends to make forecasting and budgeting more desirable. We recommend that in the future the company prepare annual budgets which include monthly figures on income and expense and that, in connection with budgeting for profits, it prepare cash forecasts which include monthly figures for receipts and disbursements. As part of the budget procedure, monthly financial statements should be presented comparing actual against budgeted figures, together with appropriate monthly analyses of exceptions. We believe that you and other members of the top management group will find that "managing by exception" through budgeting would be a profitable, as well as a time-saving, feature in directing and controlling the over-all operations of Foley Company.

Insurance coverage. We note that the officers, as well as other employees, frequently use their personal automobiles in company business, such as going to the bank, post office, suppliers, and so on. There is no record of insurance coverage on automobiles other than those owned by the company. Claims might arise against the company in the event of a serious accident involving liability. We suggest that protection against such a contingency be provided by adequate insurance.

The company should review its use and occupancy insurance coverage to determine whether the present policies are of benefit to the company. In view of the fact that operating losses have been sustained in recent years, it appears advisable to review the amount of coverage and potential risk involved. We suggest, too, that consideration be given to a newer type of "block policy" which, judging from our experience with other clients, has often produced substantial savings in premium costs.

We note that the company does not carry products liability insurance. It is our opinion that your company is definitely exposed to a risk of this nature. We suggest that management attention be directed to the desirability of adding such coverage.

We have been informed that the most recent survey of the insurance coverage was conducted over three years ago. We recommend that this be done on a more frequent basis in the future.

Use of company manuals. We appreciate the fact that no system of internal control will function effectively unless all personnel are impressed with their responsibility in connection with the performance of specific assignments. The same is true with respect to management controls. One method of obtaining the best results would be to prepare procedural manuals for use in the various departments. These manuals should explain in detail the duties of each employee and the responsibility and authority delegated to him. The employees should understand that they will be accountable for all deviations from prescribed procedures.

Purchasing. Our review of the material and supply products cards disclosed that the company has not established economic lots for most of the items it purchases, thereby foregoing the advantages obtainable from organized economic lot buying.

Our review of material and supply inventory cards also disclosed a lack of reorder points so that at times supply procurement became urgent and emphasis had to be placed on the delivery and not the price of particular items.

We noted, too, that quantities of some of the major classes of items purchased were *first* brought to the attention of the purchasing department only as the need for such materials arose, and notification came only through the medium of a purchasing requisition. In view of the significant amounts disbursed for these items, we suggest that the purchasing department be notified earlier in the year of the over-all anticipated yearly requirements so that the annual inventory requirements, as well as the proper levels for these items, can be programmed in relation to market conditions, availability of supply, delivery time, production scheduling, and so forth. This would of course be related to the budgeting procedures we have recommended for adoption.

We note, too, that not all procurement is centralized in the purchasing department. We therefore recommend that the policies governing the company's purchasing activity be reviewed.

Summary. This letter does not provide a complete survey of all phases of operating and management controls; it merely directs attention to certain areas which we believe to be especially worthy of management consideration. We appreciate that the ultimate objective of management is to achieve maximum control at minimum cost. We believe that correction of the deficiencies enumerated in this letter is compatible with that objective.

We will be pleased to discuss the foregoing with you, the Board, or other members of the Foley Company as you direct, and to assist in the implementation or correction of any of the preceding management controls.

Sincerely,

The Management Control Audit Program

The management control audit program is basically an extension of the management control (or management services) questionnaire (see pages 30-44). Research discloses that CPA firms utilize audit programs, but not nearly as extensively as questionnaires. This type of program can be extremely valuable for the CPA who feels particularly well qualified to make an extensive investigation of one or more phases of clients' operations. It ordinarily requires personnel more experienced and knowledgeable in an area under review than does the questionnaire. For example, a questionnaire prepared for use of the audit staff inspecting for basic deficiencies in management control over the purchasing function might be limited to the following key questions:

1. Who, in general, may initiate purchase requisitions?
2. Is there evidence that adequate procurement control is concentrated in the purchasing department?
3. Is there evidence of too much concentration of control resulting in production delays or other inefficiencies?
4. Is competitive bidding a continual practice?
5. Is there evidence that purchases are made from budgets, production schedules, and/or automatic reorder points in formalized economic lots?
6. Do purchasing department files and records appear adequate?

The answers to these six questions alone will reveal the more significant violations of good purchasing administration in a business. More important, the questions can be adequately evaluated and answered by any staff man who has had the benefit of a brief orientation on the principal elements of proper management control of the purchasing function.

Analysis in depth

The management control audit program is a more painstaking operation. Consider the following plan, developed for the use of an auditor thoroughly grounded in purchasing techniques and administration. This program, when adopted by a qualified staff man with an appropriate investment of time, is more apt to point up trouble spots.

1. Investigate the incidence of competitive bidding.
2. Investigate the incidence of formalized material specifications.
3. Investigate the concentration of buying within the purchasing department.
4. Investigate directed sources of supply.
5. Investigate follow-up of orders placed.
6. Determine the basis and formality of "make" or "buy" decisions.
7. Determine degree of concentration of buying in limited vendor sources.

8. Determine if economic lot buying is practiced. Describe basis.
9. Determine whether advance notice of an annual production program is given to and utilized by purchasing. Investigate for adequacy the degree of co-ordination established with the production scheduling function.
10. Investigate system of automatic supply reorder points.
11. Investigate handling of routing instructions, shipment, and discount terms.
12. Determine if vendor financial stability is periodically checked.
13. Investigate purchasing files for adequacy.
14. Investigate for price discrepancies—invoices to purchase orders.
15. Determine if technical tests are made of materials when vendors are changed.
16. Investigate procedures in effect for procurement of "trouble items"—special tooling, dies and jigs, use of outside vendors for various services, including design services, and the like.

The foregoing could be expanded further, but it illustrates the potential of a formal audit program. Is it necessary to adopt such an ambitious plan in the purchasing activity audit of a small business? Probably not. However, the above outline should prove valuable to CPAs who are qualified or who believe that additional benefits can be obtained from the development and application of management control audit programs.

How to appraise management: A check list

The following check list[1] provides a really comprehensive example of a management control audit program.

I. MANAGEMENT CONTROL

A. Company objectives

1. What are the company's objectives?
2. Are long-term programs planned to meet objectives?
3. Does the long-term plan include all major activities of the company?
4. Does the plan provide for results that can be achieved and are acceptable to management, stockholders, and employees?
5. Does the company have a long-range forecast of its financial requirements

[1]Reprinted with permission of Robert Morris Associates (originally distributed at their 1953 fall conference). Prepared by Oliver J. Greenway, Vice-President of International Resistance Company, and by Raymond A. Rich, Vice-President of Philco Corporation; reviewed and edited by William J. Wiley, Vice-President of Atlas Powder Company.

which reflects all of the company's objectives? How accurate have forecasts been in the past?

6. Do all administrative personnel understand the general objectives and are their programs and projects directed toward the same target?

7. Is the plan reviewed frequently and brought up to date?

8. Is the plan sufficiently flexible, permitting sights to be altered promptly as changing conditions require?

B. Company policies and principles of operation

1. Does the company have written policies and principles of operation which are in harmony with its objectives?

2. Are they understood and practiced by all levels of management and supervisory personnel?

C. Organization

1. Is the organization of the company set up to carry out the objectives effectively and efficiently?

2. What is the type of organization?
   a. Is the executive staff composed of specialists?
   b. Are the separate functions departmentalized?
   c. Is the management buried in details?

3. What is the professional reputation, integrity, experience, age, service with the company, and turnover of the executive personnel?

4. Does the company employ an executive development program? Are understudies being trained for every executive position to provide for contingencies and to ensure continuity?

5. Are executives rewarded in proportion to results achieved?

6. Are organization charts maintained?

7. Are functions and responsibilities for all positions clearly defined?

8. Is authority clearly spelled out and understood?

D. Control

1. How does the company effectively control over-all operations and what type of standards and yardsticks are used?

2. Are there adequate follow-ups to assure attainment of objectives? Are variances of actual results versus established goals quickly and sharply spotlighted and corrective steps promptly taken?

3. Does management keep abreast of the constant improvements and developments in its field of activity by membership in appropriate trade associations, special study courses, plant visits, and so on?

4. Does the company have its operations, practices, and methods audited occasionally?

II. MARKETING AND SALES

A. Market research

1. Is there a market research department?
2. Is it properly staffed?
3. Are markets studied before new product development?
4. Is market research used in advertising planning?
5. Is market research used in planning sales, quotas, distribution, retail coverage?
6. How big is the market—present and future?
7. Are sales trends analyzed—past, present, and future—in each product line? By geographic areas?
8. What are the changing characteristics of those areas, both geographic and product-wise (i.e., trend to suburbs, shift of market potential)?
9. Are areas analyzed on the basis of sales potential and desired sales share?
10. Are weak and strong areas checked periodically?
11. Is there a continuous coverage program?
12. Are industry and area sales figures available, and is the company using them?
13. Are internal statistics available regarding characteristics of population for product—income, number in family, buying habits, type of shelter?

B. Tools to do the market research job—are these available?

1. A skilled market research manager
2. Association information (trade information)
3. Census reports—all phases
4. Sales reports—weekly detailed analyses of sales, inventory, competitive standing on all lines
5. Government agencies (i.e., Department of Commerce)
6. Trade magazines
7. Advertising agencies
8. Field surveys—consumer, retail, distributor—both product and sales
9. Analysis of model sales by area and reasons for discrepancies

C. Sales

1. Is the company generally sales-minded, or is this confined to the sales department?
2. Is sales forecasting on a long-range basis?
3. Does the future of the industry indicate an increasing or decreasing market?
4. What are the breakeven points, financial levels, and sales levels by product lines?
5. What is the share of industry on each line? Is it increasing or decreasing?

6. Are sales policies in writing? Is direction established by policy, not by individual whim?

7. Are service policies sound and adequate for future growth?

8. Are sales quotas by each line and each area established?

9. Is the effect of volume on manufacturing overhead taken into account in sales plans?

10. What is the export market size and share by line?

D. Advertising and sales promotion

1. Is advertising and promotion expense in line with direct selling expense?

2. Is there a good co-operative advertising program, if suitable to the business?

3. Is there a well-thought-out, well-integrated, national advertising program?

4. Are there regular promotions, salesmen's contests, keyed in with national advertising?

5. Where required, are there seasonal promotions to overcome seasonal sales fluctuations?

E. Sales training

1. Is there a sales training department?

2. Are there salesmen's bulletins?

3. Is there a sales manual?

4. Are there salesmen's kits, charts—tools for both retail and wholesale salesmen?

5. Are there regular field and headquarters sales training meetings?

6. Are there field sales training crews, if required?

F. Sales control

1. Is there a sound practice of finished goods inventory control and forward buying time cycle in order to minimize working capital investment?

2. Are there regular records of weekly sales and field inventory?

3. Are there reports by territory on sales and competitive position?

4. Are there selling expense budgets?

5. Do sales managers spend most of their time in the field with the field sales organization?

6. Are headquarters and the field sales organization decentralized and divisionalized?

7. Are there regular weekly sales reports from field and headquarters?

8. Are sales overbalanced in favor of government, industry, or consumer, which might cause trouble in any of those particular areas?

9. Are inventories and warehouse space adequate?

G. Sales force

1. Are there individual product line sales managers?

2. Is there adequate sales personnel in the field?

3. Is supervision adequate—field and home office?

4. Are salesmen properly trained?

5. Is the compensation plan good as to incentive, method, amount? Does it encourage long-range building as well as immediate sales?

6. What is the morale of the sales force? Is there excessive turnover?

7. What are procedures for hiring and training salesmen?

H. Competition

1. Are there advantages over competition in product, sales, or merchandising?

2. Does competition have advantages in any of these fields?

3. What will be the impact of new competition?

4. What about future competition in the same or new products?

I. Products

1. Is product line diversified?

2. Are quality, design, and consumer appeal good?

3. Is there a long-range program on product lines?

4. Are frequent field survey methods used to keep finger on pulse of product acceptance? To get new product ideas? To confirm future development plans?

5. Are new product lines needed? If so, what's being done about it?

6. Is the product one which might become obsolete? If so, are there plans to cope with this?

7. If a product line is seasonal, are there other lines to balance factory and overheads? What are the cyclical volume problems, if any, and how they met?

8. What is the reputation of the company and its products?

J. Pricing

1. What is the pricing policy or formula? Does it allow adequately for contingencies, flexibility, and volume variations?

2. Are prices, discounts, and allowances in line with the industry?

3. Do prices and discounts allow a satisfactory profit for manufacturer, distributor, and retailer?

4. Do the right relationships of prices and discounts exist between manufacturer, distributor, and retailer?

5. Is discount structure properly established with respect to L.C.L., carload quantities, and seasonal aspects?

6. Do payment terms encompass cash discount, ordinary terms, dating-ahead terms (floor planning)?

K. Distribution

1. Is there an adequate number of wholesale outlets? What is their quality?

2. Are wholesale outlets independent or factory-owned? If the latter, is financing adequate?

3. Are wholesale areas too large to be handled properly?

4. Are key centers (depending on population or customer concentration) covered by well-staffed and properly divisionalized wholesale outlets?

5. Is there thorough retail coverage, particularly in key areas?

6. What is the wholesalers' opinion of the manufacturer and his products?

7. Are there policies and programs to aid the wholesaler in the proper management of his business with respect to overhead factors, sales promotion, advertising, and dealer aids?

8. Does the manufacturer have continuing programs to aid the distributor and the dealer in moving merchandise?

III. MANUFACTURING

A. Plant

1. In what type of facility does the company perform its operation?
   a. Where is it located?
   b. Owned or leased?
   c. Size of areas?
   d. Is any of the space unused at present?
   e. Where would any expansion take place?
   f. Cost of space?
   g. In what condition is the facility?

2. Has any consideration been given to decentralization?

3. What degree of security is there against strike, sabotage, and so on?

4. Is the plant safe from fire, explosion, and the like?

5. Is location good for raw materials, market, and source of labor?

6. Is plant well lighted and ventilated?

7. Is good housekeeping maintained?

B. Equipment and facilities

1. Are they modern and up to date?

2. What portion is general purpose equipment?

3. What portion is special purpose equipment (i.e., peculiar only to this company's process)?

4. Is it in satisfactory condition?

5. Is a preventive maintenance program used?

6. Is an equipment replacement program in effect?

7. Is all equipment being used?

8. Is there any equipment on the books at value not being used which is obsolete or worn out?

9. What is the ratio of maintenance expense to direct labor? Is this too high? If so, why?

10. Are good safety practices employed for personnel protection?

C. Plant operations

1. Is the plant well laid out to provide an efficient and orderly process of production, material handling, stores, and associated functions?

2. At what level of capacity does the plant generally operate?

3. If sales fluctuate, what is done to minimize the effect on plant operations?

4. Is the capacity greater than needed or insufficient?

5. Is there a definite program established to obtain improvement, simplification, and economies in equipment, methods, processes, materials, labor, and overhead?

6. What is the worker productivity, both direct and indirect? What is the trend?

7. Does the company use an incentive system? What type? To what extent is it employed? What is its effectiveness?

8. What effort has been made to obtain level production?

IV. PURCHASING

A. How important is the purchasing function to the operations? Are purchasing specialists used?

B. Do purchased materials represent a large percentage of the product costs?

C. Do items purchased have technical complexity?

D. What is the annual value of purchases?

E. Are adequate controls exercised on commitments by members of management such as the financial officer, purchasing agent, works management, and engineering, and sales executives?

F. In what manner are the controls maintained?

G. Do you consider the purchasing function a profit-making operation or is it used only as a facilitating service?

H. Are any of the important purchased items subject to abnormal economic conditions such as government control, patents, rareness, or monopoly?

I. Is reciprocity practiced and, if so, to what extent?

J. How is purchasing performance measured?

K. If the company has multiple plant operations, is the purchasing centralized or decentralized and what benefits accrue from methods used?

L. Are relations with vendors good? How is this determined?

M. How are vendors selected?

N. Are there automatic checks and balances for:
   1. Control of requisitioning authority?
   2. Distribution of paper work to all persons who should have information?
   3. Matching of orders, invoices, and actual receipts?

4. Inspection of receipts?

O. Does the procurement group keep abreast of technological developments and is it constantly searching for new sources of supply, new and better materials and methods, and lower prices for the operations?

V. MATERIAL CONTROL

A. Are modern and efficient methods employed to control inventories?
B. Are inventories maintained at the optimum level?
C. Is turnover rate high enough?
D. If inventory size and balance get out of line, is an explanation requested of the steps being taken to revert to a normal position?
E. Are materials properly and efficiently recorded and stored to provide a minimum of obsolescence, deterioration, and pilferage?
F. Are modern materials handling methods used for transportation and storage?
G. Is a good system for physical inventory of materials in effect to obviate any surprises in loss or value?

VI. PRODUCTION PLANNING AND CONTROL

A. Is a sound and efficient program for production planning, scheduling, and control in effect?
B. Are production schedules made as far in advance as possible to insure availability of materials, level manufacturing loading, and minimum turnover and movement of workers?
C. What is the record on meeting customer delivery promises?
D. Is there good control over movement of work in process materials and is this inventory kept at a minimum consistent with an efficient manufacturing cycle?

VII. QUALITY

A. Is top management quality-minded?
B. Does the company use modern quality-control techniques?
C. How does this company's product compare with that of competitors?
D. Are there markets of any significance which this company cannot serve because quality does not meet the requirements?
E. What is the in-plant performance on rejects and repairs? Is it excessive?
F. Is the product uniform?
G. Does the company have a materials conservation and salvage program which provides the best method of utilization and disposition?
H. Are customer returns of defective material excessive?
I. Does top management include a review of product quality reports?

J. Is the quality function used for:
  1. Better vendor and customer relations?
  2. Reducing manufacturing costs?
  3. Product improvements?
  or is it limited to inspection activity only?

VIII. COST CONTROL

A. Are costs known and is effort made with any success to control them?

B. What products are unprofitable, and are steps being taken to make them profitable? Is intelligent use made of the cost data in setting sales prices, valuing inventories, and so forth?

C. Have standard operating ratios been established and are they being used intelligently?

D. Are budgets used effectively?

E. What is the breakeven point? If it is high, what steps are being taken to reduce it?

F. How would the company fare in any recession in business? Is there a planned program of what would be done if there were a downturn in business of 10 to 20 per cent, for example? Could economies be effected immediately?

G. Are costs increasing or decreasing, and why?

H. Are cost methods adequate? Are they calculated for the purpose of providing an historical record or are they used to control operations?

I. Are sufficient reserves maintained for equipment and materials inventories?

J. Are nonrecurring expenses identified and separated from regular operating expenses?

K. Is vigorous control exercised over indirect expense?

IX. RESEARCH AND ENGINEERING

A. What importance does the company place on research for the (a) improvement of its existing products, manufacturing equipment and processes, and (b) development of new products, manufacturing equipment, and processes?

B. Are the research activity objectives in harmony with the over-all company objectives, and is the active program well directed to accomplish effective results?

C. In the development of new products, manufacturing equipment, and processes, has proper consideration been given to:
  1. Future market volume and profit potential?
  2. Product quality?
  3. Review of manufacturing considerations?
  4. Sufficient trial runs on a pilot basis to avoid "bugs" when in factory production?

5. Standardization of equipment and materials?
6. Economy in manufacturing?
7. Simplification of processes?
8. Minimum labor content?
9. Minimum of maintenance?
10. Caution against over-engineering?
11. Use of existing inventories of materials?

    Is all of this done before project authorization is given? What has been the company's experience?

D. What control does top management have over research and engineering programs, projects, and budgets?

E. How does this activity keep abreast of the (a) industry's new developments, and (b) customers' specific programs and requirements?

F. How do they keep informed of competitive developments?

G. How is the company geared to make rapid changes in its programs?

H. How much money does the company spend for this activity? What percentage of net sales? How does this compare with the competition?

I. What results have been accomplished in the past? What percentage of present sales are due to improvements from research and engineering?

J. Are the facilities adequate to accomplish the results expected?

K. Are working conditions, patent and publication policies, and salaries such that topnotch research and engineering personnel are attracted?

X. INDUSTRIAL RELATIONS

A. What is the management's attitude on industrial relations as a whole and how well is it set up to handle this important function?
   1. What is the title of the person in charge of industrial relations? (Place on organization chart will indicate to a great degree the attitude of management.)

B. Does the company employ good programs for:
   1. Employment
   2. Wage and salary administration
   3. Medical care
   4. Employee welfare
   5. Employee services
   6. Training

C. Is the company unionized? If so, how long has it been unionized? What is the union? (Suggest a review of the contract for any peculiar conditions.) What is the company-union relationship?

D. What is the morale of the employees and their attitude toward the company?

E. What is the rate of employee turnover as related to (a) the area in which the company is located, and (b) its competitors'?
   1. What is the unemployment insurance experience?

F. What is the record on absenteeism and lateness as related to (a) the area in which the company is located, and (b) its competitors'?

G. Does labor make unreasonable demands resulting in restriction of output, featherbedding, inflexibility, and so on?

H. On employee wage rates and fringe benefits, how does the company compare (a) with the area in which it is located, and (b) with its competitors?

I. If the company is out of line on employee wage rates and fringe benefits, is it not probable that it will ultimately be obliged to get in line with the area and its competitors?

   1. What are the potential long-term costs of the fringe benefits?
   a. Insurance
   b. Pensions, etc.
   Are they actuarially sound? Funded or nonfunded?

J. What effect would such a cost increase have on its operations?

K. Is there an effective training program for all key personnel?

L. Are all key positions protected with trained replacements?

M. Is the company training personnel for the expansion of its operations?

N. Is there harmony and co-operation among key employees and between departments and divisions?

O. Does the company have good two-way communications throughout the organization?

P. Does the company have an effective program to enlighten employees on the true economic "facts of life"?

Q. Is front line supervision functioning effectively and is it paid properly?

XI. PUBLIC RELATIONS

A. What is the company's reputation in the area in which it is located?

B. What does the general public think about the company?

C. Does the company maintain good relations with the press?

D. Does the company participate actively and financially in worthy community projects?

E. Does the company participate in activities which promote the general welfare of the industry?

XII. LEGAL

A. Does the company have a well-established legal service which:

   1. Routinely keeps the company management informed about:
   a. Relevant laws, public regulations, and public policy?
   b. The rights conferred and obligations imposed by company contracts and other commitments to avoid defaults and conflicting commitments?

   2. Passes upon the wording of contracts and intra-company documents impos-

ing obligations upon the company (including union documents) where accurate expression and clear understanding are essential?

3. Establishes and maintains or supervises certain corporate procedures relating principally to stockholders, the Board of Directors, security regulatory bodies, and other public authorities?

4. Passes on the maintenance and discard of documents and records?

The Management Control Questionnaire

Probably the most valuable tool in extending the regular work is a questionnaire designed to assure that review is made of the areas which most often prove troublesome. A good questionnaire can keep the staff man on the right track, confine his activities to key areas, and control the expenditure of staff time. This last item can constitute a real problem if checks are not placed on ambitious staff men who wish to demonstrate their prowess at the expense of the regular audit work.

The use of questionnaires in management controls review is relatively new, but their use is growing rapidly among most of the firms that have adopted them. Some firms have found questionnaires to be extremely productive; others have not yet experienced the same results. They are almost always used in conjunction with the internal control questionnaire.

Characteristics of the questionnaire

Research discloses that a diversity of opinion exists as to the content, extent, and form of the questionnaire. A firm that has one of the largest management services divisions in the profession, for example, uses a short, two-page, twenty-five–key-question form that basically requires only "Yes" or "No" answers. Their contention is that proper follow-up by the audit partner in charge or by a specialist eliminates the need for the staff man to go beyond locating the basic trouble areas. Others then take it from there; and through the wider experience of the partner or specialist a better and less time-consuming appraisal of the full nature and extent of the control deficiency is presumed to result.

Another firm, equally well organized in its management services division, uses a more extensive questionnaire which it believes produces better results. It consists of seventeen pages with approximately one hundred questions or reminders for inquiry. Furthermore, it requires subjective rather than "Yes" or "No" answers. For example, two of the more subjective questions included ask:

"1. Are there any data on the use of available capacity, productivity trends, inventory accumulations, and so on, that might indicate special problems in production? Explain.

"2. Is there a balance between the production facilities and market available? Explain the recent relationship in this regard."

The questionnaire used by the first firm does not ask the staff man to give explanations, let alone seek or provide answers to questions of this magnitude. Each firm, in developing a questionnaire, must consider the following:

1. The level of training, experience, and competence of the staff who will initially utilize the questionnaire, as well as the partner who will review and follow it up. The answer to this question will obviously have a significant influence on the type of questionnaire to be employed, as well as on the depth of its probe.

2. What is the size of the typical client served? This must also be considered. For example, it is not nearly as important to seek out signs of nepotism in a small business run by father and son as it is to unearth them in a large, publicly held corporation. Conversely, whereas it would be desirable for the CPA to determine by questionnaire if the owner/ managers of a small business have wills and if their estates are planned, it is certainly not within the scope of the review of management controls for a CPA firm to ask the officials of a publicly held corporation questions about their personal affairs.

Sample questionnaires

Following are illustrations of three management control questionnaires used by some CPAs, which vary in approach as well as scope. They have been selected so that a reader may: (1) obtain the best coverage of most of the areas into which his firm might extend its services, and (2) develop the type of questionnaire best suited to his particular needs.

Abbreviated type. The first (pages 32 to 33) is an abbreviated type designed principally for use by the nonspecialist staff man. While it should prove valuable in directing the staff man's thinking, it is restricted to areas with which staff men are familiar or in which they may quickly be trained. The questionnaire calls primarily for "Yes" or "No'" answers and, as such, does not require the expenditure of excessive staff time during the course of the regular work. In practical usage, the staff man is permitted to make brief comments, qualifications, or suggestions to supplement his "Yes" or "No" answers. In all cases, either the partner in charge or a firm specialist reviews the questionnaire and actually conducts, or has the staff man conduct, further investigation where it appears necessary. The partner or specialist also evaluates the significance of noted deficiencies and determines if and how they should be brought to the attention of management.

CLIENT

PREPARED BY

DATE

YES   NO

I. Organization

    A. Are organization charts in use?

    B. Are they up to date?

    C. Are management policy and operating procedure manuals in use?

    D. Are job descriptions prepared and used?

II. Budgets.

    A. Is a formal budget system used?

    B. Does it include:

        1. All divisions and departments?

        2. Forecasting of cash and budgeting of capital expenditures?

        3. Timely comparisons to actual results?

III. Office management

    A. Does office layout provide for efficient work flow?

    B. Is a good system of forms control in effect?

    C. Is there an office manual?

    D. Does the company have a written records retention program?

    E. Has a clerical work measurement program been introduced?

    F. Does the office machinery appear to be the best for the job?

IV. Data processing

    A. Does it appear that data processing applications could be used?

    B. If in use, does maximum utilization appear to be effected?

    C. Is the system well organized and programmed? Do results appear to justify costs?

V. Management reports

    A. Are internal reports to management issued quickly and timely?

    B. Are there apparent duplications in reports?

    C. Is "responsibility reporting" in effect?

    D. Is "management by exception" a company practice and are reports prepared on this basis?

VI. Cost accounting

    A. Is a cost accounting system used?

    B. Does it provide for performance measurement?

    C. Does it tie into the general ledger?

    D. Are standards and overhead rates up to date?

    E. Have the cost centers been properly established?

    F. Are cost variances analyzed and reported (as to price, usage, etc.)?

    G. Does system provide adequate information for compilation of breakeven data and analysis of profit-volume relationship?

VII. General accounting

    A. Are accounting manuals used?

    B. Does the chart of accounts provide for the accumulation of adequate financial and cost information?

    C. Are "fast closing" techniques utilized?

VIII. Personnel practices

    A. Do personnel practices include:
        1. A formal selection process including a testing program?
        2. A job classification and evaluation program?
        3. A training program (including management development)?
        4. An employee handbook or manual?
        5. Proper personnel department reporting practices?
        6. Wage incentive systems for:
          a. Sales personnel?
          b. Factory personnel?
          c. Office personnel?
          d. Supervisory personnel?

Comments. (Refer comments to appropriate question number and letter above. Include on a separate work paper brief comments on other deficiencies you have found or believe to exist in areas not covered by this questionnaire.)

(A full page is provided in the questionnaire for comments.)

Extended type. The second type of questionnaire found to be in use is one that goes considerably beyond the scope of the simple "Yes" or "No" type just described. It requires (1) that it be used by experienced staff or specialists and (2) that considerable time be devoted to it. The information called for in this questionnaire can often be obtained by an experienced audit staff man and then reviewed by the partner or specialist. This type of questionnaire was developed by a smaller CPA firm that has been asked on several occasions to "survey" the principal operations and management controls of small businesses.

The reader will note that this variant is almost a detailed program of examination for the particular area under review. Time obviously would not permit it to be employed in the course of the regular work. This questionnaire was developed principally on the basis of a survey check list included in Clinton W. Bennett's book, *Standard Costs*. The portions reproduced here by way of illustration are neither all-inclusive as to scope, nor applicable to all types of businesses.

QUESTIONNAIRE FOR REVIEW
OF MANAGEMENT CONTROLS
(Extended type)

NAME OF COMPANY

PREPARED BY

DATE

A. General information (list):

1. Plants, offices, and warehouses
2. Organization data:
   a. Type of organization
   b. Date founded
   c. Control
   d. History
   e. Kind of business
   f. Position in the industry
   g. Growing or declining
   h. Other
3. Business
   a. Nature of products
   b. Diversity
   c. Volume of sales of each
4. Executive personnel:
   a. Name
   b. Title
   c. Job
   d. Lines of authority and responsibility
5. Obtain or prepare copy of organization chart from client
6. Obtain copies of most recent financial statements
7. Obtain copies of all types of management reports
8. Remarks

B. Financial and accounting:

1. Describe nature of financial policies

2. Describe nature of accounting and control policies
3. List departments and show for each:
    a. Function
    b. Names of persons in charge and assistants
    c. Names and jobs of all employees
    d. To whom each person reports
    e. Hours worked per week
    f. Methods of wage payment
    g. How time is recorded and reported
4. Obtain chart of accounts
5. List books of account
6. Describe general accounting procedures
7. Describe cost accounting procedures
8. Obtain copies of all forms and show for each:
    a. Function
    b. Who uses it
    c. Dispositions
    d. Who controls it
    e. How many are used
9. Remarks

C. Sales:

1. Describe sales policies
2. Name and title of person in charge of sales
3. Names and titles of sales assistants
4. Territories where sold, how, and how much:
    a. Own salesmen
    b. Jobbers
    c. Mail order
    d. House-to-house
    e. Other
5. Salesmen, show for each:
    a. Name
    b. Address
    c. How compensated
    d. Specialty (if any)
6. Sales office, show for each:
    a. Location
    b. Number of employees
    c. Salaries and jobs
7. List points away from the plant at which inventories are carried and show quantities at each one
8. Describe how inventories are handled and controlled
9. Remarks

D. The order system:

Describe the phases of the order system cycle for *Purchase, Customer, Production,* and *Shipping* and show for each:

1. Procedure followed
2. Records kept:
   a. Manual
   b. Mechanical
3. Reports prepared; when and for whom
4. Name of person in charge
5. Names and duties of all other employees
6. Method of wage payment
7. Hours worked each week
8. To whom all personnel report
9. Remarks

E. Receiving:

1. List receiving locations
2. For each location show:
   a. Classes of goods received
   b. Reasons for each location and quantities received
3. Investigate whether the receiving stations are:
   a. Centrally located
   b. Provided with adequate space
   c. Properly staffed
4. Describe how goods are transported:
   a. Freight
   b. Express
   c. Truck
      1. Common carrier
      2. Hired
      3. Owned
5. Describe how receiving is recorded and reporting handled
6. Describe how, where, and when goods are delivered from receiving department
7. Describe how incoming goods are checked for:
   a. Quantity
   b. Condition
   c. Over, short, and damaged goods
   d. Partial shipments
8. List number of employees, names, and to whom they report
9. Remarks

F. Stores—raw materials; work in process; finished goods:

1. List stock rooms maintained and show:
   a. Location

b. Classes and quantities of goods kept in each

2. Investigate whether stock rooms are kept locked and list who has access to stock rooms

3. Investigate whether the stock rooms are:
   a. Properly located
   b. Adequate in size
   c. Efficiently maintained

4. Describe handling and storing devices used

5. Describe how goods are:
   a. Segregated
   b. Marked for identification

6. Show quantities on hand at each location

7. Indicate records maintained

8. Describe how obsolete or surplus goods are handled and reported

9. Describe reports made and where they are sent

10. Describe how returnable containers are controlled

11. Show name of person in charge and to whom he reports

12. Show names of other employees and to whom they report

13. Remarks

G. Manufacturing department:

Make a list of departments in the order of work flow and for each department show:

1. Name of department

2. Brief description of functions

3. List of principal operations performed

4. List of machines by major classes

5. Name of foreman

6. Number of workers:
   a. Direct
   b. Indirect

7. Names of assistants and all supervisors and clerks

8. Hours worked per week

9. How time is reported

10. Method of wage payment

11. How goods are moved into, through, and out of the department

12. Authority for starting work

13. How production is planned and controlled

14. How, when, and to whom production is reported

15. What is the maintenance policy

16. Who cleans up and when
   a. Machines
   b. Department

17. Daily reports made to management of machine utilization showing:
    a. Operating time
    b. Idle time
    c. Down for repairs
    d. Down for other reasons
18. Materials or supplies stored in the department, who is responsible for them, and how they are controlled
19. Describe inspection procedure
20. Describe how rejected work is handled and reported
21. Describe department layout
22. Describe paper work showing:
    a. Records maintained
    b. Reports prepared; to whom sent and when
23. To whom employees report:
    a. Foreman
    b. Other employees
24. Remarks

H. Packing department:

Describe functions of the department showing:
1. Name of person in charge and to whom he reports
2. Names and jobs of other employees and to whom they report
3. Location of the department
4. Authority for performing work
5. What records are kept
6. What reports are made, to whom, and when
7. What classes of materials and supplies are used
8. How they are obtained
9. The method of wage payment
10. Who delivers work to the department
11. When work is delivered and by whom
12. Remarks

I. Shipping department:

Describe functions of the department showing:
1. How many employees; their duties; how they are paid; and to whom they report
2. How work is delivered to the department
3. What materials and supplies are used, and how they are obtained
4. How shipments are made
5. How partial shipments are handled
6. Internal control procedures as to finished stores, packing, and shipping
7. Source and extent of shipping instructions

8. What records are kept

9. What reports are made, when, and to whom

10. Remarks

J. Service or nonproduction departments:

Make a list of all service and nonproduction departments and for each one show:

1. Name of department

2. Brief description of function and policy governing department

3. Location

4. Person in charge, title, and to whom he reports

5. Names and jobs of all employees and to whom they report

6. Hours worked per week

7. Methods of wage payment

8. How time is reported

9. Authority for starting work

10. Materials or supplies stored in the department, who is responsible, how controlled, how materials and supplies are obtained

11. What records are kept

12. What reports are prepared, to whom sent, and when

13. Remarks

14. List all plant services, including cost:
    a. Steam plant
    b. Power plant
    c. Light and power (if purchased)
    d. Motor trucks
    e. Other

Combination type. The third example of questionnaire currently in use lies between the foregoing two in respect to both scope and intensity, and in many ways adopts the same approach. Basically, it follows the simple "Yes" or "No" pattern, but requires a deeper study of the areas and some degree of subjectivity on the part of the user. The individual completing the questionnaire must therefore be an experienced audit staff man, who has received additional training in reviewing management controls and using the questionnaire. The partner or specialist reviews the results with the staff man.

The following illustration is not meant to be all-inclusive. A CPA or firm desiring to prepare its own questionnaire should find it possible to develop a reasonably complete one patterned on its needs by amplifying this list and referring to the two preceding ones.

In actual practice, the questions or instructions should be placed on the left side of the sheet and the right side should be left blank for answers and/or comments.

QUESTIONNAIRE FOR REVIEW
OF MANAGEMENT CONTROLS
(Combination type)

NAME OF COMPANY

PREPARED BY

DATE

I. General data:

A. Ownership and organization
   1. Obtain organization chart or charts
   2. Describe evidence of nepotism
   3. List people (and titles) who make executive decisions
   4. List large stockholders who are active in the business

B. Products and competition
   Describe (provide statistics where applicable and possible):
   1. Main product lines or products
   2. Main customers, geographical areas served, and share of market obtained
   3. Marketing plan of company and competition—list principal competitors
   4. How does net income compare with industry statistics?

C. Review of past operations
   1. Evidence of trends in:
      a. Sales?
      b. Expenses?
      c. Working capital or its elements?
      d. Number of employees?
   2. If *yes*, explain possible reasons for condition

II. Production facilities and practices:

A. Purchasing
   1. Who initiates requisition for raw materials to be purchased?
   2. On what basis are order quantities determined?
      a. Budgets?
      b. Economic lot sizes?
      c. Other? Explain
   3. Is competitive bidding practiced?
   4. Are components manufactured? If yes, is there an adequate basis for arriving at "make or buy" decisions?
   5. Do the inventories or production processes disclose problems of:
      a. Excesses?
      b. Shortages?
      c. Obsolescence?
   6. Is all purchasing, including parts and supplies, done by purchasing department?
      If not, describe
      a. Is purchase by others subject to control by central purchasing?
      b. Is there evidence of costly over-control?

B. Use of production standards
1. Are standards in use?
2. When were they last revised?
   a. On basis of time and method studies?
   b. On basis of engineering estimates?
   c. On basis of other cost studies?
3. Are they used for control of:
   a. Direct labor?
   b. Indirect labor?
   c. Indirect costs?

C. Production flow and control
1. Is there a separate production control department?
2. Describe briefly the production control system used
3. Does this system provide:
   a. A definite procedure for determining size of economic product lots or runs?
   b. For co-ordination of raw materials and parts throughout the entire production cycle?
   c. For controlling inventory levels?
   d. For scheduling of *all* production?
   e. For usage of most economical labor loads and plant capacity?
   f. Briefly describe records maintained, including unfilled order data

D. Production cost accounting
1. Is a cost accounting system used?
2. Describe type (process, job)
3. Based on standards?
4. Describe overhead allocation system
5. Is cost center approach used?
6. Is overhead segregated as to variable and fixed?
7. Is a good reporting system of cost data directed to operating people?

III. Management reporting:

A. Obtain copies of following internal reports:
1. Budget analysis
2. Financial statements
3. Sales statistics
4. Efficiency (plant) reports
5. Cost reports
6. Other important financial reports
7. Are reports issued timely?

B. Describe extent of budget system:
1. Prepared by department and division heads?
2. Who reviews and who approves them?
3. How often are actual results compared?
4. Are budgets adequately developed so that budget analysis is meaningful?

IV. Financial management:

A. What has return on invested capital been for past three years?

B. What is nature of outside financing?

C. Evidence of excess funds?

D. Evidence of deficiency in long- or short-term funds?

E. Are cash forecasts in use?

F. Forecasts used to support requests for funds?

G. Are there peak seasonal requirements for funds?
  1. Special lending arrangements established (credit lines)?

H. Is computation of inventory carrying cost made?
  1. Cost of funds tied up considered?
  2. Cost of storage space and handling considered?
  3. Cost of obsolescence considered?
  4. Is carrying cost properly balanced for needs of
    a. Customer service?
    b. Economic production runs or purchase lots?

I. What is bad debt experience in last three years?
  1. Is there a written credit policy?
  2. What is average collection period?
  3. Evidence of "bad blood"—credit—sales departments?

J. Describe extent of equipment and properties leased

V. Management planning:

A. Have long-term forecasts been developed?
  1. Describe briefly
  2. Are any major changes planned?
  3. Are forecasts periodically measured to actual results?
  4. Evidence that major projects have not been subjected to adequate advance planning in the past?

B. Is there a program for control of research and development expenditures?

C. Evidence of "one-man" control?

D. Evidence of "key-man" development?

E. Outsiders on board of directors?

F. When was the last new product introduced?

G. Who is responsible for new product development?

VI. Industrial and personnel relations:

A. Is turnover excessive?

B. Are employees unionized?
  1. Describe areas
  2. When were last contracts signed?
  3. Evidence of major disputes in past?

C. Employee handbooks used?

D. Are following fringe benefits offered?
  1. Profit sharing?
  2. Group life?
  3. Hospitalization?
  4. Major medical?

5. Pension plan?
6. Other?
7. Obtain copies of descriptive material
E. Describe incentive systems used

VII. Personnel development:

A. Definite wage administration program?
B. Evidence of on- or off-the-job training or schooling?
C. How long have management and/or key personnel held positions?
   1. President
   2. Marketing chief
   3. Finance chief
   4. Production chief
   5. Engineering chief

VIII. Orders, billing, and receivables:

A. Attach key forms used to acknowledge sales, authorize shipment or manufacture, and bill customers
B. Are sales and receivables records handled
   1. Manually?
   2. By pegboard system?
   3. By machine? Type?
C. Are accounts receivable records maintained in
   1. Book ledgers?
   2. Ledger cards?
   3. Open invoice system?
D. How are sales data analyzed for ledger entry and statistical purposes?
E. Are unfilled and back order records efficiently maintained for production and sales department use?
F. Evidence of good credit and collection follow-up system?

IX. Marketing and merchandising:

A. Briefly describe channels of distribution (number of company outlets, distributors, etc.) and how sold (number of company sales force, direct sales to customer, through independent representative)
B. Is the principal basis of pricing
   1. Competitive prices?
   2. Cost-volume factors?
   3. Are costs and breakeven volumes known for
   a. Products?
   b. Special contracts?
C. What is the nature of advertising program (media, expenditure, agency used)?
   1. Is advertising budgeted and allocated?
   a. On what basis?

D. Where are shipping points located, and which customer types and areas are serviced from each?
   1. What is finished goods turnover?
E. Realistic sales forecasts prepared and revised regularly?
   1. Following factors considered in preparation
      a. Customer inventory surveys?
      b. Industrial and economic forecasts?
F. Is there a salesman's incentive plan?
   1. If yes, describe

X. Insurance:

A. When was last insurance survey made?
   1. By whom?
B. Were coverage deficiencies noted in audit of prepaid insurance?
C. Are safety and/or preventive programs to reduce premium cost in effect?

XI. Labor cost distribution and payrolls:

A. How many employees are on the payroll?
B. How often paid?
C. What system used for preparation?
   1. Manual?
   2. Pegboard? Type?
   3. Machine? Type?
D. How many hours does it require to
   1. Record time?
   2. Accumulate labor distribution charges?
   3. Prepare payrolls?
E. How often are labor efficiency reports prepared for
   1. Direct labor?
   2. Salesmen?
   3. Clerical?
F. Attach a list of key forms used; note who initiates and approves

Industrial and Trade Statistics

Another valuable tool for the review of management controls in a business is the use of operating ratios and statistics. Comparison of a client's operations to similar businesses within the industry can often provide important clues to deficient controls. With the knowledge that a cost relationship or some other aspect of the business is inconsistent, a more intensive investigation into the areas which could account for the inconsistency may prove fruitful. The review of management controls is bound to be more productive if the CPA can develop clues with respect to problem areas.

Trade statistics and operating ratio analyses are usually available from the industry's trade associations or from Dun & Bradstreet, Inc., Robert Morris Associates, U.S. Federal Trade Commission, and the like. A comprehensive list of trade associations and other sources of such information is provided below.

Manufacturing lines

Dun & Bradstreet, Inc. "How Does Your Business Compare with Others in Your Line?" Fourteen important ratios in seventy-two lines of business; comparative ratios for the years 1957-1961. Dun & Bradstreet, Inc., 99 Church Street, New York 8, New York, 1962, 21 pages. No charge.

BUSINESSES AND EXTENT OF SAMPLE USED

Airplane Parts and Accessories (40)
Automobile Parts and Accessories (62)
Bedsprings and Mattresses (59)
Bolts, Screws, Nuts and Nails (55)
Breweries (42)
Chemicals, Industrial (62)
Coats and Suits, Men's and Boys' (127)
Coats and Suits, Women's (98)
Confectionery (39)
Contractors, Building Construction (167)
Contractors, Electrical (57)
Cotton Cloth Mills (47)
Cotton Goods, Converters, Nonfactored (36)
Dresses, Rayon, Silk, and Acetate (87)
Drugs (43)
Electrical Parts and Supplies (69)
Foundries (76)
Furniture (93)
Hardware and Tools (97)

Hosiery (68)
Lumber (66)
Machine Shops (120)
Machinery, Industrial (327)
Meats and Provisions Packers (72)
Metal Stampings (83)
Outerwear, Knitted (71)
Overalls and Work Clothing (55)
Paints, Varnishes, and Lacquers (107)
Paper (61)
Paper Boxes (57)
Petroleum, Integrated Operators (37)
Printers, Job (71)
Shirts, Underwear and Pajamas, Men's (50)
Shoes, Men's, Women's, and Children's (87)
Steel, Structural Fabricators (sell on short term) (90)
Stoves, Ranges, and Ovens (32)

Robert Morris Associates. Statement studies: Part I, Basic Study; part II, Income Supplement. Robert Morris Associates, Philadelphia National Bank Building, Philadelphia 7, Pennsylvania. $10.

MAJOR MANUFACTURING AREAS

Food
Beverages and Tobacco
Textile Mill Products
Apparel
Leather and Leather Products
Lumber Products and Furniture
Paper and Paper Products
Printing and Publishing
Chemical and Chemical Products

Rubber Products (except tires) and Miscellaneous Plastics Products
Stone, Clay, and Glass Products
Iron and Steel Products
Electrical Machinery and Equipment
Nonelectrical Machinery and Equipment
Transportation Equipment
Nonferrous Metals and Products
Instruments—Professional and Scientific

Jewelry
Toys and Novelties

Sporting and Athletic Goods
Furniture and Fixtures

United States Federal Trade Commission. Quarterly Financial Report for Manufacturing Corporations. Government Printing Office, Washington 25, D.C. $1.25.

General trade lines

Dun & Bradstreet, Inc. "How Does Your Business Compare with Others in Your Line?" Fourteen important ratios in seventy-two lines of business; comparative ratios for the years 1957-1961. Dun & Bradstreet, Inc., 99 Church Street, New York 8, New York, 1962, 21 pages. No charge.

RETAIL TRADE LINES AND EXTENT OF SAMPLE USED

Clothing, Men's and Boys' (173)
Clothing, Men's and Women's (81)
Department Stores (416)
Dry Goods (81)
Furnishings, Men's (47)
Furniture, 50 per cent or more, installment (132)

Groceries and Meats, Chain (71)
Groceries and Meats, Independent (54)
Hardware (71)
Lumber and Building Materials (165)
Shoes (79)
Women's Specialty Shops (214)

WHOLESALE TRADE LINES

Automobile Parts and Accessories (203)
Baked Goods (50)
Cigars, Cigarettes, and Tobacco (94)
Confectionery (26)
Drugs and Drug Sundries (77)
Dry Goods (150)
Electrical Parts and Supplies (123)
Fruits and Produce, Fresh (50)
Furnishings, Men's (32)
Gasoline, Fuel Oil, and Lubricating Oil (55)
Groceries (246)
Hardware (200)
Hosiery and Underwear (39)

Household Appliances, Electrical (109)
Iron and Steel Sheets, Strips, Bars, and Plates (69)
Lumber (94)
Lumber and Building Materials (101)
Meat and Poultry (41)
Paints, Varnishes, and Lacquers (32)
Paper (132)
Plumbing and Heating Supplies (166)
Shoes, Men's, Women's, and Children's (61)
Wines and Liquors (52)
Women's Wear, Coats, Suits, and Dresses (31)

National Cash Register Company. Expenses in Retail Businesses. National Cash Register Company, Main and K Streets, Dayton 9, Ohio. No charge.

LINES OF BUSINESS

Appliance and Radio-TV Dealers
Automobile Dealers
Auto Parts Dealers
Bakeries
Barber and Beauty Shops

Bars
Building Materials Dealers
Camera and Photographic Supply Stores
Candy Stores
Children's and Infants' Wear Stores

Clothing Stores (Family)
Cocktail Lounges
Delicatessens
Department Stores
Drug Stores
Dry Cleaners
Electrical Appliance Stores
Farm Supply Stores
Floor Coverings Stores
Florists
Furniture Stores
Garages
Garden Supply Stores
Gasoline Service Stations
Gift and Novelty Shops
Grocery Stores
Hardware Stores
Hotels
Jewelry Stores
Laundries
Liquor Stores
Meat Markets
Men's Wear Stores
Motels and Tourist Courts
Music Stores
Office Supply and Equipment Dealers
Package Liquor Stores
Paint and Wallpaper Stores
Shoe Stores (Family)
Specialty Stores (Women's Wearing Apparel)
Sporting Goods Stores
Super Markets
Toy Stores
Used Car Dealers
Variety Stores

Robert Morris Associates. Statement Studies: Part I, Basic Study; part II, Income Supplement. Robert Morris Associates, Philadelphia National Bank Building, Philadelphia 7, Pennsylvania. $10.

MAJOR RETAIL TRADE AREAS

Department Stores, Dry Goods, and Apparel
Drugs
Building Materials and Hardware
Furniture
Autos and Accessories
Electrical Appliances and Supplies
Paints, Glass, and Wallpaper
Jewelry
Books and Office Supplies
Sporting Goods
Marine Hardware, Boat, and Supply Dealers

Camera and Photographic Supply Stores
Luggage and Gift Stores
Fuel and Ice
Music Stores
Vending Machine Operators, Merchandise
Road Machinery Equipment
Farm and Garden Equipment
Florists
Music Stores
Road Machinery Equipment Dealers
Floor Coverings

MAJOR WHOLESALE TRADE AREAS

Food, Beverages, and Tobacco
Textile Products and Apparel
Drugs
Florists
Lumber and Coal
Paper and Paper Products
Iron and Steel Products

Electrical Equipment
Industrial Chemicals
Machinery and Equipment
Automotive Parts and Accessories
Jewelry
Petroleum Products
General Merchandise

SERVICES AND MISCELLANEOUS

Laundries and Dry Cleaners

Soft Drinks (including bottling, wholesaling, and retailing)

Specific trade lines

Appliance and Radio-TV. National Appliance and Radio-TV Dealers Association. Costs of doing business survey. Chicago, Illinois.

Automobiles. National Automobile Dealers Association. Operating averages for the automobile retailing industry. Washington, D.C.

Automotive Equipment. Motor and Equipment Manufacturers Association. Annual survey of 410 automotive wholesalers. New York, New York.

Motor and Equipment Wholesalers Association. Cost of doing business in the automotive wholesale industry. Chicago, Illinois.

Automotive Wholesalers. National Standard Parts Association. Comparative performance records and leading lines survey for wholesaler executives. Chicago, Illinois.

Beverages. National Beer Wholesalers' Association of America. Operating results for the wholesale beer trade. Chicago, Illinois.

Wine and Spirits Wholesalers of America. Annual operations survey. St. Louis, Missouri.

Building Ownership and Management. National Association of Building Owners and Managers. Office building experience exchange report—analysis of rental income and operating expenses. Chicago, Illinois.

Children's and Infants' Wear. Dun & Bradstreet, Inc., Public Relations and Advertising Department. Children's and infants' wear stores operating results. New York, New York.

Clothiers. National Association of Retail Clothiers and Furnishers. Men's wear stores annual survey of operating experience. Washington, D.C.

Clubs. Harris, Kerr, Forster & Company. Clubs in town and country. New York, New York.

Horwath & Horwath. City club operations. New York, New York.

Department Stores. Harvard University, Graduate School of Business Administration, Division of Research. Operating results of department and specialty stores, by McNair, Malcolm P., Boston, Massachusetts.

National Retail Merchants Association. Controllers Congress. Departmental merchandising and operating results by Flanel, Sam. New York, New York.

Druggists. Lilly, Eli and Company. The Lilly digest of retail drugstore income and expense statements. Indianapolis, Indiana.

National Wholesale Druggists' Association. Operating Survey. New York, New York.

Dry Cleaners. National Institute of Dry Cleaning. Bulletin service—cost percentages. Silver Spring, Maryland.

Farm Equipment. National Retail Farm Equipment Association. Cost of doing business in the farm equipment retailing industry. St. Louis, Missouri.

Food Chains. National Association of Food Chains. Operating results of food chains, by England, Wilbur B., Harvard University, Bureau of Business Research, Division of Research. Boston, Massachusetts.

Furniture. National Retail Furniture Association. Furniture store operating experience. Chicago, Illinois.

Grocers. United States Wholesale Grocers' Association. Survey of wholesale grocers' profit and loss figures. Washington, D.C.

Hardware. National Retail Hardware Association. Retail hardware survey. Indianapolis, Indiana.

Hotels. Harris, Kerr, Forster & Company. Trends in the hotel business. New York, New York.

Horwath & Horwath. Hotel operations. New York, New York.

Jewelers. American National Retail Jewelers Association. Operating statistics. New York, New York.

Laundries. American Institute of Laundering. Operating cost percentages of members of the American Institute of Laundering. Joliet, Illinois.

Lumber. Northeastern Retail Lumbermen's Association. Survey of cost of doing business of retail lumber and building material dealers of the Northeastern states. Rochester, New York.

Northwestern Lumbermen's Association. Cost of doing business survey. Minneapolis, Minnesota.

Paint and Wallpaper. Retail Paint and Wallpaper Distributors of America. Marketing survey. St. Louis, Missouri.

Paper. National Paper Trade Association. Annual survey of paper merchants' operations. New York, New York.

Plumbing and Heating. Central Supply Association. Report of operating costs for plumbing and heating wholesalers. Chicago, Illinois.

Printing. Printing Industry of America, Inc. PIA ratios for better printing management. Washington, D.C.

Shoes. Shoe Service Institute of America. Shop operating cost study. Chicago, Illinois.

Sporting Goods. National Sporting Goods Association. Costs of doing business survey, by Snyder, Richard E., Chicago, Illinois.

Stationery and Office Equipment. National Stationery and Office Equipment Association. Cost of operations report. Washington, D.C.

Super Markets. Super Market Institute. The super market industry speaks. Chicago, Illinois.

Trade Associations. American Society of Association Executives. Operating ratio report for trade associations. Washington, D.C.

Variety Chains. Harvard University, Graduate School of Business Administration, Division of Research. Operating results of variety chains, by Hersum, Anita C., Boston, Massachusetts.

Sources of information

Individual trade associations as well as other organizations and publishers have conducted single or recurring studies in a number of trades and industries. If you do not find the line of business in which you are interested among the foregoing entries, perhaps one of the following associations or other issuing agencies will be able to help you locate pertinent ratio studies. The names and addresses of the publishers of such studies are:

American College of Apothecaries, *39th and Chestnut Streets, Philadelphia 4, Pennsylvania (Pharmacies)*.

American Meat Institute, Department of Marketing, *939 East 57th Street, Chicago 37, Illinois*.

American Paper and Pulp Association, *122 East 42nd Street, New York 17, New York*.

Heating, Piping and Air Conditioning Contractors Association, *45 Rockefeller Plaza, New York 20, New York*.

Indiana University, Bureau of Business Research, *Bloomington, Indiana*.

International Association of Ice Cream Manufacturers, *910 17th Street, N.W., Washington 6, D.C.*

Michigan, University of, Bureau of Business Research, *Ann Arbor, Michigan.*

National Association of (Cost) Accountants, *505 Park Avenue, New York 22, New York.*

National Association of Furniture Manufacturers, *666 North Lake Shore Drive, Chicago 11, Illinois.*

National Association of Insurance Agents, *96 Fulton Street, New York 38, New York.*

National Electrical Contractors Association, *610 Ring Building, Washington 6, D.C.*

National Lumber Manufacturers Association, *1319 18th Street, N.W., Washington 6, D.C.*

National Paper Box Manufacturers Association, *1101 Liberty Trust Building, Philadelphia 7, Pennsylvania.*

National Restaurant Association, *1530 North Lake Shore Drive, Chicago 10, Illinois.*

National Shoe Retailers Association, *274 Madison Avenue, New York 16, New York.*

United States Department of Commerce, Business and Defense Services Administration, *Washington 25, D.C.*

How Management Controls Review Stems From Regular Work

IF A CPA or staff man habitually adopts a "management state of mind" during the course of his regular work, he will discover many opportunities for special services to management. What is being sought in the review of management controls can be illustrated by covering the extension of some of the elements of the CPA's usual work. For purposes of example, areas with which the CPA will almost always come into contact have been selected for discussion.

The audit of cash

Let us first consider the audit of cash, be it the annual audit of one of the country's largest firms or the monthly service for the local supermarket.

The bank reconciliations have been made or checked and other routine cash functions have been initialed off on the program. During the course of the financial audit of cash, the CPA or staff man has conscientiously considered all of the internal control aspects of cash handling and safeguarding. He may have promptly noted that independent listings of incoming cash receipts are not made for subsequent comparison to the cashier's deposit slips, or that supporting data are not being effectively cancelled.

This is a matter of training and a normal state of mind. But by extending this state of mind to a further evaluation of the control of cash—by continuing to search within another portion of the established definition of internal control *"to promote operational efficiency and encourage adherence to prescribed policies"* much more can be accomplished.

If it is second nature, even to a junior accountant, to automatically maintain strict control over the key to the check signer as well as over the other elements affecting the financial control of cash, then it is logically second nature to ask further questions about *management control* of cash. For example:

1. Do the management controls of cash include a system of cash forecasting?

2. What control is exerted over the potential for investment of excess funds?

3. What controls are in effect to properly plan that requisite funds shall be on hand to meet business needs?

4. Are cash reports in use? If so, are they adequate, or is a better system of reporting needed?

It might be argued that management pays continual attention to the cash position, and that a CPA will rarely have the opportunity to render a management service in such a basic area. This is a debatable point of view. Business managers may be continually evaluating whether they have *enough* cash with which to operate, but it is doubtful whether a majority of them recognize when they have too much cash or have any idea what their cash balances will be sixty days from now.

To illustrate how a business and its CPA can benefit from a review of its cash management, consider this excerpt from a CPA's management letter:

During the course of our regular work, we reviewed the controls utilized to manage the company's cash. While we will be pleased to provide more details, we wish here to present only a summarization of our findings.

Month-end cash and outstanding loan balances during the year were as follows:

	Cash	Loans payable
January 31	$17,200	$22,000
February 28	16,800	22,000
March 31	32,400	20,000
April 30	32,300	20,000
May 31	41,400	20,000
June 30	47,700	18,000
July 31	46,200	16,000
August 31	54,600	13,000
September 30	62,300	—0—
October 31	39,100	—0—
November 30	21,900	—0—
December 31	14,600	25,000

As a policy of long standing, management has arranged its borrowing requirements in December and scheduled repayment to be made in installments during the first six or eight months of the year in amounts which, at management's discretion, provided for retention of adequate cash during this period. We were further informed that management has never invested funds during periods of cash excesses as your commercial bank does not offer time deposits, nor may local savings institutions legally accept corporate accounts.

It is our opinion that a formally established system of cash forecasting will save considerable interest cost and permit the establishment of a program whereby excess cash can be invested in short-term U.S. Government obligations which will contribute substantially to profits. Detailed calculations have not been made of the saving in interest cost, or of the interest income from investment of excess cash which could have resulted from this type of program during the year, but by basing ourselves on the foregoing schedule for a quick estimate, we are confident that the contribution to profits could have exceeded $1,000. We would also like to call your attention to the possibility that time deposits in certain foreign banks, if it were possible to arrange these through your sales subsidiaries, could result in an even higher yield and resultant contribution to profit.

In this specific case, the president engaged the CPA to install a simple cash forecasting system—a move from which both profited. It is noteworthy that this particular suggestion stemmed from a semi-senior accountant's work in the regular audit of cash.

The audit of receivables

Many CPAs do not see the need or desirability of reviewing credit and collection correspondence unless it is in connection with vouching a bad debt writeoff. Experienced credit managers in larger businesses develop highly scientific collection systems involving letter series, tag codings for systematic follow-up of delinquent accounts, and so forth. Smaller businesses appear content to scan the receivable ledger once a month for evidence of slow payments and take their chances until it is next scanned. A brief review of the credit and collection system of a business, while going over bad debt writeoffs or aging the accounts, will often disclose control deficiencies that have contributed to losses.

Another deficiency found in business is that of *a too tight credit policy*. And yet, if it is a policy of long standing, it will probably never be challenged by anyone inside the company. A CPA can often serve management by reviewing the credit administration in a business that points with pride to its consistently low ratio of bad debts to sales. The alert CPA may find not only an area of lost profits through lost sales stemming from too tight a credit policy, but also evidence of overexpenditure in the credit policy administration.

Consider the company which habitually checks the outstanding balance of each account from which small orders are received. It is doubtful that it will show less loss than a company which eliminates this time-consuming analysis in favor of filling any order for less than, say, $100 unless the account is known to be delinquent. After all, 999 out of 1,000 of these orders are usually shipped to nondelinquent accounts anyway.

Areas related to receivables. The foregoing is an example of deficiencies in management control which can be uncovered through simple extension of the receivables audit. There are other functional areas to which the audit might extend. Order handling and billing are closely related to receivables and the gate is opened for inspection of these functions. For example, every CPA has probably been disturbed at one time or another by the length of time it took a client to ready customers' statements before audit confirmation work could start. However, few CPAs have investigated the feasibility of introducing cycle billing to such clients in order to eliminate this month-end problem.

The audit of inventories

Inventories—their production, purchase, and sale—are directly or indirectly the heart of any business that either makes or buys and then sells to make a profit. The cost of obsolescence, their markup or markdown, their flow, carrying costs, and turnover are the factors over which management control must be carefully and continually exerted if maximum profits are to be shown.

The financial audit of inventories can lead to a review of these important management controls. Consider for a moment how many operating areas or company functions are crossed in the conduct of the audit of inventory.

Taking the physical inventory of a business gives a CPA the opportunity to review storage and material handling facilities, plant layout and production facilities, and provides him with a picture of how production flows. The pricing of inventories results in contact with the cost system, the perpetual inventory system, and with vendor's prices and the purchase function.

The normal inspection and evaluation of obsolete or slow-moving inventories makes it possible to consider not only balance sheet pricing, but also the reasons why it has become obsolete. An analysis of this type will often reveal deficiencies in production planning, or purchasing, or perhaps in the organizational structure or communication system, which does not adequately control the co-ordinate efforts of production and sales.

Analyses of cost variances, normally undertaken in the financial audit of inventories, are sometimes dismissed by CPAs as indicative only that a client's standards are good or bad. Closer analysis of the variances is one of the easiest ways to uncover operational deficiencies in the management controls of labor, materials, or other elements of cost.

Case illustration. Let us consider a specific case in which the first annual audit resulted in a special management services engagement for a medium-sized CPA firm in the Midwest.

Their new client, a manufacturer of several types of metal products, had recently set up a relatively sizable division for a new wooden product. It was in the early months of full-scale production at the time. Although simple, this manufacturer's cost accounting system apparently provided adequate summaries of labor, material, and overhead variances. Neither cost reports nor the books reflected the variances by individual products or cost centers. The senior on the job, who was inspecting the variances as part of the inventory audit, found, merely on a basis of comparison with the over-all variances of the prior year, that some strange changes had occurred, not attributable to changes in standards made during the year. Analyzing further, he found that the typical trend of variances had changed a few months after the new wooden product had been in production. The client was inexperienced in the actual production of this item, but was confident that selling prices, based largely on competition, were producing about a 40 per cent gross profit.

The variances had taken such a strange turn that the senior first sought to determine whether the standards for the new product were a reasonable basis for inventory pricing. His conclusions, with which management agreed, were:

1. That the material cost standard had been set too high, which accounted for the favorable variance. This variance, the senior noted, was not broken down as to usage and price factors.

2. Inexperience of the operators accounted for some of the excessive labor cost, but the unfavorable labor variance was principally attributable to setting standard times too low.

3. The overhead variance appeared unfavorable because the standard plant rate had been applied to actual accumulated costs. While it was recognized that a separate overhead would have to be developed after some more experience with the operation, management was satisfied that the higher overhead was attributable only to some nonrecurring expenses incurred during the first months of production.

4. The high scrap variance was attributable to the quality control standards, which were deliberately set high so that sales introduction

of the product would not be hurt by low quality of manufacture. The sales department was properly concerned that customers might be skeptical of the company's ability to produce wood products, in spite of its long experience in metal manufacture.

In view of these reasonable explanations, and since management apparently was confident it knew what was going on, many auditors would have considered it logical to apply the information to the financial audit problems and drop the issue. Actually, however, this senior became increasingly suspicious, partly because he had found evidence that the wood product had been thoroughly engineered and test manufactured, and partly because precise specifications of manufacture had been established by a production engineering firm before full-scale production was started. Moreover, the cost system did not satisfy him. It did not provide for usage and price variances. Scrap loss included the cost of material only. No information was available regarding labor loss, rework cost on scrap work, or other factors allowing an accurate evaluation of the reasons for scrap. The overhead allocations appeared arbitrary, and under the existing system true overhead cost in this new cost center could not be determined.

Discussion between the senior and the partner in charge left both of them with the impression that their client was actually blindly entering this new venture. The partner discussed this with the president and found a receptive and alarmed ear. The partner was asked to state in writing his conclusions as to the basic deficiencies.

His letter was specific regarding the deficiencies mentioned in the foregoing paragraphs. Further, it pointed to some possibilities for generation of cost information which the present cost system would not reveal. A further check of practices in this department had disclosed deficiencies in time-reporting for the production of this item. It had also disclosed the lack of proper reporting of scrap and rework by inspectors and quality control people. The letter did not attempt to answer the question; it only pointed to the specific problems.

Before the firm was engaged to revise the cost accounting system, the production manager, to whom the partner had been asked to send a copy of the letter, had reviewed his material specifications with the purchasing agent and cost accountant. A further analysis of the material variance to determine price and usage had been suggested in the letter and had revealed that purchase price variances had been very favorable indeed. Further investigation disclosed that an inferior grade of lumber was being purchased. The lumber supplier had apparently convinced the purchasing agent that the company could save money by purchasing an almost identical product in carload lots on a drop shipment basis from a mill. The company did save money, and receiving department personnel and inspectors were unable to tell the difference in the lumber because of their inexperience with wood and wood products.

In the course of the special work for which the CPA firm was engaged, a reconstruction of the available cost records proved indisputably that raw material cost, as well as labor and scrap costs, was greatly in excess of planned cost because of the high scrap and rework factor resulting from an inferior grade of lumber.

The simple extension by a CPA of his financial audit and subsequent rendering of a separate, special service resulted in action by the client which went beyond the adoption of a revised costing system. The CPA's findings led management to review this operation. Within sixty days management had:

1. Changed purchasing specifications to improve quality and processing, and adopted new quality control specifications and reports.

2. Reinstated the use of equipment that had been abandoned when it failed to work properly owing to the poor grade of lumber. This increased machine capacity and output significantly.

3. Changed the plant layout to provide a continuous work flow, which costing procedures and revised time reporting methods had revealed was unsatisfactory.

4. Dropped the five high-cost, low-turnover items from the new line.

Thus what had started as a routine review of cost variances developed into assistance to management not only in overhauling the cost accounting and reporting system but also in improving the manufacturing operation.

Other areas of audit

Cash, accounts receivable, and inventories have received brief coverage to show that even the most common areas of audit can lead to management service engagements. A financial audit can prove equally fruitful. Extensions of the audit of fixed assets, for example, may logically range from relatively simple evaluations of the adequacy of property ledgers and depreciation or disposal policies to the more intricate evaluations of management control over make, buy, or lease decisions. The audit of sales can just as easily lead to a review of pricing policies, order-handling function, shipping, distribution or warehousing policies, and sales reports or statistics. Payroll audits provide an opportunity for inspection of management policies with respect to incentive systems, labor standards, work measurement, fringe benefits, and other personnel practices.

Pitfalls in Management Controls Review

If a CPA is to extend his work to a review of management controls, some discussion must follow as to which controls affecting which administrative or operational practices may logically be examined by the CPA. This leads to the first major pitfall in this type of work:

1. A CPA should not undertake to extend his review activity to areas of

the business with which he is not, or cannot become completely familiar, or which will involve operations requiring a technical or specialized knowledge which the CPA does not possess. The findings of the review of management controls ordinarily should have their roots in the financial audit or other regular work. The nonspecialist CPA who gives management advice in manufacturing, sales, or any other specialized area of the business will often find it difficult to obtain the confidence of management if his advice is not grounded in financial matters. Advice not supportable by figures or by a knowledge that the client is confident the CPA possesses, is often wasted. It is also potentially dangerous in client relationship. In short, the value of the review will be enhanced if the deficiencies located or recommendations made are traceable to the regular work and training of the CPA.

2. Another danger, which is perhaps similar in nature to the foregoing, lies in the method in which the review is conducted. If it is not conducted on a well-organized and programmed basis, it can lead to trouble. This danger is particularly present when the CPA does not know in advance what the problem is. For example, the client's employees may feel that the CPA has been detailed by management to appraise the employees themselves.

3. Neglect of regular work in an effort to review management controls is yet another pitfall. While an enthusiastic staff man may not be able to wait to try to uncover deficiencies in the practices and policies involved in the credit and collection function, the regular work on the receivables must come first. It is not implied, of course, that regular work would be deliberately side-stepped in favor of the review—only that this might occur unless specific care is taken.

This point should be expanded in order to relate the review of management controls to the client's over-all system of internal control. A review of management controls, or its resultant recommendations, never compromises internal control: rather, its purpose is to appraise the over-all system of internal control and enhance its value. The American Institute of CPAs has defined the system of internal control as follows: "Internal control comprises the plan of organization and all of the co-ordinate methods and measures adopted within a business to safeguard its assets, check the accuracy and reliability of its accounting data, promote operational efficiency, and encourage adherence to prescribed managerial policies."[2]

The financial audit deals primarily with those aspects of internal control that "safeguard the assets of a business" and "check the accuracy and reliability of its accounting data." It is generally concerned to a lesser degree with controls adopted to "promote operational efficiency and

[2]See *Special Report on Internal Control,* AICPA Committee on Auditing Procedure, 1949, p. 6.

encourage adherence to prescribed managerial policies." The review of management controls primarily supplements the latter elements within the definition of internal control, but does so only by following the financial controls to the operating areas and to the controls which govern the activity of these areas. Thus, the review of management controls never by-passes, nor should its results weaken, the system of internal control. Rather, it should lead to an expansion of its total value—by determining whether it is adequate and effective in assisting management to achieve its profit objectives.

4. A CPA should not believe that his discovery of a management control deficiency necessarily requires his solution to the problem. By erroneously holding this attitude, a CPA might disqualify himself from undertaking a systematic management control review program in any area where he is doubtful of his competence to provide a complete solution. For example, a CPA might hesitate to appraise the potential of a cost system if he does not feel capable of installing his own recommendations. This would mean setting up an unnecessary barrier in management services work.

The emphasis in the review of management controls is *on the location of the problem,* for its basic purpose is to identify and signal the practices or policies requiring improvement. The solution should be thought of as a separate second step, and if special training is required to solve the problem, it can generally be obtained either through further study by the CPA or through the assistance of others.

There is no reason for a CPA to deny management control evaluations to business through self-imposed limitations resulting from an inability to provide a solution following discovery of a problem. The important thing to the management of a business is that the independent CPA point up the problem and recommend an approach to its correction. Correction may be made possible by management, by the CPA, or through the engagement of specialist CPAs.

Fee Structure

Need for a clear policy. A clear policy should be established with respect to fee structure. The accounting firm as a whole must know what rates will be charged. Intrafirm understanding in this area is essential if fee problems are to be avoided. All firm members should have accurate information that they can give to interested clients when they are assisting in arranging a management services engagement. The reasoning behind the fee structure should also be understood by the entire firm.

There is evidence that small CPA firms vary as to the rates charged for management services work. This is undoubtedly the result of the development of different policies with respect to the fees that should be charged. The results of the 1961 survey conducted by the American Institute of CPAs give useful insight into the experiences of others in establishing their fee structures for management services work. Specifically, the CPA firms were asked, "How do your rates for management services work compare to those charged for audit and tax work?

Higher .... Lower ....
by 10% ......, 25% ......, 50% ......, 75%......, 100%......."

Three hundred and forty-one firms completed this section of the questionnaire. Of these, 207 reported that their management services rates were higher than those charged for regular work. Only 8 firms reported that they charged lower rates; and 116 firms wrote in that they charged the same rates. The 207 firms indicated that management services rates were higher by the following percentages:

	Number	Percentage of total
10% higher	74	36
25% higher	96	46
50% higher	30	14
75% higher	4	2
100% higher	3	2
Total	207	100

Of the 8 firms reporting lower management services rates, 6 stated that rates were 10 per cent lower and 2 stated that rates were 25 per cent lower.

CPA firms engaged in management services work generally indicate that they have been able to obtain higher fees for management services work. The preceding table bears this out. However, it should be noted that 82 per cent of the smaller CPA firms report that these rates are only 10 to 25 per cent higher.

It is believed that the management services fee structure is somewhat higher in the national accounting firms. This may be the result of (1) higher overhead (including a lower ratio of chargeable time) and salary costs of specialists, and (2) size of the typical client served. The great majority of smaller firms do not have higher costs to contend with, mainly because they do not have separate specialized management services departments within their organizations. The smaller CPA firm, too, may encounter somewhat greater fee resistance from smaller business clients. Respondents reporting that their management service rates are higher than their regular work rates should encourage firms hesitant to enter the management services field for fear they would have difficulty arranging an adequate fee structure.

Need for Referral Service

Management service activities have become firmly established as a part of the customary functions of the CPA. The validity of the CPA's role in management services has been accepted by the public and the profession.

The growth of management service activity in CPA firms in recent years has been extensive. However, the growth in management service skills has been much more disproportionate among the various firms than the expansion of auditing and tax capability. Generally speaking, practicing CPAs have kept abreast of developments in the auditing and tax field. The expansion of knowledge and technical lore in the management services field has led to certain specialized services being offered by some CPAs which are not offered by others. Whether this disparity in activity and diversity of skills has been a matter of choice or difference in size, opportunity, or financial strength is unimportant. The existence of the disparity *is* important and creates the present need for developing a procedure for referral service among CPAs which will not only permit, but also encourage consultation and direct assistance on client problems.

No CPA will undertake to perform a specialized management service engagement beyond the scope of his professional competence; however, assuming that the need exists by the client for the service, the CPA would appear to have an obligation to obtain such service for the client. Referral to a CPA qualified to perform the service or to a non-CPA consultant is the alternative. It is obvious that the profession as a whole would benefit from greater utilization of capabilities from its own ranks.

The referral machinery envisioned here embraces a service by one CPA to another and/or to the latter's client. Such a service could, in some cases, be limited to a consulting arrangement whereby the CPA referred to would, in effect, be engaged by the referror CPA to advise and prescribe certain procedures which would be undertaken by the latter. In such cases, it may be possible for the referee to remain anonymous to the client. In most instances, however, acceptable standards of practice and the degree of responsibility required for competent professional management services will compel the CPA performing the engagement to have contact with and work on the premises of the client.

Other professions

The other professions that have regularly made referrals among their own membership (law and medicine, for example) usually do so in a manner and in circumstances whereby particular matters are referred to specialists not engaged in the same line of practice (such as brain surgeon, heart specialist, or admiralty attorney); therefore, encroachment is not ordinarily a problem. However, in those instances where the specialist represents a firm or has a practice that renders the same services as the referror, long-established customs and a mutual regard and understanding between both professional parties have usually been sufficient to avoid encroachment problems.

There is little doubt that the fundamental philosophy of ethics, particularly in regard to encroachment, of the CPA profession is similar to that of other recognized professions. However, the range in size of firms, scope of practice, areas served, and other aspects of the CPA profession appear to distinguish it from other mature professional fields. Moreover, the hallmarks of specific competency in the management services area are not at this time sufficiently apparent to others, both within and without the profession, so that the selection of a specialist can be accomplished with the same degree of confidence as can be done in the case of attorneys or medical doctors (who have directories or specialized academies identifying particular fields of practice).

Larger firms

A number of the larger CPA firms have carefully developed internal controls over the quality of their services and have earned international respect for their proficiencies. These firms appear to be reluctant to accept referrals from any other CPA in a manner which might restrict or limit application of their own standards of client service. Accordingly, some of these "national" firms do not wish to extend assurances relative to encroachment on a blanket basis to another CPA who might refer a problem to them. However, it is encouraging to note that most of the larger firms interrogated on this subject indicated that they would favorably consider giving assurances on a selective basis under conditions they considered appropriate. In view of this attitude, it may be possible to provide a referral service that would protect the interests of both parties if an *elective* rather than *mandatory* code of assurances could be established. Under such a program, the referring CPA could inquire of the firm or firms he may select to assist him or his client whether or not they would subscribe to the conventions. The firm referred to would be free to accept or reject the conventions, and the referror would then be in a position to decide whether to make the referral or not, depending on the position of the specialist as to such assurances.

Smaller firms

An analysis of practice and opinion of firms considered most likely to require specialized assistance in the management services area indicated that a major obstacle to a workable referral program was a strong fear of encroachment. Most smaller firms stipulated that they would require adequate assurances that their existing client relationship would not be disturbed. As might be expected, the type of assurances desired and their relation to the scope of services varied considerably.

CHAPTER TWO

Financial Planning Engagements

Organizing for Financial Planning

Organization Planning and Charting[1]

A soundly planned organization and work classification system is an essential first step in the efficient operation of any business. The logically conceived and implemented organization permits the establishment of a compatible work climate whereby people can develop and increase their contribution to the business, and where savings will result from economical operation. Such a system is a vital management tool in that it must be considered in conjunction with the attainment of company objectives and planning for future growth.

Principles of organization

Before analyzing the subject by means of a case study, let us review a few principles and rules of organization structure, because these will have a direct bearing on the nature and direction of the evaluation.

Responsibility definition. The responsibilities of each position within an organization should be defined clearly and explicitly. In this way, an individual will know precisely what his job content is and what is expected of him. The necessity of running to his supervisor for counsel and advice every time he faces a new situation will be eliminated. Properly prepared, job descriptions will also show how a position and its work content interrelate with others in an office.

An example of a properly prepared job description follows:

[1]Pages 63-70 adapted, with permission, from an article by Alan J. Fredian in the October 1961 issue of *Management Controls*. Copyrighted 1961 by Peat Marwick, Mitchell & Co.

JOB DESCRIPTION: CONTROLLER

Report to:

The president

Basic function:

To assist the president and his principal executives to obtain maximum profits; spearheads the joint development of realistic operating and investment plans and standards, and administers a system of positive follow-up and controls.

Supervises:

Manager of Controls and Analysis
Manager of Industrial Statistics
Manager of Procedures and Audits
Manager of Cost Accounting
Manager of General Accounting
Manager of Office Services

Specific duties:

PLANNING

1. Develops and publishes the ground rules for company short- and long-range planning and the general procedure to be followed by each function. Works with department heads to co-ordinate their planning with company policies and objectives.

2. Reviews and clears all cost standards and measures of activity proposed by departments for use in plans and budgets. Initiates studies of areas where measures are not felt to be reliable.

3. Combines the proposed plans of all departments. Appraises the effects on profit, financial, and market position, and the progress anticipated. Evaluates the realism of the proposed plan against general business and industry conditions. Summarizes points of importance for the president and recommends action on the master plan of operations and investment.

4. Issues monthly projections of current operating results for several months ahead, relating changes to the original plan.

FOLLOW-UP

5. Develops and ensures timely issuance of control reports to the president and his principal executives. Administers a system of supporting reports to underlying levels of supervision.

6. Performs periodic review and appraisal of operations, involving study of performance in all operating areas and determination of factors underlying poor or good results.

7. Conducts a monthly review meeting with the president to bring out significant operating results and action points. Assists the president to prepare for his own follow-up meetings with key operating executives.

8. Works with all levels of supervision to develop understanding of quotas and budgets, the use of control reports, and the technique of holding review meetings on their own performance.

9. Reviews major pricing proposals for maximum profitability and thorough analysis of volume effect.

10. Conducts general accounting, cost estimating, cost accounting, and payroll activities, ensuring adequate control over sources of basic data and conformance with government contract requirements. Issues necessary statements, reports, and special statistics.

11. Co-ordinates the development of and publishes all interdepartmental procedures and all manuals and procedures with control significance; audits conformance to such procedures and manuals. Initiates steps to simplify procedures and cut costs.

12. Provides necessary office services.

13. Administers a reports control system covering all recurring reports in the company.

Authority. Along with responsibility, there must be a commensurate specification of authority. While this may seem obvious, it is often overlooked and couched in vague terminology. A man is assigned to a task and proceeds to work on it, but everywhere he encounters opposition. With no authority to overcome obstacles or generate support and co-operation, he either gives up or seeks to compromise on less effective alternatives. In the absence of authority, the issue frequently is settled by the stronger person, even though he may not have the better solution.

Delegation of work. Activities and responsibilities should be delegated on down the organization to the lowest level of adequate performance and control. This simply means that work which can be carried out on a subordinate level should not be conducted on a higher plane. Another way of providing for this in a company is to set monetary limits of authority: the treasurer must approve all disbursements over $500, but the accounts payable clerk can approve those under this amount. This kind of delegation allows the key officers to spend more time on planning functions.

Line of reporting. In the ordinary course of events, orders, instructions, or directions should be relayed to employees by their immediate supervisor rather than by more remote levels of supervision or others with no direct authority. Evading key men and direct transmission of orders tends to undermine the supervisor's position. This is not as easily done where the business is small in size and work relationships are quite informal or where family ties and other arrangements exist. The converse is also true, namely employees should not be allowed to go around their supervisors to seek permission from higher management levels. The burden of responsibility and authority has been placed with a supervisor for a reason. He should be allowed to exercise it without interference or complication from others. Only in this way will supervisors grow and develop fully in their positions.

Dual authority. By the same token, an individual should not receive directions from more than one line executive or officer. In a survey form used in many business organizational studies, there is a question which asks the individual to identify the person or persons to whom he reports and their job title or titles. Given the opportunity, an employee will often name more than one person, and occasionally three or more. In one company, for example, the vice-president in charge of finance is located near accountants who report to the secretary-treasurer. But when questions arise, the accountants take them to the vice-president because he is nearest to them. A close look at an organization may reveal many subtle arrangements of this nature.

Climate for change. One of the prime rules of work simplification is to explain the impact of changes before they are made, lest people resent this invasion on their work habits. The same is true with organizational changes, perhaps to an even greater degree because personalities are involved. Organizational changes should be studied with respect to their effect on all individuals involved and the entire work climate.

With these basic rules and principles firmly in mind, the phase of developing duties and responsibilities for every function or position in a business may be initiated.

Case study

This analysis of duties and responsibilities is bound to produce a few surprises when all the facts are drawn into a structured organization chart. Figure 1, page 67, shows the actual organization of a savings and loan association before the study of what, where, and by whom work is performed and sequence of individual reporting has taken place. Examination of the chart and recollection of the rules of organizational planning reveal some interesting arrangements. The secretary-treasurer, president, and vice-president are all on the same level and report to the board of directors as a committee. Since the president is not running the business, who makes the day-to-day decisions? Every time a question is asked or a problem posed does the committee convene to resolve the problem? This method is far too cumbersome to be practical. The assistant secretary for savings as well as the secretary-treasurer report to the president. The vice-president of loans has two typists reporting directly to him although the secretary-treasurer is responsible for office activity.

The above organization plan gives rise to the following questions:

Who supervises the assistant secretary?

On what issues can the president act alone?

Who hires and supervises the secretarial help?

By applying the principles of accountability, division of work, responsibility, and authority to each position, the entire organization is studied in detail and revised in accordance with the objectives and personality of the association. The latter phase is called synthesis.

From analysis to synthesis, the approach is similar to psychoanalysis. A person goes to a psychoanalyst when he is unable to function effectively as an individual. The analyst studies his personality over a period of time and then restructures it for a better orientation to his environment. The organization essentially goes through these same steps of analysis and synthesis before it emerges in restructured form. In addition to the im-

Figure I

ABC COMPANY: ACTUAL ORGANIZATION

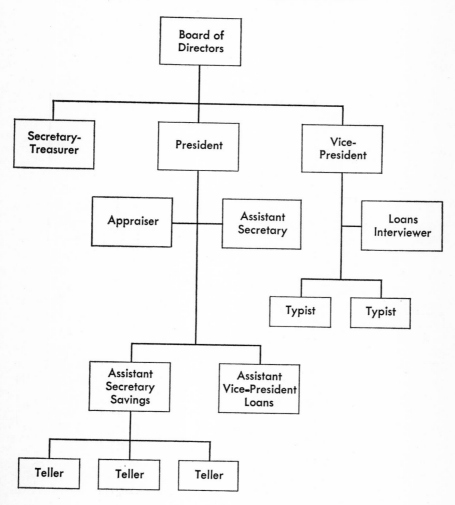

mediate day-to-day problems, plans for future growth and expansion should be considered.

Turning to the association under study, the results of this kind of evaluation are apparent in the new structure shown in Figure 2, below. Under the new organization, the vice-president in charge of loans has an appraiser and a loan officer reporting to him; his function is well integrated. The position of loan officer provides a training ground for future executives. The president now has the responsibility and authority to act as managing

Figure 2

ABC COMPANY: CHART AFTER REORGANIZATION

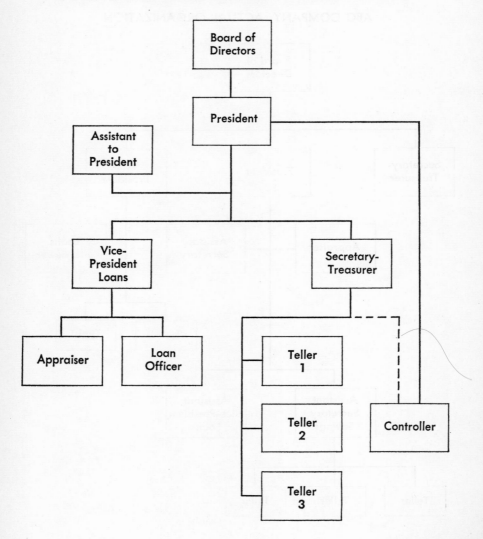

officer. He has time to plan improvement of the association's investments and devise means to increase the income of the association. The assistant secretary was made assistant to the president. Although an advertising agency handles the entire advertising operation, many miscellaneous activities in advertising and other areas can be handled by the assistant to the president. The secretary-treasurer's position is comparable to the controller's in many associations, but the controller here is basically an internal auditor and general accountant. Human factors have determined the particular development of this organization. The secretary-treasurer is a thirty-year employee of the association. He has developed a number of wonderful friends and the customers respect him. Nevertheless, he is extremely weak in terms of his accounting and executive know-how. As a result, the controller's position was created under him to combine the controller function with the internal audit function. Although the controller is functionally in the secretary-treasurer's organization, he actually reports to the president. This arrangement circumvents the awkward situation of having a man report to an officer whom he has been continually auditing.

Organization and morale

Time and patience are necessary to implement a totally new organization scheme because employee morale is sharply affected. One study on the relationship among morale, discipline, organization, and customer complaints (Figure 3, below) revealed that fewer complaints occurred

Figure 3

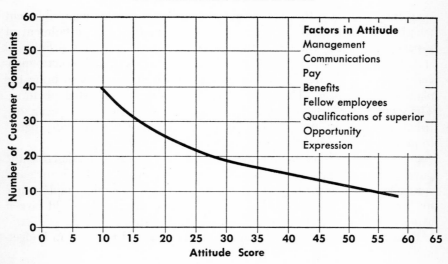

ATTITUDES TOWARD COMPANY RELATED
TO CUSTOMER COMPLAINTS

when favorable attitudes were reported concerning management, internal communications, pay rates, benefits, fellow employees, and so on. The higher the morale, the friendlier personnel were with customers. Consequently, organizational change should be conducted in an atmosphere which will boost rather than undermine morale.

The plan should be formalized, discussed thoroughly, and perhaps tied in with personnel benefits and practices.

Summary

Organization is not an arrangement of slots in a wall chart or a group of fancy titles. It is the description and logical structuring of work and the establishment of accountability and authority for efficient performance. Organization requires careful planning as well as analysis and synthesis because the results will have a long-term effect on operating efficiency and control. It is a dynamic tool for the accomplishment of management objectives, good for both small and large businesses. It is a requisite to sound budgetary planning if responsibility is to be established for the planned goals.

Budgeting for Profit

Helping the Client With His Budget Problems

Budgeting is a term that has many different meanings for many different people. One man thinks of it as a sales guess, another as a curtailment of expenditures. Others see it as estimated cash flow or a projected financial statement. Those familiar with budgeting see it as both a complete financial plan for a business and a device for control of activities to bring the plan into realization. The central idea should be co-ordinated planning. The scope should cover all operations—selling, production, purchasing, distribution, administration, and financing. Its purpose is controlled progress to profit and financial objectives.

C. E. Knoeppel coined the name "profit engineering" to describe the profit phase of budgeting. He wanted profits to be planned in advance and controlled much as plant production is controlled. The modern budget, like his profit engineering, should have a profit objective, and should give it expression in a projected income statement for a future period.

Prior Sinclair makes this statement on the financial program in budgeting:

The balance sheet at the end of the preceding year presents a situation that is to be maintained or bettered by the coming year's operation, the results of which will be written into next year's balance sheet. Between these two statements are the multitudinous details of operation which every business performs and which the budget endeavors to plan to a favorable outcome.[2]

This financial objective of the budget is best expressed in a projected balance sheet.

Cash budgeting, which is so frequently found in practice, is a projection of cash receipts and disbursements through analysis of the items of the projected income statement and the changes in balance sheet items.

The co-ordinated plan for profits, financial condition, and cash is called a master budget. The subdivision of the plan into component units consists of budgets of sales; production; expense; capital outlay; financing; and cash receipts and disbursements. Further subdivision is possible. For example, the production budget can be separated into budgets for material, labor, and manufacturing expense.

Budgetary control provides the methods for attainment of the expected results. It uses standards, timely and accurate records of actual operations, a comparison of actual with budgeted amounts, and a careful analysis of variations between expected and actual operations.

Consultants versus staff

In business planning, large businesses use staff specialists for counseling, but occasionally they engage outside consultants. Small businesses, which lack centralized staffs, frequently seek specialized knowledge and skills from consultants. The small, owner-operated businesses, especially those which gradually take on staff as they grow, seem to have special need for outside services in budgeting and other phases of business planning.

There is one basic difference between service to a large and a small business. In a large business the availability of specialized staff and operating personnel somewhat reduces the detailed work of the CPA. The CPA serving a small business frequently must do much of the work involved in putting his recommendations into effect.

One thing is certain. Business, large or small, needs to budget. Generally, large businesses, with functional divisions and staff organization, have some form of budgeting, but this often falls short of the requirements for complete and effective budgeting. Many small businesses operate with no budget at all. Perhaps this is one of the reasons why so many new business enterprises fail.

It is not necessary to have complete budgeting in order to improve operating performance. The CPA can help his client in planning one or more

---

[2]*Budgeting,* Ronald Press, New York, 1934.

phases of operating problems, which may not be thought of as budgeting problems, but which in reality constitute foundation work or basic steps in developing a budget. Typical help of this nature includes supplying or improving: organization; charts of accounts; financial accounting system; cost accounting; inventory control; procurement; job evaluation; salary and wage plans; profit planning; cash control; capital requirements; volume, price, and cost relationships.

If there are inefficiencies arising out of unsatisfactory accounting, operations, or personnel, they should not be frozen into budget standards. A budget has little chance of success if the business organization, chart of accounts, and accounting procedures do not follow functional lines and do not establish responsibility in conformity with delegated authority.

Although the budget is specifically a responsibility of top management, it concerns all lines of management. Consequently, division and department heads must have a part in setting their individual objectives. They will be responsible for the divisional or departmental action under the established budget. The CPA frequently starts the development of the budget by selling top management on the need for a budget. He can help in the job of securing co-operation of the division and department heads in forming the budget and establishing effective procedures.

Budgetary planning and control

Why are there so many small companies, and larger companies, which do not have any part of a complete program of budgetary planning and control? The answer is found in several misconceptions of budgeting which are encountered rather generally. These are that budgeting:

1. Is a complex process
2. Increases the costs of the accounting function substantially
3. Is a restrictive procedure which limits or inhibits management decision
4. Is a guessing game as to what the results and position will be sometime in the future; the budget will therefore always be missed so "why have one?"

The first step in instituting budgetary planning and control in a business is to correct these misconceptions.

Budgeting is not a complex process. It complements and parallels the accounting, cost accounting, and statistical procedures. It is simply an orderly process of planning income, costs, and capital expenditures for a period and the financial position at the end of that period, and then comparing actuals with the plans during the period to secure indications of required corrective action, or of modification of the plans. Budgeting cannot run ahead of the existing system of accounts and records. If sales are recorded only in total, then the sales budget is for total sales. If they are recorded by sales office, then they are budgeted by office. If they are recorded by product line, they are budgeted by product line. Costs are budgeted in the same detail as actual costs are recorded. This same parallel is followed for each phase of the budget.

There is some added cost when a budget is instituted. Actuals must be compared with the budget and deviations must be analyzed, and these must be reported to the persons having responsibility for the function and to top management. Experience has shown that these added costs range from 10 to 20 per cent of the cost of the accounting and statistical processes without budgeting. This added cost is recovered many times over in increased operational efficiency.

The idea that budgets are restrictive goes back to the origin of budgets in governmental operations. These were and are supposed to be fixed budgets establishing spending limits which cannot be exceeded. Recent experience, particularly with the Federal budget, demonstrates the fallacy of this concept, even in government. Business budgets must be flexible budgets which provide for the adjustment of the budgeted amounts to those which are applicable to actual conditions experienced during the period for which comparisons are made. Within this concept budgets are and should be restrictive. If the plans were sound, every management decision should be directed toward meeting the plans. There should be aversion to underruns of income and overruns of expenditures. However, the profit objective must always be paramount. If an expenditure in excess of budget will result in profits which would not be realized if the expenditure were not made, the expenditure is justified. The analysis of deviations would explain this. Therefore, budgeting provides a basis for evaluating the probable results of decisions before they are made and the actual results after they are made. It stimulates rather than inhibits management decision.

Evaluating results

It is true that actual results are seldom, if ever, exactly as budgeted. The virtue of a budget is that plans must be made in some detail, and that it tells why the plans did not materialize or were bettered. The very act of planning leads to a critical examination of what is being done. This is constructive, for even in the smallest business, under the close control of the owner-manager, practices develop which may be desirable at the time but are continued long after the reason for them has passed. Removal of these in the budget building process has a favorable effect on profits and may easily pay for the entire cost of the budget program. Then, the very fact that a budget is not being met generates questions as to why, and what can be done. These are raised during the period, long before final financial statements are prepared. There is an established procedure for bringing them to the attention of management. Instead of "flying by the seat of their pants," managers have the instrumentation and controls to tell them where they are in relation to their "flight plan" and the direction and degree of correction required to get them back on the beam. Again, the effect on profits is favorable.

There is great danger, in starting a budget in any business, and particularly a small business, that too much detail will be incorporated at the start. The CPA should sell the idea of a simple budget to his client. Later the process can be expanded as the simple budget proves its worth in operation and management feels the need of more detail for closer control.

Mechanics and techniques

Much of the accounting literature and discussions concerned with managerial accounting are devoted almost exclusively to the *mechanics and techniques* of such procedures as budgeting, standard costing, direct costing, breakeven analysis, and cost analysis. No one can deny that such techniques have excellent potentialities in appropriate settings. More important, the critical test of their potentialities in a given situation is the extent to which management uses the results in the process of decision making and in planning and controlling operations.

In any given situation, a basic problem is to put *techniques* and *application* together so that management has a system suited to the situation and fundamentally sound in principle and design, yet tangible and detailed enough for specific application as well as for broad use.

Budgetary planning and control as practiced today by the better managements provides the only systematic and tangible approach so far developed for bringing sufficient certainty to management planning and control and for applying the above-mentioned management dictates in a co-ordinated and practical manner.

Budgetary planning and control is a comprehensive system whereby all aspects of the management process may be brought into a co-ordinated whole, and where the loose ends of management action and operations may be carefully tied together. This all-inclusive concept of the budgetary process is frequently misunderstood by some managements and by some CPAs.

In order to comprehend the full importance of budgeting, a careful distinction must be made in budgetary planning and control between (1) mechanics and techniques, and (2) fundamentals or principles. Mechanics have to do with such matters as design of budget schedules, clerical methods in completing such schedules, and routine computations. The techniques of budgeting are many and varied. For example, we may note methods of developing the sales budget, breakeven analysis, capital budget procedures, cash-flow analyses, and variable budgets.

The mechanical aspect of budgeting is a "natural" for CPAs since there is much in common here with the accounting model. This fortunate situation not infrequently leads to serious pitfalls, such as an oversimplified view of the budgetary process and a possibly unjustified feeling of competence with respect to it. An unfortunate by-product is the possible failure to realize the full potential of budgetary planning and control in a given situation.

Frequently a budget program may be appropriately characterized as a mere mechanical or technical exercise with no deep-rooted management involvement. This situation occurs, for example, when the company accountant, the company budget director, or the independent CPA "draws up the budget."

Techniques are important. The characteristics and problems of the firm should determine the particular techniques to be employed as well as the way in which these should be adapted and applied.

To have an effective budgetary planning and control system, the mechanics and techniques of budgeting must be brought into complete harmony with management problems and needs. To accomplish this objective in any situation there must be a clear understanding of certain underlying fundamentals. These have much more in common with the process of management and enlightened human relations than with accounting. It is for this reason that CPAs need considerable depth of understanding of management methods, policy formulation, organization principles, and behavioral sciences.

Fundamental principles

Fundamental principles are concerned directly with the basic management functions of planning, co-ordination, and control. First and foremost, systematic planning for the individual firm for both the short run (one year or less) and the long run is essential. A recent survey of 424 better-managed companies revealed that over 96 per cent of them develop detailed and comprehensive short-range budgets on a formal basis. Approximately 65 per cent reported that they develop formal long-range budgets. A systematic and formal approach to planning is essential, particularly in view of the fact that indefinite plans seldom have meaning, are frequently forgotten or, at least, are inconsistently changed. Planning is essential to judicious employment of available resources; and a firm, no less than an individual, needs well-defined goals and objectives. Planning is the easiest function of management to put off. It seldom if ever forces our hand at the present—we can always temporize. The most effective planning in a firm generally comes from the combined efforts of the management team rather than from one individual or a single staff group.

The present-day concept of the planning budget (preferably *plan of operation*), coupled with the long-range budget, appears to be the only generally applicable, satisfactory approach so far developed to facilitate in a systematic manner the planning function of management. The planning budget expresses in financial terms management plans and policies for the period under consideration. It is the first step in effective profit engineering. From the mechanical point of view, the planning budget concept is simple for the accountant. From the point of view of technique, it becomes more involved, and from the point of view of "principles," simplicity ceases altogether. The following are important fundamentals or principles relating directly to *managerial planning* through budgeting:

1. Organization. Budgetary planning must rest upon sound organization structure coupled with clear-cut lines of authority and responsibility. Plans and budgets should be developed in terms of individual responsibilities. It is people who get things done. Planned performance must therefore be directly related to organizational responsibilities.

2. Responsibility accounting. Budgeting requires an effective accounting system tailored to the organizational structure and to assigned responsibilities so that individual performance can be measured and evaluated. An accounting system tailored to external needs and to "generally accepted accounting principles" is essential but by itself is inadequate for management planning and control needs.

3. Participation. This principle requires clearly defined responsibilities for input of planned data. It is basic that those having supervisory responsibilities should be responsible to the fullest possible extent for developing the plans for carrying out such responsibilities, in conformity with the plans and policies of higher levels of management. Achieving meaningful involvement in the planning process is not easy. Lower levels of management react favorably to participation, yet certain checks and restraints are necessary. Token participation is apt to create negative reactions. Participation by lower levels of management imposes a prior responsibility on higher levels of management to clearly define and circumscribe policies well in advance. Planning budget procedures provides a framework suitable for participating management. Accounting and budget experts may design and co-ordinate the planning system, but those who have to perform should build the budget and provide the input data. This procedure makes possible effective implementation of the participation principle in management.

4. Timeliness. This principle holds that there must be a definite schedule for planning activities, preferably in the form of a written "planning schedule." Once a management firmly commits itself in this manner to budgetary planning, procrastination in planning largely ends. Successful managements today report this result to be one of the most important indirect benefits accruing from a budgetary program. Whereas before it was practically impossible to assemble certain management groups intact for planning sessions, following adoption of such a program this activity often takes precedence similar to that of a meeting of the board of directors. In many companies executives absolutely refuse to make outside commitments during the critical phases of budget planning. Many such companies which budget effectively report that for the first time both strategic and detailed planning are on a rational and timely basis. Nothing is more devastating to effectual planning than for management to issue a budget some time after the beginning of the period involved.

5. *Confidence.* The management must be confident that it can significantly influence the course of events for the company and that it is its duty to plan such influence. It must be convinced that realistic policies and goals can be developed in advance and that it is desirable to do so. It must operate under the belief that persons having management responsibilities in the firm tend to tie their own success to that of the firm, and will therefore strive seriously and aggressively to attain *known* and *realistic* goals.

6. *Flexibility.* This principle holds that there must be recognition from all levels of management that a budget will not manage the business, and that flexibility in applying the budget must be the rule so that no straitjackets are imposed and no opportunities passed up merely because they are not covered by the budget.

7. *Realism.* In budget planning the management must exercise neither undue conservatism nor irrational optimism. The objective should be to plan realistically attainable goals and objectives.

Systematic planning as a fundamental aspect of the budgetary program and some related principles have been briefly examined. Another concept is that of *control* as a fundamental aspect of budgeting.

In the process of control, problems of human relations stand out clearly as the most critical consideration. A management does not need a budget to practice poor human relations; alternatively, a budget program may be a vehicle for accentuating either enlightened or poor human relations. The weaknesses of a management in this respect are frequently attributed to budgeting.

Principles of budgetary control

The essentials or principles related to effective budgetary control are:

1. *Individual recognition.* This is primarily a system whereby the individual is recognized, and both outstanding and substandard performance

are revealed. The system of evaluation must be fair, understandable, and reasonably accurate. It should give recognition to the abilities of the individual, his aspirations, his reactions, and to the group pressures that affect him. The individual's dignity must be respected.

2. *Organization.* This involves a principle mentioned earlier with respect to planning. Since control is exercised through people, there must be a clear-cut delineation of responsibilities from the organizational point of view as well as in terms of goals. What do we expect of the individual supervisor? Planning is fundamental in clarifying this situation; sound planning is thus basic in establishing effective control. The measurement and reporting of actual performance must be in terms of organizational responsibilties.

3. *Effective communication.* Communication implies a common understanding between two or more individuals on a given point. Communication for effective control should be such that both superior and subordinate have the same understanding of responsibilities and goals. The planning budget, built in terms of responsibilities and developed to a large extent by the supervisor himself, assures a degree of understanding not otherwise possible.

4. *Standards.* A system of goals, objectives, or standards is vital to control. There must be bench marks to which performance may be related. Basically, standards are essential (a) to provide a target at which to shoot, and (b) to provide a bench mark against which actual results may be compared in order to measure control; that is, to determine the degree of efficiency or inefficiency with respect to attainment of the goals.

5. *Management by exception.* This principle holds that the busy executive should devote his time to the unusual or exceptional items, rather than worry about those matters that are not out of line. Dealing with out-of-line items is enough of an accomplishment, without having to pinpoint them. To make this principle effective, the control system must be designed so that the exceptions stand out. By emphasizing variations, budgetary planning and control provides a method whereby the attention of successively higher levels of management is called to the exception. This principle obviously requires comparison of an actual with a realistic standard. The usual comparison with last year's results is unsatisfactory since these frequently constitute an unreliable standard. Budgeting stands far out in front as the basic, practical approach to effective management by exception.

6. *Follow-up.* This principle holds that both good and bad performance should be investigated, the purpose being threefold: (a) in the case of

poor performance, to lead to corrective action immediately and in a constructive manner; (b) in the case of outstanding performance, to recognize it and perhaps provide for a transfer of knowledge to similar operations; (c) to provide a basis for improved planning and control in the future.

7. *Flexibility*. Expense and cost budgets must not be used and interpreted inflexibly. They must not prevent the making of rational decisions merely because the expenditure is not covered by the budget.

Variable or flexible expense budgets are frequently employed to meet the problems of expense control arising from the volume differential. To illustrate the point, assume that the budget for Department X carries an allowance of $2,000 for indirect labor; 10,000 units of production are planned. Now assume that unforeseen circumstances make it necessary to produce 12,000 units. Obviously, a comparison of actual costs incurred at 12,000 units with a budget allowance based on 10,000 units would show an unfavorable, and more significantly, a meaningless variation. The variable budget provides a means of adjusting the budget allowance to the actual volume prior to the comparison. This does not mean that because variable budget allowances are available they should be allowed to influence the effort to develop realistic volume forecasts initially.

8. *Cost consciousness*. Both experience and investigation have demonstrated that attitudes of cost consciousness are fundamental to effective cost control. To illustrate, investigations have shown that if an executive is cost conscious, his subordinates likewise tend to be cost conscious by a margin of three to one, as compared to situations where the executive is not cost conscious. Here we are dealing with attitudes, with the psychology of the individual and of the work group. Our control system must be designed to take advantage of these psychological phenomena.

Summary

There are three broad aspects of budgetary planning and control: the mechanics, the techniques, and the underlying fundamentals. Mechanics are relatively simple, yet undue concern with them may cloud our thinking with respect to the budgetary process. The techniques available must be known and understood. The underlying principles of the budget process are of primary significance; they have much more in common with the process of management and enlightened human relations than with accounting. Budgetary planning and control go directly to the heart of:

Organization structure

Delegation of authority and responsibility

Accounting keyed to lines of authority and responsibility

Effective communication

Enlightened human relations

A budget program has great potential if it is designed and operated on a sound basis. The program must be sound mechanically and technically, but it must also rest on a firm foundation of basic principles. We must therefore conclude that a budgetary planning and control program is not simple, and that broad competence is essential on the part of those upon whose shoulders the task may rest.

What does all this add up to for the CPA in public practice? The area of budgetary planning and control clearly stands out as a potential for the CPA interested in expanding his services. Management, particularly in medium and small firms, is in need of this kind of assistance. It has been estimated that practicing CPAs, with their present clients, could expand their practice by at least 15 to 25 per cent by focusing on this one area alone. This is possible because it would inevitably lead the CPA into organizational studies, accounting system design and improvement, budgetary system design and improvement, internal reporting problems, and direct advice to management concerning specific decisions. Budgetary planning and control provides the practicing CPA with an unequaled service for helping the client to stay in business and make more profits. Who can question the value of a realistic, well-designed road map for the immediate future, coupled with a simple control system, for the owner of a small business?

Classification of Budgets

Three principal categories of budgets are the appropriation budget, the fixed budget, and the flexible budget.

The appropriation budget shows the amount of money which can be spent on a particular activity for a given period of time. It is usually planned at the beginning of the year and consists of a fixed amount for that year. This type of budget is used to control government expenditures. Advertising and research and development budgets are examples of appropriation budgets used in business.

The fixed (or static) budget is based on a single volume of business activity. Once a level of activity is predetermined, the fixed budget is prepared for anticipated expenses only at that one level. If the volume of activity changes, the actual expense can be compared only with the figures established in the budget. Obviously, a fixed budget has doubtful validity if a level of activity changes, since most expenses are affected by changes in volume.

The flexible (or variable) budget is a refinement of the fixed budget. It is so constructed that expenses can be adjusted to changes in business activity. It represents a series of fixed budgets established at all probable levels of activity. The flexible budget recognizes that some expenses do not remain constant but are affected by changes in production or sales. Construction of a flexible budget involves analyzing each item of expense and breaking it down into either the fixed or variable component.

Cost behavior

All costs and expenses are dependent upon (1) the passing of time and/or (2) the level of activity. When considered from this viewpoint, they fall into three categories.

1. Fixed costs. Fixed costs are period costs and tend to remain constant within a certain range of activity. It would be ludicrous to suppose that fixed costs remain the same at all possible operating capacities. However, within a relevant range, fixed costs will not vary. Although total fixed costs remain the same, fixed costs per unit of output decline with increased production.

2. Variable costs. Variable costs, as contrasted to fixed costs, change proportionately with changes in plant activity. Variable costs do not vary proportionately with activity from zero to full capacity, but their variability must be considered within the normal range of plant operations. In order to measure variable costs as they apply to some function or product, they must be related to a measure of plant activity which most closely parallels the particular cost. Variable cost per unit of output will remain constant within the relevant range of plant activity.

3. Semivariable costs. Semivariable costs are composed of both fixed and variable elements. They will increase or decrease with various levels of activity but this change will not be in direct proportion to activity. It is the semivariable costs which create the most perplexing problems in constructing the flexible budget.

The factor of variability

The factor of variability refers to a measure of plant activity which is most closely related to a particular expense. The ideal situation is one in which the expense and measure of activity are directly proportionate to one another. Some of the more commonly suggested bases of variability are:

> Unit basis
> Material cost basis
> Labor cost basis

Prime cost basis
Labor hour basis
Machine hour basis

The trained judgment of the CPA is helpful in the selection of the appropriate measure of variability. The CPA must deliberate the following three key points before arriving at a decision:

1. The factor of variability which causes costs to vary, by department if possible.
2. The factor of variability which is most sensitive to changes in volume of activity in the plant or department.
3. The factor of variability which is both easy to understand and compute with reasonable accuracy.

Once a factor has been selected for the flexible budget, it should be used only so long as it remains the most applicable measure of variability. If the production process changes or newer machines are introduced, it may be necessary to select a different factor.

Selecting expense categories

After a factor of variability has been selected for a particular cost center or department, it is necessary to study each expense item to decide in which expense classification it belongs—fixed, variable, or semivariable. The selection of a proper expense classification is not a simple task. It requires due deliberation and the exercise of sound judgment. After the fixed and variable expenses are properly classified, it is a simple matter to construct budget figures for them. The semivariable expenses cause the greatest difficulty because they should be separated into their fixed and variable components. Many methods have been suggested for budgeting semivariable expenses. Two of the more common methods are (1) the high- and low-points method and (2) the correlation method. The correlation method may be solved graphically or by a least-squares method.

Budgeting semivariable expenses

The high- and low-points method is best described with a simple illustration. Suppose a CPA is preparing a flexible budget for the Southway Company and is confronted with the problem of determining the fixed and variable components of indirect labor cost. He has found that direct machine hours provide a better measure of costs than direct labor hours, his alternative choice. He finds that the company has records which provide him with information relating to machine hours. This data, together with indirect labor costs, is shown on page 83.

Correlation methods for determining the fixed and variable components of costs are based on the assumption that the past pattern of how costs have varied is the best estimate of how they will vary in the future. A graph is prepared with cost on the vertical scale and volume on the horizontal scale. The historical data is plotted and a trend line is drawn by inspection through the plotted points. The point at which the trend line intersects the vertical scale represents the constant portion of cost. Using the information provided for the Southway Company, the graphic method of correlation would produce the results shown in Figure 4, page 84.

1. The point at which the trend line intersects the cost scale appears to be slightly less than $900, i.e., $890. This amount is the fixed element of cost for the month. The annual fixed cost would be 12 × $890 = $10,680.

Month	Direct machine hours	Indirect labor cost
January	25,000	$ 1,625
February	22,000	1,525
March	11,000	1,230
April	30,500	1,825
May	49,000	2,370
June	19,000	1,440
July	14,000	1,280
August	28,000	1,750
September	25,000	1,700
October	26,500	1,725
November	20,000	1,560
December	30,000	1,770
Total	300,000	$19,800

The variable rate and fixed element of cost are computed as follows:

INDIRECT LABOR

Activity	Direct machine hours	Expense
High	49,000	$2,370
Low	11,000	1,230
Difference	38,000	$1,140

Variable rate = $1,140 ÷ 38,000 hours = $0.03 per direct machine hour
Fixed cost = $2,370 − (49,000 × $0.03)
= $2,370 − 1,470
= $900

2. The fixed expense is subtracted from the total expense to determine the variable element of expense. Thus, $19,800 − $10,680 = $9,120, which is the total annual variable expense. The amount of variable cost per direct machine hour is obtained by dividing the variable cost by the number of direct machine hours. Thus $9,120 ÷ 300,000 hours = $0.0304 per direct machine hour.

It is often difficult to draw a trend line by inspection through the plotted data.

Method of least squares. The method of least squares is a mathematical technique which may be used by itself or to check the results obtained by the graphic correlation method. Its purpose is to compute the trend line mathematically so that the sum of the deviations of the plotted points from the trend line equals zero. In other words, the trend line, so determined, passes closest (on the average) to all the plotted points.

Figure 4

GRAPHIC COST ANALYSIS, 1960—INDIRECT LABOR (SOUTHWAY COMPANY)

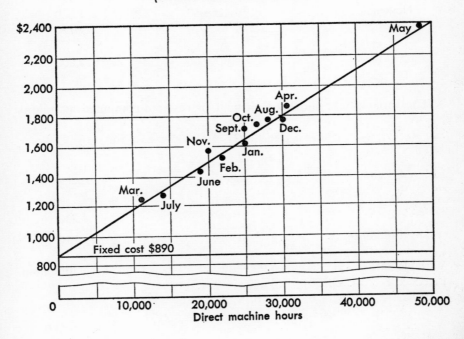

The least squares method is illustrated by the following five steps based upon the data for indirect labor of the Southway Company.

STEP 1: Compute, first, the arithmetic average of the monthly direct machine hours and the arithmetic average of the monthly indirect labor expense using the data for the twelve month period.

$$\text{Average monthly direct machine hours} = \frac{\text{Direct machine hours}}{12} = \frac{300,000 \text{ hours}}{12} = 25,000 \text{ hours}$$

$$\text{Average monthly indirect labor expense} = \frac{\text{Indirect labor cost}}{12} = \frac{\$19,800}{12} = \$1,650$$

STEP 2: The differences between the actual monthly figures and average monthly figure for both variables are determined as shown in columns 2 and 4 below.

Month	(1) Direct machine hours	(2) Difference from average of 25,000 direct machine hours	(3) Indirect labor	(4) Difference from average of $1,650 indirect labor cost
January	25,000	—	$ 1,625	$ − 25
February	22,000	− 3,000	1,525	−125
March	11,000	−14,000	1,230	−420
April	30,500	+ 5,500	1,825	+175
May	49,000	+24,000	2,370	+720
June	19,000	− 6,000	1,440	−210
July	14,000	−11,000	1,280	−370
August	28,000	+ 3,000	1,750	+100
September	25,000	—	1,700	+ 50
October	26,500	+ 1,500	1,725	+ 75
November	20,000	− 5,000	1,560	− 90
December	30,000	+ 5,000	1,770	+120
Total	300,000	—0—	$19,800	$ —0—

STEP 3: The next step requires (a) that each difference from the average of 25,000 direct machine hours be squared and the squared differences totaled; and (b) that each difference from the average of 25,000 direct machine hours be multiplied by the associated differences from the average of $1,650 indirect labor expense and totaled.

Month	(1) Difference from average of direct machine hours	(2) Difference from average of direct labor cost	(3) Column (1) squared	(4) Column (1) × column (2)
January	—	$ − 25	—	—
February	− 3,000	−125	9,000,000	+ 375,000
March	−14,000	−420	196,000,000	+ 5,880,000
April	+ 5,500	+175	30,250,000	+ 962,500
May	+24,000	+720	576,000,000	+17,280,000
June	− 6,000	−210	36,000,000	+ 1,260,000
July	−11,000	−370	121,000,000	+ 4,070,000
August	+ 3,000	+100	9,000,000	+ 300,000
September	—	+ 50	—	—
October	+ 1,500	+ 75	2,250,000	+ 112,500
November	− 5,000	− 90	25,000,000	+ 450,000
December	+ 5,000	+120	25,000,000	+ 600,000
Totals	—0—	$ —0—	1,029,500,000	+31,290,000

STEP 4: Compute the variable element of indirect labor expense.

$$\frac{\text{Sum of column 4}}{\text{Sum of column 3}} = \frac{31,290,000}{1,029,500,000} = \$0.0303 \text{ per direct machine hour}$$

STEP 5: Determine the fixed element of indirect labor expense.

Fixed expense = Average expense − (Variable rate × average hours)
Substituting:

Fixed expense = $1,650 − (0.0303 × 25,000 hours)
Fixed expense = $1,650 − $757.50
Fixed expense = $892.50

The methods illustrated to determine the variable portion of total expense have been oversimplified to demonstrate technique.

It is possible that a negative value for fixed expense could result from the use of the correlation methods; that is, a minus figure for fixed expense could be computed. This situation could result because: (1) the expenses were improperly controlled in the past; (2) the expenses were improperly classified; or (3) an incorrect factor of variability was selected. If a negative value for fixed expense results, the information must be re-examined more carefully to find the cause of the negative value.

Preparing the Budget: Breakeven Analysis

It is sometimes necessary to select a course of action among several available alternatives in preparing a budget. It would prove rather futile, for example, to complete the planning budget and find that a product selected for special promotion during the year was uneconomical to produce or market. Breakeven analysis is helpful in making decisions regarding changes in sales mix, sales price, sales quantities, and fixed or variable costs.

The value of breakeven analysis is based upon two assumptions. First, fixed and variable costs must be determined for use in the budget. Second, the factor of variable cost must be selected and computed with accuracy. Breakeven analysis would be of doubtful validity if the variable expense budgets were prepared haphazardly.

Two procedures can be used in breakeven analysis: (1) a graphic procedure; and (2) a mathematical procedure. The 196— planning budget for the Southway Company is shown to best illustrate these procedures.

SOUTHWAY COMPANY
CONDENSED BUDGETED STATEMENT OF INCOME
FOR THE YEAR ENDING DECEMBER 31, 196—

	Fixed	Variable	
Sales			$1,000,000
Budgeted Costs			
Materials		$100,000	
Labor		325,000	
Manufacturing expense	$125,000	75,000	
Selling expense	100,000	75,000	
Administrative expense	75,000	25,000	
Totals	$300,000	$600,000	900,000
Budgeted Income			$ 100,000

Graphic procedure

The breakeven point is computed graphically in Figure 5, page 89. The vertical scale represents dollars of revenue and cost. The horizontal scale shows dollar sales volume. The three lines which represent fixed costs, total costs, and variable costs are located as follows. First, plot three points on the cost and revenue scale at sales volume: the point for fixed costs, at $300,000; the point for total costs, at $900,000; and the point for sales, at $1 million. The fixed cost line is drawn parallel to the horizontal scale through the fixed cost point of $300,000. The total cost line is drawn through the total cost point ($900,000) to the point at which the fixed cost line intersects the vertical scale ($300,000). The sales line is drawn from the budgeted sales point ($1 million) to the zero point. The point at which the total cost line and sales line intersect is the breakeven point (approximately $750,000).

Mathematical procedure

The equation for computing the breakeven point is:

$$\text{Breakeven point} = \frac{\text{Fixed costs}}{1 - \dfrac{\text{Variable costs}}{\text{Corresponding sales}}}$$

The following computation of the breakeven point is based upon the assumed budget figures of the Southway Company:

$$\text{Breakeven point} = \frac{\$\ 300,000}{1 - \dfrac{\$\ 600,000}{\$1,000,000}}$$

$$= \frac{\$\ 300,000}{1 - 0.60} = \$750,000$$

The computation can be verified as follows:

Breakeven sales		$750,000
Less: Fixed costs	$300,000	
Variable costs (0.60 × $750,000)	450,000	750,000
Net profit		$ —0—

Breakeven analysis and the relevant range

Breakeven analysis serves as a useful guide to budget preparation within a certain range of plant activity called the relevant range. Breakeven analysis indicates the level of fixed costs and the movement of variable costs within the relevant range. Different conditions may exist outside this range which would change the relationship of the fixed and variable costs.

This brief introduction to the variable budget and breakeven analysis indicates that the preparation of the planning budget is not based on one set of assumptions. The planning budget must be flexible to meet changed conditions; it cannot be based upon an unchanging plan. The budget is a dynamic technique for planning. The CPA, by employing variable budget procedures and breakeven analysis, can help his client develop an effective budget.

The Sales Budget

An accurate sales forecast is the first step in the preparation of the planning budget. The operations of a company depend upon sound sales estimates. It is difficult to plan purchases accurately or estimate direct labor requirements reliably if the sales budget is constructed on a "hit or miss" basis. The accuracy of the sales budget depends upon the care exercised in its preparation and the effort expended by the firm's sales organization in attaining the goals set forth in the budget.

The executive in charge of sales usually assumes the responsibility for developing the sales budget. The CPA should be able to furnish the technical advice necessary to plan the forecast and prescribe a suitable format for presentation of the sales budget. However, the CPA may find it necessary to prepare the sales budget himself when there is no one on the company's sales staff capable of assuming the responsibility. The CPA, in any case, must equip himself to meet this challenge.

Figure 5

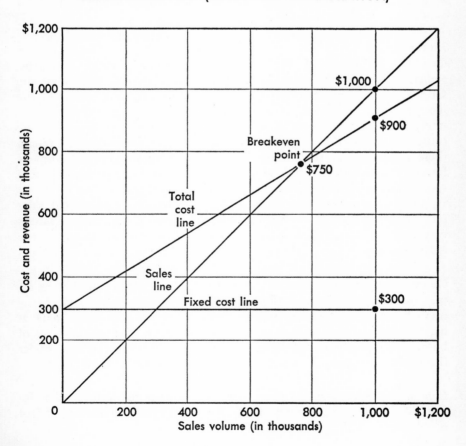

BREAKEVEN CHART (SOUTHWAY CORPORATION)

Long-range versus short-range planning

The establishment of a sales budget requires consideration of both the long-range and short-range plans of the company. The goal of long-range planning is to maximize profit over a number of years. The introduction of new products, exploration of territories for new and existing products, and improvement of selling methods are long-range objectives. Short-range planning involves the preparation of the budget for a current year. One objective of short-range planning is the maximization of annual profits. Often, however, a program is established which reduces the current year's profits so as to realize long-range plans.

Analysis of past performance

The past performance of a company offers a clue to its future performance. The past history of a business, even a small business, is related to two factors: (1) the effect of managerial policy and methods on past sales (internal factors); and (2) the effect of general business conditions (external factors).

Internal sales factors. An analysis of past sales performance requires detailed breakdowns of sales by product, territory, salesman, or customer. It may not be practical to analyze sales in such detail, but the CPA should be in a position to judge which breakdown will yield the most effective results. Sales should be analyzed by both amounts and units, if at all possible. The purpose of this analysis is to explore the causes of weaknesses in prior years' sales and to attempt to eliminate these weaknesses in the future. The analysis of past sales is a form of forced planning, where the CPA and management can probe for "sore spots" and constructively attempt to eliminate them.

The relationship of cost of sales and distribution costs to past sales provides an invaluable aid in planning the future budget. The analyses may indicate, for example, that the company has been promoting the wrong product.

General business conditions. Some small businessmen do not recognize the effect of general business conditions on their firm's sales. Some small businesses are not as sensitive to changes in national income as big businesses. However, any pronounced change in the general level of business eventually will affect the small firm. The CPA should consider the effect of economic trends on his client's sales forecasts.

Forecasting sales trends. There are two sources of information for forecasts of the general trend of business conditions: (1) the opinion of management, and (2) the use of economic indicators.

The management opinion method relies upon management's judgment of what the future level of business activity will be. Many small businessmen rely on judgment alone. Unfortunately, the opinion of management may be nothing more than a calculated guess with more guess than calculation.

A general business forecast to predict the future sales of a firm is widely used by analysts for many medium-sized and large businesses. The CPA will find that this technique can be used for sales forecasts for smaller companies if a proper economic indicator is selected. This technique is especially useful in checking on a prediction developed from internal sources.

Another factor to consider in the sales budget is the sales price. While over a long period of time the goal of pricing policies is to earn maximum profits, the CPA must recognize everyday problems in setting sales budget goals. Pressing problems, such as competitive conditions, efforts to introduce new products or enter new territories, and idle production and distribution facilities must govern immediate pricing policies.

Methods of sales budgeting

When all the facts have been compiled, there remains the problem of constructing the sales budget itself. A few of the more frequently used methods follow.

Sales department estimates. When estimates of sales originate with the sales department, one of two approaches is possible:

1. The salesman in each territory estimates the sales for the coming year by product and customer. He is given a record of past sales to use as a guide. He may make the estimates himself or consult his supervisor. Salesmen's estimates are reviewed by the executive in charge of sales.

2. The sales estimate is prepared by the sales executive group. The salesmen do not estimate their sales.

The CPA should recognize that he must prepare the sales estimates for many small businesses. The second approach does not appear feasible for a small company. The CPA must therefore be able to evaluate the salesmen's estimates.

Survey of executive opinion. Another method available to larger businesses is the combination of thinking of all department heads in the formulation of the sales program. The executives usually prepare their own independent estimates and then test these estimates in group discussion. The executive opinion method can be applied in the small business if the client, his general manager, other executives, and the CPA follow a program similar to the one outlined for the larger business.

Statistical method. The statistical method uses the economic indicators mentioned earlier. The advantage of this method is that it makes use of independent forecasts prepared by economic analysts, but a tendency may develop to rely too heavily on statistical methods and forego the independent thinking so vital to sound sales budgeting.

Combined methods. A combination of the suggested methods may be used. The use of two or more methods will result in more reliable estimates. One method serves as a check on the other.

Form of the sales budget

There is no prescribed form for presentation of the sales budget. The selection of a form depends upon the nature of the business and the detail with which the budget is prepared. The budget figures are usually analyzed by quarters. Monthly estimates are scheduled for the first quarter of the budget period. The dollar amount of products is limited. If there is a large number of products, it may be necessary to indicate only dollar amounts. An alternative approach is to show the budget for the major products separately and group the sales for minor products. The budget should be divided into sales districts if these are established.

The sales budget can be presented in summary form or in great detail. The quantity of information will depend on the circumstances; judgment will play an important part.

Production and Inventory Budgets

The sales budget furnishes the basis for planning production. The CPA must therefore turn his attention to how much must be produced to fulfill the projected goals embodied in the sales plan. He must also consider two other matters which are significant in planning production: (1) maintaining ideal inventory levels and (2) stabilizing production. When these elements are properly blended, a production budget can be formulated.

Proper inventory levels and stability of production are of paramount importance in production budgeting. Investment in inventories is substantial in typical manufacturing and trading companies. The dangers of obsolescence and possible decline in the value of inventories are ever present. Even if prevailing market conditions do not jeopardize the value of the inventory, the cost of maintaining excess inventories could strain the financial resources of the company rather severely. On the other hand, the company must be able to deliver its goods within a reasonable period of time after acceptance of the sales order. The best inventory level, then, is the one which permits filling of all sales orders quickly and yet keeps the dollar investment in inventories at a minimum.

Consideration must be given to stabilizing production in establishing inventory levels. Stability of production is desirable because it increases productivity by reducing idle plant capacity and by minimizing labor turnover. Stability of production can be achieved by many companies, in spite of sales fluctuations, by permitting the level of inventories to fluctuate within established minimum and maximum limits.

A sound management policy, established with the competent advice of the CPA, is directed at achieving a balance between production and inventory levels following preparation of the sales forecast.

Estimating the annual production budget

The annual production budget is based upon the sales forecast for the year and established inventory requirements. It is preferable to formulate the production budget in terms of units to be produced. If it is not practicable to forecast unit sales because of the variety of items sold, it will be necessary to use aggregate dollar amounts. For example, if the Southway Company could state its budget in units and inventory levels were established, the production budget could be presented as follows:

	Units
Sales budget requirements	95,000
Add: Desired final inventory of finished goods	15,000
Total	110,000
Less: Beginning inventory of finished goods	12,500
Required production	97,500

If the sales budget is stated in dollar amounts only, a different approach based upon an inventory standard may be used.

Let us consider the following example: The Southway Company's budgeted sales for 196— are estimated at $1 million. The inventory turnover rate is three times a year. The opening inventory at cost is $182,000. If one inventory turnover is the desired inventory level, the budgeted closing inventory at sales price should be $333,333 ($1 million ÷ 3). The production budget would be developed as follows, assuming that the estimated cost percentage of 62.5%[3] is the same for all products:

[3]The estimated cost percentage is computed as follows:

Budgeted Sales		$1,000,000	100.0%
Budgeted Costs			
Materials	$100,000		
Labor	325,000		
Manufacturing expense	200,000	625,000	62.5%
Gross Profit on Sales		$ 375,000	37.5%

Sales budget requirements at cost ($1 million × 62.5%)	$ 625,000
Add: Desired final inventory of finished goods at cost ($333,333 × 62.5%)	208,333
Total	$ 833,333
Less: Beginning inventory of finished goods at cost	182,000
Required production	$ 651,333

Scheduling production over the budget period. The sales budget is prepared by time periods of less than one year, that is, by months and quarters. It indicates seasonal variations. However, the short-run production budget is not determined solely by the demand for the product in the market. The ideal production budget does not vary from month to month. The amount of inventory is permitted to vary between the minimum and maximum levels to achieve a more stable production. The inventory budget is the buffer between fluctuating sales and stable production.

The production budget should not be viewed as an inflexible schedule but as a guide for planning production. It does serve as the foundation for planning material and labor needs, capital additions, and cash requirements, which are integral parts of the budget plan.

Manufacturing Costs

The production budget is the basis for the preparation of the budget of manufacturing costs. The daily activities of the manufacturing division, such as the purchase of raw material, hiring of personnel, and maintenance of machinery result in manufacturing costs. One of the most important phases of budgeting is to relate these costs to the planned rate of production. These costs are compiled in material, labor, and manufacturing expense budgets.

Materials and purchases

The production budget is the starting point for planning the quantity and cost of materials needed to fulfill production requirements. Corollary to estimating material requirements is the planning for purchase of these materials. The CPA must be in a position to advise both the purchasing manager and the production head in planning the purchase and use of materials.

Raw materials may consist of direct materials, which are specifically identified with the product, and indirect materials, which are used in the production process. The materials budget is concerned only with direct materials. Indirect materials are considered in the preparation of the manufacturing expense budget.

Estimating quantity of materials for production. It is sometimes possible to estimate quite simply the quantity of materials needed for production. If the standard quantity of material used in producing a unit of finished product is known, the quantity of materials required for production is obtained simply by multiplying the budgeted production by the standard quantity.

However, it is often difficult to calculate such standards. The CPA must then rely on less definite bases for measurement. Two alternative approaches are possible: (1) the development of material usage figures from prior years' experiences; (2) the development of costs of materials directly without quantities.

Raw materials inventory levels. Inventory levels require the same consideration in planning the raw materials budget as in setting the production budget. The CPA must advise his client of the importance of establishing policies pertaining to the level of the raw materials inventory. Just as the finished goods inventory furnishes the cushion between production and sales, so the raw materials inventory serves as the buffer between purchases and raw material requirements for production. In planning raw materials inventory levels, the following factors should be deliberated:

1. The quantities of materials required for production
2. The availability, perishability, and storage requirements of materials
3. The cash available to make favorable purchase arrangements
4. The fluctuations in the cost of raw materials
5. The availability of quantity discounts and the ability of the firm to take advantage of them if large purchases are made

Purchase budget. The planning of purchases is simplified if the company employs a purchasing manager. However, it may be necessary for the CPA to plan this budget without any assistance.

The major problems involved in determining the purchase budget are estimating (1) the amount of each kind of material to be purchased and (2) the unit cost of the material.

Establishing inventory levels for materials furnishes the basis for planning the amount of materials to be purchased. If the inventories are maintained at fixed levels, the purchase budget will parallel and precede production requirements by a predetermined lead time. If the inventory is allowed to fluctuate with seasonal production requirements, purchases will not vary widely from month to month. It is therefore apparent that the timing of purchases is greatly dependent upon inventory levels.

The unit cost of material depends upon market conditions. Application of the techniques used in forecasting sales through the use of economic analysis would be very valuable in estimating the market price of materials. Industry factors, the general level of prices, and the economy as a whole affect material prices. If the CPA can help his client save money by favorable purchasing, he will be furnishing a service seldom offered by public accountants.

Unit costs of materials will usually vary during the year. The estimated average unit cost of materials may be used to avoid the necessity of predicting each price change for the purchase budget. A study of the pattern of past purchases coupled with a projection of future materials prices may be used to establish the average unit cost.

Some thought should be given to the handling of freight charges on materials purchased in preparing the purchase budget. Theoretically, freight is an added cost of materials, but for the sake of simplicity it may be handled as an overhead cost.

As with all phases of budget preparation and operation, situations arise during the year which call for deviations from the purchase budget. If there is a sudden temporary break in prices, such as a price war, it would be unrealistic to follow the purchase budget originally established. A flexible policy is required. The purchase budget serves as a restraint on impulsive behavior; it does not replace good judgment.

Direct labor

The second element of manufacturing cost is direct labor. Direct labor is labor time applied in the fabrication of a product. All other labor time, such as that spent in maintenance and inventory control, is classified as indirect labor and is budgeted with manufacturing expense. Consequently, the direct labor budget includes only the wages of employees who work directly on the product.

The direct labor budget not only furnishes the estimate of direct labor cost, but is also used to plan personnel requirements during the year. In addition, since meeting the weekly payroll is a problem in many small businesses, the direct labor budget helps to predict cash requirements for the direct labor portion of the payroll.

The direct labor budget may be estimated from piece rates, labor hours and cost, or labor costs only. If the labor time required in production can be determined readily, the logical approach is to multiply the direct labor hours by the average wage rate. If no operational times can be estimated, it may be necessary to develop a ratio of direct labor cost to a measure of productive activity.

The method used in developing the direct labor budget depends upon (1) the method of wage payment, (2) the type of production process, and (3) the accounting records available.

Determination of direct labor hours. Direct labor hours per unit of output can sometimes be estimated by observing the operations required to perform a certain job. In the larger business, standards are usually set by time and motion studies. However, because the expense of setting standards may be prohibitive for the small business, the CPA should enlist the aid of the client or shop foremen in an attempt to establish estimates of operational times.

If this is not feasible, historical ratios may be used. If the total number of direct labor hours is related to physical output, the resulting ratio can be used to set the time needed to produce a unit of product. If the company is departmentalized and produces more than one product, a ratio must be computed for each department by product.

Estimating wage rates. The wage rates for direct labor may vary during the year as a result of changes in the over-all level of wages, changes in personnel, and differences in the amount of overtime worked. It is easier to budget direct labor through the use of average wage rates than to prepare estimates for each category of worker and then project changes in rates within these categories.

Average wage rates are estimated by first listing the number of employees in each wage rate classification. Consideration is also given to any explicit wage rate changes anticipated for the coming year and to implicit wage rate changes expected to result from changes in overtime hours worked. If each employee is expected to work approximately the same number of hours in the coming year, a simple average of the wage rates may be used. A weighted average rate is computed if there are differences in hours worked by employees receiving different wage rates. The weights are the hours each employee is expected to work.

Average wage rates may also be set by computing the ratio of total direct labor cost to total direct labor hours estimated from prior years' figures. The ratio would then be adjusted for any anticipated changes in wage rates or overtime hours worked.

Estimating labor cost directly. When no suitable means are available for estimating labor hours and rates, the CPA must estimate direct labor cost directly. He may estimate direct cost either (1) per unit of production or (2) in terms of some measure of production activity. If wages are based on production, the piece rates are the direct labor cost per unit of output. When no such measures are available, it will be necessary to relate past total labor costs to direct labor hours or direct machine hours and prepare budget estimates.

Manufacturing expense

Manufacturing expense is that part of total manufacturing cost not included in direct material or labor because it cannot be specifically identified with the product. Some of the more important types of manufacturing expense are factory supplies, indirect labor, taxes, insurance, and depreciation. The chief problem in budgeting these expenses is that such widely different costs must first be accumulated in cost centers, such as producing or service departments, and service department expenses must then be eventually allocated to producing departments and, if need be, directly to a product. Manufacturing expenses are incurred and accumulated in two cost centers in a departmentalized company: (1) producing departments and (2) service departments.

A producing department works directly on the product being manufactured. A service department does not work on the product directly, but furnishes services to producing departments or other service departments. The repair and power departments are examples of service departments.

Budgeting problems. Incurred expenses are the responsibility of the supervisor who has authority to control departmental expenses. If a company has producing and service departments, the departmental foremen are accountable for expenses in their departments. This assignment of responsibility is essential to cost control.

However, after costs have been accumulated, it is necessary to allocate service department costs to producing departments and eventually to the product itself. This allocation of costs is essential to product costing but not necessary to cost control.

In preparing the manufacturing expense budget it is therefore necessary first to budget costs for the department in which they are incurred, since they may be controlled by type of expense, and then to budget costs by allocating them to the product.

Construction of budget. Construction of the manufacturing expense budget involves the preparation of a budget of each expense of the company by time period, by departments if necessary, and according to accounting classifications.

The amount of work required to set up the planning budget will depend upon whether fixed or variable budgeting procedures are being used. If fixed budget procedures are used, it will be necessary to construct the manufacturing expense budget for the planned level of activity. When a variable budget is used, it is a relatively simple task to construct the planning budget because the variable budget figures are selected for the planned level of activity. The variable budget is usually prepared independently of the planning budget, whereas the fixed budget cannot be prepared until the budgeted level of activity is decided upon.

Allocation to product. Once the manufacturing expense budget has been prepared by organizational responsibility, there remains the problem of allocating costs to product. The first step is the preparation of a budgeted manufacturing expense distribution sheet in which the service departments are allocated to other service departments and, finally, to producing departments. This allocation procedure must be preceded by a study of how service department costs are being used. For example, power is usually measured by kilowatt hours. It is necessary to estimate how many kilowatt hours will be consumed by each of the using departments. Sometimes these factors are easily measured, but usually an equitable basis for allocation must be found.

If a plant superintendent has three departments, for example, should his salary be allocated on the basis of time spent, number of employees in each department, or units produced by each department? Here again the certified public accountant must use judgment in analyzing his client's operations.

A final step in the development of the manufacturing expense budget (to review briefly an area familiar to most accountants) is the allocation of manufacturing expenses to producing departments. It is necessary to establish departmental overhead rates to allocate expenses to producing departments. Manufacturing expenses are not incurred at the same rate as they are applied to a product, so it is important that some method be used to identify manufacturing expense with the product during the budget period. Computation of the overhead rate accomplishes this aim. The overhead rate is computed by dividing the total budgeted expense for a department or cost center by the budgeted activity planned for that department. This rate can then be applied to the product, depending upon the activity of the factory.

Cost of goods manufactured and sold. After the three elements of manufacturing cost have been budgeted, the budgeted cost of goods manufactured and sold can be completed. The inventory of finished goods and work in process can be computed following the basic assumptions made as to the flow of costs (fifo, lifo, average).

The preparation of budgeted manufacturing costs requires the association of material, labor, and manufacturing expense to the budgeted physical production. Material and labor costs are associated directly with physical production. Manufacturing expense is budgeted for producing and service departments and then allocated to production by the use of established overhead rates.

Completing the Planning Budget

Following completion of the manufacturing cost budget, the CPA must turn his attention to the cost of getting the goods to market. He must now closely scrutinize selling, delivery, and advertising expenses.

Selling expense

The chart of accounts classifies selling expense by assigned responsibility. The budget should be constructed on the same basis. For example, if a company has three regional offices, the selling expense budget should be prepared so that each regional supervisor is aware of the expenses for which he is responsible. Certain expenses included in the selling expense budget may be estimated at the same time that the sales budget is being formulated. These selling expenses are dependent upon sales plans and are estimated at a level in accordance with the over-all sales program. The advertising budget may, for example, be dependent upon the sales budget. Advertising expenses are usually incurred to achieve the proposed sales "push."

Variable budget procedures are recommended for budgeting selling expense in preference to fixed budget procedures. The usual measure of activity used in budgeting selling expense is net sales. The selling expense budget should be constructed by time periods and by organizational responsibility. Although it is part of the selling expense budget, advertising expense is budgeted on an annual appropriation basis.

Budgeting advertising. A separate budget is prepared by many firms for advertising. A definite amount is appropriated for advertising in the sales and selling expense budgets. This amount is dovetailed with the sales plan. The budgeted advertising expenses are broken down by type of advertising medium and by monthly or quarterly expenditures.

Advertising expense is commonly treated in the selling expense budget as a constant amount for each month or quarter. The accounting treatment may vary. Some accountants prefer to prepare a standard accrual each month by crediting an estimated liability account. Expenditures are charged against the estimated liability. Other accountants record advertising expense as it is incurred.

The small business need not have a formalized advertising budget, but its level of expenditures should be planned. Sometimes a businessman will spend a certain amount of advertising dollars each year without considering the amount of additional sales dollars which will result from the campaign.

Administrative expense

The last category of expense to be included in the budget is administrative expense. These expenses are incurred in the over-all co-ordination and supervision of the operation of all major functions of the business rather than in the performance of one particular function.

The chart of accounts should classify administrative expense by organizational responsibility. In a fairly large business, there may be divisions under the executive, the controller, and the treasurer. The small business will generally have one all-inclusive administrative category.

Administrative expense has traditionally been thought of as relatively fixed. However, managerial decisions and policies influence many of these costs, so variable budget procedures are recommended in budgeting administrative expense. One frequently used measure of variability is budgeted net sales volume. Many administrative expenses vary with net sales and the level of production. Additional sales and production, for example, require larger expenditures for accounting, credit control, and general supervision.

Since administrative expenses are incurred so close to top management, it is common to overlook excessive spending. By intelligently planning these expenses and relating them to proposed sales volume, the executive may find that certain expenditures can be reduced. Budgeting administrative expenses obliges management to take a long look at the future.

Final budget review

The CPA should consider any factors which may have been omitted before completing the budgeted income statement. The form of presentation is important. The budget will be examined by executives who are not familiar with accounting jargon or techniques. The budget must be presented simply and forcefully; accounting and technical terminology, which is difficult to understand, should be avoided.

After the supporting schedules have been developed, the CPA is in a position to estimate the effect of changes in price policy, fixed expenses, and variable expenses on the profits of the company. The available budgeted statistics permit the CPA or his client to reconsider some of the policy decisions made in the development of the budget estimates. Alternative courses of action can be evaluated by breakeven analysis.

Sources and Means of Financing

Determining the Financial Requirements of Small Business Clients

Forecasting financial requirements lies at the heart of the financial management of any company. There are no statistics on the number of small businesses that make formal forecasts of their financial requirements. Since very few do any budgeting, it is doubtful whether many have formalized their financial planning.

The degree of formality required in financial planning will vary according to the size of the company. Both small and large companies will need planning, but the task is likely to prove easier in the former. Greater accuracy can result from more intimate knowledge of the affairs and plans of a smaller company by a few management people and a CPA.

Cash forecasting

The determination of financial requirements must be divided into two parts: short-term and long-term fund requirements. While one will to some extent affect the other, ordinarily seasonal needs in the annual financial cycle of a company will bear no specific relation to the long-term planning of its capital requirements or to its needs for long-range expansion. It is never adequate merely to plan cash flow for the next ninety days in the business that is looking forward to growth. A majority of businesses probably plan their cash flow informally a few weeks in advance. Such a practice is defensive in nature. The informal plan is usually adopted for the sole purpose of determining whether the payroll or other current debt can be paid. While this may qualify in theory as financial planning, in practice it contributes little to an over-all plan for expansion.

However, these forecasts are on the right track. For example, to determine if the payroll will be met on Saturday, all that the owner of a small machine shop need do is add estimated receipts to his checkbook balance and deduct the expected expenditures, and he will have fulfilled his financial planning until the following week. The fundamental steps in short-term forecasting are identical in principle with those which the largest corporate entities go through.

Short-term cash forecasting for a business of any size is not an especially difficult function. The installation of a system of short-term cash forecasting is a management service area in which no doubts can arise with respect to the CPA's competence.

There are several methods of projecting short-term financial requirements. There is the familiar one of directly estimating cash receipts and disbursements. Some of the others can get to be quite involved. While the more technical methods can, in some cases, enhance the value and accuracy of forecasting, they must still rely on good judgment and an understanding of the kinds of operations in which the company is engaged. A review of some of the principles, approaches, and results of short-term forecasting may therefore not be out of place at this point.

The answer to providing accurate forecasts at close periodic intervals lies in the utilization of an operating budgetary system. If budgetary detail is unavailable, sound estimates can often be developed from the data of any company, even one that uses the simplest of accounting systems. It is obviously impossible to forecast cash requirements without knowing what can be expected to occur. The client who does so for any reasonable period of time in the absence of a *formal* budgetary program has only to formalize the process in order to develop an operating budget. The reason for this is that much of the operational planning will have been accomplished in the process of forecasting cash requirements. Cash forecasting is the conversion of an estimated income statement for a future period into a statement of receipts and expenditures. Forecasting can become simple and accurate if the budget system has produced a formal estimated income statement.

There is no formula for forecasting cash requirements. It is simply a matter of logically resolving into written figures facts and estimates already known or anticipated. The cash forecast will emerge from the application of historical relationships to these facts and estimates. Experience shows that by reducing the forecast to writing the resulting figures often differ sharply from those previously envisioned by management. As in budgeting, the system and methods selected for cash forecasting will vary in each case.

Financial planning of short-term requirements should include estimates of events throughout an entire cycle of operations. A forecast of financial condition at widely spaced intervals may be wholly inadequate because of seasonal and other business fluctuations. Cash forecasting, like budgeting, is a cumulative phenomenon. It must be continuously reviewed, and it should continuously project the entire cycle of the business; otherwise its main advantages will be lost.

Main advantages

The principal advantages of cash forecasting are:

1. It will indicate well in advance the need for obtaining funds from outside sources and determine fairly accurately the duration of loan requirements. The cost of borrowed money is always low if it produces a profit and it is always high if the funds are left idle.

2. It will make possible the enlightened investment planning of idle funds. Only a few small businesses are faced with this problem, but for those that are, the resulting profits can be important.

3. It provides for the preplanning of tax payments or the liquidation of obligations and dividend payments. Cash forecasting enables financial management to co-ordinate cash requirements for the purposes of tax planning, maintaining dividend policies, and similar short- or long-term projects developed by business management.

4. It will often enable a business to avail itself continuously of purchase discounts and permit forward planning in its purchasing policy.

5. It can help to obtain or arrange for loans or lines of credit well in advance of actual need. A continuous cash forecasting process whose soundness is demonstrated to lenders can always benefit the credit

standing of a company. Indeed, reliable cash forecasts are the best method of assuring a lender that a loan can be repaid. Moreover, by determining the need for a loan well in advance, a company may well be in a position to bargain or shop for a lower interest rate.

6. Short-term forecasting serves as a starting point for long-range cash projections. Long-range forecasting is of significant value to any business. It makes possible the determination of over-all, long-range financial policy, which must be firmly established on a formal basis. The larger corporations constantly review long-range policies and planning, and so should the entrepreneur who would like to add a third bakery to his chain two years hence.

Long-range projection

Long-range projection will evolve from short-term forecasting; only in this way will sound financial policy and growth plans be determinable.

The CPA's role in the area of determining financial requirements should not be confined to convincing his client of the desirability of cash forecasting. Forecasting will indicate when funds will be available or when they must be obtained from outside sources. But the CPA must then provide answers to the following questions:

1. Will the projections of cash determined to be available from internal sources be adequate to meet planned requirements? If not, where can the additional funds be obtained? Judging from projections of the financial position, what can be expected of lenders? If bank loans will not be available to the required extent, what other sources should be considered and perhaps contacted at this time?

2. Does the present type of business structure enable the client to fulfill his financial needs adequately? Which form of organization will result in the largest rate of return to the owners of the small business? Will it be compatible with the quest for additional funds? For example, the capitalization of the corporation must be balanced to provide for the greatest profit potential while creating a structure that will prove advantageous in arranging for future financing. It is often difficult to reconcile different objectives and still achieve the optimum capital structure. A company that elects debt financing may obtain tax benefits and a high rate of return on the equity capital employed in the short run, but it must then accept the risk of encountering greater difficulties in raising future capital. Will the capital structure be too thin, in view of the planning? The CPA can never afford to forget the tax considerations of financial planning.

3. What type of financing will be required? Are short-term funds adequate or do projections and plans indicate a need for intermediate or long-term funds? Does the analysis disclose that additional permanent capital is required?

In short, it must be determined where the money will come from and what additional planning now will guarantee its availability later.

If the client is a proprietorship, state usury laws may preclude him from accounts receivable financing with a commercial finance company. If this form of financing is profitable and is the only one available, the CPA will have to consider carefully the pros and cons of the business structure in providing financial management advice.

It is hoped that the foregoing suggestions will give the CPA some insight into the complex problem of guiding businesses in the determination of their financial requirements through forecasting and financial planning.

Methods and Sources of Financing for Business Clients

One of the most valuable services a CPA can perform for his clients is to give them guidance to the various sources of funds. Although sources are plentiful, business usually looks only to the commercial bank for capital. If the bank rejects a proposal, plans for growth, product additions, or new plant and equipment often fall by the wayside.

Many types of financing are available which commercial banks either cannot or will not provide. The policies and offerings of commercial banks vary from one region to another, partly as a result of variations in economic conditions and money markets. Since CPAs and business are both normally familiar with the offerings of their local banking connections, this chapter will be devoted to other sources of funds.

The various sources should be investigated only after a business has adequately planned its financial requirements and carefully determined the type of financing which will best satisfy its needs. We will deal here with three categories: short-term, intermediate or long-term, and permanent funds.

Sources of short-term funds

Before advising a business to seek short-term funds from an outside source, the CPA should naturally make sure that the funds are unavailable within the business itself. Several lending agencies have expressed concern over the number of small loan applications they receive for temporary funds which are not actually needed. Indeed, in most cases internal sources are able to generate the needed funds.

The CPA is in a very good position to determine whether internal sources are being properly exploited before his client needlessly incurs interest cost. The following are some of the questions he should be able to answer after he has reviewed the client's operations:

1. Do the accounting system and policy followed for income tax purposes generate the most working capital? For example, has the business chosen the most favorable treatment in establishing allowances for bad debts? What about its depreciation policies? Are other fast tax writeoffs taken? Is the basis used for tax reporting purposes cash, accrual, or installment, and is it the best method for retention of cash? Is the client on a proper fiscal basis, or are the bulk of his tax payments due when the working capital is tied up in inventories or receivables?

2. Is the business looking for additional funds while considerable working capital is needlessly tied up in inventories, receivables, or other improperly controlled assets? A relatively large amount of capital can often be tied up in inventories, particularly if purchase or production control is lacking. The CPA should be able to isolate balance sheet items that are using up more than their fair share of the working capital.

3. What of the relations with customers and vendors? Are collection and payment policies really sound, or are they simply a matter of habit? How long has it been since the collection practices were reviewed or the selling terms revised? The pattern of business selling terms has been anything but uniform in recent years, nor can any significant trend be determined. The changes have occurred by industry, through competitive influence and changing economic conditions. Business examines its own selling terms continuously, as well as those offered by the principal suppliers. Does the client buy and sell on the best possible terms? Are the collection and payment policies balanced to provide the maximum working capital at the lowest cost? For example, is the client losing 2 per cent cash discounts from vendors because it is against company tradition to offer one per cent to customers? A periodic review of such policies by the certified public accountant in collaboration with management can prove fruitful.

The preceding and other internal sources should all be explored before resorting to outside sources.

The balance sheet. A small business may have established an enviable reputation for paying its debts and for the integrity of its management. While these factors are of great value in any borrowing negotiation, they are generally insufficient to raise large sums. But the assets found on a typical balance sheet may be available as collateral for financing purposes and so become a potential source of funds.

Accounts receivable financing. Accounts receivable are often available for pledge. Some CPAs still feel that any business that has to pledge its receivables is on the verge of bankruptcy, but this is no longer a widespread attitude. Many CPAs will know of at least one client who is currently financing through accounts receivable. The practice is especially prevalent among smaller, growing businesses. Their sales strategy often requires selling terms which are unusually favorable to the customers. A liberal selling policy can leave a sizeable, though dormant, asset on the balance sheet. However, the company may need additional cash before the asset can be profitably re-employed in its operations.

Conversion into cash. Receivables can be converted into cash in a number of different ways. The most direct method, of course, is to persuade customers to pay their bills promptly by giving or raising the discount rate for quick payment. A customer will usually pay in ten days if he is offered 2 per cent ten-day terms net thirty days. The customer who is used to extended due dates or other special dating arrangements can sometimes be persuaded to pay promptly if he is reminded that a 2 per cent discount earned in ten days is worth 36 per cent per year to him. If he can borrow money at 6 per cent, he will have saved a good deal more than the loan cost.

Accounts receivable may be taken to some banks for pledge, purchase, or as general collateral for a line of credit. But since individual banking practices vary, the CPA should familiarize himself with the lending arrangements available at local banks.

Basis for loans. Accounts receivable constitute the principal basis of loans made by commercial credit companies. (These will be discussed later in this chapter.) When receivables are pledged with a commercial credit company, the amount received will of course be less than the amount pledged. The client may request that customers are not to be advised that his debt has been pledged. If the advance represents 80 per cent of the face amount pledged, interest is charged to the borrower only on the funds actually received, not, as is often thought, on the amount pledged. The words "actually received" are important. The client accepts advances only for the amount of cash he needs so as to avoid paying interest on excess idle cash.

Many finance companies report that both percentage and cost will vary according to individual circumstances. An industry representative speaking recently before a group of businessmen stated that 75 to 80 per cent of the total amount of receivables pledged is generally advanced to the borrower. A survey conducted not long ago by the Federal government found the typical advance to be 80 per cent, with a range of 65 to 85 per cent.

Cost. Statistical studies indicate that the cost of this type of financing may range from 8 to 24 per cent. The typical median rate was 14 per cent and the highest median rate was 16 per cent. This rate will almost always be higher for smaller advances. A small business must expect this when it resorts to a finance company. However, when comparing these rates with a straight 6 per cent bank loan, it should be remembered that compensatory bank balances, generally at 20 per cent of the loan outstanding, make the effective bank rate higher.

A per annum interest rate of 15 per cent may strike some CPAs as staggering. Research into business failures, however, discloses that few, if any, are the result of high interest cost. On the contrary, many small businesses have borrowed money at 20 per cent, made 30 per cent on it, and have outstanding records of quick growth to levels which would never have been reached through "economical" financing from retained earnings and character loans. The records of "growth" companies suggest that the cost of borrowing is never too high if the funds can be employed to produce profits in excess of the cost.

Outright sale. Instead of pledging accounts receivable, these may be sold outright to a factor. This is generally done on a nonrecourse basis, meaning that full liability for collection becomes the factor's problem. If circumstances require it, however, it can be arranged for the factor to have recourse. Accounts can be sold on a notification or non-notification basis; that is, the customers owing the money may or may not be asked to remit directly to the factor. Non-notification is often difficult to arrange and consequently rarely found in practice.

Importance of credit standing. A factor will want to reassure himself as to the credit standing of the accounts. Sometimes, of course, he may reject them. A factor who buys accounts makes a flat charge on the face amount, which will usually vary depending on the length of time the accounts have to run. In addition, interest is charged from the time of purchase to the maturity of the account, with a collection period time allowance of five to ten days. For example, a one per cent flat charge made on an account that has thirty days to run is equivalent to 12 per cent a year; and if an additional 6 per cent a year is charged to maturity, the combined effective cost to the borrower is 18 per cent a year.

Factoring charges. Rates charged by factors vary according to circumstances. A recent survey shows a weighted average typical rate of 6.7 per cent on cash advanced, and a median typical factoring charge of 1½ per cent. As in the case of loans by commercial finance companies, these rates tend to be higher as the volume of receivables purchased becomes smaller. The flat factoring charge is subject to the widest variation. Factors charge rates ranging from a low of one-half of one per cent to a high of 2¾ per cent.

Many CPAs seem to think that these facilities are available only to companies generating a large volume of receivables, and that only certain industries can obtain funds from these sources. Research gives no support to this impression.

Minimum receivables. There appears to be no established minimum of receivables that will be considered for financing by commercial finance companies or factors. Some place the minimum at $50,000, others at $25,000, some still lower; but each statement is qualified by the phrase "depending on circumstances." A recent survey of nineteen commercial finance companies showed that five would consider making loans on receivables to a business with less than $75,000 in annual sales; five more said they would talk to companies with $75,000 to $150,000; the next eight preferred a minimum volume in the $150,000 to $375,000 range. The minimum amounts of credit which these companies would have advanced ranged from $10,000 to $60,000. Fifteen companies also stated that they would consider providing financing to businesses having a net worth as low as $10,000. Their only other requirements were that a prospective client be potentially profitable, well managed, and of good character. They generally preferred that the business be at least two years old. Client location was rarely mentioned as a deterrent to the availability of their services.

These qualifications will exclude the corner drugstore, but accounts receivable financing is clearly available to a good number of a CPA's business clients from commercial finance companies. While no studies of the qualifications for factoring are available, discussions with factors themselves lead to the conclusion that minimum requirements are generally higher than those outlined above. Only companies having a sales volume of at least $225,000, with say $20,000 worth of receivables, are likely to interest factors.

The kind of industry appears to be immaterial, provided other requirements are met. Factoring is most prevalent in the textile and garment field, but in recent years some factors have actively sought and done business in other industries.

CPAs should familiarize themselves with certain technical aspects of accounts receivable financing in order to give a client competent guidance. While this chapter attempts only to review the general availability and cost to business of accounts receivable financing, a few of the advantages and disadvantages ought to be mentioned; the advantages may offset the high interest cost.

Accounts receivable financing, either on a pledge or outright sale basis, can become a method of long-term financing. This type of borrowing may not have to be repaid. The first $100 received, if repeatedly replaced with invoices for the same amount, can be retained for use in the business for as long as the money is needed. As sales increase, cash advances increase proportionately and constitute a revolving fund which is available as long as required.

Effect on current ratio. Accounts receivable financing will affect the current ratio in different ways—and this, in turn, may affect relations with other creditors. The factoring of receivables, for example, will almost always improve the current ratio if it is used to liquidate current debt. It is worth while to consider in advance what the effect on the current ratio will be in determining whether pledge or sale of receivables is the better arrangement. Clearly, factoring accounts receivable should not be recommended at a typical rate of 15 per cent per year just because it enhances a client's balance sheet, particularly if adequate funds are available at cheaper rates.

Other services. Commercial finance companies and factors can often offer more than accounts receivable financing. In addition to other financing, particularly on inventory, equipment, and conditional sales, commercial finance companies will often provide valuable assistance to the CPA and his client in the formulation of a sound program. Factors will also give advice, particularly on the matter of credit arrangements with customers. Factors are interested in avoiding losses; this impels them to serve as a built-in credit department for the smaller business which might not otherwise be able to afford a good credit manager. An obvious advantage of selling accounts to a factor on a notification basis is the elimination of the collection function and its attendant costs.

Reliable trade estimates indicate that at least $11 billion of accounts receivable financing were serviced by over 400 commercial finance companies and factors in each of two recent years. This is more than 2½ times the amount financed ten years before. This form of financing has therefore been on the increase, even if due allowance is made for the impact of inflation. More than 400 commercial finance sources are fairly well distributed throughout the country, but factors are generally found only in the larger cities, with the heaviest concentration in the northeast.

A word of caution is in order with respect to the selection of a finance company or factor: if it is reputable, it will never charge or demand an advance fee. This is the practice of the so-called lender's service agencies, which promise to locate a source of financing in return for a fee. Most of the time this is a complete waste of money. A prospective borrower would be far better advised to consult local banks, which can generally provide information or recommend a finance company or factor. The local bank can always check with a correspondent bank in the nearest large city. It is advisable to examine the credit rating of a finance company or factor. The National Commercial Finance Conference, Inc., at 29 Broadway, New York City, will supply a roster of members in any area. Investigation and selection, however, are left up to the CPA or his client.

Installment sales financing. While the availability of funds from accounts receivable is discussed, consideration should also be given to the possibility of selling the product on installment terms and selling the paper to a sales finance company. The nature of the product will of course be a significant factor in determining the feasibility of installment selling. Sales finance companies do not, as is sometimes thought, restrict their activity to automobiles, television sets, and jewelry. They will ordinarily consider any product which has (1) a reasonable life, (2) a value greater than the unpaid installment, and (3) economical and practical repossession possibilities. If these requirements are met, selling on the installment basis may be valuable as a technique to keep working capital in the business and may also prove to be a spur to sales.

Many sales finance companies handle only this kind of financing, as do some of the commercial finance companies. Some banks offer this service in addition to the usual automobile and appliance loans, but the general tendency has been to restrict it inasmuch as it is a specialized, heavy paper-work operation. The position of the banks is understandable. The local bank can probably recommend a reputable sales finance company. The finance rate and recourse arrangements between the client and the finance company are a matter of wide-range negotiation; they will depend on the product, size of account, type of customer, basis of collection method—direct or indirect—to be used, and other factors. The CPA and his business clients should not ignore the potential of installment selling, which has become a tremendous economic force in recent years.

Other receivables. Other receivables on the balance sheet can also be converted to cash. Notes receivable taken from delinquent customers originally sold on open account offer few attractive possibilities, but more and more businesses in recent years have notes originating from installment or deferred payment sales. These notes are generally welcomed by commercial banks either as a pledge for a note of the seller or as an endorsed discount sale to the bank. Either way, the bank has two parties from whom it can collect.

The *trade acceptance* is not extensively used, but it provides an avenue through which a small business can quickly convert sales to cash. It is nothing more than a draft upon a buyer by a seller for the amount of the sale. On the margin is the statement that the trade acceptance arises from a current transaction and that the maturity is within the usual credit period. The acceptance is sent to the customer with the invoice and the buyer writes "accepted" and signs his name. A commercial bank (or others) will discount the document, as it would any other note. If a client can utilize trade acceptances without his open account customers feeling that their character and integrity are being attacked, this can enhance the client's cash position.

Bankers' acceptances are another kind of negotiable paper arising from a sale. A buyer arranges with his bank to authorize a seller to draw a time draft on the buyer's bank for the amount of the invoice. The seller attaches the invoice to the authorization and generally takes it to his own bank for dispatch through banking channels to the buyer's bank. The draft is accepted by the bank and returned through bank channels to the seller's bank. The draft is now a banker's acceptance which may be discounted by the seller's bank. The customer relation problem is present, of course, as in the use of trade acceptances.

The CPA and his client would be well advised to talk over these possibilities with the bank. If the latter is not interested, a commercial credit or sales finance company will often purchase this form of negotiable paper. Local private sources may also be available. For example, two or more businesses will sometimes buy each other's paper when their cycles of business and working capital needs are opposed to each other.

Inventory financing. Although inventories are not as liquid as accounts receivable, much can be done with them in the way of financing. A business must generally exhaust its ability to borrow on receivables before a lender will consider inventory loans. Finance companies usually require this type of financing to be only part of an over-all financing plan.

Before a CPA helps to look for a method and a source of funds from inventories, he should review his client's inventory policy. The key to many business working capital problems is often to be found in low inventory turnover created by any of several deficiencies. Some of the questions to be asked are: Is the inventory policy sound? Are levels predetermined or otherwise budgeted? Are older items cleared out? Is there proper timing of purchase and is adequate attention given to the production planning and scheduling functions? Could all or part of the inventory be taken on consignment? In other words, can borrowing on inventory really be justified, or is borrowing necessary only because there is too much inventory? Before he entertains the possibility of financing inventories, the lender will also want to know: (1) Can the client's product be safely stored, and for how long? Is there any danger of obsolescence or deterioration? (2) Are the price and demand for the product reasonably stable, or are they apt to fluctuate sharply? How broad and consistent is its market? What would the cost of liquidation be?

Customary instruments. If the answers to the above questions are satisfactory, the following ways of raising money from inventories may be considered with reasonable assurance that the lender's investigation will conclude that there is sound economic reason for inventory financing and that the inventories will be liquidated within the normal course of business. (If the lender does not have this assurance, the client will not get his money.)

Warehouse receipts, factors' liens, and *trust receipts* are the usual instruments through which inventory is pledged. *Unless there is a specific statutory provision to the contrary,* (e.g., Uniform Commercial Code), it is a general legal principle that a pledge of inventory as security for a loan is invalid unless the property is physically delivered to the lender or to a third party to be held for account of the lender. This can obviously render inventory financing impracticable in cases where segregation will impede production and sales. To meet this problem, the factors' lien and the trust receipt have been legalized in some states. Only twenty-four states have enacted legislation authorizing the creation of factors' liens; and only thirty-one have authorized the use of the trust receipt. Furthermore, these laws are not uniform. Consequently, the point must be underscored that each client's potential for certain types of inventory financing will be contingent upon local law. The local finance company will undoubtedly have a thorough knowledge of what is legal in the states in which it operates, but the CPA should recommend that local counsel review any inventory financing arrangements to ensure that the client has a clear understanding of his rights and obligations.

The warehouse receipt comes into the picture when inventories are delivered to a public or field warehouse. When the use of a far removed public warehouse becomes prohibitive owing to transportation cost, resort is had to the field warehouse. This is actually a branch public warehouse established at the borrower's plant for a nominal rental charge, under lease, by a public warehouse company. There are many legal technicalities in arrangements of this type. Warehouse receipts, issued as collateral in either public or field warehousing, are governed by the Uniform Warehouse Receipts Act, except in states where the Uniform Commercial Code applies.

The use of warehouse receipts requires some form of distinct segregation. As already noted, this poses complications for the manufacturer who wishes to convert pledged raw materials to work in process and pledged work in process to finished goods. Other security devices must then be used. While there are legal differences, both trust receipts and factors' liens provide for additional freedom of inventory movement by the borrower. A business can reach workable arrangements by using either or both of these instruments.

Cost. The cost of inventory financing and the percentage of funds advanced vary. The rate will usually depend upon the risk occasioned by the nature of the inventory, size of loan, supervision of inventory required, general credit rating of the client, and so forth. The best information available indicates that rates are generally about the same or slightly higher than those for accounts receivable financing.

Many aggressive smaller businesses have grown rapidly through implementation of inventory financing. It is well to remember that the sale of pledged inventories can lead to the pledging of accounts receivable. A cycle is thus established that permits rapid sales expansion on limited initial working capital.

Export and import financing may be included with inventory financing. Although this form has limited applications, it deserves brief review. If a client has a product that may be saleable in foreign markets, or if a business can reduce costs or otherwise advantageously purchase requirements from abroad, discussion of possible arrangements with banks and finance companies could prove valuable. Export and import financing is either largely misunderstood by or unknown to many businessmen, according to the representatives of sources that make it available.

An often neglected source of funds is *drop shipment financing*. If a client lacks the capital necessary to establish or expand existing manufacturing facilities but can accept more orders than can be produced, a drop shipment financing plan, available from many finance companies and factors, may provide a solution to the dilemma.

Essentially, a client arranges to have an item produced and drop-shipped to his customers by a manufacturer who is guaranteed payment by the finance company or factor (since he would not otherwise grant credit). The lender will of course demand the right to inspect customers' orders and pass on them before guaranteeing the manufacturer from loss. The accounts receivable resulting from these orders serve as security for the obligations. Other factors to be considered are share of risk of merchandise returned to the manufacturer and whether the receivables will be financed on a notification or nonnotification basis.

Additional balance sheet assets may be available as a pledge for short-term loans. The customary mortgages on machinery and equipment are often helpful, and on some balance sheets there will be other items of tangible value that can be used to secure short-term money. The pledge or mortgage of land and buildings is discussed under the heading, "Sources of Intermediate or Long-term Funds" (page 115).

Subcontracting. Still other ways can be found to increase a client's cash position. A company can avoid the headaches attached to the financing of land, buildings, equipment, and inventory by contracting that some of its products be manufactured by others. It can do this for technical reasons or to avoid additional investment in facilities. If cost, quality, and trademark problems can be resolved, subcontracting can be of real value. Every business has its strengths and weaknesses. It might be suggested, without offending a sales-oriented client, that a qualified contractor can make a product as well as or better than the client; and that this approach would preserve working capital for additional advertising or promotion purposes. When prepaid insurance is present, the question might logically be asked as to why it is not being purchased on an installment basis.

Leasing. Finally, an obvious, often overlooked, method of preserving working capital is to rent rather than buy. Pride of ownership appears to be important to many businessmen; a reluctance to rent equipment, buildings, or autos seems to be based on emotional rather than economic grounds. Buying on time also appears to distress the more conservative element of the business public. Business can rent almost anything from a variety of sources: manufacturers, leasing companies, and the like. In a recent year, long-term—three years or more—leasing of production equipment, excluding real estate, buildings, trucks, and autos, exceeded $227 million. This represents an increase of 26 per cent over the preceding year.

Leasing has both advantages and disadvantages. The analysis and advice that a CPA is equipped to provide can simplify management's rent-or-buy decisions. The correct decisions cannot always be arrived at by pure mathematical formula. Each client must be advised to compare the cost of purchasing versus renting in relation to his particular circumstances. At the root of the decision lies the ability to forecast whether the profits on the capital released will outweigh the additional cost of leasing, which is what the mathematical formulas are designed to reveal. The CPA must also examine carefully the income tax implications of rental, sale and leaseback, or related decisions. Expert tax analysis or formulas by themselves rarely come up with the right answer. Actuarial validity can only be as good as the facts which constitute the formulas. All data and computations must be evaluated in the light of sound business judgment.

Sources of intermediate- or long-term funds

It is in the area of intermediate- or long-term and equity financing that small business faces its greatest problem.

Banks as a rule will not make term loans. While the revolving financing of accounts receivable and inventory can provide working capital for a considerable period of time, a finance company can generally become a source of intermediate-term funds only through equipment financing. Rental of equipment or buildings will also preserve working capital and perhaps obviate the necessity for long-term debt financing, but the decision to rent may only have been reached because long-term money was not available. What are the sources of long-term funds for small business, and under what conditions will these sources make loans?

Commercial finance companies. A commercial credit company may make equipment financing available to clients if the local bank or manufacturer does not. Finance companies specializing in equipment financing normally purchase the installment contracts from the seller of the equipment. The typical maturity with these companies is eighteen to thirty months, but it is possible to obtain longer maturities if the type of equipment and credit standing of the borrower warrant it. Typical charges for equipment financing as reported in a recent year by a group of finance companies ranged from 11 to 24 per cent per year. The median was 13½ per cent; the smaller the amount of financing, the higher the rate.[4] The company size required to qualify for equipment financing is generally the same as that required for accounts receivable financing (see page 106).

Insurance companies. Life insurance companies are the leading institutional source of long-term financing of American business. Corporate bonds and business mortgages represent by far the majority of their investments. Their fiduciary responsibilities to policy holders and a vast network of state regulations governing their investment policies tend to limit their business loans to borrowers of large amounts, with high credit ratings. They finance almost exclusively on a long-term basis through real estate mortgages.

In 1956, a group of life insurance companies controlling 75 per cent of industry's loanable funds reported that only 2 per cent of their industrial bond investments were placed with businesses having assets worth less than a million dollars, and only 15 per cent with businesses with assets of less than five million. In terms of money, 0.2 per cent went to businesses with assets of less than a million.[5] Clearly, exceptional circumstances must be present before a life insurance company will arrange bond financing for a small client.

Mortgage loans. While mortgage loans to small business constitute a minor portion of the loans outstanding, they do make up a large part of the total loans made. During 1956, the same group of life insurance companies mentioned above made nearly 5,000 business mortgage loans. Nearly 2,000 were for amounts lower than $50,000; and over 4,000 were for sums not exceeding $250,000.[6] However, it is not as easy as these statistics might lead us to believe for most small businesses to obtain mortgage loans. It is a very difficult task for the millions of small businesses with assets of less than $100,000, and a virtually impossible one for the new business.

In 1956, only 16 per cent of the total mortgage loans made by life insurance companies went to businesses with assets of less than $100,000. Numerically speaking, only about 800 of the 5,000 mortgage loans arranged in that year went to these firms. Thirty-eight per cent of all

[4]*Financing the Small Business: Report to the Committees on Banking and Currency and Select Committees on Small Business,* Parts 1 and 2, April 11, 1958, 85th Congress, 2d Sess., p. 462, Washington, D.C., 1958.

[5]*Ibid.,* pp. 512, 517.

[6]*Ibid.,* p. 514.

mortgage loans went to firms whose assets ranged from $100,000 to $500,000; and 22 per cent went to those with assets of $500,000 to $1 million.[7] In other words, over three-quarters of all loans went to businesses with assets of a million dollars or less. The purpose of these statistics has been to clearly identify that segment of business able to secure mortgage loans.

Incidentally, maturities ranged up to thirty years on these loans, with most falling into the fifteen- to twenty-five-year category. Interest rates ranged from 5 to 6.5 per cent, with the smaller loans generally bearing the higher rate.[8]

Law and tradition dictate caution in the investment of institutional funds. The most important factor in the investment policy of life insurance companies is safety of principal. They do not seek high-risk loans, regardless of interest rate; this immediately precludes consideration of businesses that are not firmly established, are undercapitalized, or have weak management. Even those businesses that do qualify may expect to find one or more financial covenants in their mortgage document pertaining to continual maintenance of working capital, dividend restrictions, and the like.

An instruction sheet used by one of the large life insurance companies in requesting information from prospective borrowers is reproduced on page 126 so that clients can have a better idea of the degree of investigation they can anticipate from the companies.

Loans on life insurance companies and mortgage of residential property to raise business capital are another source of funds made available by life insurance companies. Businesses in need of money are quite familiar with these fund-raising methods.

Other institutional sources. The loan policies and practices of life insurance companies establish the character of institutional lending in general, but there are other institutional sources, namely, fire or other insurance companies, savings banks, pension funds, universities or educational foundations, investment trusts or banks, and charitable organizations.

Sources of bond issue financing. Since institutions have been virtually eliminated as purchasers of small business bond issues, to whom can the smaller company sell its long-term obligations? Its officers, employees, customers, vendors, and other local investors are always possibilities, but they are apt to yield only modest amounts. If a small business wishes to sell its obligations to a broader segment of the public, how should the CPA suggest that his client go about this? What are the results likely to be?

[7] *Ibid.*, p. 516.
[8] *Ibid.*, pp. 518, 519.

The CPA's first technical consideration should be the SEC registration requirements. These should be investigated and the specific effect on the contemplated issue determined before it is decided to adopt this form of financing. The regulations and related costs of registered issues could have important implications. (See the discussion on equity financing, page 122.)

A second important step is the selection of an underwriter. The main problem here will be to find an investment banker willing to attempt the distribution of an unknown company's small issue. Few if any small issues are ever purchased by underwriters on a firm commitment basis. In other words, underwriters will not buy an entire issue and then resell to others. They will act instead as agent for the seller on a "best effort" basis and earn a fee commensurate with the number of units they sell. Cost data reveals that the most economical method of debt financing through underwriters usually is direct private placement. Underwriters will frequently know of private groups or investors interested in all or a sizeable portion of an issue. If an agreement is concluded, the client will be charged an agent's (or finder's) fee.

The costs of floating a small debt issue through underwriters will reduce proceeds to a significant extent. Average costs for the smallest bond issues are proportionately about ten times as high as those of the largest issues. In the case of recent bond issues of $750,000—of such manufacturing companies as underwriters have been willing to work with—average flotation costs have come to about 12 per cent of the face amount issued.

We can logically conclude that debt financing through underwriters is not a practical solution for most of the country's small businesses.

State development credit corporations. One of the often neglected sources of long-term funds is the offerings of local industrial development groups that have been formed on the state and community level. Local CPAs are undoubtedly familiar with the very numerous community groups.

The state development credit corporations are relatively new, the first one having been organized in 1949. They are private financial institutions whose purpose is to use financing as a method of developing the economies of their states. They are distinctly different from the State Credit Authorities, which are public agencies using public funds for development work. The corporations aid the economies of the states by increasing employment through the use of a specially created pool of private funds. Though financing small business is not their explicit goal, most of their assistance has benefited smaller businesses. They generally lend funds to three types of companies: (1) profitable companies having expansion plans that require more financing than can be obtained from conventional sources; (2) businesses that will begin operations in a community if financing can be obtained to provide the necessary facilities; and (3) marginal businesses that will probably discontinue operations unless their financial position can be strengthened. A concern may formally apply to a credit corporation only if it cannot obtain enough credit from conventional sources, namely, commercial banks. It is therefore reasonable to infer that commercial bank standards regarding earning ability, capital, and collateral are more stringent than those of the credit corporations.

Credit corporations provide loans in various ways for fairly long terms. For example, the experience of a group of New England development corporations indicates that less than 10 per cent of the loans, in terms of both number and total amount, had maturities not exceeding five years. Most fell in the six- to ten-year range, and about 8 per cent were for periods of more than ten years. Almost all the borrowers involved were manufacturers, which generate more income in a given area than most other lines because of larger payrolls. Less than 5 per cent of the loans were issued to nonmanufacturing businesses, 75 per cent to businesses having less than 100 employees, and almost 35 per cent to businesses with less than 20 employees. Borrowers with from 10 to 19 employees received an average of $26,000 each; those with from 50 to 99, $81,000. Interest cost experience indicates that rates average between 6 and 7 per cent, just a few points above the prime rate. There are circumstances in which a CPA is well justified in recommending a development corporation to his client.

According to the latest information available, over 1,500 development companies in the United States have an estimated capital of about $5 million.[9] In 1959 thirteen states had development companies. Now practically every state has a development organization of one kind or another. Some are regional but most are local in the scope of their operations.

Government sources of long-term funds. Any review of sources of funds must include a discussion of the facilities offered by federal government agencies. The following three sources are of diminishing importance and limited applicability but still deserving of mention.

1. Under certain conditions, it is still possible to obtain Federal Reserve bank loans. This program was relatively important through the early forties, but is of little practical value today.

2. Under the Defense Production Act of 1950, the Departments of the Army, Navy, Air Force, Commerce, Interior, and Agriculture, the General Services Administration, the National Aeronautics and Space Administration, and the Atomic Energy Commission have been authorized

[9]*Hearings on Small Business Financial Problems* (Report of the Subcommittee of the Committee on Banking and Currency, U.S. Senate, 85th Cong., 2d Sess.) Washington, D.C.: U.S. Government Printing Office, 1958, p. 408.

to guarantee loans for defense production made by commercial banks and other private financing institutions. The Federal Reserve Banks act as fiscal agents of the guaranteeing agencies under the Board's Regulation V.

During 1961 the agencies authorized the issuance of 13 guarantee agreements covering loans totaling $103 million. Loan authorizations outstanding on December 31, 1961, totaled $202 million, of which $157 million represented outstanding loans and $45 million additional credit available to borrowers. Of total loans outstanding, 74 per cent on the average was guaranteed. During the year approximately $103 million was disbursed on guaranteed loans, most of which represents revolving credits.[10]

3. The Fisheries Loan program was established in 1956 to assist commercial fishermen with their financing problems. Some 360 applications for direct loans were filed in the program's first year of operation. About half of them were approved at a rate of 5 per cent and an average maturity of eight years. Clients in this particular industry should contact the Department of the Interior for further details.

Small Business Administration. The Small Business Administration is the only Federal agency having a loan program specifically designed to promote the welfare of small business. This program was inaugurated in 1953 to provide funds to small business on either a participation or direct loan basis when longer term financing is unavailable on reasonable terms from banks or other private lenders. It also provides for loans to victims of disasters such as floods, hurricanes, and droughts. The SBA's share of a loan cannot exceed $350,000, except when groups of small concerns request a pool loan. The law governing the SBA originally set a maximum interest rate of 6 per cent in 1953 for business loans. The Small Business Act of 1958 reduced the rate to 5½ per cent, and all loans issued since have been at or below these rates. The maturities may run up to ten years. In its first 3½ years of operation, the SBA approved about 8,600 business loans and 6,900 disaster loans for the rehabilitation of homes and businesses. The business loans were granted to 19,500 formal applicants; the average amount of a loan was $45,000. Thirty per cent of the loans was made on a direct basis and the remainder on either an immediate or deferred participation basis with a private lender. The SBA will make a direct loan only if participation is unavailable.[11]

While most of the money went to manufacturers, much of it also went to wholesale, retail, and service businesses. It should be noted that pro-

[10]*Forty-eighth Annual Report of the Board of Governors of the Federal Reserve System Covering Operations for the Year 1961*, Washington, D.C., 1962.
[11]Ralph B. Tower, *A Handbook of Small Business Finance*, Small Business Administration SBM Series No. 15, 6th ed., p. 68, Washington, D.C., 1962.

fessional people can now also apply to the SBA for a small business loan.

SBA loans are assisting more small businesses as the program develops. During 1961, 13,680 business loan applications were filed for a total of $894,351,000, and 6,836 loans were approved for a total of $369,400,000.[12]

The SBA has recently attempted to simplify its processing procedures so as to expedite its lending program. Until 1955, authority to take action on applications was largely restricted to SBA officials in Washington. Since then, regional offices have been granted additional authority, and regional directors have in turn been permitted to delegate authority to SBA branch managers. As a result, more than one-half of the branch offices are now authorized to take final action on business participation loans up to $15,000 and disaster loans up to $20,000. Some offices have been authorized to approve participation and disaster loans up to $100,000 and $50,000, respectively. Some can approve or decline direct business loans up to $20,000. Regional directors can now approve business participation loans up to $100,000 where there is at least a 25 per cent bank participation; and they can approve disaster loans up to $50,000. This delegation of authority has resulted in improved service to small business concerns and led to the elimination of some red tape.

SBA requirements. There are some important SBA requirements that must be met. All loans must be secured by adequate collateral. In applying this rule, however, the SBA in each case weighs both collateral and earning ability. This is particularly significant for prospective non-manufacturing borrowers having less tangible collateral than the typical manufacturing business. Furthermore, loans are rarely granted to finance a change in ownership, unless such a change is necessary to keep the business in existence. Loans will generally not be issued to recreational or lending institutions.

In order to qualify for an SBA loan, the client must fall into one of the following small-business categories:[13]

(b) *Manufacturing.* Any concern primarily engaged in manufacturing is classified:
    (1) As small if its number of employees does not exceed 250 persons;
    (2) As large if its number of employees exceeds 1,000 persons;
    (3) Either as small or large depending on its industry and in accordance with the employment standards set forth in Schedule A of this part, if its number of employees exceeds 250 persons, but not more than 1,000 persons;
    (4) As small if it is primarily engaged in the "food canning and preserving industry" and its number of employees does not exceed 500 persons ex-

[12]*Twelfth Annual Report of the Select Committee on Small Business,* U.S. Senate, 87th Cong., 2d Sess., Report No. 1491, p. 8, Washington, D.C., 1962.

[13]*Code of Federal Regulations,* Title 13, 121.3-10 (*Federal Register,* vol. 27, pp. 9761, 9762, effective October 3, 1962).

clusive of agricultural labor as defined in subsection (k) of the Federal Unemployment Tax Act, 68 A Stat. 454, 26 USC (IRC 1954) 3306.

(c) *Retail.* Any concern primarily engaged in retailing is classified:
   (1) As small if its annual sales do not exceed $1 million;
   (2) As small if it is primarily engaged in making retail sales of "groceries and fresh meats" and its annual sales do not exceed $2 million;
   (3) As small if it is primarily engaged in making retail sales of "new or used motor vehicles" and its annual sales do not exceed $3 million;
   (4) As small if it is primarily engaged in the operation of a department store and its annual sales do not exceed $2 million . . .[14]

(f) *Wholesale.* Any concern primarily engaged in wholesaling is small if its annual sales do not exceed $5 million. Any wholesale concern also engaged in manufacturing is not a "small business concern" unless it so qualifies under both manufacturing and wholesaling standards.

There are also specific rules for construction, services, shopping centers, transportation, and warehousing. Additional information can be obtained from either the local or Washington offices of the SBA.

Equity financing sources for small business

Small business clients who elect to sell stock to raise capital or who are considering taking such a step, will almost invariably require their CPA's advice. Small stock issues sold privately to vendors, customers, friends, employees, or other local sources do not present the problems encountered in registering with the SEC. Regardless of the market to be sold, the CPA can offer advice on the type of security to be issued, be it preferred or common stock, or a convertible debt issue. He is also in the best position to recommend an attorney in equity financing situations if the need should arise. Equity financing is based less on the assets of a business than on its earning power. When a small business has been operating long enough to develop an earnings trend as well as the potential for higher earnings, a market for equity funds can generally be found, and the CPA should be instrumental in this search.

At what price can a client's equity be sold? Another important opportunity for service by the CPA lies in providing the answer to this question. The market, be it Wall or Main Street, tends to value stock in proportion to earnings and risk of the operation. For a few of the larger blue-chip growth corporations, there seems to be no limit to an acceptable price/earnings ratio. The market will pay up to and even above $50 for every $1 they earn. A price/earnings ratio of ten to fifteen is common for the average company. For the small business, however, the price/earnings ratio can drop to three or five times earnings. *These ratios will of course*

[14]*Federal Register,* vol. 27, p. 11313, effective November 16, 1962 (adding subparagraph 4).

rise and fall with investor sentiment and economic conditions. For small, indeterminate-risk businesses, public offerings of common stock are always expensive and their success often unpredictable. The CPA's advice with respect to alternative sources, offering price, estimated expenses of flotation, and timing of sale can be inestimably valuable to business management.

Selling stock to employees. It is worth repeating that *local* sources of stock sales should be fully explored before the expensive public offering of a small issue is attempted. Particular consideration might be given to employee sale. Many large companies make stock available below market price to employees, not so much for the purpose of raising funds, but rather because experience shows that such a step greatly enhances employee motivation and morale. The investment capacity of a group of fifty clerks, toolmakers, and assemblers may not be impressive, but the cumulative effect of an annual $300-stock purchase by each individual is unmistakable. A small business *could* thus raise $75,000 in five years at very modest expense.

Private investors. Some private investors, not necessarily local ones, may be interested in equity purchases in unusual situations. The investment banker or other specialists who handle private placements of equity issues can help to locate them. Confidential connections may sometimes be made with these people through a local banker or his correspondents in larger cities. Nor should advertising what one has to sell in financial media be overlooked as a means of interesting a private investor.

Venture capital. Another source of equity capital for manufacturing concerns is firms which operate in the venture capital field and seek capital gains mainly through investment in radically new products. They seek investment in new, small, and financially weak companies. Generally they buy a substantial stock interest. As capital requirements increase with growth, they often increase their investment, and usually obtain voting control (an important point to bear in mind).

Small Business Investment Companies. Still another source is the Small Business Investment Companies, or SBICs, licensed under the Small Business Investment Act of 1958. These are private corporations chartered under state law or by the Small Business Administration, whose specific function is that of providing long-term funds to small business through the purchase of convertible debenture bonds or through loans. It is well to remember that SBICs are also authorized to provide consulting and advisory services to small businesses on a fee basis. While SBIC activity is actively policed by the SBA, its advisory fees might compensate for its low interest rates. An SBIC should be investigated as any other

123

lending agency would be. Incidentally, the SBIC program does not supplant the regular loan program of the SBA.

To date, forty-three states and the District of Columbia have SBICs licensed by the SBA. As of December 1962, there were over six hundred licensed SBICs, excluding branch offices.

Minimum capital. A minimum capital of $300,000 is required to form an SBIC; the SBA will supply up to half of this amount. A few SBICs will attain considerable size. The Bank of America, for example, recently announced plans to invest $7.5 million in sponsoring a West Coast SBIC. The Electronics Capital Corporation recently filed an SEC registration statement covering a stock offering of $12 million in what they call a nondiversified SBIC. It intends to provide equity capital to selected electronic companies. Additional information on the SBICs organized in each area can be obtained from the SBIC division of the SBA.

Small Business Investment Companies are authorized to make long-term loans to incorporated or unincorporated businesses, as well as to provide funds through the purchase of convertible debentures. This aspect of the program appears to have been generally de-emphasized in the literature. It is of questionable advantage for an SBIC to simply lend long-term money at the nominal rate authorized. The success of an SBIC will be measured by its ability to pick good growth companies, help them along, and sell their equity for capital gains. How many small businesses lose voting control will remain to be seen. Since the program is still in the experimental stage, the value of SBICs to small business will be recorded in the future.

Public offerings. Public offerings can be a complicated method of raising equity funds for a smaller business. We will not in this chapter undertake a detailed discussion of the SEC requirements with respect to public offerings. CPAs who are not familiar with these requirements will necessarily have to do research work before they can advise a client in this area. The following points are especially significant: (1) a review of the types and sizes of security transactions exempt from registration (generally those aggregating less than $300,000); and (2) the form and content of information required to be filed under circumstances that often vary in small issue offerings.

The CPA can also help in the selection of an investment banker. As already mentioned, investment bankers are seldom interested in handling small issues. The larger investment bankers will not ordinarily undertake public issues below the $500,000 to $1 million range. There also seems to be a general agreement among them to the effect that a smaller company cannot obtain capital from the securities markets on reasonable terms if a company's net earnings after taxes fall below the $100,000 to $150,000 range. However, not all security underwriters or investment bankers are big businesses. Many are small businesses themselves specializing in the sale of small issues, and small offerings are considerably more attractive to them. There should be little difficulty in locating these through either a local banker or a large investment banker willing to guide other interested parties. A fellow CPA in a larger city may also be of assistance.

The CPA can do much for a client in reviewing the fees and expenses of security distribution. Compensation to underwriters takes the form of a spread between the price paid by underwriters to purchase a security issue and the price at which the issue will be sold in firm commitment underwriting. As previously mentioned, the small issue of an unknown company stands little chance of acceptance on this basis. A client's cost of flotation will probably be for best-effort underwriting, based on the number of units sold. In addition, there will be the costs attributable to SEC regulation, if the issue is subject to regulation, and other costs not related to SEC regulations. Compensation to underwriters ordinarily represents 75 to 85 per cent of the total stock flotation costs.

The cost of flotation is proportionately greater for small security issues than for large ones. Total costs for a $1 million issue on a registered basis average slightly less than 20 per cent of the proceeds; for a $500,000 issue, about 25 per cent. A common stock issue costs more than a preferred issue, and both cost considerably more than a debt issue of comparable size. A client's costs will vary according to industrial activity and other factors that may make averages misleading. In general, however, the costs of public issues are high, often prohibitively so.

Helping Business Clients to Obtain Funds

The CPA should make sure that the audit report, either in short-form presentation or by means of supplemental information, will give the lender a thorough insight into operations and the over-all financial picture. A lender will almost always be concerned about the following items:

1. The aging of receivables and details regarding any concentration in a few customers, details of notes receivable, and full information regarding the provision for bad debts should be disclosed.
2. Inventories, which are always scrutinized, should be presented by classification, with comments on saleability and turnover.
3. Investments, fixed assets, and other assets should be detailed in supplementary schedules. Market or appraisal values should be noted where applicable.
4. Liabilities and reserves should be fully explained and the latest tax year examined should be indicated. As a general rule, the lender should be given as much information as possible: this will almost always help the client, and rarely if ever hurt him.

Mention has been made of audit reports, but supplementary information such as the following will help greatly:

1. Budgets and forecasts. The lender will be particularly interested in operating forecasts and anticipated cash flow. Wherever practical, past budget and cash forecast data should be submitted, together with comparisons of actual results with budget to prove that forecasts are being utilized.
2. Repayment provision schedule. Any lender would naturally want to know how the money is going to be repaid. The precise need and purpose of the funds can also be outlined in this way.
3. A document describing the history and basic facts concerning the client. This should include:
   (a) A statement of past earnings and other historical financial data, explaining any past year losses.
   (b) Date formed, history of growth, and changes in the financial structure, if any.
   (c) Data relating to the management and officers, such as ages, background, experience, attitudes.
   (d) Explanation of business operation (products, markets, customers, and so on). If new products are involved, explain the marketing plans. A catalogue should be submitted.
   (e) Competitive position. This information can be important to a banker. Evidence of the client's status should be supplied by means of records of sales to some of the better customers or other available data.

Information required by life insurance companies. Following are the instructions of a typical life insurance company on the letter of information to be furnished by an industrial company applying for a mortgage loan.

Audit reports. Furnish complete, original, annual audit reports for the last ten years certified by independent certified public accountants. These will include balance sheets, earnings statements, surplus accounts, and supporting schedules. If the last annual statement is over three months old, include the latest available interim earnings and balance sheets with comparative data for the previous year.

History of the company. Give an outline of the growth of the business to include significant changes in financial structure, management, physical plant, products, processes, and any important contracts or agreements— either new or old. List location of all plants and offices presently occupied. Explain any loss years or poor earnings during the past ten years. For the past five years, state separately sales to the government and to domestic civilian customers.

List of products and marketing scheme. Describe market area covered or to be covered, selling organization and methods, advertising policy, effects of important patents or royalties, sources of raw materials, and principal vendors. Indicate if all products are manufactured by the company or if some are purchased. Submit sample catalogues and circulars.

Competitive position. Include a list of principal competitors and their relative standing with relation to the company (annual sales, net worth, and so on). Relate how the company secured its standing in the industry and what steps are taken to maintain this position, such as product or market research.

Principal customers. List names and sales records for each customer during the past five years. In addition, state length of association with each.

Forecast of future sales and earnings. Give a brief explanation of the basis of the estimate. State the current backlog of orders by products or departments. Describe budgeting practices and other methods of expense control.

Real estate. Briefly describe real estate offered as security. Include land area, building (including square feet of usable floor area and gross area), cost when acquired or constructed, and estimated cost of any new construction. Indicate what additional property the company owns, such as machinery or other plants, and how title to real estate is held. If a change is being made, include for each of the last ten years previous rental costs which are to be eliminated and explain what further economies are anticipated.

Purpose of the loan. Explain the benefits to be obtained and the application of proceeds. Include a proforma balance sheet giving effect to the proposed loan at the time it is contemplated to be closed.

Equity funds. Explain the source of all required funds if purchase or construction of additional facilities is planned.

Officers and directors. List these with their names and operating titles. Show the principal stockholders or stock control by number of shares or percentage of total.

Principal executive and technical experts. State background and experience, age and compensation. Discuss availability of "second men."

Labor information. Include number of employees, membership in unions, strike history, and labor relations. Give number of employees hired and number terminated in each of the last three years.

References. List bank and trade references.

The client can help himself in other ways. He can, for example, maintain a continuous relationship with lenders or prospective lenders. He can send them financial statements and inform them of new products or other significant changes in operations. Moreover, he can establish a line of credit in advance of actual need. Many CPAs have reported that nearly every commercial client has been helped to obtain a credit line. Although many clients never use their line, should funds be required, even in excess of the established amount, faster and generally more successful negotiations will result.

Through his knowledge of finance, the CPA can perform a very real service to business clients who are generally unfamiliar with lenders' requirements and attitudes. Providing supplementary data for a business should not require much additional time. It will aid clients to obtain the top dollar and often transform what may appear to the lender to be a marginal situation into a good risk.

The decision to make funds available to a business lies essentially in the determination of management effectiveness. This will manifest itself through the financial statements, as well as through management attitudes and practices. Lenders are sophisticated financial experts. Consequently, the first weaknesses they are likely to spot in a small business applicant will be in the area of financial management. The opportunity to evaluate the soundness of production control or personnel practices will probably not present itself. When lenders cite unbalanced management as a common reason for turning down a loan, it can safely be assumed that much of this imbalance is evident in the financial management area.

CPAs can fill the financial management void in many businesses. By investing only a little additional time, a CPA can capably function as an advisor to his business clients. By so doing, he will contribute to the strength and profitability of both his clients and himself.

CHAPTER THREE

Inventory and Production Controls

Inventory Management

EVERY SO OFTEN, the subject of inventory management emerges from relative obscurity to a prominent position. These periods of interest usually coincide with periods of substantial decline in business activity. The interest wanes as soon as business activity recovers.

These on-again off-again attempts at inventory management seldom result in maintaining inventories at the most effective level during all phases of the business cycle. They are almost always accompanied by periods of slippage during which more is produced or purchased than should be, and vice versa. The attempts to correct the situation are then more drastic and more prolonged than need be. The subject of continuous, effective inventory management should command universal attention because it is important to all of us in our roles as businessmen and as individual citizens. It has a significant effect on individual companies, on industries, and on the behavior of the economy of the country as a whole.

Importance to Business

From a purely business standpoint, why is it important to have effective inventory management?

First, effective inventory management is essential in order to provide the highest type of service to customers. If back orders or stock-outs become prevalent, competition is invited to take business away on the basis of more dependable service.

Second, without effective inventory management, a company is not able to produce at maximum efficiency. If the required raw materials or parts are not available at the proper time, it becomes necessary to delay production, shift schedules, and perhaps move men or materials, or both, to different machines or operations.

Third, the cost of carrying inventories is directly affected by the skill with which inventory levels are managed. Carrying costs of inventory have been estimated to range from 15 to 25 per cent of the value of inventories. These costs include such items as interest on invested capital, personal property taxes, storage facilities, warehouse space, insurance, and so on. If the company is in an industry with a rapidly advancing technology, the factor of obsolescence becomes of major importance. Consider the potential reduction in annual carrying costs if a company could reduce an inventory of $20 million by 10 per cent, or $2 million. Assuming a carrying cost of 15 per cent, a potential annual savings of $300,000 may be realized.

Elements of Inventory Management

Effective inventory management requires the development of a highly integrated and co-ordinated system. In fact, there are few systems used in managing a business that require a higher degree of integration or co-ordination. What aspects of business activity are involved in inventory management? They can be enumerated so easily that their significance is often overlooked when inventory management problems are considered. Inventory management involves:

Sales forecasting
Purchasing
Production
Receiving, storing, shipping
Actual sales (as distinguished from sales forecasting)
Engineering (changes)

These activities encompass nearly all the major functions of business, and there is an interrelationship among them that affects inventories every time a change in any one of them occurs. If, for example, a sales forecast is revised, there is an implied need for adjustment in inventory levels. This gives rise to adjustments in purchasing or production scheduling. If the time required for crating, packing, and shipping finished goods increases from two days to four days, or if the purchase lead time for certain items decreases from ninety days to sixty days, there are again implied changes in inventory levels. It is hardly necessary to mention the effect that engineering changes can have on inventory levels and production schedules.

Fluctuation of Inventory Levels

Why do companies make changes of the kind mentioned? Why do not all the factors remain constant so that it would never be necessary to revise sales forecasts; so that companies would not have to reschedule production or make engineering changes? It is beyond the purpose of this book to go into all the economic and social factors that give rise to changes in the volume of business activity. Insofar as individual companies are concerned, these changes in business activity are almost universally the result of external conditions over which the companies have no control and little recourse, except to adjust to the new conditions. Just a few of the external factors that force companies to change the level of their business activities are changes in international relations, new products and processes, droughts, floods, or bumper crops. Some of these factors will have a cumulative effect on our entire economy; some will not. Any of them, however, will almost certainly affect certain companies or entire industries and will usually require a change in the level of production if a company is to continue to be profitable.

There are, then, two important points to remember:

1. The control of inventory levels is affected by and in turn effects changes in interrelated functions of every business enterprise.
2. The need for changes in these interrelated functions is most often imposed externally by forces beyond company control and predictability.

This is why a successful inventory management system requires a high degree of integration and co-ordination. It must be sensitive to change and it must generate the required changes in other functions such as purchasing, production, shipping, and the like. Inventory management is not a sometime thing; it cannot be turned on and off at will and still work effectively. It must function as an organic part of the business, so that adjustments can be made as soon as any important factors change, and not six months or a year later.

Over-all Inventory Appraisals

A number of traditional methods have long been used in attempting to control inventories. One of the first that comes to mind is the inventory turnover ratio. It is a measure useful for financial analysis of units within a company or of companies in an industry. It may indicate a desirable or undesirable condition in the aggregate, but it cannot, of course, assure that inventory imbalances do not exist with respect to specific items. It will not answer the important inventory questions of "how much?" and "how often?"

Another device used to maintain over-all control of inventories is the inventory budget. A budget is usually somewhat more sensitive to short-term control requirements than the turnover ratio because it is predicated on sales forecasts and production schedules which may cover relatively short periods, such as a quarter or a month. The inventory budget, of course, is often expressed in aggregate dollars which will not disclose inventory item imbalances even though the total actual inventory may be very close to the budget.

Another measure of control sometimes employed is the return on investment. This is useful to top management because it can be used to measure performance against a planned objective. In a sense, it does indicate a relatively efficient or inefficient use of inventories, but usually many other revenue and expense items are included in calculating the return on investment which are only incidentally related to inventories or, in some cases, wholly unrelated.

These three control measures—turnover ratio, inventory budgets, and return on investment—are valuable tools which enable the CPA to make an over-all appraisal of a company's performance and to compare such performance with predetermined goals or past performance. However, they cannot provide the information necessary to actually carry out an integrated inventory control system. That requires information in far greater detail so that decisions which must be made about specific items can be made intelligently.

Factors Affecting Inventory Levels

The problem of controlling individual inventory items is usually approached by establishing minimum-maximum levels. There are many factors which must be considered when establishing stock levels and it is the care with which these factors are used in establishing inventory levels that determines the effectiveness of the control.

The first factor, of course, is the anticipated demand. This demand may be based on historical records or it may be based on a sales forecast. Whatever the basis, the anticipated demand must frequently be modified to allow for fluctuations since rarely will the estimated demand coincide with actual usage.

Another factor is lead time, both vendor lead time and production lead time. Lead times are not always exactly predictable, and while it may be established that six weeks would be a good average figure for an item, it may be necessary to allow for a one- or two-week deviation either way from the average.

A third factor is the value of the item. High-value items are controlled more rigidly than low-value items. Many companies now stratify their inventories into groups of relative values in recognition of this factor. In many companies, 10 to 15 per cent of the number of items may comprise 60 per cent or more of the total inventory value.

A fourth factor is storage space. This does not only involve consideration of the cost of storage, but availability of storage space, or the lack of it, and often influences decisions regarding inventory levels.

Another influence on inventory levels is price. This may be illustrated by two examples. One of these is the frequent necessity to decide whether or not to order a larger quantity to obtain an additional discount. A second is buying in anticipation of price increases.

The cost of carrying inventories is a factor which should influence inventory levels, but too often is not given proper weight because it is not always convenient to determine what the cost really is.

One other factor is the expectation of engineering changes or the danger of obsolescence. In industries where technological changes are rapid, or where style changes are traditional, a much higher degree of risk attaches to a high level of inventories than in those industries not characterized by these conditions.

All the factors above can influence stock levels; no attempt was made to be all-inclusive. A sufficient number were mentioned, however, to make this point: if you can envision trying to take all of these factors, and others, into consideration simultaneously, applying valid weights to each, and then deciding on two specific numbers—an order quantity and a reorder point—the CPA is not unlike a juggler. The biggest difference is in the consequences of failure. If a CPA loses track of one of the factors influencing inventory levels, the consequences are much more serious for the client. There may be lost sales, permanent loss of customers, disruption of production, and loss of cash.

Need for Objective Methods

Until recently, not too many attempts had been made to use methods expressing the factors which influence inventory levels in a definite relationship, with specific values assigned to each. Setting minimum and maximum levels has usually been pretty much of a judgment matter, rather than the result of any objective, organized procedure.

To be sure, the classical economic lot formulas have been with us for years. There are a number of them, and their common objective is to determine the order quantity which will result in a minimum setup or ordering cost and carrying cost per unit. Amazing as it may seem, however, these formulas are not used at all by many companies, even as a check on decisions reached solely through the judgment process. They have not been used more frequently for three reasons.

First, the formulas are expressed as mathematical equations, and as such make use of symbols which sometimes completely baffle many CPAs and businessmen.

Second, the use of an equation requires the determination of finite values which may not always be readily available. For example, how much does it really cost to store an inventory? What does it cost to issue a purchase order or a production order? These costs do not appear on any conventional financial statement. They require special analysis, and this requirement is often a deterrent to using the formulas. Other factors may not even be determinable by analysis, but may have to be imputed. How much is it worth to a company, for example, never to run out of stock?

A third deterrent has been the large number of inventory items to which formulas must be applied. Many companies just never considered such a formal approach to inventory control practicable.

Even where sincere efforts were made in the past to maintain current minimum-maximum levels, the objectives were frequently defeated because of a lag in recording usage of material in the stock records.

Recent Developments

Two important developments have occurred during recent years, however, which constitute major breakthroughs in efforts to establish effective, integrated inventory control systems on a practicable basis. First, industrial management is beginning to recognize that the use of mathematical techniques affords a more reliable method of inventory control than intuitive or judgment methods. Second, the use of electronic data processing equipment not only overcomes the problem of transaction volume associated with inventory accounting, but it can also facilitate the use of the mathematical techniques referred to above.

Production and Inventory Control[1]

How DO THE developments just cited affect the CPA? How can he aid the business community in general, and his clients in particular? The confidential relationship of the CPA with his clients provides many opportunities to learn the nature and extent of a company's problems.

[1]Pages 134 through 142 were reprinted from *The Illinois CPA,* Winter 1958-1959. The author is Vance A. Wadhams, Principal, Management Advisory Services, Price Waterhouse & Co., Chicago.

Working in many office departments, making plant tours and visits to branches, and engaging in discussion with employees provide an observant auditor with an insight into the need for improvements in organization and procedures. His experience will assist him to suggest practical ways of achieving these improvements. If he does not do so, he is not making the most of his opportunities to provide effective service to his clients.

Company Objectives

Two of the most important objectives of a manufacturing company are customer satisfaction and production at a cost which will assure a reasonable profit. To achieve these objectives, delivery of product conforming to specifications must be made promptly as required, and efficient use must be made of labor and capital invested in equipment and inventories. To a considerable extent, these basic requirements conflict with each other and one of the most difficult problems is the planning and control of production to achieve a proper balance between them. Therefore it is apparent that one of the most important problems encountered by a manufacturing company is that of the co-ordination of production with sales and inventories. How well the planning and scheduling of production is carried out may mean the difference between successful operation of the company and its ultimate failure.

Successful production control usually begins at a high level in the organization with top management making the decision as to quantities of product to make for a given or forecasted volume of business. Each such decision has a direct effect on operating costs and on the amount of inventory. If sales are substantially greater than anticipated, finished product inventories may be depleted to a point where orders cannot be filled, resulting in loss of sales and profit. If sales are substantially less than expected, inventories may become excessive, resulting in high carrying costs and possible obsolescence. On the other hand, if the rate of production is frequently changed to meet each minor fluctuation in sales, operating costs may become excessive. The problem is to maintain the best balance between keeping the customer satisfied and keeping the costs in line. Business involves many calculated risks, and here the calculation is concerned with the extent to which a company may risk possible customer dissatisfaction in the interests of keeping costs low and the extent to which costs, such as those of carrying inventories or making short production runs, may be incurred to insure customer satisfaction. In certain types of operations there is little choice if orders are for small quantities requiring specialized manufacturing operations and few repeat orders. Under these circumstances each order may become a special production control problem.

Company Methods

Although in a broad sense the principles of effective production and inventory control are applicable to all manufacturers, the specific methods best suited to a particular company vary considerably depending upon the nature of its operations. In a small company the principal executive, from his personal knowledge of sales orders, production facilities, and inventories, may be in a position to make the decisions for production scheduling with a minimum of records. His daily observations of work in the shop and materials on hand may be all that is required. Contrast this with the problems of planning and timing involved in scheduling work for a large automobile assembly plant where detailed arrangements must be made with company-owned plants and outside suppliers to have all required parts in specific quantities on railroad cars at various points along a route so that a freight train can be assembled and arrive at the assembly plant at the proper time. These schedules are so planned that no more than a three-day inventory of parts for assembly is on hand at any time. All of this requires plans, records, and co-ordination far beyond the ability of one man.

One of the greatest advances made in the development of management techniques for manufacturing enterprises was the separation of the planning function from the physical execution of production. There are still a few plants in which orders are entered and then transmitted directly to the shop where foremen interpret them, requisition necessary materials, plan and execute the work. It is easy to see that even in these small plants it would be much more effective to plan production in advance, group like orders, arrange for needed materials, and transmit orders to the shop only when everything is in readiness for uninterrupted production.

Examples of Production Control Systems

A brief discussion of several effective production control systems will serve to illustrate the manner in which such systems function under different operating conditions.

Precision instrument manufacturer

Consider first a company which is supplying the avionics industry, which is in a state of constant technological advancement. This involves the manufacture of control devices which are physically small and require extremely close tolerances and precision manufacture. As the demands for missiles, rockets, and aircraft increase, the demands for improvement in components increase. Thus the company is required to produce in small lots with very short lead times and delivery schedules and undergo frequent engineering changes during production.

When a customer's order is received, it is posted by a member of the planning group to a production schedule board. This group estimates from flow charts of this or similar jobs the production time required for the job, consulting, when necessary, representatives of the engineering department. This production time is converted to card form on a Sched-u-graph board which shows the length of production time for each job and the total work load in the plant. A weekly summary of all jobs by type assures proper work loading in each department of the plant.

The order is reviewed by the dispatcher and work orders for each manufactured part and assembly are prepared from the parts list. Fabrication times are obtained from the production flow charts for the job and are posted to the work orders. The average fabrication and assembly time for a job is five weeks. After work orders are prepared, requisitions for purchased material are issued by the material control group to the purchasing department. All work orders are then filed by the week of release to each particular department.

A summary of all jobs scheduled for a two-month period is issued each month. The work orders are released weekly for the coming two-week period. Records of the material control department are posted from the work orders for withdrawal of material from stock. The work orders are sent to the stockroom and are used as material requisitions. They accompany the material to the specific manufacturing department where they are used by the department dispatcher for issue control. A simple dispatch pegboard is used by the dispatchers for visual control of material released to the operating departments and of its progress through the manufacturing processes.

The dispatcher in the department and the department foreman have authority to arrange the work assigned to the department for the week in any desired order so long as it is completed by the dates assigned from the flow chart. This allows the dispatcher and the foreman maximum flexibility consistent with schedule requirements. When production problems arise that affect schedules, the foreman and department dispatcher are responsible for working out any adjustments. If a satisfactory solution cannot be reached by them, the chief dispatcher is notified and corrective action is taken.

In effect, this represents control by exception. The control group plans the work flow and schedules it by week through the departments. The department dispatcher has complete control over specific day-to-day machine assignments within this framework. No reporting to the control group is made unless an event takes place which will affect the schedule. The completed work order for each part or assembly is forwarded to the central group to match with the original orders in file which are then pulled and destroyed. The only posting is for the exceptions. An audit of orders by the control group on a regular sample basis assures that proper controls are being exercised.

Home appliance manufacturer

A somewhat different system is required in the case of a home appliance manufacturer producing both for specific orders and for stock. Fabrication of the parts manufactured requires only a few days' time. The major production steps consist of assembly, painting, and packing. A full production cycle can be completed in one week. Long-range production requirements are established first on a basis of sales forecasts using past experience and management's judgment of future prospects. Weekly production schedules are based on specific orders and existing inventory levels reflected by the finished stock inventory records.

Bills of material are prepared, first by subassemblies, next by assemblies, and finally into completed units. At each level of the bill of material all the points of usage are noted. This provides the basis for development of requirements for orders as well as the points of common usage. Standardization of parts to the extent practicable minimizes their number and eliminates minor and unnecessary variations. Application of this procedure in this particular case reduced model variations from 1,200 to only 40 production combinations.

A combination "where used" production work sheet and material requisition form is used. On this form columns are provided for the forty production combinations and the individual parts are listed down the left side. In each column under the appropriate combinations are noted the usage requirements. On the right-hand side of the form is a tear-off section on which the combined requisition quantities are noted for each part. As orders are received from customers and work orders for stock are issued they are analyzed to determine the combinations required. The combinations are summarized for the week and these totals are then entered at the top of the form and extended for the various usages in the appropriate columns. This procedure permits an early determination of requirements and eliminates separate computation and preparation of material requisitions.

Routing sheets are used which parallel the bills of material. These sheets show, for each operation, the labor hours and the material required for production of one hundred pieces. Provision is made for costing the route sheets and the cost department has developed standard costs directly from these sheets.

A form similar to the one for determining material requirements is used to reflect the operating times required. This facilitates loading individual departments to their capacity to permit efficient production runs and minimize setup time.

With the exception of the analysis of orders into the forty categories, which is performed by means of a key selection technique on a bookkeeping machine, the entire material and production control system is on a manual basis using the preprinted requisition work sheet and scheduling forms.

Inventory control of such low cost and numerous items as bolts, nuts, screws, and washers is on a nonrecording basis. Under this plan minimum quantities, sufficient for use during purchase lead time, are packaged or set aside and when needed for production, routine reorder procedures assure a new supply.

Machine parts manufacturer

A more sophisticated type of production and inventory control system is required for a manufacturer of units which are sold to a variety of machinery producers, including automotive companies. In this case manufacturing lead times are considerably longer and various parts must be produced simultaneously. Production levels are set according to sales forecasts and contracts; minor short-term deviations are absorbed in inventories. Sales and production are plotted along with established control limits. Significant changes which fall outside the control area call for a new sales forecast and production schedule. Control limits for finished goods inventories are established, keeping production in line with sales.

Finished product requirements next are translated into specific material and labor requirements. A precise job of scheduling and material control is necessary due to the high volume and relatively few basic finished models, the integrated manufacturing processes, and limited storage space.

To the extent practicable, bills of material have been standardized to minimize their number, all materials have been coded numerically, and common usage of materials in various parts and subassemblies identified. Extreme care has been taken to assure that bills of material are in agreement with blueprints.

Routing sheets showing steps in the manufacturing process, subassemblies, and final assemblies have been carefully checked. Decks of punched cards carrying all necessary information represent the bill of material and, by standard "explosion" procedures, required quantities of parts, subassemblies, and final assemblies are computed readily. By utilizing these figures, all operations from purchase of materials through processing, subassembly, final assembly, and packaging may be scheduled concurrently.

The schedule for parts and subassemblies is finally expressed in quantities to be produced each day and it backs up, step by step, from shipping and assembly requirements, to subassembly, to parts, to raw material, due consideration being given to lead time in each instance.

Bills of material and route sheets are also prepared mechanically from the punched cards. Changes in the deck can be made readily by removal of superseded cards and insertion of new cards. Using these cards together with cards representing inventory quantities on hand and on order, stock status reports are prepared as required.

The procedures followed contribute toward minimizing the work in process inventory. A further aid toward minimizing inventories in this case was found in the application of advanced mathematical techniques (operations research) to major items of raw material and finished goods produced for stock. These methods involve development of a mathematical model based on the interrelationships among three primary costs: (1) the annual cost of carrying inventory, (2) the annual ordering or replenishment cost, and (3) the annual cost associated with actual or potential stock shortages. Under this method a plan of least cost is developed which minimizes the possibility of excessive inventories or, conversely, an out-of-stock condition. Use of electronic data processing equipment is planned by this company to permit greater use of the mathematical techniques and to make possible even more rapid schedule charges.

Because so many different departments are affected, deficiencies in production and inventory control can cause trouble throughout a company with adverse effects on its progress and profitability. The need for co-ordination in planning and controlling production and inventories is not restricted to the large companies. Even in a small manufacturing company the personnel involved in these problems, in addition to manufacturing and production control people, include the sales and order personnel, storekeeper, purchasing agent, design engineer, process or industrial engineer, personnel director, maintenance supervisor, treasurer, traffic manager, and cost accountant.

The CPA's Role

What can the certified public accountant do to aid management in improvements of production and inventory control systems? He can further his own knowledge and experience in this field and thus further qualify himself to furnish such services to his clients. He can make special reviews of production and inventory control systems and assist in the development of improved systems. If the size and type of his practice warrant it, he may engage experienced specialists in this field to assist him in furnishing such services. However, without becoming a specialist, the CPA can do much to aid his clients by being alert to the need for improvement. The evidence of inadequate production and inventory control is not confined to the production department. In the conduct of an examination of financial statements, symptoms may be observed which indicate deficiencies in these functions.

Signs of Faulty Control

Since cost accounting is closely concerned with production, the review a CPA makes of a company's cost accounting and reporting procedures and inventory accounts often discloses symptoms which may indicate deficiencies in production and inventory control. Examples of such symptoms follow. (For a suggestive check list, see Table 1 below.)

Large material usage and labor variances in cost, indicating inadequate control to performance standards.

Substantial over- or under-absorbed overhead, reflecting inefficient utilization of equipment.

Excessive inventories of raw material, work in process, or finished goods, indicating ineffective production control.

Large writedowns of obsolete inventories, which may have arisen from purchases or production not properly co-ordinated with sales requirements.

Material shortages, which indicate that production needs have not been planned properly.

Table I

PRODUCTION AND INVENTORY CONTROL CHECK LIST

Area in which symptom may appear

Symptoms which may indicate a need for better production and inventory control	Accounts payable	Accounts receivable	Budgeting	Cost accounting	Financial reports	Fixed assets	Forms	General accounting procedures	Operating reports	Order billing procedures	Organization	Payroll	Purchasing	Receiving	Sales policies and procedures	Traffic	Tour of factory—inventory observation	Analysis of financial statements
Excessive sales returns and allowances	x	x		x	x			x	x						x	x		x
Delay in filling customer orders		x						x	x						x	x		
Promised delivery dates not met									x						x	x		
Inability to provide rush service to customers															x			
Too many back orders		x						x	x						x			
Excessive number of rush purchases	x			x									x	x		x		
Purchases in uneconomical quantities	x			x									x	x			x	
Fluctuations in the labor force			x	x							x							
Excessive number of stock chasers or expediters			x	x						x	x				x			
Unusually large production control staff			x	x						x	x				x			
Sizeable material usage and labor usage variances			x	x	x			x										x
Under- or over-liquidation of burden			x	x	x			x										x
Numerous handwritten forms, with excessive copying of data				x		x	x				x	x					x	
Circuitous routing of production				x													x	
Excessive inventories of raw, in process, or finished materials			x	x				x					x	x	x		x	x
Material shortages				x				x					x	x			x	
Machine down time from lack of work				x				x			x						x	
Absence of accurate production information, e.g., bills of material, engineering drawings, timed operation lists				x			x										x	
New buildings or new equipment not being used				x		x											x	
Employees loafing																	x	
Production supervisors doing clerical work																	x	
Large amounts of in-process material not being worked on				x													x	
Excessive handling of materials																	x	
Excessive amounts of spoilage, scrap, or rework				x				x									x	

Machine down time from lack of work, which may indicate inadequate planning and scheduling of production.

A review of payroll records and procedures may reflect unusual fluctuations in the labor force, indicating a need for better production planning. An excessive number of stock chasers or expediters on the payroll usually reflects inadequate material control or production scheduling. An unusually large production control staff may indicate that this function is not properly organized or that the possibility of mechanization of procedures has been overlooked.

Clear indications of need for improvement in production planning and inventory control which may be observed in reviewing sales order, billing, and accounts receivable procedures include excessive sales returns and allowances, delay in filling orders, inability to provide rush service to customers, and numerous back orders. In addition to customer dissatisfaction these lead to excessive clerical and accounting costs.

A review of purchasing procedures and accounts payable may disclose an excessive number of rush purchases, or purchases in quantities which do not appear to be economical. These too point to a need for improved planning of production and inventories.

When symptoms are encountered which indicate that production or inventory control may be deficient, the circumstances must be examined carefully and all facts ascertained before any recommendations are made to the client. Upon closer scrutiny it may be concluded that production control is satisfactory, but something else is causing the trouble, such as lack of adequate communication, ineffective quality control, inadequate material handling, or inefficient control of operator performance.

This area of service to management is only one of many in which CPAs can furnish helpful assistance to their clients. New methods, equipment, and techniques are being developed at an accelerated pace.

How to Reduce Inventories Quickly

A Case History[2]

The control and valuation of inventories is vital in manufacturing companies because inventories are one of the largest assets, if not the largest, and because excess and obsolete inventory can make the difference between profit and loss. The CPA would do well not only to broaden his

[2]Pages 142 through 151 are reprinted from the October 1960 issue of *The Arthur Andersen Chronicle*. The authors are Messrs. John B. Robinson and H. D. Kennedy, Jr., partners in that firm.

audit competence but also to assist clients in independent production and inventory control projects. These projects may have objectives such as improving customer service, reducing the cost of operating production and inventory control departments, leveling shop loads, shortening production cycles, and reducing inventory investment. This case study illustrates short-range methods for accomplishing inventory reduction.

The Marinus Manufacturing Company was in trouble. Although sales of its farm machinery and tractors had risen 25 per cent in the last two years, net profits had shown a slight decrease and the investment in inventory had gone up 50 per cent. The company's financial statements for the last fiscal year are summarized on page 144.

As indicated, the company's cash position was precarious. It was losing $100,000 annually in cash discounts because of inability to pay vendors' invoices on a current basis. Cash was not available to pay dividends to stockholders, who were beginning to grow restless. But, worst of all, the company's banks would not extend their lines of credit and were exerting pressure for a reduction in the outstanding loans. The production control people had assured the executive vice-president six months earlier that the investment in inventory would be reduced by $1 million by the end of the year, and on this basis the executive vice-president had informed the banks that a corresponding reduction would be made in the outstanding loans. Actually, the inventory had risen $400,000 during the six months instead of dropping $1 million.

The company was turning its inventory only twice a year, which was considerably less than competitors turned their inventories. If the inventory could be turned three times a year or once every four months, which the production cycle indicated was feasible, the inventory would drop to $6,700,000. This decrease of $3,300,000 would, in effect, generate an equal amount of cash. This inventory reduction would also increase annual pretax profits by at least $200,000 at a bare 6 per cent cost of money. If it is assumed that the carrying cost of inventory is about 20 per cent, over $500,000 annually would be added to pretax profit.

The executive vice-president realized that he could probably obtain some long-term financing secured by mortgages on plant and equipment, but this step would not solve the basic problem. It was obvious that in order to correct the cash situation the company had to make a substantial reduction in its investment in inventories immediately.

Short-range Program

After consultation with various members of the management group, the CPA instituted a short-range program for immediate inventory reduction with primary emphasis on outstanding purchase commitments and high annual dollar usage items. The first major step was to:

Report purchase commitments on a current basis. Before the company's inventory could be reduced, steps had to be taken to keep it from growing larger. The objective was to shut off deliveries of the larger open purchase orders if they were not needed. This meant either deferring deliveries to future periods or outright cancellations.

The company had never had a purchase commitment report. Contemplated cutoff difficulties and inaccuracies had been used as an excuse in the past. The CPA concluded that a purchase commitment report would

MARINUS MANUFACTURING COMPANY

BALANCE SHEET
December 31, 196-

Assets

Current assets:

Cash	$ 50,000	
Receivables	2,500,000	
Inventories	10,000,000	$12,550,000
Fixed and other assets (net)		5,450,000
		$18,000,000

Liabilities

Current liabilities:

Notes payable to banks	$ 3,000,000	
Accounts payable	3,000,000	
Accrued payroll, taxes, etc.	1,000,000	$ 7,000,000

Stockholders' equity:

Capital stock	$ 5,000,000	
Retained earnings	6,000,000	11,000,000
		$18,000,000

MARINUS MANUFACTURING COMPANY

INCOME STATEMENT
Year Ended December 31, 196-

Sales	$27,000,000
Cost of sales	20,000,000
Gross profit	$ 7,000,000
Selling, administrative, and interest expense	6,000,000
Profit before income taxes	$ 1,000,000
Income taxes	500,000
Net profit	$ 500,000

be helpful even though it might contain some inaccuracies. He was instructed to have the purchasing department initiate and maintain records for such a report.

An adding machine tape was run of all 5,000 open purchase orders for productive materials. Because only substantial accuracy was sought, whole-dollar accounting was used and estimates were made in those few cases where firm prices were not available. An analysis of this tape indicated that 300 open orders of over $2,000 each represented $4,200,000, or 75 per cent of the total. Consequently, only these 300 orders were included on the commitment report because the quickest payoff would come by concentrating effort on these high dollar value commitments. The first purchase commitment report as of July 31, 196—, spread the $4,200,000 by delivery dates shown on vendor acknowledgments as follows:

Month due in	Amount
Prior to July 31	$1,000,000
August	1,400,000
September	1,000,000
October	600,000
After October	200,000
	$4,200,000

The revelation that almost 25 per cent of these major purchase orders were overdue came as a shock. Because shortages really were not excessive despite these overdue purchase orders, it became apparent that too much was being asked for too soon, and that the cash position would have been even more precarious had vendors delivered requested but unneeded material when scheduled. Apparently a defense mechanism had grown up on the part of the material ordering clerks to the effect that "if a little cushion was good, a big one was better." On the other hand, a comparison of the dates on the purchase requisition with the requested dates on the purchase orders showed that the purchasing department was also involved in advancing requested delivery dates.

A tip-off on inaccurate input scheduling was obtained by comparing delinquent (overdue) purchase orders with current production shortages. Parts which did not appear on shortage lists but which did appear on delinquent purchase orders obviously were not needed currently. Immediately after beginning this comparison, the name of the particular supplier emerged.

Excess engines

Engines on open order from the Combustible Engine Company totaled $200,000 and were worth approximately $1,000 each. A comparison of engines on hand and on order with the requirements for laydown in factory assembly showed:

ENGINE SCHEDULE COMPARISON

Week beginning	Engines on hand and on order		Per factory assembly schedule (4)	
	Units	Dollars	Units	Dollars
Aug. 1	150 (1)	$150,000	8	$ 8,000
	130 (2, 3)	130,000		
8			18	18,000
15			16	16,000
22			14	14,000
29			18	18,000
Sept. 5	70 (2)	70,000	20	20,000
12			16	16,000
19			18	18,000
26			14	14,000
Oct. 3			16	16,000
10			14	14,000
17			12	12,000
24			16	16,000
Totals	350	$350,000	200	$200,000

NOTES:

(1) Engines on hand
(2) Engines on open purchase orders
(3) 250 engines had originally been scheduled for August 1, but 120 engines had already been received prior to August 1
(4) Adjusted to purchase order acknowledgment schedule date by allowing a week for receipt, inspection, and placing in assembly position and an additional week's safety cushion

Review of the shipping performance of the Combustible Engine Company revealed that almost without exception shipments were received two weeks to a month early and invoices were received usually even before the engines were received in the receiving department.

Furthermore, a requisition for fifty more engines was about to be placed for an October 3 delivery at the time of the review of the open order position. When this was called to his attention, the CPA suggested that all requisitions for material which exceeded $2,000 be personally approved by an executive and that the requisition for fifty engines be canceled.

Upon analyzing the schedule comparison and talking with the Combustible Engine people, it developed that weekly shipments would be no more expensive than monthly shipments if the quantity never fell below ten per shipment. A further agreement was reached with Combustible to the effect that shipments would not be made more than two days before schedule or in excess of schedule. Upon reviewing the internal processing time for receipt, inspection, and laydown on the assembly line, it was discovered that the present period of a week was excessive and that there was no reason why these engines could not clear through the receiving department in half a day and through the inspection department in a day and a half. It was finally agreed that the one week safety stock could be reduced to three days. The net effect of these changes gave the following "before and after" view in terms of inventory investment in engines. Average usage was three engines a day.

	Working days		Number of engines in inventory		
	Before	After	Before	After	Reduction
In process	10	10	30	30	—
In stores—					
Delivery frequency	20	5			
Average inventory	10	2½	30	8	22
Safety cushion	5	3	15	9	6
Premature delivery	10	2	30	6	24
In receiving and inspection	5	2	15	6	9
Totals			120	59	61
Average investment			$120,000		$59,000

It should be noted that the 150 engines on hand per the Engine Schedule Comparison exceeded by 30 the 120 engines called for as an average inventory investment per the "Before" column of the preceding schedule. The net result of tightening up on the procurement and internal processing times of engines was a reduction of 60 per cent in the average inventory investment; a $150,000 investment was cut to $59,000.

Excess axles and transmissions

Axles and transmissions were two other expensive components for which there were $100,000 and $80,000, respectively, in open purchase orders appearing on the purchase commitment report.

Upon reviewing the plant-wide physical inventory of axles as a prerequisite to rescheduling open purchase orders, some 170 axles at $100 each were discovered in various stages of disassembly, rejection, or obsolescence. Some of these axles were three years old.

As to the disassembly, it developed that finished axles had been stripped to satisfy customers' service requirements, and no effort had been made to replace the borrowed parts and reassemble the usable axle assemblies.

The rejections had occurred because, after receipt and initial inspection approval, axles had been stored outside and exposed surfaces had rusted badly. Disassembly, sandblasting, and repainting were required, but had never been done. Instead, the axles had been set aside and forgotten in the business of daily production.

Obsolescence arose because of a change in design. Actually, the change in design was to have been made effective only after all axles on hand (and those on order which could not be canceled) had been used. However, this procedure had not been followed.

When all the facts regarding incomplete, rejected, or obsolete axles were brought to the CPA's attention, he immediately suggested that: (1) the production control manager reschedule work (and requisitions as required) to complete any incomplete axles and to disassemble, sandblast, and paint any rejected axles; (2) the engineering department utilize obsolete axles in future specifications and use up the excess supply even though a more expensive axle was substituted at no price increase to the customer.

The plant-wide inventory of transmissions revealed 250 transmissions, or a four-month supply. Investigation disclosed that repeated overshipments by the vendor had never been applied to decrease subsequent orders, and that a 5 per cent purchase price discount policy had contributed largely to the overstock. As a result of a top level meeting between the executive vice-president and the vendor's president, a blanket purchase order arrangement which called for a firm quantity commitment by the company, to be released in the quantities and at dates specified later, was worked out for the next year. The price discount was reduced 2½ per cent because of the fact that the vendor agreed to carry the inventory until delivery was requested. Although deliveries during the next six months would be almost nonexistent, the vendor could use the firm purchase order as a basis for producing ahead and thus utilizing what would otherwise have been idle time.

The company was not too successful in its attempt to cancel $150,000 of other open orders not really needed for six months. They did succeed in canceling about $50,000, and they deferred and rescheduled an additional $75,000. They received the balance of $25,000 within a week after they requested cancellation.

After rescheduling, a comparison of the purchase commitment report for the "over $2,000 each" open purchase orders "before and after" was as follows:

Month due	Before	After
Prior to July 31 (overdue)	$1,000,000	$ —
August	1,400,000	1,600,000
September	1,000,000	1,100,000
October	600,000	500,000
After October	200,000	950,000
	$4,200,000	$4,150,000

Note that the receipts scheduled for the next three months were reduced by $800,000 as a result of the rescheduling. Of course, new orders were placed during the three-month period, some $50,000 of which called for delivery and were delivered before the end of October. On the other hand, there were $100,000 of open orders delinquent and overdue at October 31.

After the major dollar open purchase orders had been reviewed and unneeded orders canceled or deferred where possible, the next major step in the company's inventory reduction program was to:

Analyze annual dollar usage of all parts, both purchased and manufactured, and then concentrate close controls on the high value items. Note that the purchase order review covered only open purchase orders over $2,000. Consequently, large dollar usage purchased parts escaped attention entirely if they were not on open order at the time of the review, and no manufactured components or assemblies were covered at all. This second step, that of analyzing annual dollar usage of all parts, was basic to establishing permanent control policies for all classes of parts—expensive, medium, and nominal. The company's short-range program dealt only with policies for the expensive parts.

A program and timetable was established for analyzing and classifying annual usage. Responsibilities for specific projects were assigned to specific individuals, with estimated start and completion dates.

In brief, annual usage for the past six months and a forecast period of six months was computed by extending appropriate bills of material. Resulting parts and assemblies were then costed to obtain the total dollar value of the annual usage. These parts and assemblies were then ranked in descending order of annual dollar usage.

The data on page 150 resulted from this analysis.

The same intensive controls, illustrated for engines, axles, and transmissions, were applied to all other expensive (Class A) items, both purchased and manufactured, which were identified in the preceding analysis.

These controls applied equally to presently outstanding purchase and production orders and to all future purchase and production orders.

Other areas for inventory reduction

In connection with the work on purchase commitments and annual dollar usage, certain additional areas where inventory reductions could be accomplished were disclosed.

Inventory crews noted considerable congestion in the receiving rejects area. This condition was called to the attention of the production control manager, who, with the backing of the factory manager, arranged to have a complete physical inventory taken of the receiving rejects area. This inventory, when priced, amounted to $175,000, of which $75,000 was over a month old. Analysis of a few of the more expensive and older items indicated that rejects were not returned promptly to vendors when they were unquestionably defective, but instead letters were directed to vendors requesting permission to return or rework at vendor expense. After reviewing this situation, the executive vice-president authorized the immediate return to vendors without their prior permission of all receipts defective beyond question. He recognized that initially some vendors would object to this return policy but felt that this reaction could be surmounted satisfactorily if care was taken not to abuse the policy by returning material where the company's purchase orders, drawings, specifications, or test equipment were at fault.

The production control manager, now fully engaged in the inventory control program, walked through the machine shop after the day shift

Class	Per item annual dollar usage	Number of items	Total annual dollar usage* (In thousands)	Per cent of total Items	Dollar usage
A	Over $2,500	1,000	$10,500	10%	70%
B	$500 to $2,500	2,000	3,000	20	20
C	Under $500	7,000	1,500	70	10
	Totals	10,000	$15,000	100%	100%

*Similar classifications should be made in terms of unit costs and inventory values. Note that the above annual usage of $15 million is $5 million less than the $20 million annual cost of sales shown on the income statement. This is because only standard components and assemblies were included in this analysis.

had gone home. He began to count the jobs in front of each machine. He was amazed to find that material for some jobs had been sitting for two to four weeks while material issued only that day for lesser priority jobs was already being worked on. He expanded his test checks to the drilling and milling departments and found that the same situation existed. From these observations he was forced to conclude that workers were picking the jobs they were going to work on and were continually avoiding and delaying other jobs. Therefore, the production control manager immediately instructed his shop dispatching people to start cutting down on the number of jobs being started so that there would be less opportunity for workers to ignore disagreeable or tightly rated, low-bonus jobs. After three months, the net effect of tightening up on the number of orders and amount of material in the shop was a reduction of $200,000 in the work in process inventory. In addition, shortages actually decreased because unattractive jobs were no longer buried on the factory floor, and the housekeeping improved because there was less material on the floor.

Accounting treatment

Because such a small number of expensive items constituted the bulk of the dollars invested in the company's inventory, simplified control was achieved by segregating all Class A receipts and usage in a separate ledger account. The mechanics behind this segregation consisted of identifying all Class A parts on bills of material, inventory records, purchase requisitions, and purchase orders. Subsequent identification on receiving tickets and vendors' invoices was routine. Inventory was relieved by pricing the Class A components in shipments. Because the month-end balance in the Class A inventory account could be secured by manual explosion methods over a week before the rest of the inventories were costed, it provided management with a quick fix on progress in inventory reduction.

Net reduction effected

In three months the inventory was reduced $1,200,000, and customer service was maintained. Management was confident that an additional $2 million could be eliminated through continued application of the short-range practices illustrated above and through a long-range inventory control program (not described here) which would encompass forecasting, parts standardization, and possible further mechanization.

Statistical Inventory Control

Mathematical Techniques

Progress in the use of mathematical models and statistical inventory control methods has been due largely to efforts made since World War II to apply operations research techniques to business problems. Although many types of business problems have been solved through the use of OR techniques, success in the area of inventory control systems has been outstanding.

As the use of mathematics is a prominent characteristic of the OR method, it would be well to dispel some of the uneasiness that unnecessarily disquiets many businessmen when mathematics is mentioned. It is not necessary to be a mathematician to use the inventory equations. Anyone who has successfully passed high school or college algebra or applied statistics could, with a little refreshing, carry out the calculations required in most of the equations. Much of this calculating can even be eliminated because devices such as ordering tables and nomographs can be used in place of the equations for everyday inventory control.

In the classic economic lot formulas, the computation of a square root is the most advanced mathematical calculation required. This is elementary if a slide rule or a reference table is used. Camp's formula, one of the simplest economic lot formulas, for example, is:

$$Q = \sqrt{\frac{2SO}{KC}}$$

where Q = quantity, S = total estimated demand, O = cost of placing production or purchasing order into process, K = inventory carrying cost, and C = unit cost of item. Solution of this equation requires three multiplications, one division, and one square root. Using an ordinary desk calculator and a slide rule it takes less than a minute to perform the arithmetic.

This, of course, is the simplest of the economic lot equations. More sophisticated equations have been developed which require somewhat more time to solve, not because of the difficulty of the arithmetic, but primarily because of the additional number of factors included in the equations. Such equations provide for deviations in demand, deviations in lead time, cost of a stock-out, and so on. This is explained further on in this chapter.

One point should be emphasized here. The use of empirical formulas yields empirical results. The answers obtained as a result of solving the equations should, of course, be tempered by judgment and common sense. What is advocated here is a reversal from the customary use of "guesstimates" to a method which is predicated on objective techniques and which uses judgment as a double check.

EDP Equipment

A second major breakthrough has been the introduction of high speed data processing equipment. Punched card equipment has been available for years and considerable progress has been made by many companies in production and inventory control systems through efficient utilization.

Where speed and volume requirements so dictate, electronic equipment can be used in lieu of conventional punched card equipment or bookkeeping machines. Systems utilizing magnetic disk files or magnetic drum files can be searched rapidly and items can be selected from thousands on a master file in a matter of seconds. The use of such equipment permits recording related transactions in successive steps which, heretofore, have been recorded separately and often with considerable lapse of time between them. A sales transaction, for example, can be processed so that the customer's account is up-dated, statistical and accounting sales data recorded, inventory balances up-dated, and cost of sales recorded at virtually the same time, requiring far fewer pieces of paper than with other methods. Thus, in addition to providing current data for inventory control purposes, use of such equipment can serve several other purposes. This possibility of multipurpose use should be kept in mind when evaluating the cost of electronic data processing equipment for an inventory control system.

A Practical System for Small Businesses

Let us suppose that a company cannot justify the cost of a computer, or even a punched card system. Is there any practical way by which an integrated and co-ordinated system of inventory control can be developed? The answer is yes, and it can best be explained by an actual case history of a system which is now being put into effect by a very small company.

This company has twenty production workers, most of whom are female, and it manufactures about thirty different models of electronic instruments. The inventory consists of about 1,500 items having an average total dollar value of about $100,000. Last year the company was using rule-of-thumb methods for inventory control and got into trouble overnight. Management realized that what was on order plus what was on the shelves amounted, in some cases, to a two-year supply. Since drastic action was required, they sent out telegrams cancelling almost all outstanding purchase orders. They then set to work to develop a system preventing a similar occurrence in the future.

Under the new system, a sales forecast is going to be prepared each month for the next twelve months. Emphasis will be placed each month on the forecast for the succeeding three months. Forecasting, incidentally, is not new to the company, and has been accomplished in the past with a good degree of accuracy. It had not, however, been tied in to an inventory management system. The sales forecast, by instrument model, is going to be "exploded" into parts requirements using punched cards which have been prepared from bills of material. This work will be done by a service bureau since the cost of a tabulating installation could not be justified in this company.

The inventory items are going to be stratified into two groups. The first group, comprising most of the inventory value and including about four hundred items, will be maintained on card records. Order quantities for these items will be based on a simple economic lot formula. Nomographs will be constructed which the purchasing agent can use to determine the proper order quantities. The quarterly demand figures will be obtained from the parts "explosion" based on the sales forecasts.

In this particular case it was not considered necessary to use sophisticated techniques to determine the reorder point. Vendors' lead times, production lead time, and safety allowance will be determined by experience and the reorder points established accordingly. Each new forecast will be compared with the previous forecast and, in the absence of a major change in the requirements of any part or in lead times, no adjustment in the order quantity or reorder point will be necessary.

The plan also includes a method for reaching a dollars-and-cents decision about when to order the next larger quantity to obtain a lower price. Basically the method compares the added inventory-carrying cost with the price savings.

The second group consists of low-value items. The order quantity and reorder point will be established in the same manner as for the first group. However, no card records will be maintained for these items. Safety packages will be used to signal the reorder point and no posting of quantities will be required.

The company hopes to reduce its average inventory to about $75,000 as a result of these controls. In addition to reducing the investment in inventories by $25,000, the company should save about $4,000 a year in inventory-carrying costs, not a small sum to a small company. They will not require any additional employees to operate the system and their only added cost will be a nominal monthly charge from a service bureau for the parts "explosion."

A practical inventory management system can be established by small companies. With larger companies, the problems become more complex and the system must be expanded to take care of these complexities. Some companies may find bookkeeping machines an efficient way to maintain inventory records. They may estimate their parts demands and calculate order quantities manually or by using charts or graphs as described previously. Next up the ladder, a company may have its own punched card installation and maintain inventory records using such equipment. They may also use their own equipment to explode bills of material for parts requirements. Punched card electronic computers can be used to calculate economic lot order quantities. Plug board computers can be used to calculate order quantities and reorder points, although not to maintain inventory records. There are several medium-scale systems that permit a high degree of integration of all data processing affecting inventory accounting and control. For companies which are characterized by extremely large transaction volumes and extremely variable and complex conditions, the more powerful large-scale equipment may be warranted. Each case must be considered individually, and the system tailored to the specific requirements. There is, however, a practical system for every company, regardless of size.

Basic Concepts of Inventory Control

How reliable are the estimates of savings which have been attributed to the inventory control systems adopted in specific instances? Generally, the most accurate basis for deciding which type of control system might be best suited to specific circumstances consists of a series of retrospective tests in which the so-called "decision rules" of the new system are applied to available historical demand and lead-time data. The results are then compared with those obtained by the company in following its previously established practices. Since it is characteristic of a good model, inventory control or otherwise, that the results of its applications are predictable and reproducible, the savings indicated by these tests have as a rule a high degree of reliability.

Statistical inventory control methods have been developed and tested in actual practice over a period of several years through operations research. A brief discussion of their powerful technical features may be of general interest.

In approaching the problem of developing a sound program of inventory management in any company, it has been found convenient to relate the total program to four basic considerations: (1) nature of the business; (2) goals; (3) type and extent of uncertainties; and (4) problems of implementation.

The first consideration is, of course, the nature of the business. Some of the questions to be answered are:

1. Is the business a manufacturing or service organization?
2. If it is a manufacturing organization, are the company's products

more or less standardized or are we concerned with a job-shop type of activity? Is manufacture for inventory feasible? Does the company have many customers or relatively few? How are the orders received, processed, and filled?

3. At what stage is the greater part of the company's inventories maintained? Raw materials? In process? Finished goods?

4. What levels of availability of finished goods or supplies are required in view of the competition—or customer service requirements in the case of a public service?

5. In relation to raw material and in process inventories, what are the production scheduling requirements of the company in view of available production facilities?

6. Are there any special situations relating to purchase lead times or manufacturing cycle times which must be carefully considered?

7. Are raw material inventory replenishment requirements critically affected by widely fluctuating price or availability considerations?

8. Are inventories centrally located or distributed in many warehouse locations?

These are only a few of the more important questions to be considered. For the most part, these questions involve conditions over which management has relatively little short-term control. Good inventory control procedures, however, will assist management in "living within" the restrictions imposed by these external factors.

As will be made clear in the later discussion of a basic inventory control model, it is essential that the relationships between the foregoing factors and others be expressed in such a way as to be operationally meaningful. A good inventory control model gives explicit recognition not only to the factors within management control, but also to the influence of factors outside management's immediate control. For example, if it is a "fact of life" that the demands for certain inventory items are subject to wide fluctuations from one period to another, or if purchase lead times are long for particular items, then the model must reflect these conditions. More will be said about these particular uncontrollable factors when we consider the role of "uncertainty" in stock control.

Determination of Goals

"Cheshire-Puss," she began, rather timidly . . . "Would you tell me please, which way I ought to go from here?"

"That depends a good deal on where you want to get to," said the Cat.

"I don't much care where . . ." said Alice.

"Then it doesn't matter which way you go," said the Cat.

This quotation from Lewis Carroll may serve to introduce the second important factor in inventory management goals. Contrary to the situation presented by Alice's lack of a goal, in controlling inventories management is faced with a multiplicity of seemingly conflicting goals which affect, to a greater or lesser degree, the direction to be taken in the design of a sound system. Besides being often conflicting, goals relating to inventory management frequently appear to have an intangible or immeasurable quality about them which creates difficulties when one attempts to establish reasonably explicit inventory control policies and decision rules which depend upon the desired goals.

One all-inclusive goal of good inventory management which is frequently voiced by businessmen is that it should provide the proper quantities of materials *where* they are required *at the time* they are required. But to this is generally added the requirement that this feat be accomplished at the lowest possible cost.

In the first place, businessmen obviously recognize the need for establishing "proper" order or delivery quantities of individual inventory items, and by implication realize there are penalties—generally expressible as costs—associated with "improper" order or delivery quantities. Such penalties may be added carrying costs, if the quantities ordered or delivered are too large, or excessive ordering, shipping, and shortage costs, if the order or delivery quantities are too small.

Second, it is obvious that the materials should be available where needed. In the case of multiple warehousing facilities, for example, available quantities of materials or products must be allocated among the warehousing facilities in relation to individual requirements. And third, there is the question of time. If materials arrive too early, excessive carrying costs are generally incurred; if too late, the penalties might include production downtime costs, excess transportation and expediting costs, substitution costs, lost sales of finished products, or strong regulatory and public censure as a result of a disruption of a critical public service. These factors combine to create the problem of providing a balance among them so as to keep the sum of inventory carrying, replenishment, and shortage costs at a practicable minimum.

That some of these goals are in conflict with one another is clear. For example, minimum inventory carrying costs are as a rule incompatible with taking full advantage of long production runs, large purchase quantities, or low freight rates. Or again, very close timing of replenishment orders to keep carrying costs down might result in stock shortages because of variations in the period-to-period demand for materials or variations in the time required to obtain delivery. More will be said about the effects of variations of this type in connection with the third basic consideration in an inventory management program—uncertainty.

Another complication is the difficulty of correctly evaluating the effect of each factor having a bearing upon the attainment of the distinct goals in inventory management. For example, what is the dollars-and-cents penalty to be associated with an out-of-stock position for a finished product when a lost sale, or even worse, a lost customer may be involved? Or in the case of a public utility what "cost" can be assigned to "stock-outs" of materials critically affecting, and altering in varying degrees, the continuous operation of the service facilities? These are difficult questions but they must be faced in every sound inventory management program. Suitable answers frequently cannot be found directly, and we must rely upon indirect measures which are operationally capable of being acted upon.

For example, in most instances management is generally hard put when it comes to expressing the "cost" of stock shortages in dollars and cents. Since the cost implication of a stock shortage of an item is one of the main cost elements to be weighed against the cost of carrying protective stock, it is clear that some means must be found for establishing the direct or indirect costs incurred as a result of such a shortage. In most cases it thus becomes necessary to devise alternative measures for giving dollars-and-cents expression to actual or potential stock-outs. Naturally these alternative measures must be designed for full utilization of the intuitive judgment of management regarding the level of service that must be provided, with due regard to the more directly measurable costs of maintaining such a level of service. The approach to these alternative measures of finding the cost of stock shortages will be more fully dealt with later.

The Role of Uncertainty

A contemporary philosopher has suggested that success, however measured, is primarily influenced by the manner in which a man adjusts to the constant stream of both major and minor uncertainties which confront him. In the establishment of controls over inventories, this thought hits the nail right on the head. The proper treatment of "uncertainties" surrounding a given inventory situation is of vital importance as will be attested to by those who have had uneconomically high inventory levels or damaging inventory shortages because of a failure to appraise properly the effect of the uncertainties of consumer demand or vendor supply.

In the course of initial discussions with management on the application of statistical inventory control techniques, there is one reservation which is almost invariably cited and which threatens to arrest any attempt to introduce this type of control. This is the belief that "in their case" the demand characteristics for raw materials, in process inventories, or finished products are unique in relation to "other" companies where statistical procedures might be applicable. Some specific objections are: "The period-to-period demand for stock items is too erratic; our customers' requirements are unpredictable." Or again, "Average demand means nothing in our business; it's the variations in demand from one period to the next which cause us headaches."

The answers are simple. In the first place, unless the company is approaching financial disaster, it must have succeeded somehow in meeting this condition, perhaps imperfectly, in the course of establishing its present inventory control system and its decision-making procedures. And second, the fact that the demands for stock items are erratic from one period to the next does not preclude the use of well-established statistical principles in designing procedures which give recognition to the "pattern" of such erratic demand. In fact, it is for precisely such random variations in the occurrence of events that statistical techniques were developed.

In other words, the existence of erratic period-to-period demand does not necessarily mean that this variation has no pattern which, when properly understood, can be usefully applied through recognized statistical procedures. Our multibillion dollar insurance industry depends upon this fact. The millions of dollars saved annually by industry as a result of statistical quality control is but another instance of the benefits to be derived from the application of statistical principles to problems arising from uncertainties generically the same as those faced by companies attempting to control inventories.

Besides uncertainties of demand, the uncertainties of erratic lead periods in replenishing inventories call for the use of statistical procedures. Again, it is not only the "averages" which must be considered but also the variations, both assignable and random, about such averages. It is the random variation in both demand and lead periods about their respective averages which creates the need for "safety stocks." If there were no variations in demand or replenishment lead times brought about by extraneous and largely uncontrollable factors or arising from company policies or other internal matters, then the problems of inventory management would be drastically (and pleasantly) reduced. In fact, the only major problems would then center about the determination of economic production, purchasing, or delivery quantities so as to balance the costs of carrying stock against the costs resulting from the initiation and receipt of replenishment orders, and considerations relating to price discounts for quantity purchases. Means for solving these more restricted problems have been available for decades and involve the application of so-called "classical" lot-size or purchase quantity formulas. When uncertainties of demand or replenishment lead periods are significant (which is the rule rather than the exception) such classical approaches are inadequate in establishing an inventory management program of maximum effectiveness.

Before a full program of implementation is undertaken, tests are carried out to provide management with some indication of the results which might be obtained from the use of statistical inventory management. Normally, a few of the items which the company closely controls by its usual methods are selected for test. Rough approximations are made of the various cost data and operating characteristics. Using historical demand and lead-time data, calculations are made to determine inventory levels which would result from the generalized formula developed in the past. Comparisons can then be made between the levels of inventory actually carried and those which would have resulted if statistical methods had been used.

Problems of Implementation

Having established by tests of representative stock items that a statistical inventory management program is economically justified, a CPA must enter upon the implementation phase. The problems which arise in the implementation phase of the program fall into four broad classifications:

1. Organization of the implementation program
2. Integration of related functional activities
3. Partitioning of inventories for varying levels of control
4. Continuing control after implementation

Organization

Experience has shown that in implementing a statistical inventory control system it is desirable to form two company groups, one technical and the other advisory. The technical group consists of one or more persons responsible for the day-to-day work of supervising the accumulation of cost and operating statistics relating to individual stock items, processing such data in accordance with the recommended statistical inventory control procedures, and supervising the incorporation of the results as to each processed item into the over-all control system. The second company group acts as a committee and consists of a number of officials representing the several functional activities related to inventory control, such as purchasing, production, sales, and finance, and possibly a representative of engineering when design changes are frequent. It is the function of this advisory group to provide policy guides to be followed in relation to the inventory control program. Meetings with this group are arranged as the needs for guidance on matters of policy arise.

Integration of functional areas

The second problem of implementation is the integration of related functional activities. It is clear that if the policies established in the various functional areas related to inventory control are not properly integrated, economies effected in one area may be offset by increased costs in one or more related areas. Further, sound inventory management requires that the flow of information to and from the functional activities related to inventory control, such as engineering and sales, be consistent and provide an efficient means for taking timely corrective action when unusual circumstances arising in one area might prove disturbing in other areas. For example, engineering changes might be contemplated which would make certain materials obsolete, or sales emphasis might be changed which would affect the demand pattern for an item.

Partitioning of inventories

It is generally recognized that all items of inventory need not be controlled to the same degree. For this reason, the problem arises of segregating or grouping individual items comprising the inventory according to economically and operationally justifiable degrees of control. Parenthetically, it might be mentioned that the term "control" as used in this discussion relates to operational and managerial control rather than to internal control in the sense in which that term is used by CPAs. One of the first steps consists of tabulating and arranging all items in decreasing order of annual consumption costs. Generally, such a tabulation will show that a relatively small percentage of the items accounts for a large percentage of the annual cost of materials consumed and a correspondingly large part of the total investment in inventories. (See page 150, for example.) As a general rule, the greatest degree of continuous control would be exercised over the items which account for the largest expenditures in material consumption and inventory value. This classification of the inventories leads to the application of another general rule. As one approaches the low-cost end of the scale, the average inventory in that group of items should be relatively large so as to eliminate the need for close attention to a large number of stock items which in the aggregate comprise a small part of the total inventory carrying costs. At the other extreme, those relatively few high-cost items would warrant almost continuous review and call for a relatively low average stock level.

Continuing control

Once the statistical inventory control system has been completely installed along the lines discussed above, it is necessary to establish procedures for updating the ordering policies on individual stock items as the various factors affecting such policies undergo significant change from one period to another. This is the problem of continuing control after implementation. If, for example, the average demand rate for an item over a future time period is expected to be significantly different from that on which the current ordering policy is based, it will be necessary to make a recomputation so that a new ordering policy may be established based upon revised order quantities and reorder points. Procedures related to statistical quality control, using control limits based on average demand rates and normal deviations therefrom, have been used for the purpose of signaling the need for a change in the ordering policy of individual stock items.

A great deal more could be said about the problems of implementation, particularly since it is in the implementation stage that most of the practical difficulties arise and the more unique features of a company's inventory operations must be adequately dealt with. Much of whatever "art" is needed in the establishment of a scientifically oriented inventory management program must be exercised during the implementation period. The more scientific aspects of inventory control will be described in the following illustration of one type of generalized statistical inventory control model which has served as a guide in numerous inventory control engagements.

Statistical Inventory Control Model

The following illustration is of necessity somewhat technical but may be of interest to those struggling with an inventory management problem and having or desiring some technical training.

This model is based upon interrelationships among three primary costs: (1) the annual cost of carrying inventory; (2) the annual ordering or replenishment cost; and (3) the annual cost associated with actual or potential stock shortages.

The sum of the variable parts of these costs constitutes a measure of effectiveness and expresses this so-called Total Annual Variable Cost (TVC) as a function of two factors which are under the control of management, namely, the Order Quantity Q (how much) and the Reorder Point R (when).

The TVC formula also incorporates factors not generally within the control of management (or possibly fixed by management policy). These include variability in the item demand rate, variability in lead time, and cost elements such as the unit item cost, the cost per replenishment order (production or purchasing), the unit cost associated with actual or potential stock shortages, and the carrying charge factor (the latter factor when multiplied by the unit cost of the item gives the annual cost of carrying the item in stock). The optimum ordering policy for any given item is then mathematically determined by finding the values of the Order Quantity Q and Reorder Point R which minimize the Total Annual Variable Cost (TVC). The order quantity and reorder point thus obtained are called the "Integrated Economic Order Quantity" and "Basic Reorder Point," respectively.

How does this model differ from, and in what way is it an improvement over, models based on "classical" lot-size formulas? The main difference lies in the explicit recognition which is given to the cost implications occasioned by uncertainties of demand and replenishment lead periods and relating them to the more tangible costs of carrying and replenishing stock. In Exhibit 1(a) (see page 175) the main elements entering into the determination of classical economic order quantities are indicated. In the upper diagram is shown the stock level variation over successive time periods for two different policies relative to the size of the order quantity. The average stock level in each case is one-half of the order quantity, and the number of replenishment orders in a given period of time is inversely proportional to the size of the order placed. The annual carrying cost in each case is found by multiplying the average stock level by the cost of carrying one unit of an item in stock for one year. The variable part of the cost associated with the replenishment of a year's demand is obtained by multiplying the number of replenishment orders placed per year by the variable part of the cost per replenishment order.

The diagram shown in Exhibit 1(b) illustrates the influence of the choice of the order quantity on the annual carrying and annual ordering costs as well as the sum of these annual costs. It is seen that the classical economic order quantity Q corresponds to the point where the annual carrying and ordering costs are equal.

The mathematical derivation of the formula for the classical economic order Quantity Q is shown in Exhibit 1(c). In this formula S represents the annual demand in units, O is the variable cost per replenishment order, and K is the carrying charge factor which when multiplied by the unit cost (price) C of the item gives the annual cost of carrying a unit of the item in stock.

How the model works

Exhibit 2 (page 176), on the other hand, illustrates new dimensions added by the statistically oriented model and graphically portrays the situation as it might actually appear in the case of a variation in the stock level over successive time periods when uncertainty is introduced through variability in the item demand rate as well as variations in the replenishment lead period. Suppose that prior to time zero the stock level is above the Basic Reorder Point R and that through usage the stock level is reduced to the Basic Reorder Point at time zero. At this point a replenishment order of the size Q is initiated and after a lead period of duration L, the replenishment order is received in stock.

As usage continues, the stock is again reduced to the reorder point and another replenishment order of size Q is initiated. After a lead period of duration L (not necessarily the same as that for the previous order), the replenishment order is received in stock. Continuing in this manner, occasionally the demand rate or lead period will deviate to such an extent from that expected that a stock shortage will be incurred unless special expediting action is taken. In this exhibit the Average Upper Stock Level represents that level about which the stock level "peaks" oscillate with half of the peaks being above this level and half below—on the average. Similarly, the Average Lower Stock Level or "Safety Allowance" (denoted by the symbol ρ) represents that stock level about which the stock level "valleys" oscillate with, on the average, half of the valleys being above this level and half below. The usage over a typical lead period is denoted by X and the average value of X is called the "expected lead period demand" and is represented by the symbol μ. The reorder point R is the sum of the expected lead period demand μ and the safety allowance ρ. The fundamental problem, therefore, consists in establishing an Order Quantity Q and Reorder Point R which minimize the sum of the annual variable costs of carrying stock, replenishing stock, and being actually or potentially caught short of stock.

Stock control work sheet

Exhibit 3 (page 177) shows the "Stock Control Work Sheet" by means of which eight basic inputs (see Data section) are "manipulated" (see Computation section) to yield the optimum ordering policy (see Ordering Policy section). This model represents a rather strict control system and would normally be used only for a limited number of stock items of a really critical nature (constituting a high percentage of the dollar volume of activity). A less stringent method would be used for less critical items. However, making the necessary computation even for this model is not a serious problem. As a matter of fact, one company, in the process of implementing the model, had the computations programed on a small-scale electronic computer and found that the entire set of calculations indicated on the work sheet took 1½ minutes per stock item. Even on a manual basis the time involved in the computations is not prohibitive when it is realized that the recomputation to arrive at an ordering policy need not take place more than once or possibly twice a year, depending on the magnitude of the secular or cyclical changes in demand or lead time (or upon significant changes in the other input factors listed in the Data section of the work sheet).

Aside from its inventory control features, the model also has potential value as a budgetary control tool. For example, the cost implications of varying levels of item demand can be projected by merely carrying out the computations on the work sheet for several values of the "expected item demand rate." Or again, a dollar value can be placed on different levels of vendor service as measured by the "mean lead period." This type of analysis was carried out by one company, and when it was demonstrated in dollars and cents what it was costing to carry additional safety stock for the excessive lead periods caused by red tape in the purchasing function, steps were immediately taken to reduce the lead period. As the company's management itself pointed out, the inefficient practices were so well entrenched that no action would probably have been taken without such a practical demonstration of the costs of excessive lead periods.

Basic stock card

Exhibit 4 (page 178), shows a form of "Basic Stock Card" used to maintain continuing control on the inventory position of an item based upon ordering policy established by the "Stock Control Work Sheet." This exhibit is self-explanatory, except possibly for the column headed "Current Reorder Point." The Current Reorder Point equals the "Basic Reorder Point" R minus the number of units "on order." When the stock level is reduced to or below the Current Reorder Point, a stock replenishment order is initiated for an "Integrated Economic Order Quantity" Q. Equivalently stated, when the stock on hand plus the stock on order is reduced to or below the Basic Reorder Point R, a stock replenishment order is initiated. The initiation of a stock order is indicated by an asterisk in the column headed "Review Period Usage." The work sheet and basic stock card illustrate a case where the estimated "Unit Cost of a Stock Shortage" A is 50¢ for each unit short. Similar analyses were conducted for unit shortage costs of 25¢, 33¢, and $1. The effects on the stock position of the item for optimum ordering policies corresponding to each unit shortage cost estimate are shown on Exhibit 5 (page 179).

Exhibit 5 shows that as the estimated unit shortage cost increases from A = ¼ (25¢) to A = 1 ($1), the inventory model automatically reduces the frequency of stock-outs in order to maintain a balance among the annual carrying, ordering, and shortage costs in such a manner that the sum of these costs is minimized by the ordering policy corresponding to each of the unit shortage costs considered.

Benefits achieved

Exhibit 6 (page 180), is an illustration of the typical benefits realized through use of the inventory model in an actual situation. The characteristic control features of the model are clearly recognized by the model's ability to stabilize the range of stock level variation within relatively narrow and predictable control limits.

One feature of this application is of special interest in that a basic relationship was discovered in the course of the development of this particular model. The mathematical relationship was originally introduced into the analysis merely for computational convenience, but it was subsequently found that the principle which it embodies was capable of practical interpretation. The principle states:

> Under conditions of optimum inventory control, the mean tolerable number of years between stock-outs (or potential stock-outs) of an item is equal to the ratio of the unit cost of an actual or potential stock shortage to the annual cost of carrying one unit of the item in safety stock.

In other words, under optimum inventory control conditions there is a balance between the number of years one would be willing to incur a carrying charge on an item in safety stock and the cost one would be willing to incur by either sustaining an actual stock-out of an item or by exerting special effort to prevent the occurrence of a stock-out of the item during this period. As a practical matter, insofar as inventory control applications are concerned, this principle has assisted companies in obtaining a better estimate of the level of safety stock to be assigned to an item to minimize the sum of the costs associated with carrying and replenishing stock on the one hand, and the cost associated with actual or potential stock shortages on the other.

Under what conditions can this rather sophisticated system for controlling individual items of inventory most profitably be introduced? As previously stated, it will generally be found in analyzing the composition of inventories in a company, that a relatively small number of items account for the bulk of the dollar usage of all items carried in inventory. It is for these items that more precise control "tools" are justified—provided that the aggregate incremental dollar savings attributable to this use can be expected to yield a reasonable return on the investment involved in their installation and operation. It is not possible to state where the breakeven point lies because of the many factors involved. Among them are the relative importance, dollar-wise, of the items in the group, the quality of the original control system, the nature of the business, and many others. It is for these reasons that any plans for revising a company's inventory control system should be preceded by preliminary tests of an objective and quantitative nature to establish the potential value of system revision—there being no reliable substitute for such a preliminary evaluation.

To control a system one must understand its dynamic characteristics. There is much more to learn about the dynamics of inventory behavior. However, statistical inventory control models may provide insights into inventory behavior which can be used to guide many companies in establishing sound inventory management programs.

The Punched Card and the Electron in Inventory Control[3]

The Requirements of Control

There are several basic requirements which inventory control must satisfy if it is to function as a part of the system of capital management. First, it must provide financial and physical accountability; that is, how much should be there, not just what is there. If the system is to maintain control, the tail cannot wag the dog, for management must be satisfied that its record keeping process is reliable. It is in this area that the authority of the documents supporting inventory movement must be established. All receipts should be covered by receiving records and all shipments by invoices. Production records should generally account for internal movement, but in some instances additional documentation may be desirable to record transfers, and requisitions should account for self-consumption.

Second, the procedure must provide data on the status of inventory and inventory movement frequently and in a timely manner, for it is axiomatic that turnover is the basis of profitable capital utilization. Without this information at timely intervals, a business can die of indigestion caused by obsolescence long before it starves to death for lack of products to sell. Thus, it is desirable that the control system include perpetual inventory records so that the status of inventory and its movement can be readily ascertained at all times.

Third, the procedure must recognize the costs of storage and handling in satisfying the first two requirements, for these costs in relation to turnover must be considered in terms of the economical handling of quantities or sizes. It accomplishes little to create high turnover and high gross profit if the warehousing or handling cost per unit cannot also be re-

[3]Pages 167 through 174 are reprinted from Haskins & Sells' *Selected Papers*, 1957. The author is William W. Gerecke, a manager in the Los Angeles office of that firm.

duced or minimized to leave a higher net profit. Yet it is easy to lose sight of this fact when only the dollar value of inventory is considered in the evaluation of turnover. Hence, our ideal inventory control system must balance the costs of inventory ownership and the costs of handling in order to maximize the net return on the investment in inventory.

Control systems have been commonplace in manufacturing operations for years, but they are relative newcomers to the field of financial management. It is surprising how closely the requirements compare. First, there must be a continuous flow of current operating data so that operations can be checked with plans. Second, the mechanism or medium for collecting this data must be integrated into a reporting system to permit fast interpretation and action, for only through an orderly process of review can bottlenecks or shortages be anticipated. Finally, the data must be summarized as a record of what has happened and as a guide for future planning. Industry has long relied on a wide variety of meters, gauges, overflow valves, thermostats, and other continuous recording instruments to facilitate control of operations, while too frequently management has relied on intuition to control inventory. The investment in inventory cannot be treated haphazardly. It is deserving of controls as critical as those employed in creating the inventory.

Decisions and Data Processing Equipment

When it comes to supporting management intuition with facts, the punched card and the electron offer a tremendous potential to the businessman. Each of these tools can provide a wide variety of management and accounting functions in its basic program when the economics of the situation justify their consideration. They permit rapid processing of data under controlled programs, which may perform a number of functions simultaneously. For example, through the use of tabulating equipment the billing function can reduce the inventory, prepare the invoice and related shipping documents, including total weight and warehouse location, and prepare a punched card with sales statistical information by product, customer, and salesman. To perform the same functions manually would require several clerks and a large number of invoice copies if the volume exceeded roughly one hundred invoices a day.

On the surface, the processing problems of the manual system may not appear large enough to bring them under close scrutiny until the consideration of decision making is studied. Neither the punched card nor the electron is a panacea in itself in this problem area, but they do offer the facility of handling routine decisions with a high degree of reliability. This facility, in addition to the speed of processing, is the most important aspect of tabulating and electronic data processing equipment. This point should be stressed: Historically, tabulating equipment has been thought of as a sorting and listing device used for the routine analysis of historical facts, yet it has the capacity to make certain limited comparisons, which are, in effect, decisions. It can compare current data with standards to determine the amount of deviation and can select either the positive or negative deviation, or both, for listing for visual review. The complexity of the decision process can be increased beyond this point, but the amount of card handling also increases so that the procedure can become burdensome. On the other hand, the electronic computer, which is the newcomer in the data processing field, brings both greater speed and increased mental capacity. Where tabulating equipment makes a comparison in approximately half a second, the electronic computer will flash through the same steps in speeds varying from a few thousandths to a few millionths of a second, depending on the size of the computer. The mental capacity of the computer is its greatest asset, for within its memory device may be stored from ten thousand to several million digits of information, all of which may be virtually instantaneously accessible under certain circumstances. This vast memory system permits the storage of complex programs for processing data against a large file of current information, such as the model of a warehouse inventory. Hence, as the computer's memory increases in size, so may the complexity of the decisions which it can make. The principal limitation on its ability in this area will be the inability of the human planner to define the criteria which influence or determine the decision.

The Data Processor in the
Inventory Control System

The choice between punched card and electronic data processing equipment would have to be based on volumes, complexity, and economics. As a basic ground rule, the computer is more sophisticated in its internal processing of data and is faster than tabulating equipment. In all other respects what will be said can be equally true of each type of equipment.

In evaluating the requirements of an inventory control system, the continual review of the current condition of inventory was set forth as a basic necessity. Data processing equipment lends itself naturally to this problem, for a warehouse model can be constructed and maintained with relative ease, thus satisfying the requirement of financial and physical accountability. The model can contain, in addition to the quantity on hand for each item, such information as the location, unit of storage, economical handling unit, unit weight, and recent history of the movement of the item. As invoices for sales orders are processed, it is possible to perform several steps. First, it is possible to test the availability of inventory to fill the order; or, if stock is not available, to indicate a back order and to signal an out-of-stock condition; or, if a minimum condition is reached, to signal that the reorder point has been reached. Second, if inventory is available, it is possible to indicate the location, the extended weight, and the cubic measurement, to reduce the quantity available, and to prepare shipping instructions. Third, after completing all sales invoices for the day, it is possible to sort orders by items and by warehouse location for the purpose of facilitating picking for shipment and thereby minimizing costs of handling. This phase of the work is one of the most fascinating to speculate with, for as the age of the automated warehouse moves closer it is easy to visualize where these same punched cards or magnetic tapes may actuate the warehouse order assembly system and materially reduce the costs of storage and handling.

The Model Inventory

Based on the requirements of the business, the status and movement can be reviewed daily, weekly, or monthly, but at all times the system is working against predetermined maximums. These maximums need not and should not remain inflexible, but should be changed in accordance with shifts in seasonal patterns or consumer preferences. The reporting from the system need not be in complete detail, but may be designed to be selective to provide management by exception. This can be accomplished by determining in advance which information it is desirable to have, such as all out-of-stock conditions, all items below the minimum quantity, or all items whose turnover is less than the standard expected of each item. By utilizing the basic inventory compatible with available capital resources as a standard for measurement, it is possible to keep the inventory under continuous scrutiny without jeopardizing either warehouse efficiency or sales commitments.

The model inventory concept can become a valuable tool in warehouse management, for it encourages the most efficient utilization of space, people, and equipment. Attainment of this goal requires the cooperation of the purchasing and selling functions of the business, for their operating decisions and policies can aid or defeat the warehousing program. Success requires that consideration be given to (1) buying and selling where possible in economical handling units, (2) providing advance information on incoming shipments so that storage problems can be anticipated, and (3) planning delivery schedules which minimize peak loads. The acceptance of these ideas is fundamental to the maintenance of a model inventory and the rewards of good management.

The slot system

One method of warehouse management which draws on the ideas stated above is the slot system, whereby inventory is directed to a specific location when received. This location is then associated with the item for purposes of preparing order-picking instructions until the stock is depleted or moved, at which time the area is assigned to another item. This random approach to assigning storage areas is well suited to data processing equipment, which has the ability to sort data into a logical sequence very rapidly. Thus the slot system takes advantage of turnover to minimize warehouse space requirements and of the sorting ability of the processing equipment to facilitate order assembly. The flexibility of machine processing permits it to be equally effective under other systems of warehousing, such as the ton-mile concept or fixed storage areas so that the services of the equipment can be used to advantage in a program of positive inventory control.

Organizations which presently operate data processing equipment should explore the economics of bringing inventory control into the system. Since other applications have already justified its existence, this work can probably be added at nominal cost. If there is no machine accounting installation, investigation may reveal that, with the inventory control application as a starting point, other applications will naturally dovetail into an economically sound data processing operation. Once the investigation of the inventory application commences, it will be natural to consider the billing operation and proceed from there to payrolls and payables. This path is not without its pitfalls, but the rewards for success are impressive.

Case Studies of Data Processing Applications

Following is a description of two inventory control systems which utilize machine methods. One has been proposed for a manufacturer and distributor in the retail field; it will use punched cards and conventional tabulating equipment. The other system has been designed for a merchandiser; it will use two medium-sized electronic computers.

Punched card application

In the first instance, the company had been through a series of years of unsatisfactory earnings and was faced with shrinking working capital. Sales had remained steady and, in fact, were growing in some areas. In several of these locations, branch managers had requested additional warehouse space to accommodate the inventory which they felt was necessary to support their increasing volume of sales. Management was very anxious to satisfy these needs, but the precarious working capital condition just did not warrant additional fixed charges. In addition to stocks in branch warehouses, the company maintained a large inventory at its principal warehousing location and at its factory, and was able to draw upon stocks of manufacturers of its other products upon short notice. Inventory turnover at the branches and main warehouse ranged from approximately six to eight times a year.

In seeking a better understanding of their business, management began to re-examine what was basically necessary to the conduct of the business. They first looked at working capital, and here their attention was called to inventory, which represented 50 per cent of the current assets. If the annual turnover could be improved by only two turns, the investment in inventory might be reduced by about $2 million, not including the related interest charges. How to accomplish this without arbitrary cutbacks became the next problem.

The core of the problem rested on the fact that the company had no inventory control. Each unit had been given almost complete autonomy in building its inventory, without planning for return on investment. Management had set no criteria on the amount of inventory which each branch should have to meet its sales budget and had given no thought to how to reduce warehouse stocks and still maintain sales.

The search began with a review of the sales order, billing delivery cycle to determine the time requirements of customers. It was found that in almost all instances there was at least a one-day processing cycle from the time the order was received until it was shipped, and in some instances the cycle might extend to three days without injuring the customer relationship. With this knowledge it became possible to work on the inventory pipeline, for if turnover was to be improved and the need for additional warehouse space eliminated, it would be necessary to replenish branch inventories rapidly.

Operation. By installing one of several card punching mechanisms in conjunction with billing operations at the branches, it would be possible to produce punched cards representing tomorrow's planned deliveries. The cards would be shipped air express to the principal warehousing location at the close of business each day and would be available for processing the following morning. The product cards would be summarized by products and by branches in the centralized tabulating installation and would be merged with the master deck of product cards which contains the economic replacement quantity and the cubic measurement of this quantity. The merged decks would then be run through a tabulating machine which would compare sales with the economic replacement quantity and prepare a shipping list of products to be replaced. The tabulating machine would also be wired to compare the accumulated cubic measurement with the capacity of a van or rail car so as to preclude less-than-carload shipments. The file of products not replaced because of less-than-economic-lot quantities or of less-than-carload quantities would be merged with the following day's sales, and the process repeated, starting with the last product shipped. This procedure would require approximately forty-five minutes per thousand products. At times of special drives or promotions it would be possible to increase the shipments in advance of these drives and reduce the replacement at the close of promotion periods.

Benefits achieved. This approach will provide management with positive control over the value and quantity of inventory at all branch locations and gives promise of increasing the annual turnover to at least twelve to sixteen turns. At the same time, it will satisfy the needs of branch managers in meeting sales commitments. With a shipping list geared to economic shipping lots, the warehouse will be in a position to prepare the day's shipments to the branches without delay, and the pipeline to the branch will be refilled with today's sales. Branch inventories need not be any larger than the average sales for the elapsed time of the replacement cycle. The significant point of this approach is that the program will minimize handling problems at the shipping end by providing preplanning for carload shipments and so relieve the warehouse of the need to juggle shipments to obtain freight economies. At the same time, inventories at the receiving end should be reduced by about one-half to permit more efficient handling and better utilization of warehouse space and employees.

Electronic computer application

The second example concerns a national merchandiser who supplies a large number of branch stores through ten regional warehouses. The company used a large tabulating installation and employed over two hundred persons for controlling merchandise at the regional warehouses and branch stores. The extent of their problem is pointed up by the fact that the inventories consisted of close to six hundred thousand individual items, accounted for at branch and regional locations. While only fifteen hundred items might be present at any one location, it was necessary to maintain records of inventory balances of each item at every location. The company was acutely conscious of the time delay in processing data, both for replenishing the stocks of the branch stores and in keeping the buyers at the company's headquarters advised of the status of inventories at the regional warehouses. In addition, the stock status reports of the warehouses failed to reflect sufficient information for the buyers to anticipate the needs of the warehouses. The result of these problems was a tendency to overstock inventory, thereby complicating the role of financial management and the physical handling of merchandise.

Operation. In this instance a program was designed to utilize two medium-sized electronic computers. The branches were to continue filing weekly reports of merchandise movement, except that they would be sent to the head office. The movement by items would be converted into a paper tape and read into a computer to reorder in logical shipping units, and to adjust the record of balance on hand by branches and by warehouses. The two last-mentioned records would also be read into the computer from magnetic tape—the warehouse data into the memory device and the branch data into the comparator—as each item in the inventory is processed. The output of the computer would consist of (1) a stock status report for each branch, which would include fifteen months' past experience, turnover computations, and the balance on hand; (2) an order on the warehouse for goods to be shipped to the branch; and (3) a record of out-of-stock conditions when the warehouse is unable to fill the branch requirements. When all the branches controlled by one warehouse have been run, the process is repeated for each successive group until all the warehouses have been up-dated for branch movement. The total processing time for each group of roughly forty branches controlled by one warehouse would be about three hours.

Main advantages. This basic program would then be repeated for the warehouses by comparing the balances on hand with a model of each warehouse inventory as a basis for issuing purchase orders for replenishment of the company's inventory. The principal advantages gained from this system would be the speed of handling the mass of data—total processing time would be about thirty-five hours—and the fast reporting of inventory position in time for positive action and control.

Conclusion. Each of the instances discussed has dealt with the operation of multiple units, but the same principles are equally applicable to the single-unit warehousing operation. The economics of the single unit may not justify the use of an electronic computer, but a punched card system may be well within reach if there are other job applications within a company.

Data processing equipment can be the catalyst in a successful inventory control system, for it has the capacity to (1) maintain physical and financial accountability on a timely basis, (2) present visual records of inventory status and movement, and (3) consider the economics of handling and storage by measuring logical handling and shipping units.

Exhibit I

CLASSICAL ECONOMIC ORDER QUANTITY FORMULATION
for Securing an Optimum Balance Between the Cost of Carrying and Ordering Stock

(a) Ideal stock level variation with time for which demand rate and lead period are fixed and known

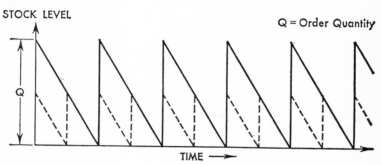

(b) Graphical representation of variations in annual carrying and ordering costs for varying order quantities

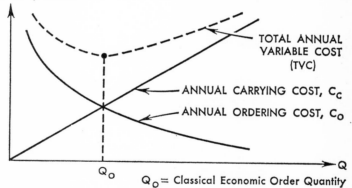

Q_O = Classical Economic Order Quantity

(c) Algebraic development of Classical Economic Order Quantity formula

$$TVC = C_c + C_o = KC\frac{Q}{2} + \frac{S}{Q}O$$

Where K is annual carrying charge factor, C is unit item cost, S is annual demand and O is variable ordering cost.

MINIMUM TVC OCCURS WHERE $C_c = C_o$ GIVING:

$$Q_o = \sqrt{\frac{2SO}{KC}}$$

Exhibit 2

REPRESENTATION OF TYPICAL STOCK LEVEL VARIATION WITH TIME,
Indicating the Added Consideration of the Cost
of Actual or Potential Stock Shortages

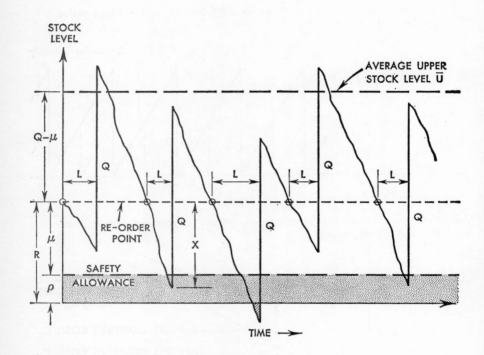

Q = Order Quantity   X = Lead Period Demand

R = Re-order Point μ = Expected Lead Period Demand

L = Lead Period ρ = Safety Allowance

Exhibit 3

A STOCK CONTROL WORK SHEET DESIGNED TO DETERMINE THE OPTIMUM ORDERING POLICY

DATA

REVIEW PERIOD = 1 WK

Code	Symbol	Description	Code	Value
(1)	$\bar{L}$	Expected lead period (weeks)	(1)	13
(2)	σ_L	Std. dev. in lead period (weeks)	(2)	3
(3)	$\bar{D}$	Expected item demand rate (units/wk)	(3)	200
(4)	σ_D	Std. dev. in item demand rate (units/wk)	(4)	50
(5)	C	Unit cost of item ($/unit)	(5)	5
(6)	O	Unit ordering cost ($/order)	(6)	8
(7)	K	Annual carrying charge factor (/yr)	(7)	0.20
(8)	A	Unit cost of a stock shortage ($/unit)	(8)	0.50

COMPUTATIONS

Code	Operation		Value	Code	Operation		Value
(9)	(7)(5)	KC	1	(29)	0.78 (25)		0.094
(10)	(8)/(9	N	0.5	(30)	(26)(26)		0.0061
(11)	52 (3)	S	10400	(31)	(29)(29)		0.0088
(12)	2 (6)		16	(32)	2 (28)		1.616
(13)	(11)(12)		166400	(33)	2 (30)		0.0122
(14)	(13)/(9)		166400	(34)	(32)(33)		0.0197
(15)	$\sqrt{(14)}$	Q_o	408	(35)	(31)+(34)		0.0285
(16)	0.5+(1)		13.5	(36)	$\sqrt{(35)}$		0.169
(17)	(16)(3)	μ	2700	(37)	(29)+(36)		0.263
(18)	(4)(4)		2500	(38)	(37)/(32)	P	0.163
(19)	(3)(2)		600	(39)	32 (38)		5.216
(20)	(16)(18)		33750	(40)	4.85+(39)		10.066
(21)	(19)(19)		360000	(41)	15.2 (38)		2.478
(22)	(20)+(21)		393750	(42)	1+(41)		3.478
(23)	$\sqrt{(22)}$	σ	628	(43)	(40)/(42)		2.894
(24)	(11)(10)		5200	(44)	0.5−(38)		0.337
(25)	(23)/(24)		0.120	(45)	(44)(43)	t	0.975
(26)	(15)/(24)	P_o	0.078	(46)	(23)(45)	ρ	610
(27)	1.6 (25)		0.192	(47)	(17)+(46)	R	3310
(28)	1−(27)		0.808	(48)	(24)(38)	Q	848

ORDERING POLICY

Code	Symbol	Description	Code	Value
(48)	Q	Integrated Economic Order Quantity	(48)	848
(47)	R	Basic Reorder Point	(47)	3310

Exhibit 4

BASIC STOCK CARD
Designed to Control the Order of an Item in Accordance with Optimum Policy Shown in Exhibit 3

Q= 850
R=3310

$$A=\frac{1}{2}\ \frac{\text{Dollar}}{\text{Unit Short}}$$

Receipts	Stock Level	Review Period Usage	Current Reorder Point	Receipts	Stock Level	Review Period Usage	Current Reorder Point
	3310	(*)			816		
		189	2460			220	760
	3121				596	(*)	
				850	1446		
		204				290	760
	2917				1156		
		163				197	
	2754				959		
		240				227	
	2514				732	(*)	
				850	1582		
		207				246	760
	2307	(*)			1336		
		202	1610			229	
	2105				1107		
				850	1957		
		212				347	1610
	1893				1610	(*)	
		163				244	760
	1730				1366		
		140				249	
	1590	(*)			1117		
		175	760			252	
	1415				865		
		195				174	
	1220				691	(*)	
		229				209	−90
	991				482		
		175				176	
	816				306		

Exhibit 5

WHAT DOES IT COST TO BE OUT OF AN ITEM?
A Graphic Representation of the Stock Position of an Item as a
Function of the Unit Cost of a Stock Shortage "A"
Under Conditions of Optimum Control

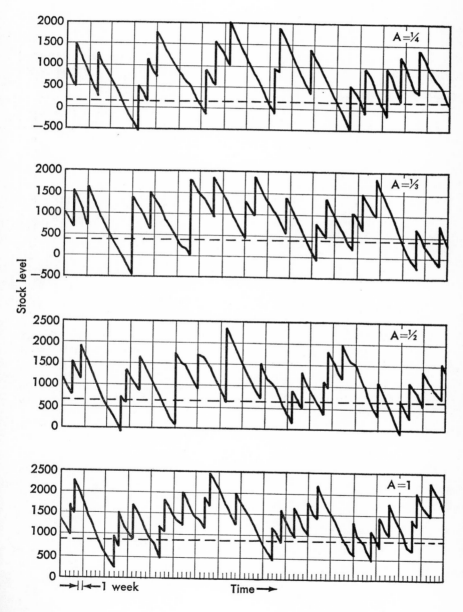

Exhibit 6

AN ACTUAL APPLICATION OF THE NEW STATISTICAL INVENTORY CONTROL MODEL

Showing by Graphic Representation the Economic Benefits Realized by Its Use Over that of Less Formal Methods

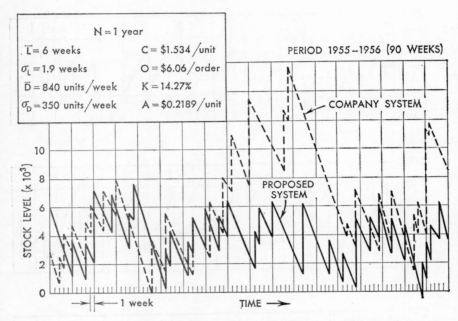

N = 1 year

$\bar{L}$ = 6 weeks   C = $1.534/unit

σ_L = 1.9 weeks   O = $6.06/order

$\bar{D}$ = 840 units/week   K = 14.27%

σ_D = 350 units/week   A = $0.2189/unit

PERIOD 1955–1956 (90 WEEKS)

COMPANY SYSTEM

PROPOSED SYSTEM

STOCK LEVEL (x 10³)

→ ⊢← 1 week   TIME →

Note the greatly decreased stock level which was economically realized through the proposed system, and resulted in a 17 per cent reduction in the total annual inventory cost of this particular item

PROPOSED SYSTEM
ORDERING POLICY
  Q = 2,550 units
  R = 8,340 units

STOCK NUMBER 12345678
INSULATOR, SUSPENSION,
6″ DISK, PORC.

ANNUAL COSTS

C_C	C_O	C_S	C_e	TVC
$1,315	118	0	?	1,433 + C_e
$ 909	104	175	0	1,187

Systems and Procedures Analysis

SYSTEMS AND PROCEDURES are terms which are often used interchangeably by the laity. However, systems and procedures have separate and distinct meanings to the informed.

A system is a collection of events which conform to a plan and represents the plan itself. In designing a system a practitioner or analyst provides a means whereby the required information is made available to management for the purpose of control and correction in operating decision areas. An equally important function of system design is to make available all information possible from which the most effective course of action can be chosen.

The design is accomplished by providing the most effective method and implementations that will furnish timely, efficient, and economical means for recording, assembling, and classifying informative data to each decision or operating area.

Systems analysis therefore is often involved with major decision areas and their interrelationships with each other. The structure and execution of the management function are molded by the particular system involved. Analysis is required therefore to ascertain whether the specific system in fact provides management with proper information in order to carry out their objectives.

Procedure analysis refers to the documentation of each succeeding step which may be performed within a specific system. This may include form design, motion studies, work flow and/or distribution, work measurements, and methods analysis. Procedures should indicate who is responsible for the function, what the function is designed to do, under what set of circumstances, and what steps are involved.

The certified public accountant can do much in this area of activity. In fact, there are indications that this is one of the areas of activity in which most CPAs have become involved to some extent. The reason for this activity (whether it be formal or informal) is that an accountant becomes somewhat familiar with the client's system and procedures through his audit relationships.

This chapter does not purport to describe all the techniques of a systems engagement. It is hoped however that it will give the accountant some insight into this area of activity. An accountant may get into the systems and procedures area (1) as a normal extension of his audit engagement or (2) at a specific request from his client.

Types of Systems Problems[1]

MANY OF us visit the doctor every year to have a general check-up. We are all familiar with the procedures he uses to check our personal system of internal control. If anything is wrong with that system—assuming he discovers it—he tells us, and he prescribes a medicine or course of action to overcome it.

Clients are exposed to CPAs in a very similar way. CPAs are able to gain a detailed picture of clients' internal business operations every year by doing their audit or by attending to their tax affairs.

Identifying Weaknesses

However, some CPAs are inclined to be careless. Their principal concern is with the immediate work at hand—to prepare or report on financial statements, or to prepare tax returns. During this process they encounter a variety of conditions which reveal internal weaknesses. Such weaknesses can be grouped into three broad categories:

1. Deficiencies in the system of gathering, classifying, and summarizing data, which can be described as the accounting system
2. Unsound practices of a managerial nature which do not have a bearing on the accounting system
3. Conditions other than these two which lead to the economic or financial weaknesses of the client's enterprise

The last two are generally the more difficult to detect and to remedy. They are more difficult to detect because they extend beyond the field to which CPAs devote their principal attention in the audit or tax matters

[1]Pages 182-187 first appeared in the *Proceedings of the Fourth Annual Systems Conference,* October 27-28, 1960, Los Angeles Chapter of the California Society of Certified Public Accountants. The author is Maurice B. T. Davies, partner, Lybrand, Ross Bros. & Montgomery, Los Angeles.

before them. They are more difficult to remedy because they generally require extensive and highly skilled study which some CPAs are not qualified to provide.

Recognizing problems in the client's accounting system is only half the battle—the diagnostic side. A few thoughts will later be offered on the curative aspect. First, CPAs should try to typify the accounting system problems met by their clients. They should also recognize the danger of attempting any precise categorization, because most problems embody features common to several of the types described in the following pages.

Slowness. One of the major types of deficiencies of an accounting system is its inability to produce information promptly. The businessman needs his information speedily if it is to be of use to him. If costs are too high, he wants to know it *now* so that he can get them down. If there is too little money in the bank, if debtors are slow, or if too much is tied up in inventory, the sooner he learns these facts the faster he can do something constructive about the situation and thus improve his profits or financial position.

What causes the system to produce data too sluggishly? We have all encountered these causes many times. Let us consider a few of them:

1. There is the accountant's mental attitude. Often he considers himself controller of the archives rather than a managerial intelligence officer.

2. A desire for unrealistic accuracy is another cause. How many times does one find the accountant who refuses to close the books until all the vendors' invoices have been received? Had he decided to estimate the amounts of the invoices not yet received, or—in many cases—had he even decided to omit them altogether, his accounts would still be reasonably accurate as a guide for management.

3. A third cause is an unhealthy belief in the magic of double entry. The accountant hesitates to release any figures before he has first agreed his trial balance or proved a control account.

These are just a few reasons. But the result is that the accountant is short-changing his management. He is feeding them stale information. And the older this information is, the less valuable it becomes, and the less likely it is that the management can use it as a basis for earning profits.

Inaccuracy. Another problem that auditors often observe is the existence of errors so material in nature or in number that they destroy the reliability of the accounting statements. Management ceases to rely on its accounting reports, or, worse still, is led into making erroneous decisions because it relies on erroneous data.

Many causes contribute to this condition. Three more important ones are as follows:

1. Incompetent accounting leadership is perhaps the most prevalent cause. The client's chief accountant is unqualified either as an accountant or as a supervisor to make sure that the direction is sound and that his staff is following directions.

2. Understaffing is a common cause. An overburdened accounting staff is prone to make mistakes and to have too little time to check its work.

3. Inadequate communication with operating management gives rise to many errors. In one instance, the accounting department may fail to get all the facts or may fail to get them correctly. And, in another case, operating management may fail to examine the accounting reports and tell the accounting department about obvious errors or inconsistencies.

Overstaffing. Man—and that includes woman—is a most ingenious creature. If there is insufficient work to keep him occupied, he finds countless ways to create unnecessary work and keep himself on the payroll. How often have we come across situations such as these:

1. Duplication of routine work
2. Preparation of unnecessary reports
3. Excessive and unnecessary checking of data
4. Reading inconsequential material
5. Use of highly trained people to perform low-grade work

The cause may stem from poor management, conscious empire building, or contraction of work without a corresponding contraction of staff. In any event, staff members are generally so wedded to unnecessary duties that eventually they honestly believe in their necessity and feel that serious damage would be done if a pruning operation were started.

Complexity. When procedures become too complex, they generally give rise to each of the problems previously discussed, namely: (a) too great a delay in producing accounting data; (b) too many errors; and (c) too many people in the accounting department.

There are four predominant causes for this condition:

1. An inherently complex business will always tend to create complex procedures. There is often little we can do about this.

2. Muddled procedural development is another cause. Perhaps the procedures have grown complicated over the years because of failure to discard unnecessary features. Perhaps the development of a new procedure has been conceived by an illogical mind.

3. Excessive concentration on trivia invariably tends to give rise to complicated methods. This is often stimulated by an almost pathological fear of making mistakes or leaving the door open to the remotest possibility of fraud. It results in such phenomena as accounting for inventories of paper clips while matters of fundamental importance to the business sometimes escape attention altogether.

4. Perhaps one of the most significant causes is the endeavor of the

accounting staff to comply with unrealistic demands, policies, or procedures imposed by the management or the operating departments. Unless these are corrected, the accounting procedures can rarely be improved.

Laxity. CPAs have an ingrained understanding of the need for efficient internal check: it helps to provide for more accurate accounting data and to guard against the more prevalent risks of error, loss, and fraud. The smaller business is often unable to afford the luxury of such a system. Yet, as the business grows, it sometimes tends to continue its previous deficiencies instead of realizing that, with a bigger staff, it is now in a position to provide better internal protection. In such cases the CPA, who is also human and who has worked with the client year after year, is equally exposed to the risk of overlooking the opportunity for a change for the better.

The more common types of problems that beset accounting systems have so far been considered. At the risk of oversimplification, they have been grouped into five general types:

1. When data are produced too slowly
2. When data are produced inaccurately
3. When too large a staff is employed
4. When procedures are too complicated
5. When the system of internal check is weak

Course of Action

How can the CPA identify these situations? In his capacity as auditor, he is not making a systems examination as such, but is rather confining his observations to the regular study of internal control, which forms an integral part of his audit, aided by his natural powers of observation and inquisitiveness.

The CPA should extend his exposure, in terms of lunch meetings and other client contacts, beyond the accounting staff. He should try to meet and talk with such people as the sales manager, the credit manager, the advertising manager, the purchasing agent, the plant superintendent, the safety director, the production control manager, the personnel manager, other officials in the client organization, and, of course, the president. There are generally good reasons why he will need to speak to them in the normal course of his audit. Their comments and attitudes should give him a better feeling of the pulse of the over-all enterprise. The CPA should endeavor to look for such straws in the wind as the following, and then evaluate their importance as evidence of problems, as symptoms, or as causes:

1. Are there excessive backlogs of work?
2. Is overtime work high?

3. Is there evidence of idleness or sluggish habits?
4. Are internal reports produced long after the period to which they relate?
5. Are operating departments keeping informal accounting records?
6. Is it difficult to find information readily?
7. Is a large number of accounting corrections made, either by the client's staff or by the auditors?
8. Do people perform work without knowing why they do it?
9. Is there evidence of weakness in the system of internal control?
10. Does the purchasing department's power extend unduly beyond the sole task of purchasing?
11. Is there evidence of a high level of customer complaints or of returns by and allowances to customers?
12. Is it difficult to extract data from the books for purposes of (1) management information, (2) tax returns, or (3) SEC renditions?
13. Is inventory mounting at a faster rate than sales, and are there substantial writeoffs when physical counts are made?
14. Does animosity or lack of understanding exist between the accounting staff and the operating departments?
15. Is there an absence of realistic sales data?
16. Are financial results analyzed in excessive depth or, on the contrary, is the analysis too superficial?
17. Is there a lack of yardsticks, such as ratios, forecasts, and budgets, for measuring performance?
18. Is it difficult to correlate managerial responsibility with data contained in accounting reports?
19. Are accounting reports produced with inadequate narrative material to explain what they mean and imply?
20. Is there a failure to plan cash needs in advance?

It is desirable for the CPA to limit questions to a controllable number because this enables him to make his approach systematically without having to refer continuously to a check list.

Helpful reminders

The CPA should bear the following thoughts in mind when he attempts to help his client solve problems:

1. *Be sure of the facts.* This means getting all the facts, getting them correctly, and interpreting them properly.

2. *Concentrate on the more material items.* If the client has a variety of problems, the CPA should not waste time worrying about the little ones and letting the big ones go unattended—unless, of course, the client asks for the CPA's help in the little ones.

3. *Figure out the best solution.* There are generally many choices of a

solution. The CPA should examine the more likely ones, select the best, and be prepared to justify this selection.

4. *Present recommendations convincingly.* When the CPA offers advice to the client, he should tell him these four things: (a) What is being done, or not being done, now; (b) what difficulties this creates or is likely to create; (c) precisely what he should do instead; and (d) how he will benefit by following the advice.

This sounds easy, but it requires an experienced and logical mind, patience and understanding of one's fellow men, thorough technical competence, and a convincing attitude to ensure that the client accepts and benefits from professional advice. These demands are exacting, but they are part of the burden of the certified public accountant. If he acquits himself well, he will achieve the greatest reward a professional man can have: a grateful and satisfied client.

The foregoing then gives the accountant some indication as to what symptoms he may look for in the normal course of his audit engagement. Surely all would agree that if the accountant finds one or more of these symptoms he should point them out to management.

Suppose, however, that a client requests his accountant to perform a systems engagement, either as a result of the accountant's recommendations or at management's initiative. What approach does the accountant take and how does he execute the engagement?

A Sound Approach in Systems Practice[2]

A SYSTEMS engagement is only successful if the client benefits. The client benefits only if he takes effective action, on a sound recommendation, directed to a real problem. Therefore the objective is not a comprehensive report of findings and conclusions which may be masterful but which does not result in action.

Engagement Criteria

To be assured that the client will benefit requires selectivity in seeking and accepting engagements. CPAs will do well to assure themselves that:

[2]Pages 187-195 were excerpted or adapted from an article by Gordon L. Murray, partner, Haskins & Sells, Executive Office, New York, which appeared in that firm's *Selected Papers,* 1957 ("Management Services by Local Practitioners—Accounting Systems").

1. The client has a real problem.
2. They consult with the client on the real problem, not a symptomatic one.
3. The client recognizes or is led to recognize that he has a problem.
4. The client needs help.
5. They are qualified.
6. The climate is such that the client will act on a sound recommendation.

These criteria provide the basis for evaluating the opportunity for a successful engagement. The absence of any of these factors in a particular situation may well give cause for declining the engagement.

This also means that the CPA does not necessarily undertake to perform those specific assignments requested by a client. A professional obligation exists to assure oneself that the assignment is compatible with these criteria and, if not, the scope of the assignment should be changed or the work declined. It may be difficult to deny a client's request, but this is painless when compared to the problem of explaining later that things did not work out well because the client's request was not sound in the first place.

The Consulting Approach

The client is most apt to benefit through use of a consulting approach in systems work. A consultant guides the client in recognizing and solving his problems; he does not perform these functions in his stead. In this way he assists the client to do a more effective job and attain a more effective operation, rather than assume management's prerogative by working on the problem independently.

The consulting approach implies a small staff on most engagements, working closely with client personnel, and requires client participation in all phases. A consultant's role is to help the client help himself. Such services are of a relatively high order and represent the sale of technical know-how, skill, and experience rather than manpower or man-hours.

Fortunately this approach works out to the advantage of the practitioner as well as of the client. Efforts can be directed toward building a relatively small staff of highly qualified persons who can serve a considerable number of clients, on a consulting basis, over any given period of time. Such a staff can command reasonably high rates for a high order of service. Staff problems are minimized.

This approach is somewhat exceptional and is not universally recognized or practiced by those engaged in this work. It is also difficult because it requires that the consultant develop in the client a real desire to act on a problem and to obtain effective results. This is more difficult than doing the job for him or writing a long report as though that were the objective. This approach also requires that the problem be viewed from the standpoint of the general management of the business. There is an obligation to consider the best interests of the company as a whole rather than any particular individual or group. A high degree of objectivity is required.

It must be recognized that the consultant has no authority within the client organization. He consults through fact finding, analysis, suggestion, and assistance, and therefore must gain client confidence in himself and his proposals as the work proceeds.

This is the most rewarding approach when performed effectively. It provides training and experience to client personnel through participation, so that they become qualified to carry on the program when the consulting phase is completed. Cost to the client, in fees, is held to a minimum consistent with the objectives.

This basic approach must be applied with common sense. The degree to which it can be applied will vary in different client situations and different types of engagements. However, the adoption of these objectives offers a very effective approach from the client's, and therefore the practitioner's, viewpoint.

Executing Engagements

THE EXECUTION of systems engagements includes the solution of problems. Problem solution requires a definition of the problem, identification of alternative courses of action, evaluation of alternatives, and selection of the alternative which most nearly meets the requirements of the objective.

In systems engagements this approach is usually applied in the seven steps of (1) problem definition, (2) fact finding, (3) analysis, (4) drawing conclusions, (5) making recommendations, (6) installation, and (7) follow-up. This represents an orderly progression of the phases making up practically every systems engagement, whether it be for a large or small client or for a broad or narrow problem.

Problem Definition

Definition of the problem and objectives is the first step in performing any type of systems service. Occasionally this can be accomplished easily through conversation with the client, based upon knowledge the consultant already possesses about the company's operations. However, definition is most often achieved through a preliminary survey of the client's facilities, procedures, reports, and the like. Such a survey usually contains all the steps in engagement execution, but in limited scope. It is in the nature of a miniature engagement performed to define the nature and scope of the problem, to serve as the basis of a proposal to the client, and to permit an evaluation of the situation against the engagement criteria previously discussed.

Survey Techniques

THE PROBLEMS and techniques entering into initial surveys of an existing accounting system are sufficiently important to warrant further remarks. The quality of the survey will directly affect the success of all other phases of the work. The points made here are particularly applicable to assignments for the general over-all survey of a system, but are generally applicable to more limited surveys as well. How does one conduct an over-all survey of a system?

Background information

Appropriate background information should be obtained prior to undertaking any extensive work on the client premises. There are internal and external sources of valuable information.

Internal. Discuss the client's operations with the partner, principal-supervisor-manager, or others in the CPA's organization. Secure the background of the business: what it does, history, plant sites, etc. Obtain their views as to areas or clues to areas which are susceptible of improvement. Review weaknesses revealed by reviews of internal controls. Obtain the background on the personalities concerned so as to be able to anticipate in some degree personality and political problems. Review financial statements for an appropriate period (perhaps ten years) and look for trends indicative of strong or weak profit performance.

External. Review, through publications and/or through personal contacts, the production and marketing characteristics of the industry. Become acquainted with significant trade practices. If there is a trade or industry association, find out if they have published uniform charts of accounts or manuals and review these publications. Some of them are particularly valuable, such as the MAPI accounting manual of the Machinery and Allied Products Institute, the manual of The National Electrical Manufacturers Association, a manual on construction cost control published by the American Society of Civil Engineers, and others. Publications of the

American Institute of CPAs, the National Association of Accountants, Financial Executives Institute, and similar organizations are valuable in obtaining information on specific industry characteristics and practices.

Client arrangements

Review with the client official for whom the survey is being made what is proposed to be done, plans for going about it, and actions required of client personnel. Arrange for the client to call together the key people in the organization concerned for full explanation of the nature and scope of the survey. Everyone affected must understand who the consultant is and what he proposes to do, so that an atmosphere of co-operation is created. In attempting to develop such an atmosphere, the consultant should refrain from suggesting displacement of employees as a primary objective and should indicate that he is attempting to help by smoothing operations and procedures. Phrases like "checking up," "cost cutting," and "installing efficiency" should be avoided.

Organization chart

Obtain or prepare an organization chart if a recent one is not available. Review this chart with the client executive sponsoring the project to obtain knowledge of how the company is organized, what functions are performed, where they are performed, who is responsible for their performance, and other over-all company facts usually developed from a discussion of the organization chart. (See also Chapter 2, page 66.)

Plan and schedule

Based upon this review, determine which persons are to be interviewed and lay out a sequence and time schedule for these contacts. This permits you to budget your time and allows you to arrange appointments in advance. Lining up appointments at least a day in advance avoids loss of time, is courteous to the client's people, and gives the person an opportunity to consider the matter of your visit in advance, so that he is prepared.

Plant tour

A plant tour should be made early in the survey, preferably with someone from the production organization. A production man is better able to explain his operations than an accountant. He is also less likely to resist changes which may affect his operation if you have dealt directly with him and provided him with the opportunity to explain his side of the problem. In touring a plant, follow, as far as practicable, the flow of production from raw material, through work in process, to finished goods and shipment. Often your guide will take you by the most convenient route from a mileage standpoint rather than by a logical route from a production standpoint.

The plant tour should precede work on the specifics of the accounting system, since it provides a basis for evaluating the accounting and paperwork phase of operations through knowledge of how production flows and the operations take place. It should be borne in mind that an accounting system is meant to report on the results of operations. Some accountants make the mistake of expecting operations to conform to their information system.

During the plant tour you should observe evidences of shop controls—shop order, move tickets, schedule boards, timekeeping, material requisitions, scrap tickets, and the like. Should the production man indicate his problems, it is often desirable to check the functions immediately preceding and following his particular area of responsibility. This often avoids a clash due to procedure or paper-flow changes which may disturb the requirements of another control center. Observe also housekeeping, orderliness or degree of confusion, storage facilities and methods, equipment groupings or centers, material handling, condition of equipment, tool cribs and tool controls, and other factors.

Control reports

Obtain a set of the top-control reports on financial position, cost, schedule, quality, and other pertinent areas which go to the top executives. Review these reports and outline the questions you wish to cover during your interviews.

Conducting interviews

After these preliminary steps have been taken, the consultant is ready to conduct interviews of the persons concerned with the functions being surveyed. In an initial survey, interviews are often limited to department heads or key supervisors. However, the coverage and depth of interviewing depend upon conditions in each case. Deciding how much the consultant needs to know to be entitled to an opinion and have a sound factual basis for his conclusions is largely a matter of judgment and experience.

Conducting a successful interview is a complicated problem. It means listening more than talking, asking the right questions, avoiding expressions of opinion or criticism, and seeking to obtain the interviewee's opinion on what is done, his ideas for improvement, things previously tried and abandoned, and things that are being planned.

The persons interviewed should include all key persons who may be affected by your recommendations even if not considered necessary from a technical standpoint. Unless such persons have had a hearing, there is a possibility of later resistance and resentment.

During the interviews, material which will be of help in analyzing and evaluating the findings should be collected, including forms, manuals, flow charts, reports, and other materials.

Some organizations engaged in this work feel that guides or questionnaires are useful in conducting surveys. There are hazards in this practice to the extent that a stereotyped approach may result in standard conclusions and "pat" systems. There should be ample latitude for exercising judgment and for allowing the systems man to pursue the facts wherever they lead.

Organization of facts

All of the facts obtained in the survey must be organized in such a way that they can be analyzed and evaluated. There are a variety of techniques including schematic diagrams, flow charts of various types, outlines of notes, and others. The methods used depend largely upon the complexity of the situation and personal preferences.

Systems evaluation

Evaluation of the facts developed during the survey in terms of management control is frequently effective. Management control implies that areas in an operation requiring control are identified; that plans in the form of forecasts, budgets, standards, and the like are applied in each control area; that there is an accounting or other measurement of actual results; that results are reported by comparing plan and actual and pointing to exceptions; and that reports are distributed according to the division of responsibility under the plan of organization. In effect the consultant must determine what constitutes an adequate control plan, what parts the client already has, and what parts of the plan are missing. During this process many alternatives are usually considered before conclusions are reached.

Next, consideration is given to the effectiveness of present methods and what methods are appropriate for the new control procedures it is decided will be required. These are matters of mechanized versus manual procedures, centralization versus decentralization, clerical costs, timing, and so on.

This two-step approach—first, management control requirements and then methods—usually has the most appeal for the top executives in the company who are the real audience, but who are not usually technical accountants. It is almost always a mistake to attempt to present survey findings to such an audience in terms of forms, number of copies, routing, journal entries, and other procedural details.

Presentation of recommendations

The consultant's presentation of recommendations requires attention to such strategy questions as:

1. If he is reporting to the president, does he present findings to the controller first? In which direction does he seek acceptance: from the lower echelons up, or from the top down?

2. Should the consultant have one general meeting to hear the recommendations? Will this embarrass anyone? Will the size of the meeting cause problems?

3. Should the recommendations be prepared in final report form prior to review? After review? Preparation of a report in final form before presentation is almost always poor strategy. Carrying such a report into a presentation meeting indicates that the consultant has fixed and final conclusions, that he does not intend to discuss or negotiate, and that he is not receptive to any suggestions or new ideas from those present. Deferring the final report permits him to adjust the emphasis based upon his sensitivity to the reactions of his audience. He can be a purist and insist on an all-or-nothing acceptance, or he can be a realist and strive to get his most important proposals accepted. After all, the consultant's objective is to get the client to act in his own best interest. A sound program should not be lost because some unessential point proves to be unacceptable.

The submission of a full and formal report after a personal presentation is generally unnecessary, and even undesirable, because a written report is a wonderful aid to procrastination. It can be too easily filed for future reference without action. The absence of a report tends to prey on a client's conscience as he realizes he has done nothing, not even filed the consultant's report. Also, reports are very expensive; in some instances they cost more than the survey work.

This does not imply that such engagements should not be adequately documented with progress reports or summaries of actions taken. However, reports should not be relied upon to get action or be considered the products of the consultant's work.

4. Should an oral review ever be omitted? The answer is that there should always be an oral presentation and only seldom a formal written report. Oral presentations provide the best means for explanation: points readily accepted can be disposed of quickly and more controversial items can be emphasized.

5. Effective oral presentation requires keen sensitivity to people. Everything the consultant proposes to say must be weighed in terms of the reaction of each person present. A point might make a great hit with the controller and embarrass the treasurer. The presentation should be aimed at the men who have the authority to make the decisions. The positive approach of explaining how to move from "where they are" to

"something even better," is far superior to the negative approach of reciting all the deficiencies in "what they have." A recital of deficiencies may evidence insight but does not result in acceptance or action. Full credit should always be given to the ideas of others. The consultant's role is not necessarily to supply all the answers, but to act as a catalyst to bring action on the best thinking on a problem.

Action program

An action program should conclude the presentation of recommendations. The action program sets forth in specific steps all actions required to move from where they are to where it is proposed that they go. It should later include the names of client people responsible for each step and scheduled dates. This provides the basis for client actions to implement the program. It also indicates at which point the consultant should review and consult as the program is carried out.

This then represents the two ways in which the consultant may become involved in a systems engagement. Based on such engagements many types of problems may be uncovered. Two particular problems are used in this chapter to indicate how diverse they may be. In the first instance a report problem was uncovered and secondly a procedural problem is described. These are discussed in order to give the accountant more insight into specific problems which he may carry over to other areas.

Control Report Problems[3]

The foregoing has dealt with an initial survey directed toward development of the areas warranting attention in depth. This survey may uncover an attractive opportunity to improve the system of management reporting. If so, how would such a study be conducted? What constitutes a sound approach and what are some of the techniques to be used in executing such an engagement?

There are indications that many companies approach the problem of control reports through the screening procedure. An assistant to the president, a vice-president, or even a secretary, goes over reports, picks out trivia, and decides what should go to the head man. This position "next to the throne" can become powerful and also frustrating to the

[3]Pages 195-204 were excerpted or adapted from an article by Gordon L. Murray, partner, Haskins & Sells, Executive Office, New York, which appeared in that firm's *Selected Papers,* 1958 ("An Effective Approach to Report Control Problems").

rest of the organization. This results in the "screener's" judgment being substituted both for the judgment of the president and for the person submitting the report. We can conclude that this approach fails to face up to the real problem. Rather, a new set of problems is substituted for the problem of too many reports.

The basic objective of a sound control reporting system can be stated in simple terms. What should be done is to make certain that each person in an organization has the information needed to perform a job effectively and also that unnecessary information is eliminated. This implies that the information is adequate as to content, form, timing, integration, and so on. If management were certain this condition prevailed it could not help but be satisfied. Report costs would be acceptable if at all reasonable.

This sounds like a rather obvious and basic objective and, of course, it is. Generally it is not adopted, however, for several reasons. Management and staff personnel in an organization may not have time to tackle the problem. The scope of such an undertaking may serve to frighten management off. There may not be anyone in the organization in a position to be sufficiently objective to carry through such a program, or the techniques for such a project may not be known.

Basic principles

The principles to serve as a guide in developing a plan to meet this objective are as follows:

1. First of all there should be a recognition that control reports represent a problem area susceptible of study as a separate problem. Reports can only be produced from information and data generated by systems, procedures, and methods. However, report requirements can be approached separately. Many procedures exist partially or solely for reporting purposes. Therefore, it is logical that report requirements be resolved first and that attention to procedures and methods should follow.

2. There should also be an acceptance of the desirability of studying all types of control information together, i.e., financial, cost, schedule, quality, service, work load, personnel, and the like. From a top management standpoint all areas of the business are interrelated, and therefore an integrated reporting system requires inclusion of all controllable areas relating to profits. Management expects balanced performance; it expects not just production on schedule, but production on schedule at proper costs and up to quality standards.

3. There should also be a recognition that the development of a reporting plan must include a review of company policies. A consultant should ask these questions: What are the objectives and policies of the company? What needs to be controlled? How are the over-all business and its various operations to be planned and controlled? What are the

factors affecting profits and how can they be measured and reported for planning and control purposes?

4. There must be an acceptance of the premise that organizational questions are an essential consideration in arriving at a sound reporting system. Management has been defined as *the art of getting things done through people*. This definition implies that one of management's prime responsibilities is to know how well things are being done—how well people are performing. Reports must be based upon a determination of who controls as well as what must be controlled if performance is to be measured. This is the means for making organization and accounting work for you.

It also follows that if the objective is to see that each key person has the information he needs to do his job effectively, the planning and control responsibility assigned to each position must first be determined.

5. There should also be a realization that a review of reports now being issued is but one phase of the project. Individual reports can be reviewed, the format can be changed, the columns can be moved about, and so forth. However, the opportunity to make major improvements by using this method is limited. An over-all plan should be set up first to provide a basis for evaluating individual reports later on. It is a mistake to begin sifting a collection of reports before the ground rules and criteria for evaluating these reports, with regard to both coverage and content, have been established.

A case study

Now that the nature and importance of this problem have been considered, the opportunity it presents to CPAs and how the problem can be properly approached, will be reviewed in the following case.

This particular company is a very successful and substantial company with first-class management personnel. Their management control report problem was typical of that encountered by many companies. In short, no integrated plan of reports existed. Various reports had been initiated over the years and had been continued after the original need no longer existed or the person requesting them had moved elsewhere. No conscious effort had been made to look at the whole body of reports as a separate problem requiring planning and integration.

The immediate causes for concern about the report problem arose from several factors.

1. Since World War II the company's operations had expanded from one location to several locations and there were plans for further expansion. In some instances they had purchased a going business and inherited a reporting system different from their own. In other instances they had started a new operation themselves and needed to develop a reporting system. In every case the volume of control information multiplied. These

facts had added to the problem of integrating information and required that over-all management delegate authority and responsibility and divorce themselves from detailed operating data.

2. Management responsibility had been transferred in recent years to a more or less new generation of executives, many of whom had had experience with other companies. Therefore, more diversity of opinion existed on how operations should be controlled and reported, which had to be reconciled.

3. Certain shifts in emphasis and policies within the operation had occurred. For example, sales were being made to a more diverse group of customers, under new conditions, and on new terms. These and other policy changes had resulted in new areas requiring controls and report coverage.

4. A number of organizational changes had been made from time to time. These shifts in the assignment of duties and responsibilities resulted in changed report requirements which had not been provided for.

5. Owing to the existence of a small, closely knit group of owner executives and keen competition, much data on company operations was traditionally held in strictest confidence. There was need to expand the dissemination of certain information to permit key personnel to function effectively. In other words, there was need to decentralize authority and responsibility but still to provide central control on performance.

6. Report coverage was inadequate. Some areas in the operation were covered by a multiplicity of reports, while other areas were the subject of few, if any, reports.

7. The controller was a relatively new employee and had initiated a number of progressive programs for improving management controls. To a considerable extent the success of these programs depended upon an improved system of reports.

8. There was the usual criticism in some quarters that there were too many reports, while other executives were critical of the lack of information on certain phases of operations.

The approach used in resolving these problems consisted of a number of basic steps, as follows:

Current organization chart. In co-operation with the controller and other key executives, a current organization chart was developed and the functions and responsibilities assigned to each organization unit were spelled out.

Management reports scheme. The next step was to develop a tentative over-all control report scheme. This scheme identified the major elements in the operation which had to be controlled and the positions having control responsibility, as well as positions which should have had data for information and planning purposes.

This can be termed the *imaginative* phase of the program, as opposed to the *analytical* phase, when specific reports are evaluated. Up to this point no detailed examination of present reports had been made. Rather, effort was directed toward predetermining objectively what the reports structure should be so there would be a basis for evaluating actual reports and reports coverage later on.

Figure 1 (pages 200-201) illustrates an approach to developing a management reports scheme. Major control areas are shown in the left-hand column, and in practice these may be further detailed to the degree appropriate. The planning column specifies the basis to be used to predetermine performance and information to be used for comparative purposes, followed by specification of data required to be provided by the accounting and other information systems. The content of reports is then summarized along with report distribution. In practice the report distribution column is divided into a subcolumn for each key executive. These subcolumns are coded to indicate whether a position receives information on that control area and, if so, whether it is for control, planning, or information purposes. The principle here is that no more than one position can be designated as having primary control responsibility, provided the organization plan is sound. If it is not clear as to which position controls, such conflicts should be cleared up at this point.

Once the over-all control report scheme was developed and approved, a major step in the work had been completed. This constituted a definition of the problem and positioned the goal posts by indicating what coverage was necessary for the complete program. Organizational questions had been resolved at the start and the necessity to negotiate the questions throughout the rest of the program was minimized. All the rest of the work could be tied back to this plan, which also provided a means for budgeting time and determining when the work was complete.

Criteria for report adequacy. This over-all management control scheme was supplemented by a set of criteria for appraising the adequacy of an individual control report, such as simplicity of format and use of comparative data showing trends.

Reports prepared. All divisions, departments, and sections were requested to submit a copy of each report prepared in their unit together with a list indicating for each report the frequency of issue, distribution, and person to contact. Actual copies of reports were requested rather than blank forms, and the date of daily, weekly, monthly, and annual report samples to be submitted was specified. This provided actual report samples as of common dates so actual data on one report could be related with another.

Reports received. All units were also requested to submit a list of reports received, indicating the names and sources of each report. This provided a means for cross-checking between lists of reports issued and received to

Figure 1

AN APPROACH TO DEVELOPING A REPORTS SCHEME

Control areas	Planning	Accounting	Reporting	
			Content	Distribution

Sales:
Volume
Price
Mix
Profitability
Type customer
Customer
Geographically
Size order
Per cent of market
Equipment vs. service parts
Backlog, etc.
 	
Production level vs. capacity
 	
Cost:
Labor
Material:
  Usage
  Price
Overhead:
  Expense:
    Variable/fixed
    Controllable/ noncontrollable
  Rates
  Product
  Cost center/department
 	
Scheduling:
Performance
Shortages
Load
	Planning may be in form of:
	Forecasts
	Budgets
	Standards:
	  Internal
	  External (published industry indexes, etc.)
	Lead times
	Turnover rates, etc.
		Records of actual results:
		Dollars
		Units and quantities
		Hours
		Number of occurrences, etc.
		
		Includes accounting or measuring in broad sense—accounting, statistical, operating data
			Adequate coverage of each control area to show:
			Position
			Performance
			Variations from plan
			Cause
			Responsibility
			
			Integrated to bring together related factors —show cause and effect
			
			Pyramided from low to higher echelons
				Distribution tied to assignment of authority and responsibility under organization plan. Only one position receives report for control purposes; others may receive report for information and planning purposes if it is related to their assigned functions

Other Illustrations of Major Control Areas

Department store

Over-all operating results

Financial position:
Balance sheet
Cash position
Accounts receivable status
Collection performance
Inventory position and trend
Fixed asset budget status

Industry and competitive position:
Sales performance vs. competition
Comparative merchandising
Sales, stock, expense, and profit performance vs. other units or stores (NRMA or other industry data)

Port operation

Revenues:
Operating revenues
  Department
  Major type:
    Dockage, sheddage, tollage, leases, etc.

Nonoperating revenues:
Subsidies
Investments, etc.

Activity statistics:
Facilities usage
Current activity and trend
Competitive position

Sales:
Store
Department:
  Dollars
  Transactions
  Cash, charge, contract, etc.

Departmental performance:
Merchandising departments:
  Sales
  Pricing, markups/markdowns
  Anticipation and cash discounts
  Stock shortages
  Selling expense, etc.
Workrooms
  Work load
  Costs, etc.
Work centers
  Expense, etc.

Buying

Quality or service

Publicity

Personnel

Research

Property and facilities

Insurance

Costs and expenses:
Revenue producing departments:
  Docks:
    Wharfs and sheds
    Banana conveyers
    Harbor patrol
    Administration, etc.
  Commodity warehouse, etc.
Nonrevenue producing departments:
  Engineering:
    Design and construction:
      Costs and expense
      Application of charges to projects:
        Direct
        Through overhead, etc.
    Operating gain or loss

Construction program:
Long range:
  Major projects:
    Cost
    Schedule
    Source of funds
Short range, etc.

Balance sheet items

Other

Procurement:
Competitive prices
Schedule performance/shortages
Economic purchase quantities
Single/multiple sources
Quality—receiving inspection

Profit:
Dollars
Return on investment
Per share
Breakeven points

Cash

Receivables

Inventories:
Class
Level
Turnover/days of supply
Obsolescence

Personnel:
Manpower/headcounts
Turnover
Promotability

Quality:
Rejects
Scrap
Returns

Research and development, etc.

be sure all report samples were accounted for and distribution lists were accurate.

Interviews. Interviews were then conducted of all appropriate personnel, starting with departments preparing the greater numbers of reports, and working from the bottom of the organization chart upwards. In this way as much background as possible was acquired before talking to report users. It helps to know how each report is prepared and what a subordinate's opinions are before interviewing the superior.

These interviews also included a discussion of the control responsibilities of each position, the importance of the various factors in the job, and the incumbent's ideas as to what he should have. In effect, the man was asked: "What is your job? How do you operate? What needs to be controlled? How do you control? What do you think of the reports you get? What do you need?" This permitted refinement of the over-all control scheme as work progressed.

Report forms. The facts obtained by interview were recorded on two forms, one covering information on the preparation of each report, called a *report inventory,* and the other covering information from each user of each report, called a *report user data sheet.* When the interviews were completed a complete file had been compiled on each report, including a sample report, inventory sheet, and data sheets from each user.

Classification. As a practical matter each interview covered all reports prepared and used by the individual interviewed. However, reports are evaluated and the new structure is built by first evaluating all reports falling in each control area. Once a pyramid of report data is decided upon for each control area, then all areas are considered together to build an over-all reports pyramid and provide for integration of information.

To accomplish this, all reports were listed and classified by control area. This immediately showed up areas not covered by reports and areas covered by many reports.

Critique. It will be found that it is better to develop the reports structure from the top down rather than from the bottom up. In the case referred to, it was concluded early in the evaluation phase that there were many opportunities to improve individual reports in the files. However, there was a complete absence of any top-management report or series of reports which would permit the over-all operation of the business to be reviewed. The present reports did not represent an integrated set of data to indicate where performance was good and where major problems existed from a top-management point of view. Almost every report was given a "shotgun" distribution, with the section head, department manager, division head, and president all receiving the same report. The president wound up receiving a copy of almost every report and was left to sort, analyze, and digest the data himself.

In this company the need for a top series of reports covering all phases of the operation was accentuated by the existence of a management committee, including the president and the head of each major function. This group met weekly to discuss various problems and to pass on most major business decisions, but had not been recognized in reporting practices. Members received only those reports appropriate to their individual positions rather than broader company-wide data. Therefore, this group was not sufficiently informed to give adequate consideration to the questions brought up for decision at the meetings.

Improvements. A completely new series or package of reports was developed for the use of this top executive group. These reports cover all control areas in summary form and clearly indicate responsibility for performance in each area. As this group is most concerned with major company decisions, the reports emphasize trends rather than short-term results.

At the first meeting following the issuance of this series of monthly reports, each person is called upon to review the report schedules covering the activities for which he is responsible. By having the reports ahead of time, each person is expected to indicate the action he is taking on the problems showing up in the reports. This results in a very different type of meeting than one where problems are revealed for the first time and the responsible official has had no opportunity to plan a course of action. Here time is spent considering positive solutions rather than excuses.

This case illustrates that the purposes of the various committees in an organization and their information requirements should be included within the scope of a reports survey.

Other management meetings should also be given attention, as some meetings are required because of deficiencies in control reports or are held to get a group decision which would not be required if control responsibility were properly defined in the first place.

Evaluation and recommendations. Following the design of this set of top summary reports, all of the other reports were evaluated. This evaluation covered report content and coverage, format, timing, accuracy, distribution, and integration with the top set of reports which formed the top of the pyramid of reports. Recommendations were then made for eliminations, changes, and new reports. The objective was not to give everyone what he thought he should have but rather what he required as part of an over-all plan related to the assignment of control responsibility, organizationally speaking.

A reports numbering system was adopted for administrative purposes. Authorized reports were entered on a reports plan which classified all reports by areas of control and showed the distribution of each report.

A reports co-ordinator was appointed on the controller's staff with responsibility for maintaining the reports plan. The development of a comprehensive reports plan is not a one-time proposition but rather serves as a starting point. Continuing effort is required to improve it and adjust it for changes in the organization structure and in the operations of the business.

By-products of report review

A company stands to benefit from the by-products that often result from systematically reviewing reports. It is not unusual to find need for information that is practicable to obtain but which is not currently available. Other information is not available soon enough to be of value.

A good report usually compares actual results to planned results. In order to conclude that a certain result is good or bad it must be compared with what that result should have been. Very often a study of reports will disclose instances where no standard or goal has been established. This points up areas where planning procedures and techniques can be improved.

The easy way out is to make comparison to the prior period or to last year. Then if your report shows a gain over last year, you conclude the results are favorable. This could also mean that the results were less unfavorable. After all, there is nothing sacred about last year's results which reflect previous sins as well as virtues.

In the case example just discussed, almost every reference to last year has been eliminated except for trend data in planning reports. Once the plan has been approved, management expects planned performance, not last year's performance. As a compromise, a few reports showed both plan and last year's performance. It was found that this led to a rationalization like this: "Well, I missed my planned performance by 10 per cent, but I am still all right because I am 5 per cent over last year." This is not an acceptable answer.

Another important result should be a better understanding of their jobs by all executives and of the relationship of their jobs to the over-all operations of the company. The plan should clearly spell out who controls what, who is responsible and accountable for each phase of operations, and the importance attached to each phase of an activity. Often this represents the first time everyone has had an opportunity to really consider these questions.

Organizing Systems Work

ASIDE FROM management reporting, many other opportunities for service arise as a result of an initial survey. Among these are work studies involving process charting, mechanization, and cost reduction programs. The first will be discussed presently, and the last two in following chapters.

Organization of fact-gathering techniques for a systems analysis engagement will of course depend on the functional activities as well as the complexity of relationships of the activities to be studied.

One of the first tasks to be performed is the construction of a flow diagram. A flow diagram represents a schematic drawing of the present system. It identifies all of the activities involved and indicates the path followed in the particular area under study. This provides a pictorial view of current operations, which will subsequently yield the insight necessary to solve the problem.

Process charting symbols[4]

For analytical purposes and to aid in detecting and eliminating inefficiencies, it is convenient to classify the various actions which occur during a given process into five classifications. These are usually known as operations, transportations, inspections, delays, and storages. A number of professional organizations have suggested standard flow-charting symbols, but as yet none has achieved universal acceptance. The symbols used are therefore largely a matter of individual preference. For purposes of illustration, however, clerical functions may be represented by the following symbols.

Activities defined

Operation. An operation occurs when an object is intentionally changed in any of its physical or chemical characteristics, is assembled or disassembled from another object, or is arranged or prepared for another operation, transportation, inspection, or storage. An operation also occurs when information is given or received or when planning or calculating takes place. If it is an originating activity, a circle is often placed within the circle. The addition of supplemental information is usually indicated by enclosing parallel lines within the circle.

Transportation. A transportation occurs when an object is moved from one place to another, except when such movements are a part of the operation or are caused by the operator at the work station during an operation or an inspection.

[4]Pages 205-206 originate from the Work Study Training Centre, Canadian National Railways, Montreal.

Inspection. An inspection occurs when an object is examined for identification or is verified for quality or quantity in any of its characteristics.

Delay. A delay occurs to an object when conditions apart from those which intentionally change the physical or chemical characteristics of the object do not permit or require immediate performance of the next planned action.

Storage. A storage occurs when an object is kept and protected against unauthorized removal, shown by an upright triangle.

Combined activity. When it is desired to show activities performed either concurrently or by the same operator at the same work station, the symbols for those activities are combined, as shown by the circle placed within the square, to represent a combined operation and inspection.

When unusual situations outside the range of the definitions are encountered, the intent of the definitions summarized in the following tabulation will enable the analyst to make the proper classifications.

Classification	Predominant result
Operation	Produces or accomplishes
Transportation	Moves
Inspection	Verifies
Delay	Interferes
Storage	Keeps

Flow-charting the procedures[5]

Drawing a flow chart of the procedures is a useful and rapid method for committing to working papers the different steps used in a given procedure. This technique is the procedure analyst's way of recording facts and expressing ideas in "shorthand," much as engineers use drafting techniques. It becomes much easier to understand and visualize the interrelationships of numerous steps in a complex procedure through a study of well-drawn flow charts than through the reading of lengthy procedure descriptions. Also, the flow-charting technique forces the analyst to make sure that he has not overlooked a procedure step and that all documents are traced to their ultimate destination. Finally, flow charting

[5]Pages 206-211 were excerpted from an article in *The New York Certified Public Accountant,* July 1959 issue. The author is Henry Gunders, partner, Price Waterhouse & Co.

helps the analyst to be certain that, in reviewing the procedure, he has not overlooked important procedural steps.

The main purpose of a flow chart is to show the interrelationship between documents in a system and to portray the sequence and nature of the various processing activities. This means that the various documents must be graphically represented, that the flow of information must be shown (usually by a line), and that the nature of each processing step must be described by suitable symbols.

The shape of each symbol signifies something about the general nature of the function being performed. If greater specificity is desired, code letters can be used in conjunction with these symbols. For example, addition could be coded as "A," posting as "P," transcribing as "T," and so on. At times, one or two words might be used on the flow chart to further describe the operation. It is also desirable to indicate the documents being worked on by representing them by rectangles and describing their nature in a few words.

The number of copies of a document that are being prepared should be drawn. Working papers should also include a photocopy of each form —not blank, but rather showing all of the entries that would have been made in a typical transaction. The facts needed to construct a flow chart should be obtained by actual interview and observation of the employee who does the work. This is necessary because experience shows that even his immediate supervisor may not know precisely what is being done, though he may know what should be done. Flow charts of existing procedures should be drawn as the interview proceeds. They can be drawn much more quickly than longhand notes of procedures could be written. Also, the technique of taking notes is much more likely to result in failing to trace each procedure flow to its conclusion than the flow-charting technique because note-taking does not force the analyst to notice and resolve loose ends.

The best method to be used when questioning a clerk so as to elicit complete information is difficult to describe. It depends on whether the one being interviewed is naturally articulate and communicative or merely answers specific questions put to him. At best, it is a skill learned from experience. The CPA should also go over the flow chart with the interviewee before ending the interview, to be sure that nothing has been missed.

Illustration of flow-charting technique

A sequence of clerical procedures for recording cash receipts in the branch offices of a consumer loan company is described and then charted below.

1. Cash or checks and a passbook are received from the borrower at the cashier's window.

2. The borrower's detail loan receivable ledger card is pulled from a file that is arranged in alphabetic sequence.
3. The borrower's detail loan receivable "due-date" ledger card is pulled from another file that is arranged according to date on which payment is due.
4. The "alphabetic" ledger card is posted.
5. The posting in step 4 above is transcribed to the "due-date" ledger card.
6. The borrower's pass book is posted.
7. A receipt—in duplicate—is written.
8. The pass book and, on request, the original of the receipt are returned to the borrower.
9. The duplicate receipt is retained in bound-book form.
10. Both detail ledger cards are placed in the cash drawer, together with cash remittances, to remain there until the close of the day's business.
11. After the close of the day's business, a report of the day's collections is prepared in duplicate.
12. Cash receipts are listed on a duplicate deposit slip.
13. Totals shown on the deposit slip and the collection report are compared.
14. The collection report original is mailed to the general office.
15. The collection report duplicate is filed at the branch office.
16. The deposit slips and the remittances are sent to the bank.

A flow chart of this procedure is shown in Figure 2, page 209; the number shown next to each step relates to the procedure description above.

The symbols used in the flow chart help the analyst spot functions that are basically unproductive, such as transcribing, filing and refiling, and so forth.

Flow chart analysis

The purpose intended to be served by each step shown on procedural flow charts should be questioned during the analysis of existing procedures. This questioning should serve to reveal any principles of good procedural practice to which existing procedures do not adhere.

When this questioning process is applied to the brief case study set forth above, the analyst will find the symbol T on several occasions, indicating that the same data is rewritten several times. In ascertaining whether this is necessary, he would form the opinion that posting of the two ledger cards could be combined, and that the collection report could be prepared simultaneously at the time of ledger card posting. He would ask himself whether, in place of the pass book, a prescheduled list of the diminishing loan balances and a coupon book would make it unnecessary to use a pass book, and would also save the cost of returning the pass

Figure 2

FLOW CHART I

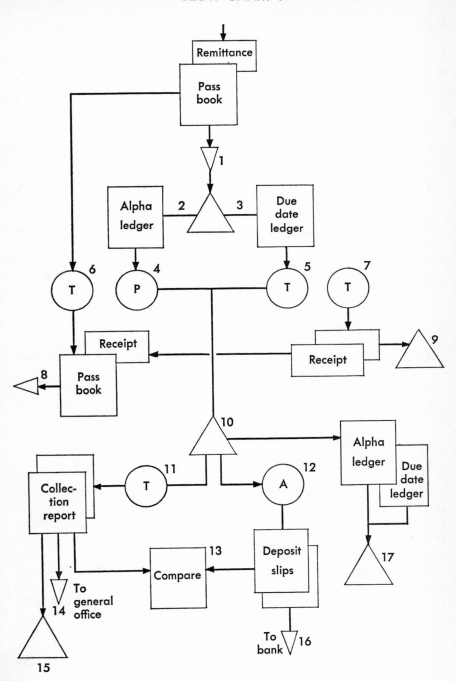

book to the borrower. He would question the need for maintaining two detail loan ledger cards for each borrower. He would wonder why the ledger cards cannot be replaced in their proper place in the files immediately after posting, so that it would be unnecessary to refile them later. The need for a receipt and its duplicate in book form would be challenged in favor of stamping a coupon stub "paid," or having the borrower's canceled check be considered as a receipt.

Procedure simplification

The CPA would then attempt to translate the answers to each of these queries into an approach for simplifying the procedure. Figure 3, page 211, illustrates a revised cash receipts procedure in simplified form.

1. Cash or check and the payment coupon are received from the borrower at the cashier's window.
2. The borrower's detail loan receivable ledger card is pulled from a file that is arranged in alphabetic sequence. (Due date is notched in the margin of each ledger card for rapid determination of delinquent loans.)
3. Postings are made simultaneously to the borrower's detail ledger card, collection report, and receipt (in the event the borrower has failed to bring his payment coupon and pays in cash). A multicopy board is used for this purpose. The ledger card is refiled immediately after posting.
4. The receipt is given to the borrower, or the payment coupon stub is stamped "paid" and returned.
5. Cash receipts are listed on a duplicate deposit slip.
6. Totals shown on the deposit slip and on the collection report are compared.
7. The collection report original is mailed to the general office.
8. The collection report duplicate is filed at the branch office.
9. The deposits slips and the remittances are sent to the bank.

The revision of this procedure sequence has accomplished (1) reduction of clerical work from seventeen steps to nine, (2) consolidation of five postings into one, (3) lessening of the likelihood of making posting transcription errors through posting all documents simultaneously, and (4) faster release of receipts to bank.

The technique of paper work simplification is another one of the tools available to the CPA. By using paper work simplification principles and procedures, he can render constructive services that will aid his client's clerical staffs to increase their productivity and efficiency.

What to look for. In analyzing flow diagrams the consultant should look for lengthy moves between operations. Long distances can become expensive, particularly when they involve the time of productive personnel. Conveyers, fork lifts, and the like, will usually remedy this situation.

Flow charts will often point out changes in work flows and backtracking. A change in procedure embracing the U-shaped layout would overcome backtracking to a considerable extent. In the physical movement of

Figure 3

FLOW CHART II

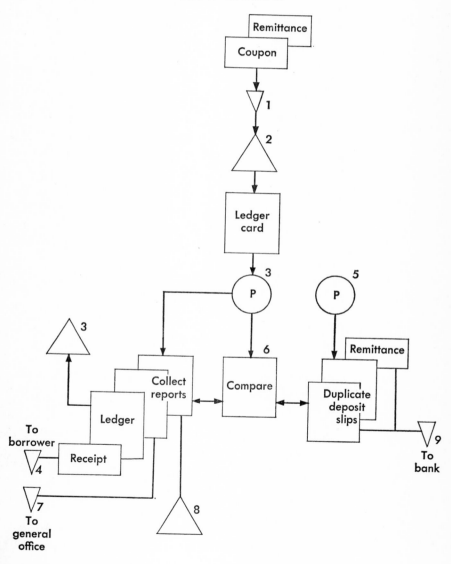

equipment, it is often expensive to move heavy equipment, whereas lighter equipment involves little expense or interruption. Improvements can also be obtained by combining related activities.

Process chart. Another method of graphically representing the co-ordinated activity of men, machines, or both, is to use a multiple activity process chart. Such a chart lays stress on timing problems. It is used to direct attention to idle capacity, to balance work loads, and to reduce job cycle time. It is also helpful in assignment problems.

Once the procedures have been charted and committed to working papers, the next step is to determine productivity in a systems analysis.

A Case Study

Another problem is dealt with in this chapter in the form of a case study, and as such gives the accountant the opportunity to review a problem in its actual surroundings. The example which follows is a real one, but for obvious reasons is not to be identified with the operation of any particular company. It is intended as an introduction to a few specifics of systems and procedures.

Paper-work problem

The procedure deals with paper work in connection with a sales order. Most companies have this problem and are strongly aware of the fact that the elapsed period from the time of agreement with the customer until the engineering, production planning, stock selection, or shipping departments can take action to satisfy the customer is just as important, hour for hour, as the elapsed time in manufacturing. Yet most delivery promises to customers are usually predicated on present backlog and manufacturing time.

Objectives of reorganization

A few years ago, management in this particular case realized that the need for improvement in processing sales orders demanded better procedure and organization. Management direction was therefore to establish an effective order department having three principal functions:

1. Receive original customer or dealer orders, edit, produce sufficient copies for all purposes, and consistently complete this work, regardless of peak loads, within a maximum time of one elapsed day. Also process invoices and back orders within one day after shipment. It is to be noted here that the average elapsed time with previous procedure often exceeded two weeks.

2. Make all contacts with customers concerning delivery information.
3. Advise planning and production departments of customers' anticipated needs.

One of the major benefits expected from the new procedure and organization was to relieve the sales departments of clerical details and delivery follow-up contacts, and so enable them to focus all their attention on their real job of selling products.

The first stage in systems work, after management has specified the objective policies, is to gather all the facts concerning present methods and jobs and ascertain the reason or lack of reason behind each step. The new procedure and organization must accomplish the function the old one tried to do in all its intricate detail, but the job must be smooth, well timed, and at the lowest possible cost in order to justify a change.

Previous organization on order processing functions was by several distinct product lines, each within its own separated group. No two had identical methods. Even the order forms differed. The order typing department covered several but not all product lines and the invoicing and back orders were completely retyped in another section, which reported to the accounting department. Each product division exerted pressure on the accounting typing section to give preference to its own work, and when that pressure did not produce results, some elected to do their own typing to achieve the desired results.

Assembling all the facts

Numerous detailed process flow charts and forms distribution charts were made picturing the travel and paper work in connection with the orders of each product line. This was done in consultation and co-operation with the respective key personnel, who were sold on the management objectives that the order department was to be established for their benefit (this is really important!). It is noted that all personnel who furnished information during this study were asked to sign the respective portions of their chart. Invariably, more factual information was discovered from this request. This is also very important because one simply *must* have all the facts.

How were improvement and acceptance developed? First all possible ideas were solicited from those who live with the task. The process flow charts were reviewed with the same people who helped to make them and with their immediate superiors. Many suggestions for improvement were noted and carefully considered. Then the charts were compared and several tentative solutions prepared. From all this a single flow pattern for all product lines was devised and subjected to the criticism of all personnel affected.

It was apparent from the step-by-step study of previous methods that there was nothing mysterious or complicated about the several product lines. All operations could be classified into functions. In all this work if people can be so dealt with that the problem becomes theirs and there is a common interest to do a better job, much of the resentment to criticism and change disappears. Management policy was that no one should lose his job because of work simplification—that helps too.

Importance of precise information

Editing orders was a rough job that supposedly required much experience and know-how. However, this secret could be spelled out so that the original order could be properly and completely written. Much time and money can be spent in correspondence, wires, and phone calls just because certain information is vague or lacking on the order. To write orders correctly, we must have tools. The answer to the question, "Why so much editing?" was found in the design of check list order forms and thus, by management direction, responsibility was placed where it belongs, namely, directly at the source. In addition to eliminating the delay in producing a complete order, the arrangement of data on these forms made preparation of typed copies easier and therefore faster. Editing became auditing and not a new creation of the order record.

The next problem was to produce all needed copies for order, invoicing, and back orders by the method best suited to that particular case. It involved products of complicated industry, having large and small units, variables, and with an obligation to furnish service parts for almost every unit ever built. The volume of orders ranged from nine thousand to fourteen thousand per month.

At some point in the study, the systems man is wise to solicit the services of forms representatives, but not before he has fully studied the problem, determined definite objectives, and arrived at several practicable solutions. In this case, real need was found for twenty copies of the order for all purposes, including planning, shop, engineering, order follow-up, unit construction records, shipping, notification of shipment, invoicing, and back ordering. Naturally, the idea was to do this job in one writing.

At this stage, the forms people were allowed to compete for the best solution of the task. Their respective proposals were carefully compared by giving proper consideration to the following points:
1. Which would do the most satisfactory job in quality, smooth operation, flexibility?
2. Cost of operation; personnel
3. Cost of forms and equipment
4. Speed of delivery after ordering forms

The flexibility of the duplication process as compared to carbon set forms is an important factor when one has a varying number of forms dependent upon use; so is the fact that duplicating masters can be combined with carbon set forms if needed for a particular purpose. The duplicating master process was selected in this case. Other problems may work better with continuous or one-time carbon set forms, or perhaps with punched card accounting.

Results of group procedure thinking

The results of group procedure thinking in this case were:
1. Management's objectives were realized in prompt processing of orders and invoices at low cost.
2. The sales department was relieved of customer contact in respect to deliveries.

In achieving the first objective, operational and forms cost reduction were affected by:
1. Eliminating separate typing of order, back orders, and invoices
2. Eliminating separate typing of "notification of shipment" forms
3. Eliminating retyping of parts orders through the use of a combination master and carbon set (this comprised about 40 per cent of all typing work)
4. Avoiding copying errors

In achieving the second objective, relieving the sales department of customer contact in respect to deliveries, orders were consolidated for all products into one central order file and order register controls set up whereby the status of any customer's order could be determined at a moment's notice.

In addition to the installation of the procedure, task distribution charts were made, the organization of the department charted, and job duties written for all important functions. A daily status of order and invoicing report was given to management to permit them to judge results quickly. The procedure job does not end there. Everyone in the organization is encouraged to make suggestions and to criticize the services of the order department. It exists to perform an important service at a reasonable cost. A net savings in cost of about 25 per cent was realized with 11 per cent increase in personnel and 50 per cent increase in volume.

Arousing interest in procedures

The basic thinking which governs procedures work has been discussed and a typical systems study examined. Now what about arousing enthusiasm for better procedures in the entire clerical task force? This teamwork method can be referred to as "participation thinking." The lone technician can usually present his case to top level management so beautifully that it seemingly will operate itself. Sometimes, however, when an experted procedure is installed there is a rude awakening; it just doesn't work mainly because:
1. The operating people did not participate in building the structure.

As the cake can be no better than the ingredients that are mixed together, so the solution can be no better than the basic facts, which must be obtained from the man on the job.

2. One man cannot possibly live long enough to know as much as the group does about the details which make the delicate mechanism tick.

In the fact-gathering stage of procedures work, the chief interest of the idea clearing house should be to stimulate attention and interest in the project. The line supervisor or worker is usually more interested in improving the status of his job than is the systems man or anyone else. He should be made part of the team.

How procedure studies benefit the worker

The worker is told that procedures studies eliminate only the unnecessary, reduce costs, and thereby permit his company to pay better wages. Management must back up that statement, together with a policy that will enhance the feeling of security.

Each person contacted in the survey should be given an opportunity to study the work flow charts. These questions should be asked:

1. What can be eliminated?
2. Is there some step that can be combined with some other operation?
3. Can the sequence be changed to improve the work flow?
4. Is there too much travel and why?
5. Do we need to accomplish the tasks by a completely new method?

Surely the systems analyst should know most of the answers, but he gets the co-operation of others by letting them think and make the suggestions for improvement. Then—and this is important—he gives them full credit and tells their bosses about it. The systems man has nothing to lose and everything to gain, multiplied by as many people as he works with.

Clear presentation encourages participation

A good way to encourage participation thinking is to clearly work out alternative procedure chart solutions. The advantages and disadvantages of each should be lined up just as in a ledger account—debits and credits. The one best way then becomes obvious. The important thing is to let the line supervisor or operator choose the right answer. It then becomes his solution and has a good chance to live.

The systems man has no mysterious tools that others cannot, with a little patience and practice, be taught to use. A few tools for systems work are:

1. Forms distribution charts
2. Work flow charts
3. Work distribution charts
4. Procedure charts

The important thing is to get the clerical work story down on paper.

It requires just a little imagination to get the knack of writing it down, preferably in picture form. Line personnel must be taught to do this—it is much easier than writing a narrative story on the procedure, much more coherent, and, most helpful of all, the procedure chart is invaluable in enabling the line supervisor to see the room for improvement himself.

In small groups the proposal is then talked over, changes are made, and finally all agree. It is no problem to get management approval when all concerned have their signatures on the proposal.

Line supervisors really like job analysis work and many become enthusiastic. Soon a chain reaction results, and the systems administrator has many thinking assistants with no need for an elaborate department of experts.

Data Analysis[6]

The analysis of data, while a separate intellectual process, invariably follows fast upon the gathering of facts in the hands of a competent systems man.

Just as the data to be gathered will depend on the objectives of the survey, so also will the analysis itself. However, the alert systems man will be on constant watch for subsidiary advantages he can offer to his client. As examples:

In a study to speed billing, he should watch for possibilities that goods shipped are not billed.

In a study to protect against pilferage of inventory, he may observe opportunities for economies through a better ordering system.

These facts should be conveyed to the client as by-products for further study on the client's part; their detailed examination may be time-consuming and of little immediate consequence to the client.

As a matter of common working practice, the CPA should endeavor to analyze facts as soon as they are collected rather than completing his entire data-gathering process and then setting about analysis. The underlying reason is that effective analysis invariably demands that (1) more facts be developed, (2) data already gathered requires questioning, or (3) factual interpretation may require revision.

The process of analysis calls for a study of the facts derived to reveal points leading to the solution of the problem.

Illustration. In a study designed to accelerate the billing process, the CPA flow-charts the handling of shipping reports. He develops the fact that

[6]Pages 217-223 are excerpted from an article in *The California CPA Quarterly,* December 1961. The author is Maurice B. T. Davies, partner, Lybrand, Ross Bros. & Montgomery, Los Angeles.

217

shipping reports are transmitted to a clerk for invoicing, and that this clerk has the additional duties of (1) accepting telephone orders from customers and (2) acting as secretary to a salesman. These three duties are such that invoicing takes third priority, thus leading to a backlog. The CPA's analysis brings him to the conclusion that he should explore the possibility of a change in work distribution.

Points that should be borne in mind during analysis are as follows:

Establish a firm bridge between the facts and the analysis. If undetermined facts have to be assumed, endeavor to substantiate these assumptions.

Analytical conclusions in a systems survey often have a direct bearing on volumes. Be sure that volumes are considered.

Considerations of internal check often conflict with considerations of speed, streamlining, simplicity, and economy. Be sure they are not overlooked.

Redistribution of work tasks often needs to be studied. Break work tasks down by reference to basic elements of the flow charts, and develop separate work sheets to show work tasks by individuals, specifying approximate time data.

Where analysis requires anything but the most obvious reasoning process, record the analytical thinking in the working papers.

Above all, be sure that the analysis makes a direct contribution toward approaching a solution or possible solution, derived from the initial facts.

Developing conclusions

To summarize, at this point the CPA should have pursued his survey by determining the client's needs and establishing an orderly process for conducting his survey, gathering relevant facts, and analyzing the implications of those facts.

His next task is one of drawing conclusions, which becomes the final step before defining a recommended course of action. Conclusions should generally be expressed in terms of: (1) an interpretation based on the analysis of facts, and (2) a tentative course of action which should be explored.

The CPA should check his conclusions with the client before taking additional action. This affords the following advantages:

It permits the client to validate the conclusions and to raise any questions regarding the CPA's data, analysis, interpretation, and reasoning.

It enables the CPA and his client to discuss the merits and disadvantages of alternative courses of action and to discard those which are unacceptable.

It eliminates any element of surprise and thus establishes a degree of receptiveness on the client's part for the eventual recommendations.

We have intentionally broken down the CPA's approach into a series of progressive actions. At the risk of repetition, we would emphasize that, in point of time, they might easily follow each other in such rapid succession that it is barely possible to separate one from another. In a single element of a system, for example, the CPA might easily get the facts, analyze them, and draw conclusions in less than an hour. However, in a complex situation these three processes will tend to become clearly definable and separate tasks. Recognition that they are in fact separate will help protect the CPA from errors of judgment in conducting his survey.

Producing recommendations

The purpose of a systems survey is generally to produce recommendations for adoption by the client. Each recommendation should meet two criteria: (1) its adoption, either alone or in combination with the adoption of other recommendations, should resolve the problems which gave rise to the survey, and (2) it should be acceptable to the client in terms of its being practical.

Very often the CPA's most difficult task is that of convincing his client to accept his recommendations. For this reason he should be guided by the following approaches:

Explain why the recommendation is made.

If alternative courses exist, explain why the selected course is chosen in preference to others.

Describe how it should be installed.

Explain the benefits to be gained by adopting it.

Be sure that it is not too complicated for handling by the client's staff, and, in any event, aim for simplicity.

If it consists of component parts, break it down into a series of component recommendations.

Prepare the client in advance so that he accepts partial authorship for the recommendation and is not caught by surprise.

Having developed his recommendations, the CPA should plan an orderly program for gaining acceptance. No uniform procedure is applicable for this, but he should consider the following processes:

Where recommendations require the co-operation of subordinate staff members, endeavor to gain acceptance at their level in advance.

Even though individual recommendations may have been discussed with and approved by the key client executive, arrange a meeting with him to cover the recommendations in their entirety.

Finally, present the recommendations in terms of a written report, procedures, or flow charts for permanent reference by the client and as a guide for him in installing them.

The CPA may encounter opposition from his client to one or more of his recommendations. In such cases, he is faced with these alternatives, the selection of which must depend on his judgment:

Convince the client of the validity of the recommendation through justifying it.

Modify the recommendation to make it acceptable to the client, provided that this does not prejudice its effectiveness.

Develop a substitute recommendation that will achieve similar results.

If convinced that the client's position is correct, abandon the recommendation. (Careful work by the CPA during the conclusion phase should preclude this alternative.)

If convinced that the client's position is untenable and no other way exists, include the recommendation in the report, recognizing that it will probably not be accepted.

The method of presenting recommendations is described in the following section.

Concluding report

A report, whether oral or written, is the essential conclusion of the systems survey. It is the communication between the CPA and his client in response to the task originally assigned.

The client engaged the CPA by saying, in effect: "This is my problem. What do I do about it?" The CPA's report should say, in effect: "Here's what you do about it."

An oral report is most desirable. At this stage, the CPA should describe his recommendations and attempt to gain the client's concurrence. He should arrange for this presentation: (1) at a predetermined time, (2) in a relaxed and unhurried manner, (3) with key people present, (4) using visual aids where necessary, and (5) covering his complete recommendations.

In addition to securing advance acceptance, the CPA is thus protected, to some measure, against client conflict and is able to present his written report in less detail.

Unless the client requires a comprehensive written report, the CPA should limit it to bare essentials. The following format should generally be adequate:

A brief letter of transmittal summarizing the major points
An index to the report
A short introduction summarizing the objectives of the survey
The recommendations themselves (see page 219) presented in logical sequence and numbered serially, describing for each: (1) existing conditions, (2) the disadvantages inherent in them, (3) the precise course of

action recommended, and (4) the benefits to be derived from taking this action

Plans for installation

Other matters revealed during the course of the survey which should receive the client's attention

The written report should be given to the client as soon as possible after completion of the survey. It should preferably be submitted in person, rather than by mail, so as to permit discussion between the CPA and the client. (The style of binding the report should be a matter of discretion for the CPA.)

The written report should serve as a permanent record for the client to enable him to adopt and install the recommendations, to follow progress, and to use for reference purposes. It should be carefully edited so as to leave the client with a clear course of action devoid of inaccuracies or obscurities.

Assistance in installation

The client derives value from the CPA's work only when the recommendations are put into effect. In most smaller businesses the client will expect the CPA to provide major assistance in this phase.

The CPA should establish a clear understanding with his client at this point to the effect that:

He will not *install* the recommendations, since this is a management function, but will rather *assist in installing* them. The extent of this assistance may be as superficial or comprehensive as a client and his CPA mutually agree.

Assistance in installation is an engagement separate from the preceding systems survey.

Just as in the case of the survey itself, a written understanding of the objectives, approach, and cost should be defined.

While it is not the purpose here to discuss the installation following a survey, it may be in order to mention a few salient points to guide the CPA:

The work should be broken down into a series of projects, and deadlines should be set for each.

Maximum participation by the client organization should be encouraged—both to assure continuity and to reduce costs.

Written procedures and/or flow charts should be prepared and published wherever needed.

Training or orientation sessions for the client's staff may be needed.

The key executive should be kept informed by means of periodic— but brief—progress reports.

While speed in installation is generally desirable, the pace should be dictated by the ability of the client's staff to absorb the new practices.

Studied attention should be paid to details; neglect of such details can destroy the effectiveness of the system.

It may be necessary to modify some of the recommendations made in the original survey.

Decisions made during the installation should predominantly be those of the client rather than of the CPA, who is an assistant and adviser.

The question of fees should also be considered. As distinct from his position when conducting a survey, the CPA is rarely able to estimate the time he will spend in an installation, since this depends almost entirely on conditions within the client organization, the degree of assistance received, the extent of co-operation and opposition encountered, and the pace at which the client is able to move. For these reasons, the CPA should arrange fees in terms of hourly or daily rates and should submit his bills at regular intervals—say monthly.

Follow-up visits

No matter how valid the recommendations and how effective the installation, the new system is in constant danger of deterioration through human failings, changes of staff, new or changed operating conditions, increased or reduced volumes of activity, changes in management philosophy, new demands on the system, changes in procedures, and misunderstandings of the system.

The significance of these conditions may not be apparent to the client. However, their effect on the system will tend to be adverse.

For these reasons, the CPA should arrange with the client for periodic follow-up visits. (These may well become a part of his regular audits.) Through these follow-up visits, he can evaluate the effectiveness of the system, identify needs for change and/or corrective action, and can provide for his client an assurance that the system is kept up to date and provides permanent value and benefits.

A *typical recommendation arising from a systems survey*

Discontinue keeping the general ledger by manual methods. Your chief bookkeeper personally keeps the general ledger in pen and ink and prepares a monthly trial balance. He estimates that this activity consumes never less than fifteen hours a month, and, because of the continuing interruptions he experiences, he frequently has to spend additional time to locate and correct errors.

An outside agency prepares all your accounting data on punched cards with the exception of about ten journal vouchers a month, which the chief bookkeeper posts manually to the general ledger. The remaining entries he posts from totals of tabulated punched card listings.

The present practice exposes you to these disadvantages:

1. There is a time lag of about three to five days from receipt of the tabulated listings to preparation of the trial balance.

2. The chief bookkeeper works extensively beyond regular hours and is being paid overtime at the rate of $4.80 an hour for late work.

3. As the general ledger is posted principally from totals of tabulated listings, reference to the content of any individual account requires examination of these listings. (It is not practicable to estimate the average time spent monthly on this type of reference.)

We recommend that the general ledger no longer be kept manually. Instead, the few journal vouchers that are posted manually should be given to the punched card tabulating agency, and instructions should be given to submit, on a separate page for each general ledger account, a listing of the postings to that account with opening and closing balances. These listings should be filed chronologically by account in replacement of the general ledger as now kept.

Adoption of this practice would provide you with these benefits:

1. The general ledger and trial balance would reach you at the same time as the other tabulated reports. This would enable you to receive monthly balance sheets, profit and loss statements and other financial reports three to five days earlier than you are now getting them.

2. Your costs would be reduced by at least $62 a month. (The agency would charge an additional $10 a month for this service. However, you would save at least fifteen hours overtime—$72—paid to the chief bookkeeper, as well as the cost of time spent in locating errors.)

3. Reference to detailed items in the general ledger accounts could be achieved more rapidly, as all data would be kept in one file rather than be spread between the manually kept ledger and the tabulated listings.

Clerical Work Measurement

Having successfully met the challenge of data analysis, the systems man is now ready to devote his attention to the subject of work measurement.

In the realm of the controller's function, clerical cost control has been considered of prime importance. Such control presupposes the ability to *measure*—with as much accuracy as is necessary and practicable—the magnitude and cost of the various clerical tasks required to carry on a business. Various techniques have been developed to measure clerical work, all of which are designed to answer with varying degrees of precision the need for clerical cost control.

Basically, the requirements of a work measurement system for the office are quite similar to those for the factory which have been well established in the form of stopwatch and formula time study over several decades. Frequently one finds companies whose system of controlling direct labor through the medium of time study and cost accounting leaves little to be desired; yet, payroll costs for clerical labor, often of substantial importance, are subject to no control whatever.

To illustrate, it is unusual to find productivity variances of as much as 100 per cent in the productivity of, for example, two experienced drillpress operators; by way of contrast it may be added that reading speeds of 300 to 400 words per minute are average, but speeds in excess of 1,000 words per minute have been observed.

It may appear at first glance that the need for measurement of clerical productivity will be substantially minimized by reason of the introduction of high-speed electronic data processing equipment into the office. However, the impact of the potential of such equipment will probably not eliminate the need for clerical operatives performing manual office work. In fact, among the most advanced installations of clerical work measurement systems are those of companies which have consistently been in the forefront of exploring the uses of high-speed electronic data processing and late model tabulating equipment.

The establishment and maintenance of a work measurement system serves a number of purposes:

1. It serves as a means for determining what productivity may be expected as a fair day's work.

2. It provides the necessary data for budgeting costs, based on work standards, according to various levels of activity. Frequently, such budgets call attention to possible reductions in overhead expenses previously thought to be "fixed," when shrinking sales volume demands that such reductions be made. Moreover, in businesses subject to seasonal peaks, the need for additional work force may be forecast with reasonable accuracy, both as to the time and the numbers required.

3. It gives management a method for appraising the efficiency of supervision. Ofttimes, a supervisor may be thought to be efficient by reason of his prompt submission of reports and other accounting data. This apparent efficiency may be merely the result of overstaffing in his department. A quantitative analysis of clerical tasks tends to disclose such situations and to provide management with a tool for continually measuring departmental efficiency against a reasonably accurate yardstick.

4. It serves as a formal procedure for constantly reviewing accounting methods and systems, with a view to lowering clerical costs. Such review represents an area where the accounting practitioner can render his clients a substantial service. In the process of making system studies, there are usually a number of alternatives meriting consideration. One of the most important considerations in selecting the best alternative is that of labor

cost. Clerical work standards provide the means for forecasting the respective labor cost of each of the alternatives; in addition, it becomes practical to state the costs of the present system in the same terms as the projected alternative system. This can prevent the common mistake of comparing the productivity under the *present* system, together with the inefficiencies it may contain, with that of an *ideal* projected system, and the resulting disappointment when the new system falls far short of expectations.

5. It can provide the chief accounting officer who has supervisory responsibility over sizeable clerical staffs with the necessary controls over the volume of clerical work, and the staff required to process it.

6. A clerical work measurement system helps in the development of a system for employee upgrading and salary adjustments in the clerical field, based on productivity rather than on length of service, or on a general impression that the quality of work has been satisfactory. During the process of setting clerical work standards, it is generally discovered that the productivity of various experienced clerks performing essentially the same type of work varies widely. This information is useful for determining what salary adjustments shall be made. As a corollary, these standards may well serve as a guide in pre-employment testing. While it is quite usual to require typists, key punch operators, and the like, to be able to produce a specified quantity of work in order to qualify for employment, the same requirement is not usually applied to file clerks, posting clerks, and so on. The reason may be found in the unavailability of proper productivity criteria to be applied to these areas of manual clerical work.

Clerical incentives

7. A clerical work measurement system greatly facilitates setting up clerical incentives. There are many indications that the proper application of incentives to clerical work can produce substantial benefits. Researchers in the field of work standards believe that productivity for tasks performed under incentive exceeds that of nonincentive work by approximately 30 per cent. It is not suggested that such incentives are applicable to all types of clerical work; nevertheless, increases of as much as 60 to 100 per cent have been noted as the result of the installation of the incentive system. It should be noted that such incentives may be of various types, financial or otherwise, for groups of employees or for individuals. Usually, the mere introduction of a clerical work measurement system will result in some increases in production, based on nothing more than the feeling of the employees that the amount and quality of work turned out by them is to be subjected to constant review and evaluation. Clerical work standards, coupled with continuing reporting

of work volume, can provide the necessary facts for critical review of employment requisitions.

8. It is frequently discovered during examinations of areas of excessive clerical expense that no control exists over additions to the payroll. If any review of requisitions for additional employment is made, the resulting decision is often based on nothing more than the clerical supervisor's insistence that additional clerks are needed. Clerical work standards, coupled with continuing reporting of work volume, can provide the necessary facts for critical review of employment requisitions.

Any discussion of the purposes and techniques of clerical work measurement would be incomplete without a discussion of the work content to be analyzed.

Segregating unmeasurable jobs

Many clerical supervisors, while agreeing in principle that the establishment of clerical work standards may produce beneficial results, contend that too many jobs in their offices depend on the use of judgment and are therefore unmeasurable. However, detailed analysis usually shows that what generally passes for judgment may actually be nothing more than comparison, inspection, selection, or classification, all of which may be measured. Doubtless there will be a number of tasks of a true judgment nature, requiring creative thought not subject to measurement. The segregation of such tasks from those of a routine nature is frequently productive of substantial benefits because it pinpoints those tasks where compensation is based on the exercise of judgment which may—in point of time—comprise only a small portion of the task. For example, a detailed study of work done by credit men, sales correspondents, buyers, and certain types of professional workers may disclose an inordinate amount of rather routine clerical work which could be performed far less expensively by lower-paid clerks.

What technique should be used to translate the general objective of establishing control over clerical expenses into a system of clerical work measurement and volume and efficiency reporting? Experience indicates that no one best technique exists. Rather, there are a number of possible approaches which will be discussed in detail. Each situation must be analyzed, considering such matters as the size of the clerical staff to be studied, the complexity of the tasks under review, and the likelihood of realizing clerical cost reductions greater than the costs of installation and maintenance of the system.

The first and most obvious technique is that of *simple comparison* of the productivity attained in one's own office with that of other companies in a similar line of business. A number of rather ambitious projects of this type have been undertaken by such groups as the Life Office Management Association, the National Office Management Association, and the National Retail Dry Goods Association. Although the com-

panies participating in these studies often have fairly comparable procedures and have submitted their production statistics in accordance with
uniform questionnaires, attempts to get a reasonable amount of correlation
from these statistics have not generally been successful. An exception is
represented by those data relating to clerical tasks where productivity is
largely controlled by electrically driven equipment, such as tabulating,
duplicating, and addressing machines.

What are the reasons for this lack of conformity? Principally, it may
be due to the difficulties involved in attempting to state the detailed
conditions under which given production was attained, and to the problems encountered when trying to adjust the raw production data for
differences in conditions whose dimensions are not usually expressed
quantitatively.

Most office tasks, in point of total time consumed, are of a manual or
semimanual nature. Even though productivity rates for these tasks are
compared for companies within the same industry, substantial variations
are usually encountered. One is forced to the conclusion that industry-
wide productivity statistics have greatly limited usefulness for setting
clerical work standards.

A modification of the comparative technique may be used for companies whose operations in their various offices are reasonably comparable.
Compilations of production data for each task performed in each of the
offices may be undertaken with a view to comparing the respective efficiency of each office. It is possible to obtain fairly reliable data in this
manner, provided that every attempt is made to maintain uniformity in
the performance of the various tasks. However, these data can do no
more than permit a ranking of the offices in the order of their efficiency;
thus, this technique merely affords knowledge as to what *is* being done,
not what *should* be done.

Unit time standards

The second technique is that of the compilation of *historical unit
time standards*. Unit time standards may be defined as statements of
the time required to process a given unit of work, as reported by the
employee doing the work. For example, a claims adjuster may report
the completion of 160 pending claims cases during a 40-hour workweek;
the historical unit time standard would then be 0.25 hours, or 4 cases
per hour.

It is believed that this type of study, while perhaps not particularly
sophisticated, can nevertheless produce substantial benefits. To begin
with, it does not require the skill of an industrial engineer, as do certain
of the more complex techniques to be subsequently described. It is
perhaps more universally applicable than the other techniques, because
of its usefulness in studying the work content of relatively small offices.

The application of the technique usually begins with the selection of a department (or an employee) whose tasks are fairly repetitive, require the use of key-driven machines or of simple manual operations, and are subject to a minimum of exception cases and disturbances. Examples of such tasks might be billing, posting of accounts receivable ledgers, extension of time cards, and the like. Each of the employees performing these tasks is interviewed, and a detailed listing of the various operations is prepared. At the same time, the interviewer should note the general working conditions, impressions concerning the tempo of the office, and any other pertinent matters. It is important that the nature of the work units chosen be described in sufficient detail to permit adequate comparisons of production times. For example, a unit described simply as "type a letter" is not sufficiently descriptive of the magnitude of the task to be useful. The number of lines in each letter would be a far better indication.

It is often advisable to have the departmental supervisor work together with the analyst, beginning in the early stages of the study. This tends to give the supervisor an appreciation of the importance of clerical cost control and productivity. Moreover, his participation will tend to facilitate his subsequent administration of the system when time standards have been set. Finally, if the supervisor is convinced of the fairness of the standards, he will be better able to justify them if that should become necessary.

After all of the operations in the department have been listed, they should be suitably coded or otherwise described. Reporting schedules are then prepared which will permit uniform recording of the work done during the time to be reported on. One type of schedule provides for vertical listing of the tasks performed by each employee, while the column headings indicate the days being reported on (see Figure 4, page 229). Another type, developed by a leading insurance company, consists of a daily report sheet called a "time ladder" which graphically shows the hours and parts of hours of the working day. This report sheet is completed by the employee by merely marking the starting and ending times of a given operation, the code number of the operation, and the volume which has been processed (see Figure 5, page 230). Both types of schedules must include the operation code number, the elapsed time, and the volume, for each employee, reported on a daily basis.

It is well to prepare written instructions to employees describing the method to be used in completing the time report and to append completed time reports as exhibits. During the first few days of installation of time reporting, a daily review should be instituted to ascertain that the data is being properly shown. Time reports should be maintained for a period long enough to cover any weekly peak periods and should preferably include a month-end peak period as well.

The completed schedules should be summarized on work sheets showing total productive time used for each operation, number of units processed, and production per hour. The hourly production may be considered the actual *historical* unit time required for each operation.

After these analyses have been completed, comparisons of individual employees' productivity may be made if the work performed by them is sufficiently comparable. Substantial differences should be recorded and the reasons therefor analyzed. Such an analysis requires a close examination of the following points: method used, effort displayed, skill, and working conditions.

Actual observation of the employee will usually be required.

A modification of the technique is found in the application of sampling methods to time reporting. The advantage of this type of approach lies in its lower cost. The end use of the data which the sampling of clerical work is to provide should be considered in determining the sample size.

The result of all of the analysis completed up to this point has been merely the gathering of historical data. No attempt has been made as yet to determine what *should* be considered a fair rate of productivity.

Determining actual productivity

Inasmuch as the initial process of gathering of data requires merely that the employee account for all working hours, these initial data may contain excessive personal time. The purpose of the next step is the determination of the *productivity actually attained* by employees. This

Figure 4

EMPLOYEE TASK SHEET

		Department	**Personnel**
Employee's name	Noreen Smith	Supvr. approval	HDV
Duties	Secretary	Date	6/26/6-

Activity code	Description of task	Start time	Stop time	Elapsed time (minutes)	Volume
M1	Open mail	9:00	9:10	10	21
M2	Scan mail	9:10	9:30	20	21
M3	Rerout mail	9:30	9:35	5	17
TL	Type letters	9:35	10:20	45	7
PL	Proofread letters, etc.	10:20	10:30	10	7

Figure 5   **TIME SHEET**

Employee's name   **Noreen Smith**   Date   **6/26/6—**

8:00		11:05	2:10
8:05		11:10	2:15
8:10		11:15	2:20
8:15		11:20	2:25
8:20		11:25	2:30
8:25		11:30	2:35
8:30		11:35	2:40
8:35		11:40	2:45
8:40		11:45	2:50
8:45		11:50	2:55
8:50		11:55	3:00
8:55		12:00	3:05
9:00		12:05	3:10
9:05	M1: 21	12:10	3:15
9:10		12:15	3:20
9:15		12:20	3:25
9:20	M2: 21	12:25	3:30
9:25		12:30	3:35
9:30		12:35	3:40
9:35	M3: 17	12:40	3:45
9:40		12:45	3:50
9:45		12:50	3:55
9:50		12:55	4:00
9:55		1:00	4:05
10:00	TL: 7	1:05	4:10
10:05		1:10	4:15
10:10		1:15	4:20
10:15		1:20	4:25
10:20		1:25	4:30
10:25	PL: 7	1:30	4:35
10:30		1:35	4:40
10:35		1:40	4:45
10:40		1:45	4:50
10:45		1:50	4:55
10:50		1:55	5:00
10:55		2:00	
11:00		2:05	

Code

TL	Typing	M1	Open mail	M3	Reroute mail
PL	Proofreading	M2	Scan mail		

may be accomplished by measuring the time which will actually elapse during the completion of what was previously reported by the employee to be an hour's work. To illustrate, let us assume that the daily employee time reports showed an hourly typing production of 21 average invoices. A group of 21 reasonably average orders should then be given to the employee, and she should be asked to record the time required to complete the typing of invoices. Assuming that she reports an elapsed time of 40 minutes, the actually attained production is then 31.5 invoices per hour, or half again as much as was developed from the original data.

It should be noted that this actual attained productivity does not contain any allowance for personal time, fatigue, or unavoidable delay. The total allowance for all three factors is usually between 10 and 15 per cent. In addition, the actual attained productivity will have to be subjected to "leveling." The purpose of leveling or, as it is sometimes called, "performance rating," is to weight a given rate of performance so as to reflect its relation to that operator whose performance has been decided upon as "normal." For the previously cited example, the typist in question may be the best in the entire department. It would be unrealistic to expect others to equal her production. Therefore, the figure of 31.5 invoices to be produced per hour will have to be lowered in accordance with the analyst's concept of normal. Despite continued efforts of the industrial engineering profession to evolve truly scientific procedures it is believed that performance rating is still essentially subjective in nature.

The technique of clerical work measurement through the use of historical unit time standards lends itself rather readily to small offices and to those situations in large offices which require that one employee perform many different tasks each day. Further, the standards thus developed are easily justified. The main disadvantage of this technique is its limitation to *already existing* procedures; it cannot be used to determine the time requirements of a *projected* procedure.

Techniques for setting standards

To overcome this limitation, attempts have been made to develop techniques for setting clerical work standards on a predetermined basis through the use of micromotion film. While this technique is initially quite costly and is therefore used chiefly by large organizations and certain professional firms, it has produced results which have rather general applicability.

Micromotion film time study consists basically of filming operations with a special type of motion picture camera. The film of the operation to be time studied is analyzed by using a special time and motion projector. This projector permits showing the film at various rates of speed.

The projector also has a clutch which may be released to stop the film at any point. By means of a hand crank, the film can be projected, backward or forward, frame by frame, or can be stopped at any point. The number of frames projected can be determined through the use of a counter which is geared to the projection mechanism. A counter reading of 500 frames (assuming a filming speed of 1,000 frames per minute) indicates, for example, that film equal in length to half a minute has passed the projector lens. Any operation or part thereof can thus be accurately timed by counting the number of frames between the start and completion of an operation.

A brief explanation of certain terms customarily used in industrial time study and frequently used in measuring clerical work may be found useful.

Elements. Subdivisions of an operation which can be definitely recognized and described. An example is the insertion of a ledger card into a bookkeeping machine.

Constant elements. Those operation elements which are generally performed in a similar manner and hence should require a similar period of time to complete. An example is the single key stroke as performed on an electrically controlled keyboard.

Synthetic time formula. The process of *combining similar elements* in a procedure in order to arrive at a total time required for that procedure. For example, it may be established that a given procedure for posting to a perpetual inventory card may involve 63 key strokes, 2 document insertions, and so on. Total time per posting is determined by multiplying the time per key stroke by 63, multiplying the time required to insert the inventory card by 2, and so on, and adding all the products.

Cyclical time. The time elapsed for one complete performance of a given clerical procedure.

Analysis. The process of determining the lengths of time consumed by each element of an operation. This is done by counting the number of film frames through the use of the time study projector. A film of several cycles of the operation to be studied is usually taken. The detailed procedure followed by the operator must then be listed, by elements, in sequence of occurrence (Table 1, page 233), taking care that quantitative variations of each element—e.g., number of digits—are recorded. Several cycles of the film are then analyzed by determining the number of frames which have elapsed for each element of the operation, and reasons for unusual variances are determined and recorded. Finally, a table of constant elements is developed (Table 2, page 234).

Table 1

LIST OF OPERATION ELEMENTS FOR PAYROLL PROCEDURE AND APPLICABLE ACTUAL TIMES AS DERIVED FROM FILM ANALYSIS

Oper. no.	Description of operation	No. of digits and motor bar stroke	Actual no. of frames*	Time in seconds
1	Set up-to-date balances on keyboard:			
	(a) Gross earnings	7	27	1.7
	(b) Taxes withheld	5	17	1.0
	(c) Social security deductions	5	17	1.0
2	Pick up proof balance	7	26	1.6
3	Print cipher proof (automatic)		10	0.6
4	Insert earnings card		36	2.2
5	Insert check		36	2.2
6	Set up total hours worked	5	18	1.1
7	Set up regular earnings	6	20	1.3
8	Set up overtime earnings	5	16	1.0
9	Print gross earnings (automatic)		10	0.6
10	Enter taxes:			
	(a) Manipulate rotary taxmeter		39	2.4
	(b) Set up taxes withheld	4 or 5	13	0.8
	(c) Set up social security deduction	4	15	0.9
11	Reading from earnings card, write:			
	(a) N. Y. State disability	3	11	0.7
	(b) Union dues	3	11	0.7
	(c) Group insurance	3	11	0.7
12	Type name (about six key strokes)		20	1.3
13	Move to numerical keyboard, and strike motor bar		6	0.4
14	Print automatically:			
	(a) Date and check no.		9	0.6
	(b) Net amount of check		9	0.6
15	Tabulate carriage (about 15")		32	2.0
16	Print automatically:			
	(a) Gross pay to date		10	0.6
	(b) Taxes withheld to date		10	0.6
	(c) Social security to date		10	0.6
	(d) New proof total		10	0.6
17	Remove check and earnings card		37	2.3
	Total time for cycle		486	30.1

*16 frames equal one second.

233

Use of the elements

These elements subsequently serve as building blocks in the establishment of additional time standards for other tasks performed on the same equipment and under similar conditions. For example, it is possible, by using the constant data derived from the films, to "build up" standard times for other bookkeeping machine applications, such as posting to accounts receivable ledgers. However, the use of this technique is limited to rather high-volume, repetitive clerical tasks, preferably involving the use of an office machine. Also, the problem remains to determine whether the production rate of the operator who was filmed represents a "normal" pace.

There is yet another relatively new technique of predetermined work measurement, which has been much discussed and adopted for industrial time study in a number of companies. A predetermined time standard may be defined as "a procedure which analyzes a manual operation or method into the basic motions required to perform it and assigns to each motion a predetermined time standard which is determined by the nature of the motion and the conditions under which it is made." (*Methods— Time Measurement*, Maynard, Stegemerten and Schwab, McGraw-Hill, 1948.)

It is believed that the use of this technique in the clerical work measurement field is limited to high-volume tasks by reason of the minute analysis of motions which is necessary and which demands a great deal of time. In certain cases, formulas can be developed for substantially similar, recurring tasks, and can save a good deal of effort. While the scope of this chapter precludes a full discussion of other uses of predetermined

Table 2

LIST OF CONSTANTS DERIVED FROM ANALYSIS OF FILMS OF PAYROLL PROCEDURE

Operation element	Elemental time (no. of frames)	In seconds
Pick up from stack and insert (card or check)	36.0	2.25
Remove from machine and put down (card or check) or refile in open ledger card tray	37.0	2.3
Key stroke (alphabetic or numeric keyboard)	3.5	0.22
Carriage travel (per inch)	2.0	0.13
Manipulation of taxmeter (rotary drum type)	39.0	2.44
Automatic printing	10.0	0.63

systems of work measurement, these systems provide an excellent, highly formalized method for work simplification studies and afford an opportunity to apply methods engineering to office tasks.

Regardless of the type of technique which may be used in developing clerical work standards, a system of continuous comparison of performance with these standards must be developed. This is accomplished through the use of standard clerical hour budgets, which should be designed to facilitate adjustments required by reason of volume fluctuations.

To maintain the usefulness of the budget, clerical volume and productivity must be constantly reported. The amount of effort required in such reporting must be kept to a minimum. It has been found possible to gather the necessary volume data with a minimum of effort by selecting a few key activities which have been determined to be primarily responsible for generating clerical work. For example, the number of orders received may have a rather direct effect on the number of invoices and bills of lading to be typed, on accounts receivable ledger postings, on sales analysis and sales commission computations, and so forth. If the past relationship of these activities to the influx of orders has been fairly constant, sufficiently accurate inferences as to their volume may be drawn from merely an incoming order count. Another inexpensive method of counting volume is to count mechanisms available for various types of office machines or to measure standard documents such as punch cards.

The types of clerical volume and productivity reports issued generally fall into two categories:

The first level of reports indicates productivity and quality of work of individual clerks, and is directed to the departmental supervisor. He should use this information to take immediate action when output falls short of expectations.

The second level is usually directed to an executive having line responsibility over all clerical employees. This type of report shows departmental volume and efficiency and serves as a means of appraising the effectiveness of supervisors. It is also useful in determining what interdepartmental transfers may be made. Finally, it serves as a continuous means for clerical cost control.

It has often been said that the areas of material handling and administrative practices are the last frontiers of substantial increases in productivity. As such, the creation of effective clerical cost controls represents a real challenge to the accounting profession.

Achieving economies

Economies are often obtained through work measurement by combining skills into homogeneous groups (see Figure 6, page 236). After the activities have been combined, responsibility for homogeneous functions is centralized under certain employees. This permits specialization which will ultimately produce greater skill. Nonproductive delays caused by waiting for work are also highlighted.

Once systems work has been organized, the problem remains of how the system will be implemented—manually, automatically, or electronically? This will be the subject of Chapter 5.

Figure 6

OFFICE PRODUCTIVITY STUDY

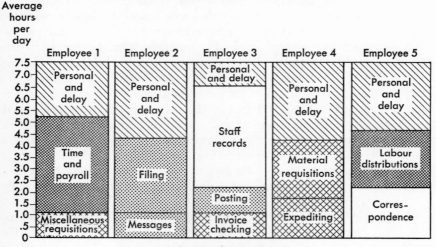

Before combining activities

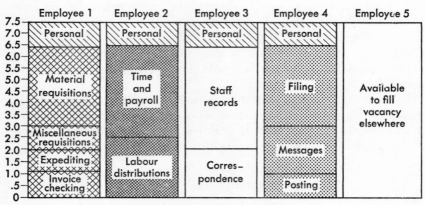

After combining activities

SOURCE: John Hockman, Manager, Office Systems and Procedures, Canadian National Railways, Montreal.

CHAPTER FIVE

Systems Mechanization

A NATURAL EXTENSION OF systems analysis is to determine how the system is to be made operative. Once an appropriate system has been charted, it can be executed manually, by means of one-write devices; automatically, by means of various bookkeeping and other automatic equipment; or electronically.

Classification of Office Machines

Office machines can be classified roughly into four categories: (1) general office machines (including adding machines, four-process desk calculators, typewriters and typewriter billing machines, and cash registers); (2) multiple-purpose accounting machines; (3) punched card machines; and (4) electronic data processing equipment. A practitioner should familiarize himself with categories (3) and (4). He must learn how to go through an elaborate process required to reach judgments as to whether a punched card or an EDP system would be suitable for a client. Situations encountered in this area tend to categorize themselves into those that are clearly too small for EDP, those clearly so large that they can justify a computer readily, and those in a twilight zone, perhaps the majority. A rather extensive feasibility study may be necessary.

Manufacturers' representatives can be relied upon to explain their distinct machine or system features. However, the practitioner must exercise caution. He should bear in mind the salesman's goal before he commits his client or recommends a piece of hardware. Manufacturers of electromechanical bookkeeping machines will very seldom suggest a one-write system. Therefore they can point to the legitimate savings of a bookkeeping machine as well as claim for their equipment the advantages of creating several records at one time, something for which a machine is not needed. However, the most enthusiastic salesman of pegboard systems will have to admit that there is a time and a place where the handwritten system, no matter how well laid out, should give way to a bookkeeping machine.

Mechanization of the client's accounting system has raised a number of questions as to how a CPA determines that an accounting system should be mechanized, how he decides what equipment should be used, and how he can most helpfully implement the installation. In a large firm, these questions are not as difficult because specialists are developed by the firm to cope with such problems. The objective here is to investigate the problem of accounting system mechanization to see if a framework can be developed to aid the smaller practitioner in deciding whether to suggest that a client's accounting system be mechanized or further mechanized. However, the possibility must always be kept in mind that the practitioner might be better off staying away from this work or appropriately delegating it to people who have had extensive experience in it.

Cost Considerations in Mechanizations

One question which will inevitably arise is, "With basic machine accounting advantages, why aren't all accounting systems mechanized?" The answer is mainly one of comparative cost. However, there are other considerations, which become more significant as the scope and cost of a mechanized system increase.

In order to install a complete machine accounting system in almost any business, adding machines, cash registers, and a multiple-purpose accounting or bookkeeping machine are needed. For these a large capital outlay is not unusual. There are also hidden expenses such as an increased average office wage necessary to hire the additional skilled personnel needed to operate the various machines in the system, as well as the cost of converting old files and related equipment to the new system. In a situation where the number of office employees decreases because of the machine installation, the increased average office wage is not a serious factor. If costs, both apparent and hidden, can be offset by savings in other costs through the installation of the new system, it would seem that the basic question of economics could easily be solved.

Cost summary. The following cost summary (Table 1, page 239) illustrates hypothetically elements that should be considered in a proposed system change.

In a situation where a clear-cut savings in office operating costs cannot be computed, some of the intangible benefits of a machine system should be carefully examined with the client before a decision not to install a mechanized accounting system is finally made. Questions to be considered include: Can the increased cost of obtaining the business data be offset by the fact that the data for decision-making purposes are available more quickly and more accurately under the proposed system than they would be under the old? Is the volume of business expected to increase

Table I

COST ANALYSIS SUMMARY

Proposed Installation of a Punched Card Accounting System

	Present system	Proposed
A. Equipment		
Annual depreciation	$ 8,600	—0—
Personal property tax	1,600	—0—
3% interest on capital invested	2,580	—0—
Machine rental, taxes, etc.	—0—	$ 24,000
	$ 12,780	$ 24,000
B. Personnel		
35 people @ $58 weekly	104,000	
23 people @ $65 weekly		77,740
C. Supplies		
	2,500	2,750
Total	$119,280	$104,490
Additional one-time costs:		
site preparation, file conversion, etc.		$ 6,000

so that in a short while mechanization could be justified clearly on a dollars-and-cents basis? If the clerical staff is not expected to decrease under the new system, is it because the old system was seriously understaffed? It seems axiomatic that, based on the machine advantages described above, mechanization of an accounting system may be desirable even if the savings fall somewhat short of a complete economic justification. The practitioner should be aware of this and advise his client accordingly.

In any extensive innovation of a paper-work system, there are significant costs, usually not contemplated in advance, which flow out of the substantial frictions created by extensive innovation, especially using machines. These costs frequently can throw the economic evaluation of a systems mechanization program out of kilter.

Other considerations

Some CPAs are naturally reluctant to take an active part in the purchase and installation of accounting machines. To begin with, no new system works too well at the beginning. It is so much safer not to get involved in the difficulties and frictions which a new system creates. If a CPA has originally recommended the purchase of the machine, he will get the blame if things do not work out. A suspicious client may wonder whether the accountant had any financial interest in the installation. Some clients expect results too quickly and are not willing to install those procedures which a machine accounting system requires. In addition, no system, handwritten, electromechanical, tab card, or computer, can cure such basic ills as poor organization, faulty source documents, or bad management. In such a case, machines may enable one to get the wrong answer faster, and even that may not happen. It is easy to ridicule as old-fashioned the CPA who tries to steer clear of this kind of situation. It is much harder to salvage an account in such circumstances.

Most CPAs will prefer to risk losing a client than continue an outmoded system of record keeping, but without careful preparation and painstaking analysis of the client's procedures a recommendation to install a bookkeeping machine can easily boomerang. There is a danger if a clean conversion is not made from a manual system to a bookkeeping machine. In the case of a one-write system the investment in permanent equipment is small; a poorly laid out form can be improved at the next printing. But there are greater hazards in the move from bookkeeping machines to punched card equipment and even greater hazards in the move from punched card equipment to computers. In moving from a bookkeeping machine to a punched card system, there is conversion of source information and files to machine-sensible forms. This is a difficult conversion. In moving from punched card equipment to computers, there is a transition to the development of a stored program, this kind of program being much more rigorous than the methods used to guide machines in systems below the computer level.

When an office reaches the stage where a machine should be purchased, office politics and idiosyncrasies will come into play. The purchase price of the machine in the range of several thousand dollars will loom large. Some clients will get very upset when they realize that in addition to, for example, $5,000 for a machine, they will have to spend another $1,000 for furniture, filing equipment, and forms (an expense which the machine salesman perhaps conveniently forgot when he submitted his proposal).

On the other hand, when a large system is called for, the company is big enough to have some fairly competent people in the office. In addition, a population explosion may have taken place in the lower clerical ranks and the client may have expressed his desire to cut costs or at least check the constant increase in clerical salaries. He may therefore be much more receptive to the idea of a data processing system.

Knowledge of machines

In order to recommend that mechanization or increased mechanization is worth contemplating and to advise his client on the type of mechanization to consider, it is presupposed that the accountant has sufficient knowledge to give sound advice. The reluctance among the small practitioners to perform a systems service of this type may be sufficient to suggest that a necessary minimum knowledge concerning mechanized systems is lacking. If it is, what can the practitioner do about it? First, the basic machine advantages developed below should be studied and evaluated. Second, it is suggested that the practitioner whose knowledge of machine systems is weak embark on a program of self-education.

It is not necessary to be completely familiar with the operational fine points of all machines available, but it is necessary to know the level of mechanization to recommend. For example, should an adding machine, desk calculator, and some type of pegboard one-write system be used instead of an adding machine and a multipurpose electric accounting machine? Should a punched card data processing system be installed in lieu of an intermediate scale electronic computer system?

Basic machine advantages

In general, machine accounting systems have certain advantages over manual systems. A mechanized accounting system will (1) produce more legible records; (2) reduce transcription error probability; (3) reduce the number of calculation errors; (4) process data more rapidly, with less people and in less space than a manual system, provided a certain minimum volume of processing exists; and (5) reduce unauthorized system changes because of the more formal nature of mechanized procedures. It is also reasonable to assume that the more legible characters and figures produced by machines are less likely to be misinterpreted than are handwritten data. A sales invoice, for example, is used as a basis for recording debits to accounts receivable, credits to various sales categories, reductions in inventory amounts, and in various types of sales analyses. Invoice legibility is important to the accuracy of the records and analyses based on the invoice.

Machine systems reduce the need for manual transcriptions and, hence, reduce transcription error probability. Bookkeeping and general accounting machines utilize the one-write principle where through carbonization several records are prepared simultaneously. Punched card and electronic data processing systems accomplish the same result by utilizing a unit record principle. After basic transaction data has been converted into a unit medium capable of being processed either by the punched card machines or by an electronic data processing system, the initial data is rarely if ever transcribed manually. (It is acknowledged at this point that manual systems utilizing pegboards reduce transcription error probability, because this system also uses the one-write principle. In this respect pegboards also improve bookkeeping efficiency. While not a machine system, a pegboard system is a step above a manual system.)

Faster data processing. This machine advantage, while valid, must be qualified. In a machine system, data can be processed more rapidly with fewer people and in less space than by a manual system, provided a certain minimum volume of processing exists. One advantage of a machine system over a manual system is speed, although with more powerful systems the differences in competence are substantially greater than speed. If a sufficient volume of processing does not exist, speed is not an important factor. However, the volume necessary to begin using machines in the data processing system is much less than one might surmise. Corner grocery stores utilize cash registers and adding machines, as do service stations and other small retail businesses. As these small enterprises grow, the accounting system must grow with them. Increased accounting system mechanization becomes desirable when increased volume of data cannot be processed rapidly enough by hand to permit efficient use of the information generated.

Machine systems and procedures are more formal and therefore less subject to change without permission by employees performing specific operations. Manual systems are difficult to control in two respects: first, individuals can deviate from instructions in the manner of performance of a certain procedure; and second, because of this, job descriptions are difficult to formalize in a procedures manual. As a result, the data may not be processed as efficiently as possible and certain internal control procedures may not be functioning. It is more difficult not to follow procedures correctly in a machine system. This system formality helps maintain control procedures and permits job descriptions to be properly established. The use of job descriptions in turn helps to improve employee training.

Link with data processing systems. An additional advantage of machine accounting is the link with data processing systems. Practically all machines are able to produce punched paper tape or punched cards as a by-product of producing the hard copy. Additional analysis is possible either by data processing equipment of the client or in a service bureau. This is particularly valuable for future expansion. Today the client may not need more than a conventional bookkeeping machine, but tomorrow when he has to install punched card or more sophisticated equipment, he can still use the present machine.

Inasmuch as most accountants are familiar with one-write and conventional equipment, the remainder of this chapter will deal mainly with EDP equipment.

Punched Tape Accounting for Business

PERHAPS THE MOST PROMISING solution to low-cost punched card processing for smaller companies is pooling the more efficient tabulating equipment through the use of punched paper tape. By using punched paper tape, economies are achieved in two major areas: (1) elimination of manual card punching and repunching for verification; and (2) reduction of manual time required to reconcile differences. Since the tape which is received by the service bureau must be arithmetically proved beforehand, there is little chance for the tabulated report to be out of balance.

With the development of a simple and comparatively inexpensive tape input device, smaller companies can afford to create their own tape and thereby make use of the reduced cost of processing.

The tape input device referred to is the tape adding machine. Use of this machine to perform punched card accounting services leads to the belief that small companies can gain many of the benefits of punched cards without installing their own tabulating machines.

The Tape Adding Machine

In appearance, the tape adding machine is a regular ten-key or full bank adding machine with a tape punching mechanism attached, so that a punched paper tape as well as a printed adding machine tape is created with each stroke of the motor bar keys. Because of its simplicity, the tape adding machine does not require a skilled operator; it is operated exactly like a normal adding machine.

Its function, however, is quite different from that of an adding machine in that its ability to add is only collateral. Its primary purpose is to enter information on a punched paper tape for further processing by tabulating or computing equipment. However, its ability to add and develop a proof total and, in addition, provide a visible printed tape of what has been entered, insures arithmetic accuracy of the punched tape. Since errors would be repeated many times throughout the processing phase, the accuracy of the input material is of paramount importance.

A *specific application.* While the tape adding machine is suitable to any job involving the distribution of amounts, as for example in the analysis of sales by salesman, product, customer, and the like, or in the analysis of labor and material costs to different jobs or departments, the illustrations chosen here and described below indicate its use for a particularly complex task—that of creating a complete set of books of account and preparing monthly and year-to-date financial statements which might contain budget, forecast, or prior-year information as well as current figures.

Each entry is made by placing the figures in the adding machine keyboard, starting with the column furthest to the left. Reference number refers to check number, invoice number, date, or any other type of reference desired, as follows:

1. *Reference number:*   *General ledger account number:*
   (4 digits)   (3 digits)
   Depress nonadd key.

2. *Dollar amount:*
   Depress plus bar for debit, minus bar for credit.

For example, if check number 1001 in the amount of $234.56 is being charged to account number 348, the entry would appear on the adding machine tape as follows:

$$1\ 0\ 0\ 1\ 3.\ 4\ 8\ \text{N}\quad\text{(nonadd)}$$
$$2\ 3\ 4.\ 5\ 6\quad\quad\text{(plus)}$$

Fixed information such as month, year, and journal source number is entered one time only, and is automatically repeated throughout the run. A split transaction, where several different accounts are affected, is handled in much the same manner, that is, by entering the account number and dollar amount for each portion. Errors in account code are detected by a rapid sight check of the visible tape and are corrected simply by entering the appropriate ledger account number and reversing the dollar amount.

A reasonably skilled operator can enter three hundred such transactions in an hour, in contrast to the one- or two-day job of writing up the books and preparing, typing, and reviewing financial statements by hand.

The punched tape and adding machine tape are mailed in a manila envelope to the service bureau, and within a few days the bureau returns printed journals, general ledger, and financial statements.

Getting Started With Punched Tape

Tape adding machines are now manufactured by several accounting machine companies. Some are available on as much as a four-year purchase option plan wherein the monthly rental is one forty-eighth of the purchase price. There are two types: a ten-key tape adding machine and full bank machines.

In some parts of the country, finding a service bureau to process the tape will be the major problem. While the service bureau industry is growing rapidly, many of the bureaus are not yet equipped with tape converting equipment.

Once the tape adding machine is purchased or made available on a trial basis, and arrangements have been made with the service bureaus to process the tape and produce the desired reports and records, there remains very little to be done. No printed forms or specially trained operators are required. Where the machine is acquired by an accounting practitioner, it may be applied to the general ledger work of a particular client simply by sending the chart of accounts to the service center together with carryforward account balances. Clients are identified by code number only, never by name. In some instances it may be desirable to set up a new chart of accounts to take care of additional detail or special reports which may be desired, such as condensed or consolidated statements, income tax return groupings, or departmental breakdowns. Where accounts receivable, payroll, or other subsidiary work is appropriate, account numbers would be assigned to each individual in the group. Unlike major machine accounting installations, there is virtually no delay in starting the job, nor is there any need to parallel the punched tape application with a hand operation in order to insure accuracy, since the operation of the machine is simple and easily controlled.

Conclusions

The simplicity and low cost of the tape adding machine, together with the trend on the part of service bureaus to process punched tape, provide a formula to solve much of the data processing needs of smaller companies. Through the use of this formula, the smaller company is able to pass the burden of heavy investment and skilled technicians to an outsider specializing in this field, and yet take full advantage of the more efficient machine accounting methods. But while the need for technical skill can thus be avoided, the need for accounting skills becomes greater. The CPA will therefore take on an important role in the use that his client may make of punched tape accounting.

The Punched Card: a Unit Memory Device[1]

Characteristics of the Punched Card

What is the make-up of the card? How does it store the facts of a business transaction? What are some of the interesting uses of this unit record memory device?

For purposes of illustration we will restrict our comments to the cards

---

[1]Pages 245-54 appeared as a paper in the *Proceedings of the Fourth Annual Accounting Systems Conference,* October 27 and 28, 1960, California Society of CPAs, Los Angeles. The author is George E. Staininger, Manager, Management Advisory Services, Price Waterhouse & Co., Los Angeles.

of International Business Machines and Remington Rand, although punched card equipment of other manufacture is available.

The make-up of the punched card is most important to the proper functioning of punched card processing equipment. In order to obtain proper registration of stored information, the card must be manufactured within the exacting tolerances found in the processing of metals (3.250 in. wide by 7.375 in. long by 0.0067 in. thick, with a maximum variation of ± five to ten thousandths of an inch).

The usual corner cut which is used to facilitate handling and filing may be placed in any one or more corners. Many significant and important uses have been made of this hallmark of the punched card. This is exemplified by the installation of a large national wholesale drug firm. The pricing of their thousands of items is complicated by various discount groups. By use of an indicative corner cut for each group the price clerk is alerted to the possibility of a discount so that he may allow the proper amount.

The IBM card contains 80 vertical columns. Each column contains 12 positions—0 to 9, 11 and 12. The 11 and 12 positions are at the top of the card and are used for storing special control indications as well as for indicating alphabetical and special characters when used with punches in the numerical positions (0 to 9). (See Figure 1, page 247.)

The Remington Rand card contains 90 vertical columns arranged in two banks of 45 columns each, in the upper and lower halves of the card. Each column consists of six positions (0, 1, 3, 5, 7, 9). Combination patterns of these six positions permit the storing of up to 54 different numerical, alphabetical, or special characters.

Before the punched card can accept data that is intelligible to machine and operator, information areas or fields must be assigned and labeled. The use of these fields must be maintained with consistency and continuity.

The facts of a business transaction are stored in the card through a series of punched holes. The punching of a single hole in a tabulating card can mean a surprisingly large number of different things. What it means depends upon the field in which it is punched and upon its location within that field. For example, the number 6 may mean June, or the 6th day of the month, or man number 6, or payroll check number 6, or part number 6. It may signify 6 crankshafts forged, or 6 hours' work forging those crankshafts, or 6 feet, gallons, or pounds of material. It may indicate 6 whole things, or 6/10 of a thing, or 6/100, 60, or 600. It may mean 6 dollars, or dimes, pennies, or mills. It may be the part of a combination of holes which causes the machines to print alphabetical or special characters.

It is the grouping into fields that controls the numerals so that six men are not added to the sixth month. Six men would be stored in a field headed "number of employees," and the sixth month in another headed "date." The positional significance of each column within its field has the same importance as the columns on working papers.

The hole punched into the card enables the various machines to do a number of things, such as:

1. Sort cards to numerical sequence
2. Merge cards in the proper place in a previously established file
3. Compare one number with another, and take one action if the two are equal and another if they are not equal
4. Print a number on the same card in which it is punched
5. Add, subtract, multiply, or divide one number by another

Figure I

ARRANGEMENT OF INFORMATION ON AN IBM CARD AND CARD CODING

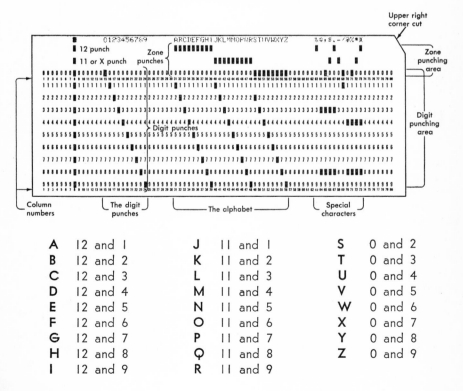

A	12 and 1	J	11 and 1	S	0 and 2
B	12 and 2	K	11 and 2	T	0 and 3
C	12 and 3	L	11 and 3	U	0 and 4
D	12 and 4	M	11 and 4	V	0 and 5
E	12 and 5	N	11 and 5	W	0 and 6
F	12 and 6	O	11 and 6	X	0 and 7
G	12 and 7	P	11 and 7	Y	0 and 8
H	12 and 8	Q	11 and 8	Z	0 and 9
I	12 and 9	R	11 and 9		

6. Print on forms to create a report
7. Eliminate data
8. Select data
9. Control spacing of the automatic carriage on the accounting machine

There are other purposes to which the punched hole may be put, but this will serve the purpose of illustrating the wide diversification of interpretation that may be placed on a single hole in a card.

Applications of the Punched Card

There are many interesting uses for the punched card. The variety of card designs and uses is almost as extensive as the many paper business forms with which CPAs are familiar. A few examples of these are:

1. *The payment coupons* for installment payments may be made up as a group of prepunched interpreted cards which are sent to the customer to be returned individually with each payment. These provide an automatic identification and payment recording media as direct input to the system.

2. The punched card *invoice* when postinterpreted is an inexpensively prepared document of billing. The summary cards from which the invoices are printed become the charge to accounts receivable.

3. As a *check*, the punched card has found wide usage. The principal reason for this popularity is the facility with which it may assist in performing that accounting department stepchild, bank reconciliation. Many of the larger banking institutions will provide this service for only the maintenance of a compensating bank balance. One of the newer examples of the punched card check is its integration with a multipart paper voucher check.

4. The punched card *time record* also has wide acceptance. All static and semistatic information regarding an employee is prepunched and interpreted on the card. Variable information is posted on the face of the card for future manual transcription. In certain ideal situations where working hours, rates, and conditions remain relatively static, the entire time record may be prepunched and selectively interpreted to include the earnings for the period.

5. As a *media for addressing*, the punched card brings great versatility of selectiveness to mailing applications. Because of the speed with which the cards may be sorted, merged, or segregated, numerous addressing machine suppliers are using them as application media for addressing. Two interesting examples are: (1) information recorded on the face of a punched card in a significant type font so that it may be electronically read and printed on strip mailing labels popularly used in magazine mailings; and (2) the direct transfer of addresses from punched cards, which have also been recorded in reverse image on the back of the card

through a special carbon. This provides a rapid, relatively inexpensive means of maintaining a mailing list with high selectivity.

6. The *tissue overlay* on a punched card has made possible a low-cost supplemental by-product of card preparation. For example, an item packing slip may be prepared simultaneously with the billing card.

7. The *aperture card* provides a versatile carrying medium for microfilmed records. Engineering drawings, individual property records, personnel history, and valuable documents are only a few of the many applications that have been found for this type of card.

Coding of data

The coding of data into significant numerical digits has been one of the most formidable obstacles to the acceptance of punched card methods. And yet the traditional chart of accounts, which is almost universally a numerically coded equivalent to an account name, has become the backbone of the data collection system, which has served its purpose well in reporting the dollar profit and loss and the dollar financial status of both large and small companies.

We are surrounded by innumerable instances of numerical coding for simplification of identity which do not have machine processing as their motivating purpose: shoe sizes, car licenses, telephone numbers, freight cars, counters in supermarkets, street addresses, and many, many others.

The complexity of coding methods and systems is an exacting science too comprehensive to be covered here. To obtain efficient, significant results, adequate time and experience must be devoted to the establishment of codes for use in both punched card and electronic systems.

Recording of data

The recording of data into a card through a series of punched holes may be accomplished in a number of ways:

1. The key-driven machines are numerous in specific design, but fall primarily into a single category. The key punch machine operator reads data from the document of original entry and, in effect, types it on a keyboard which causes the machine to punch holes in the card.

Key verifying is essentially the same as key punching. The verifier operator repeats the functions of the key punch operator with the same group of documents and cards to prove that the original punching was correct.

2. Manual punching without key-driven machines:

IBM Port-a-punch uses specially die-cut cards placed in a plastic template holder so that the operator may punch out the desired position with a stylus.

Remington Rand Spot-punch uses a special pilot hole punched card and a hand punch. The punch is designed with a pin under spring tension in the center of the die. This pin must find the pilot hole before a hole can be punched.

Mark sensing was first introduced by IBM and may be considered a form of manual punching. It requires a specially designed card with printed spaces for entry of handwritten marks. The marks are sensed electrically in a subsequent operation and the required holes are punched into the card. This method has been in use for many years and has many successful applications.

Remington Rand has recently introduced a similar method of sensing handwritten marks on punched cards. The punching is activated by optical, or photoelectric-cell, scanning of the penciled marks.

3. The punching of cards through master cards is an efficient and effective method of card preparation. The primary benefit of the master card method is the ability to assign codes selectively. For example, a sales order card need only be coded with the customer number in order to punch into the card from a master card such additional information as: customer name, type of customer, terms, salesman, state, territory, and the like. In small installations where the cost of a calculator cannot be justified, a similar method of pre-extended master cards may be used to make extensions as long as the master cards required do not greatly outnumber the cards to be extended.

4. The intercoupling of the punch with other key-driven machines has provided a means of obtaining distribution cards simultaneously with the posting of such accounting records as customer, vendor, or payroll ledgers.

An interesting variation of this marriage of two machines is the key punch with a wide-carriage adder. As information is punched on the keyboard of the IBM punch, a multiple-columned hard copy recording is prepared on the adder. Through sorting of these cards, a rerun through the punch adder will prepare other analytical hard copy listings. In effect, a punch adder and a sorter can be a limited punched card installation. The cards may be sent out to a service bureau for more complex reporting.

5. Tape-to-card conversion is receiving growing acceptance. The early forerunner of this communication system was the use of teletype to transmit data from widespread operations into a centralized data processing installation. Many variations of transmission of data are being developed. Several suppliers are announcing data collection systems whereby information is transmitted directly card to card or card to tape to card. Each such system has many of the advantages of the master card file.

6. The special usage machines are varied in scope but probably the most noteworthy are:

The tag-to-card reproducer which is bringing automation to the garment industry. To the well-known garment tag has been added an area of small punched holes. These holes are read by a special reproducer in order to produce punched cards to be used in automated sales audit and distribution applications.

The point-of-sale recorder has been primarily a punched tape machine that records sales information at the cash register in a form that can be automatically fed into punched card machines after conversion to cards.

7. Optical character recognition equipment could well become the most important news in business automation since the advent of the punched card. Optical scanning equipment has the ability to read a document as long as the data is printed with a particularly distinctive special type face. The scanner translates what it reads into machine language and records it on punched cards, punched paper tape, or magnetic tape. The efficiency of a character-sensing system, whether magnetic or optical, is predicated primarily upon its ability to accept variations in legibility of printing.

To date, companies have used the optical scanner for such operations as processing travelers' checks, converting sales reports to cards, book club record processing, dividend checks and stockholder records, cash accounting, and credit card purchases. At such time as these machines are technically proven for general application and receive a degree of wide acceptance, their impact will be felt severely in the larger punched card installations. Eventually these scanners may become direct input to computer systems and by-pass the conversion to punched card, punched tape, or magnetic tape.

Arranging and classifying

The arranging and classifying of information stored in the punched card is accomplished by relatively high-speed machines:

1. The *sorter* has probably been the most interesting piece of demonstration equipment in the punched card line. Its speed varies from 250 to 2,000 digits per minute. The sorting sequence is not dissimilar to that of manual sorting, one digit at a time. However, because of the high speeds involved, the operator normally follows a sequence of units, tens, hundreds, and thousands, unless unusually large volumes of cards are involved. These are then blocked into major groups so that subsequent machine operations may be performed concurrently as each grouping is sorted.

2. The *high-speed collator* has become an important adjunct to most punched card installations. At relatively high speeds, this machine performs efficient procedures with two files of cards, such as interfiling, matching, segregating, sequence checking, substituting, eliminating, and searching. This machine has added high-speed automation to formerly tedious manual or semimanual functions.

Computing and calculating

The so-called "punched card computers," although relatively small, have created a major revolution in automatic data processing. They perform complex functions in fractions of a second. These may include a series of multiple computations, comparisons, and logical choices. Previously such operations required combinations of numerous and often awkward steps on other punched card machines, such as punches, sorters, collators, and reproducers. Such abilities have given punched card systems the quality of effectively bridging the gap from the small firm which is controlled by the memory know-how of man to the giant business which requires a large electronic system.

The application of an hourly payroll is a good, familiar example of the small computer's prowess in performing sequential operations during a single function. From a punched card containing only date, employee number, and pay hours, together with the previous earnings-to-date card, the complete payroll record for an employee is updated. The computer

1. Computes gross earnings (rate × hours)
2. Develops new earnings to date
3. Develops new taxable earnings
4. Computes deductions for state and Federal payroll taxes (automatically partials taxes when the exempted earnings or tax amount is reached)
5. Computes withholding tax deduction amount
6. Develops amount of new withholding tax to date
7. Deducts total taxes to develop new earnings after taxes
8. Punches out new earnings-to-date card from which the payroll is printed and the next period's payroll is updated

The ability of these machines is not limited to the computation of logical business problems. They are able to perform commendably in the fields of science, operations research, marketing, and production, to name only a few. Arithmetic operations can be performed on an average of 100 to 150 per minute. Certainly this is slow when compared with the productivity of the large-scale computing systems, but in their field they are economically unequaled. Such machines are available for the cost equivalent of about three clerks.

Reporting of data

The speed and accuracy of automated processing has made it possible to arrange and classify the data stored in the punched card so that management may be provided with timely information necessary for effective decision making.

The accounting machines, or tabulators, currently available represent a wide range of reporting versatility. Speeds from 50 to 150 cards per minute, 40 to 120 characters printed on a single line, and counter capacities from 30 to 150, fit them into practically every report preparing requirement and cost strata.

Printers are available in two basic types, the numerical or statistical machine, and the alphabetic-numerical or accounting machine. In applications where only a minimum of alphabetical information is necessary, such as employee and vendor names and addresses, the less expensive numerical machines may be augmented by the use of addressing plates or other such media.

Special devices are available that make the printing possibilities of these machines appear to be limitless. Probably the most versatile and singularly important is the automatic form feeding carriage. Form feeding is the rapid, accurate positioning of reports and documents on which the processed results are reported.

The automatic carriage feeds continuous paper forms, single or multiple copies, such as registers, reports, and checks. A bill feed carriage positions single cut forms, such as ledger sheets, envelopes, or cards. A dual feed carriage is available to feed two different forms simultaneously, for printing some or all of the same machine results but with different spacing requirements such as a payroll register and payroll check.

As an intercoupled companion, the summary punch automatically converts into punched hole form the information developed by the accounting machine. The summary punch serves two basic purposes:

1. To reduce card volume and carry summary data. This process is exemplified by the punching of an invoice total card during the billing operation, which becomes an automatic recording to accounts receivable.

2. To carry balance figures forward. An example of this is the preparation of a balance forward type statement where the previous balance is followed by the current period detail. As the tabulator prints the new net total, a balance forward card is punched for the next period.

Once looked upon as only an auxiliary machine used to print the translation of punched holes onto the card to facilitate handling, the interpreter has been developed into an important piece of reporting equipment. Four examples of its versatility as a document printer were outlined in the discussion on interesting uses of the punched card. Another example of the application of its capabilities is the posting to a ledger history record. From a card in which are stored the data of a single transaction or the summary totals for a single account for the period, each activity may be posted on a fixed or variable line of the punched card history record. Only the account number need be punched into the history card for posting accuracy control.

From this brief discussion, it is evident that the available variations in reporting of the data stored in the punched card is limited only by the ingenuity of the systems and form designer.

Conclusions. The increasing statutory record keeping requirements placed upon business, both large and small, make it almost mandatory that large volumes of data be processed and reprocessed without intermediate recordings. Except for the very small firm, punched card methods and machines have become an integral part of most data processing functions. The ability to capture the important elements of an accounting transaction in a unit record provides the accountant with a near optimum method of processing data at nominal cost. The importance and future of the punched card as a unit record memory device seem to be confirmed by the fact that the manufacturers of all electronic data processing systems use the punched card as an input, output, and external storage medium.

Installing Punched Card Systems[2]

SINCE THE END OF World War II, many significant advances have been made to mechanize paper-work procedures through the use of punched card equipment. Each year we see a wider range of mechanized applications as well as an increasing number of punched card installations. The advent of smaller scale equipment has today made installations feasible even for the smaller businesses. Scores of successful installations are functioning well and producing significant advantages from punched card data processing methods. Generally, these advantages can be summarized as follows:

1. Reduction of costs that permits a greater margin of profit and strengthens the competitive position
2. Much-needed management control reports essential in making important business decisions
3. Promotion of better customer relations through prompt processing and improved appearance of records
4. Ability to overcome the shortage and training of skilled clerical personnel
5. Better preparation for meeting the challenge of continued growth and increasing paper-work needs

However, many companies have experienced difficulties when installing or expanding their punched card installations. These difficulties have

[2]Pages 254-65 appeared as a paper in the *Proceedings of the Fourth Annual Accounting Systems Conference,* October 27 and 28, 1960, California Society of CPAs, Los Angeles. The author is Paul W. Kuske, formerly a manager with Peat, Marwick, Mitchell & Co.

frequently had an adverse effect on customer service and sales, accounting and production controls, or operating costs, which was not originally foreseen. In order to guard against unfavorable results and costly installation failures, a conversion to advanced data processing methods must be adequately and carefully planned. The steps, techniques, and major planning phases required for a successful installation of punched card systems will now be described.

Initial Planning

During the initial planning phase, a detailed review of present methods must be conducted to determine the nature of basic system requirements, provide a sound basis for estimating equipment and personnel requirements, and develop a realistic timetable for each conversion project.

Basic system requirements

A study of each pertinent task is made to become familiar with the required clerical operations, processing problems inherent in the system, and the extent and complexity of exception cases. Present procedures are then flow-charted to eliminate unnecessary steps and to establish a basis for planning the new system. The next step is to analyze the purpose and timeliness of all forms and reports as well as the need for additional information. Careful attention should be given to processing schedules, deadlines, and bottlenecks existing under the present system. Finally, transaction volumes must be accurately tallied and summarized throughout the processing cycle, including peak load periods.

After the present system has been thoroughly reviewed, all the collected information is correlated into a set of basic requirements for the new system. A general flow chart of punched card procedures is developed to meet these requirements; by means of this technique, time estimates can be prepared and rough document and report formats sketched.

Cost projections

No plan for a major systems change should be considered complete unless a projection of operating and conversion costs has been made during the initial planning phase. In projecting operating costs, each step of a punched card procedure is assigned a realistic time based on transaction volume, machine speed, and schedule frequency. These times are accumulated and measured against available processing capacity so that personnel and equipment requirements can be properly established for either a proposed or an existing installation. It is then possible to estimate the operating costs of the mechanized system and compare them with those of the present system in order to determine the economic advantages or disadvantages. While operating costs are the primary factor in determining whether to mechanize, the effect of "one-time" conversion costs should not be overlooked or minimized. Some examples of such costs are:

1. Personnel training costs
2. Salaries of employees engaged in planning work
3. Costs associated with coding source documents, assigning account numbers, and key punching master records
4. Electrical wiring, structural changes, and other space preparation costs
5. Machine rental and employee salaries during test runs and conversion periods
6. Equipment purchases of desks, files, control panels, and the like
7. Freight charges for equipment delivery
8. Initial cost of cards, forms, indexes, and other printed material

These costs vary widely and can involve a sizeable cash outlay; therefore, they should be carefully estimated and controlled in order to avoid embarrassment when the bills arrive.

Conversion timetable

To provide for a smooth conversion, it is advisable to prepare a detailed timetable, which has starting and completion dates for each project and specific responsibilities assigned to participating individuals. Since a mechanization program may affect many functions or areas within a company, each major application should be scheduled separately so that system changes can be made on a piecemeal basis. A good systems planner will fit space preparation and equipment delivery to this timetable in order to minimize machine rental costs during the conversion period. Besides providing a basic guide for conversion activity, such a timetable becomes a valuable management tool in measuring and controlling installation progress. If the schedule is not being met, the responsible executive is in a position to investigate the causes for the delay and take corrective action to improve progress.

Installation factors

In preparing for an installation program, management should be aware of certain factors which greatly influence the success or failure of a major systems change. These factors are:

1. *Management support.* Each manager whose functions are affected by a proposed change should be notified and briefed on the mechanization plans. Resistance to change or lack of co-operation can create numer-

ous installation problems. Therefore, a series of meetings should be held to "sell" the program and promote active support at all management levels.

2. *Executive responsibility.* Punched card equipment normally should be placed under the direct control of the executive who has primary responsibility for the systems being mechanized. His background should preferably include a basic knowledge of punched card operations so that he is able to provide guidance, evaluate progress, and control conversion activities skillfully. Because most systems changes are best accomplished as a joint effort, this executive should have the authority to assign installation projects to specific individuals within the organization.

3. *Employee orientation.* Employees should be given an idea of the basic changes which are contemplated as well as an explanation of management policies regarding the installation. It is extremely important to continue the orientation meetings throughout the entire program in order to maintain good morale and to develop a spirit of co-operation.

4. *Training program.* A detailed training program should be established and approved by management to instruct personnel in the operating techniques and methods required for punched card equipment. Preferably, key punch and tabulating operators should be selected from within the organization, provided that they have the willingness and aptitude to learn. Attending equipment manufacturers' schools and on-the-job training are the most common ways to gain the needed technical skill. Instruction in new clerical routines must also be planned, although this training is usually performed immediately prior to system conversion.

5. *Selection of supervisor.* Experience has shown that the supervisor's ability nearly always determines the final efficiency and effectiveness of punched card systems. Thus it is extremely important to have a well-qualified supervisor. He can either be selected from existing personnel or be recruited from outside the company. An employee within the organization would have the advantage of knowing the present system, but would lack the essential technical knowledge; the reverse situation would usually be true for an individual from the outside. In either case a few months' training or orientation is required to prepare the selected supervisor for his part in the installation program.

6. *Policy changes.* Decisions on policy changes which affect the system design must be made before moving into the mechanization program. Processing requirements (for example, schedule dates, accounting structure, report information, and so on) must be established. An agreement must be reached on such points as inquiry methods, availability of historical data, and necessary organizational changes.

If these six factors receive management's close attention during a change to punched card systems, the final success of the installation will be greatly enhanced.

Systems Planning

After the initial planning phase has been completed and the mechanization program is under way, technical planning and design of the basic system is then required.

Major considerations

Punched card systems should always be designed to provide an efficient method of data processing tailored to the specific needs of a company. It is important to understand this concept because many executives feel that systems of similar businesses can be exactly copied for their own use. Although certain basic ideas may be adopted, identical systems are rarely found.

Other major points which should be considered in systems design work include:

1. Providing an adequate audit trail from source documents to general ledger entries and a tight control over input and output data in order to satisfy requirements for good internal control.

2. Examining the exception processing routines to determine which ones must be continued on a manual basis and which ones can be incorporated in punched card procedures.

3. Designing each system to fit the card and report formats developed for other mechanized applications. As an example, account numbers should be located in the same columns of both the labor and the accounts payable distribution cards.

4. Eliminating unnecessary steps, revising coding systems, and generally taking advantage of the punched card equipment's processing ability so that maximum benefits can be realized. A big mistake is made whenever a system is mechanized to include only the essential manual operations without considering related areas which might readily lend themselves to punched card processing methods.

5. Building into the reporting system additional management information needed to achieve basic company objectives. There is a tendency on the part of some punched card supervisors to use equipment or schedule limitations as a reason for not being able to make this vital information available. Such action should be closely scrutinized by the executive responsible for the installation to determine the validity of each case and take the corrective measures necessary to improve the management report system.

Procedure design

Basic systems requirements established during the initial planning phase are expanded to provide a master blueprint for procedural design.

Figure 2

DATA FLOW CHART—TYPICAL APPLICATION

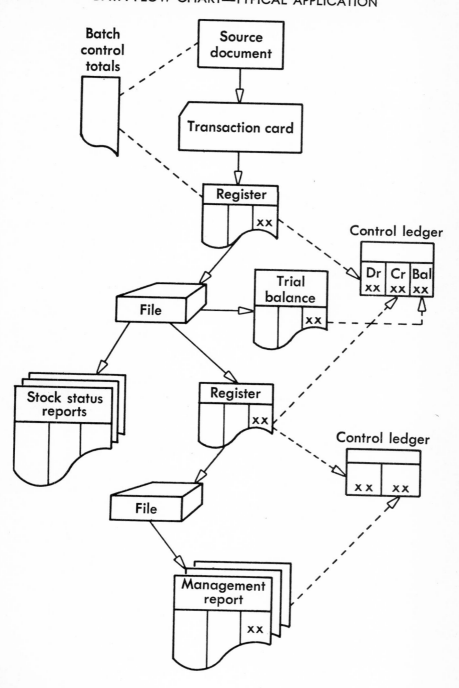

This consists of a detailed flow chart which includes individual operational steps, exception routines, and control features. (See Figure 2, page 259.) New identification codes are developed, existing coding systems are revised, and changes in the accounting system are outlined at this time. See Figure 3, this page and following, for an illustration of an IBM charting and diagramming template jacket (front and back).

During the development of the new procedure, control points must be properly inserted within the framework of the master processing plan.

Figure 3

IBM CHARTING AND DIAGRAMMING TEMPLATE

The symbols shown in this figure are recommended for use in the preparation of flow charts and block diagrams of systems and procedures utilizing IBM data processing machines and systems.

A detailed description of "Flow Charting and Block Diagramming Techniques" can be found in the IBM Reference Manual by that name (Form C20-8008).

Block Diagram Symbols		
Symbol	Stored Program	Stored-wired Program
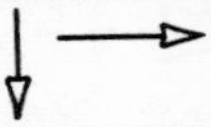	Direction of flow	Direction of flow
	Decision function	Program exit
	Connector or step identification	Branch identification
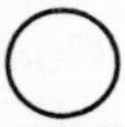	Table-lookup (650)	
	Console operation, halt	Step connector
	Priority routine identification (7070)	Communication
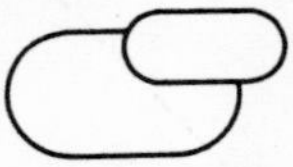	Input/output function	
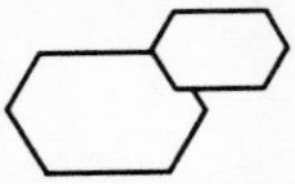	Program modification function	Control panel function
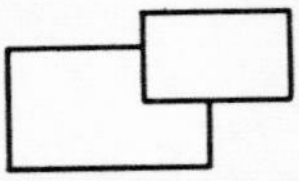	Processing function	Stored program step

Flow Chart Symbols	
↓ →→ ↓	Direction of flow

Document Symbols	Data Processing Systems Symbols
Source document	Central processing unit
Report	Input-output controls
Transmittal form	Auxiliary magnetic drum storage
Punched card	Auxiliary magnetic disk storage
Paper tape	Card reader Card punch
Magnetic tape	Magnetic tape unit
Document file	Paper tape reader Paper tape punch
Card punching, verifying, and other keying operations	Printer
Sort, collate	Typewriter
Accounting machine operations	Inquiry station
Auxiliary machine operation	Auxiliary machine

Features of the IBM Charting and Diagramming Template

Relative position of card columns and mark-sense positions.
Other side: Interpreter printing positions.

Vertical punching positions and size.
Other side: Card volume gauge.

Scale of tenths-of-inches; 407 printing positions.
Other side: Scale of 402-403-404-405-416 printing positions.

Standard line spacing: 6 lines per inch.
Other side: Optional line spacing: 8 lines per inch.

Notch for positioning actual cards. The template is card size: in width, edge-to-edge; in length, left edge to notch.

Shadowed portion is silhouette of the housing over the punching station of 24-26 card punches. When the clear strip is placed over a card column to be punched, the shadowed area represents that portion of the card which is NOT visible to the operator.

Adequate controls are a requisite for punched card procedures; in fact, lack of planning in this area can cause more headaches than any other point which may be slighted in an installation program. The basic purposes of such controls are to (1) produce accurate information, (2) prevent manipulation of accounting data, and (3) provide an independent check over operations. Methods of control are discussed later in this chapter.

Coding schemes are another important part of procedure design. These codes normally can be classified as machine codes and identification or accounting codes. Machine codes must be planned and assigned by the technician doing the plugboard wiring because they serve the purpose of controlling the punched card machines to perform various logical decisions. Identification or accounting codes are numbers assigned to such items as customer, employee, salesman, location, and the like, for the purpose of being able to arrange or accumulate data for processing and report preparation on the punched card equipment. The machines are much more efficient working with numerical codes; existing coding systems may therefore have to be revised. Another factor to consider in mechanization is that statistical information or accounting data too costly to produce by manual methods can be provided by punched card processing. Thus, new codes may have to be devised and master records may require a complete review in order to achieve this potential benefit. One excellent example of this type of information would be sales analysis reports by salesman, product, territory, and customer.

Design of all internal and external reports and forms to be produced on the punched card equipment is the next project. This work must be performed by a technically competent person to make sure that the processing ability and printing limitation of each machine has been carefully considered. It is good practice to have a test run made on complex forms to minimize the possibility of last-minute changes, which can be disastrous. Multiple use forms and reports should be planned to minimize printing costs, allow for a larger stock supply, and reduce the number of operator and key punch set-up changes. Where practical, preprinted codes on source documents should be used to reduce errors and clerical effort. Printing orders should be scheduled to meet the target dates outlined in the conversion timetable. Although these orders are generally awarded to suppliers on the basis of cost, lead time, grade of paper, and the need for proper registration are other points to consider. Proofs should be required on all orders of cards and continuous forms as an additional safeguard.

When the detailed flow chart, control points, coding systems, and document and card formats have all been developed into an integrated procedure, the finished product should be referred to each interested executive for his final approval.

Machine scheduling

As part of the system planning phase, a detailed hour-by-hour and day-by-day machine schedule must be made. Each mechanical operation is assigned a realistic processing time based on transaction volume and operating speed. These times are then recorded on a Gannt chart. By this method, the punched card supervisor is able to determine machine loads and sequence-schedule all steps of the procedure according to equipment capacity and availability. Schedules of other applications may have to be changed to meet the report deadlines of the new procedure, or alternate processing methods may be used to gain fuller utilization of machine time.

Of course, machine utilization records are necessary after the installation has been made in order to compare the actual performance against the scheduled time and adjust the schedule for bottlenecks and delays. These records can also be used to pinpoint down time and maintenance troubles.

Plugboard wiring

Plugboards must be wired to perform the various machine operations in conformity with the card and report formats which have been designed. This requires a high degree of technical skill and knowledge in order to exploit the features of each machine fully. A control panel with a normal complement of wires can cost as much as $150 for a punched card tabulator. For this reason, wherever possible more than one setup should be included in a single plugboard. It is mandatory to have board wiring diagrams prepared for both flexible and fixed control panels; these diagrams should become part of the detailed operating instructions. Test decks and set-up instructions should be prepared for use by the machine operators as the procedure is being followed.

Usually control panel wiring is not a problem for a competent tabulating supervisor; however, management must remember that this work is very critical to punched card operations and should insist that all necessary precautions be taken in testing results before the final conversion is made.

Operating instructions

The final activity of the system planning phase is to write detailed operating instructions from origination of source documents to preparation of final reports. Although methods of preparation vary widely, basic requirements are that each step be simply and completely described in a form which is readily understandable and usable by all personnel. Samples of card and report forms, explanation of balancing routines, wiring diagrams, test decks, and other pertinent processing information should be included.

Many installations do not have adequate operating instructions. As a result, problems of large rework time or long operator training periods are experienced. Another even more frustrating problem is created when a punched card supervisor leaves his employer without having performed this work. In order to guard against this possibility, the executive responsible for the installation must see that detailed operating instructions are prepared as each application is planned for punched card processing.

Conversion Planning

The final phase before putting the new system into operation consists of conversion planning. This involves testing the procedures, converting the master records, making parallel runs, and performing other preparatory work.

Procedure testing

Procedures are tested by simulating an actual run of selected data through the detailed clerical and machine operational steps from start to finish. During this test source entries are created and processed to prepare the final reports. As a result, all the related system planning work, including controls, codes, document and report formats, plugboard wiring, and operating instructions, receives a thorough check. In this way, procedural problems can be located and corrected before any real damage is done. If procedures are not thoroughly tested, chaos may well result during parallel runs or actual operation of the new system.

Master records. Master records must be key punched and verified from information provided from the existing system. Basic data should be revised and in proper condition for mechanization by the time the master punched card decks are ready for preparation. This means that all codes are assigned and that the data is in a legible and convenient form for punching operations. Examples of master records are bills of material, beginning or opening balance cards, name and address cards, and so forth. Because these master records are used repeatedly in punched card operations, it is essential that all data be verified back to the original information either by manual or mechanical methods.

Parallel runs. Parallel runs must be scheduled to enable comparison of punched card procedure results with existing procedure results. Not until punched card procedures are completely adequate and correct can the existing system or controls be dropped. This involves running duplicate systems until the tabulating function has proved itself to be operating satisfactorily. It may require one or two months for each application or control which is mechanized. This step is the final check over the new punched card system, and it is imperative for management to make certain that results are in exact agreement with planned objectives.

Other preparations. During the conversion planning phase, machine operators and clerical personnel should be given thorough instruction in the system requirements and the new or revised duties necessary for the punched card application. Another necessary step is to incorporate the new procedure in machine scheduling and utilization reporting. Due-in and due-out dates should be carefully established in order to meet deadlines for final reports that will tie in with processing schedules of other mechanized applications or manually prepared information.

Conclusions. By following the steps and techniques outlined for initial planning, system planning, and conversion planning, a punched card system is now ready for actual operation and the replaced system can be discontinued.

A successful installation for any business, regardless of size, requires adequate and careful planning. At best, a change to punched card procedures is extremely difficult and trying. Even with the most careful planning techniques, there will be unexpected problems that must be solved "on the move." If planning is haphazard or inadequate, these problems can develop too rapidly to be handled at the last moment, often resulting in complete chaos.

Under such circumstances, a company can abandon the installation or slowly correct the errors on a postinstallation basis. Either solution is far more costly than the expense of careful early planning conducted in a complete and professional manner.

The Drawbacks of Punched Tape

Punched tape applications may also have certain disadvantages. The following case study, based on an actual experience, illustrates some shortcomings found in practice.

A case study

1. *Delay in processing tapes.* The service center in this particular case attempted to schedule work by individual CPAs and not by CPAs as a class. This resulted in a contract providing for two servicings per month with a set-up charge for additional services. To provide the kind of service to which our clients had been accustomed, the costs appeared to be

prohibitive. We tried various combinations of bimonthly schedules and found that no matter what combination was devised, some clients during the month did not meet the deadlines. As much as three weeks elapsed from the time data was given our office until a finished report was delivered to the client. We also found that, with the utmost co-operation from the client, the fastest we could deliver a report via punched tape machine accounting was a week to ten days. Our clients were most unhappy with the delay.

2. *Difficulties encountered in correcting mistakes.* We found that frequently two months were necessary to correct the mistakes made in accumulating data for processing. If a wrong code number was used by the client or by our staff, it was frequently discovered too late to correct in the next month's accounting run and the error had to be corrected in the second run following. This caused numerous memorandum-type adjustments in the intervening months and wasted a considerable amount of time on the job.

3. *Difficulty encountered at end-of-year closings.* Many of our clients do not provide inventories, accounts receivable, or accounts payable immediately upon close of the fiscal year. Frequently, inventories were taken at the date of closing but priced and extended at later dates by the clients' employees when it would least interfere with their regular work. It is not uncommon for a client to fall two or three months behind at the close of his year. If we attempted to catch up on a month-by-month basis through the punched tape machine, we found it would take six months to catch up a client who had fallen behind three months. The answer to this situation was to process transactions monthly without an opening balance sheet or to catch up with the work in one lump; but either solution required spending extra time on the job.

4. *Employee fatigue.* The punched tape attachment sounds like a machine gun operating in the office. This noise was partially eliminated by putting the machine and operator in a private office to which the door was closed, but the machine noise was responsible for an excessive amount of employee fatigue. We found that the efficiency of a person's work decreased sharply after the first hour of running the machine; and after the second hour, efficiency decreased to a point where the work had to be almost entirely redone. It is our opinion that no employee should be scheduled for more than a sixty- to ninety-minute shift each morning or afternoon.

5. *Employee antagonism toward machine accounting.* We found that as the punched tape machine was new, a natural antagonism and resentment arose among our employees. This, coupled with the difficulties of correcting errors, caused the employees to blame human errors on the accounting machine in conferences with a client. Such action resulted in certain clients demanding that their accounts be taken off the punched tape machine; these demands were unwarranted.

6. *Clients not suited to punched tape machine.* Only the work of some of our clients is adaptable to machine operation—the so-called "clean" accounts. It is most difficult to process information for clients whose records are not up to date, fairly accurate, and for which the coding has not been correctly maintained. With certain other clients, machine production was constantly delayed while the operator attempted to obtain information from the client.

7. *Difficulty in analyzing certain accounts.* We have had several occasions to analyze certain accounts for clients or Internal Revenue Agents. We found that the records produced by punched tape accounting showed disbursements or purchases by folio and amount thereof, but there was no ready identification of the folio. When working from handwritten records, the vendor or payee frequently disclosed the information desired in analyzing the account in question, but with the punched tape machine it was necessary to look up the check or voucher to ascertain the needed information. By the time we attempted to analyze said accounts, this original posting information had been returned to the client's office and was sometimes not available or difficult to recover. Greater difficulty will probably be experienced in attempting to analyze records three to five years old.

8. We were advised that it would be extremely impractical to make one run of data and prepare subsidiary records therefrom. The processing center should be able to prepare accounts receivable, accounts payable, and/or cost records from a single run, depending upon the wishes of the client, without the necessity of an involved setup. The set-up charges proposed when this was requested from our existing service facilities were prohibitive and discouraged several clients from having records processed in this manner.

The above defects are not insurmountable, but they present problems to which ready solutions have not yet been found. Electronic computers are capable of producing better results than mechanical processing, but at the present time the rental of an electronic computer is too great for a small firm.

Weaknesses of punched card bookkeeping[3]

Punched card bookkeeping is at its best when the various sorting and reproducing machines are utilized. This usually occurs in summing up masses of data. However, the machines which involve punching (and thus verifying) and printing of data are slow by comparison and unable to

[3]Pages 267-70 are excerpted from an article entitled "Mechanical Accounting Machines," which appeared in the *Proceedings of the Fourth Annual Accounting Systems Conference,* October 27 and 28, 1960, California Society of CPAs, Los Angeles. The author is **Walter** R. Hyman, CPA.

furnish daily information. Why are tabulating service bureaus now so popular? Principally because the bureau can furnish *monthly* statistics and because the punched card often falls short of the mark in the furnishing of *daily* statistics.

To illustrate, some companies find it far more practical to receive monthly job cost data from a service bureau than to purchase their own equipment in order to receive daily job cost data. Other companies receive a complete listing of inventory items at month-end from a service bureau. This listing is then used to verify the manual inventory records which still must be maintained at the companies' offices. Even the largest companies still obtain from standard accounting machines (or manually) daily totals of major sales categories, for management purposes. This occurs despite the presence of a massive punched card installation capable of furnishing the figures, but not on a practical daily basis. One should be very wary of the punched card man who promises to furnish, at reasonable cost, all the daily information now obtained by other means.

Inability to furnish daily historical ledger card information is another weakness. This item could probably be classified under "inability to furnish daily data." However, this category needs special emphasis because of the widespread belief that punched card bookkeeping can be adapted to any standard accounting machine application. And what can be more standard than an accounts receivable or historical inventory ledger card? Yet it is this category which has completely defied solution by even the staunchest punched card advocate.

Maintaining an historical ledger card usually involves continual day-by-day posting to the same card. Punched card equipment does not provide for insertion of the same forms into the printing machines. Its only answer is to reprint all of the data on a sheet at given periods. There is a punched card machine called a transfer poster. In essence, it is merely a printing press. No control or proof of posting to the correct ledger card exists; consequently, balances, though correct on the journal, can be incorrect because they appear on the wrong ledger.

In punched card installations, reports and statistical information are generally considered to be more important than historical records. The reason for this thinking is that reports *must* be completed first before an historical record can be created in a punched card setup. But history records are usually essential. Very often a punched card installation is combined with a basic accounting machine retained for creating history ledgers.

Prepunched cards are often used in billing and inventory control punched card applications. Price and style number changes, if frequent, require constant change in the cards and can involve a complete waste of thousands of cards. This presents the problem of a lack of flexibility. The wired boards are no more flexible than a standard accounting machine panel or bar. If a mistake has been made in wiring or in the cards, the mistake will not be located until a complete run has been made.

Punched card accounting is notorious for its complete absence of journals. Adding machine and accounting machine prelists are still very much a necessity for proof purposes. Not infrequently do we find that a complete machine or manual reverification is necessary, sometimes involving visual scanning of thousands of cards. Adding and accounting machines, punched tape, and card hookups are a major step forward in eliminating bookless bookkeeping. The advent of the punched tape adding machine is also a partial solution to the prelist problem.

Any complete punched card installation has punched card verifiers in addition to regular key punch equipment. The verifier is similar in appearance to the card punch and its operation is the same. To verify, the operator enters the same information from the media that the key punch operator entered. The machine will lock if there is a discrepancy in the card. In essence, to have an accurately coded card, it is necessary to repeat all information, digit for digit, a second time. In practice, only parts of cards are verified (e.g., quantity and price) and then only for a portion of the cards (as low as 10 to 15 per cent of the cards). The possibility that an error will still exist after these processes is substantial.

There is only one more process in which an error can possibly be located: If the cards are passed through a collator and matched with a master deck of prepunched cards, which is quite common, an error might be located. Finally the cards reach the tabulator (a high-speed printer). There is now no chance of locating an error until a complete run of cards has been made. Grand totals are then compared with a prelist of the media. Very seldom is any control provided at this point as to accuracy of style numbers and quantities. Only total dollars or units are verified.

Since the main function of a punched card system is to provide month-end reports and statistics, it follows that there will be definite overloads at that time, particularly on the tabulating (printing) equipment, causing peak periods. If payroll and billing (or either one) are part of the installation, some operation must be deferred. In addition, around-the-clock, twenty-four-hour shifts are not uncommon, including resulting time-and-one-half wages to high-priced personnel.

Generally speaking, punched card systems do not reduce, but often increase office costs, which include equipment costs. Their dollar-saving features occur in the management decisions prompted by the reports and statistics not hitherto available to the organization. A few factors creating high office costs include (a) cost of renting the equipment; (b) wages of punched card specialists, and particularly overtime premiums during peak periods; and (c) high form costs.

Conclusions. Despite the problems involved in punched card accounting, there is no doubting its rapid growth in an age where statistics are vital. Nevertheless, the value of the statistics in relation to the cost and difficulties of punched card accounting must be considered. A thorough and exhaustive review by management of the necessity for various data is of prime importance before considering any mechanization, particularly punched card. Management must be thoroughly warned of the short-comings and high costs of punched card accounting before making any decision.

The CPA's Role

The CPA is often faced with a situation in which he is only a bystander while his client ponders the purchase of one or more accounting machines. Doesn't the CPA have a responsibility at least to determine whether there will be enough savings to justify purchasing machines? The CPA has responsibility, fee or no fee, if for no other reason than the purely selfish one, namely, the desire to avoid a dissatisfied client, faced with an unproductive accounting machine. A CPA who looked on helplessly while such a machine was purchased cannot exactly feel proud of himself.

What can the CPA do in a minimum of time to avoid any grave mistake by a client contemplating the purchase of an expensive accounting machine? Possibly some or all of the following procedures might be adopted by the CPA who wishes to help his client make the right decision:

1. Determine the area in which the volume of bookkeeping work is greatest. A knowledge of the client's business will enable an almost immediate determination.

Type of company	Probable peak volume area
Retail store	Billing, inventory control, payables
Job shop	Payroll records
Aircraft parts company	Cost accounting
Distributor	Receivables, payables

2. Make certain that the recommended machine specializes or excels in the "volume of bookkeeping" areas just mentioned. If billing is the major area, verify that a billing machine is contemplated, and not the standard accounting machine adapted to a billing operation.

3. If possible, insist on visiting one or more installations in a similar industry using similar equipment. Even a few telephone calls may produce interesting results. Note that since the machine salesman will usually suggest a good installation, it might be advisable to have the client suggest names of a few similar companies which he knows are using modern methods. He might even have a few friends in the industry.

4. Verify volume count. Take a peak period in the volume area. Examine the media for a segment of that period and count the media (number of lines, distributions, quantity of invoices, and so on). Count the data that will be mechanized. Check with the machine salesman's figures. Always remember that a machine must be adapted to the peak period of a

concern. In this sense, any other period of time loses its significance when the peak arrives.

5. Determine the reason for the interest in the machine.
   (a) Is the main criteria "elimination of employees?" If so, then a brief review of the employees' duties other than the area to be mechanized might be in order.
   (b) Does the machine salesman suggest a shifting of duties? A chat with the office manager might indicate whether the retained employees are capable of assuming new responsibilities.
   (c) Is immediate information the major factor? If tabulating is recommended will it supply, at a reasonable cost, this daily data? Will month-end peaks instantly cause the machines to fall behind?
   (d) Are the so-called "intangibles" factors?
       (i) Machine-printed statements
       (ii) Improvement of office morale
       (iii) Increase in accuracy
       (iv) Statements to be mailed faster
       (v) Bills to be paid on time

The big question here is: Do the improvements in the intangibles justify the cost of the machine?

6. Verify the number of accumulators necessary in the standard accounting machine. The price of a standard accounting machine can vary substantially depending upon the number of built-in accumulators in the machine. It is the CPA's duty to see to it that the client is not being oversold. In the volume area the number of *major* classifications requiring automatic addition must be determined. This count will determine the number of accumulators really necessary. The minor classifications can be added manually in a few minutes after the distribution operation.

7. Verify the necessity of a typewriter accounting machine. Normally the use of a typewriter consumes 30 to 60 per cent of the time in an accounting machine operation. Numerical systems are often better and faster. A few general conclusions regarding the use of a typewriter in different bookkeeping classifications for volume jobs follow:
   (a) Receivables: Typewriters generally not required
   (b) Sales analysis: Typewriters generally not required
   (c) Payables: Optional, depending upon the time spent referring to unit ledgers and cash disbursement journals
   (d) Payroll and quarterly reports: Desirable.

It should be noted that the additional cost of a typewriter sometimes makes it a nice feature.

8. Analyze peak periods. This topic has already been discussed briefly. However, it is wise to determine whether the client decided on the necessity of an accounting machine after the hectic strain of a peak period arrived. Is he buying the machine for the two- or three-month peak, and if

so will it pay for itself? The facts of each individual situation will require some review on the part of the CPA.

9. Invite competition. All too often a client, unfamiliar with the various machine companies, calls in the one company he has personally heard of. It would be a simple matter for the CPA to awaken his client to the fact that there are additional machine companies, highly competitive in all phases of mechanization. The client will thus receive the benefits arising out of a competitive situation, in which price, style, and application may vary considerably from company to company. Moreover, he will benefit from the competition of the individual salesmen, who now realize that they must do more than sell equipment to an already anxious customer.

What Is EDP? *

Introduction

The term "electronic data processing" was originated in the early fifties. At that time it referred to the use of electronic devices for scientific and pure mathematical computations. The equipment then used was primitive compared to present-day computers, and its use for business problems was virtually nonexistent.

Within a few years, however, there has been a remarkable change. Refinements in the electronic components increased the reliability of EDP. The capacity of the units and the speed of operation increased considerably. This encouraged experiments in the use of EDP for business, and these proved to be very successful.

There are now two general areas. The term "data reduction" is usually applied to scientific computations, while EDP generally refers to business problems; but there is no clear line of demarcation between them. Electronic data processing is now being used in every phase of business. For small companies there are electronic punched card calculators costing only a few hundred dollars per month. Then by easy stages the monthly rental increases to one thousand dollars for small electronic computers, five thousand dollars for intermediate computers, and up to fifty thousand dollars per month or more for the very large ones, whose purchase price runs up to several million dollars.

⁴Pages 272-78 appeared as a paper in the *Proceedings of the Fourth Annual Accounting Systems Conference,* October 27 and 28, 1960, California Society of CPAs, Los Angeles. The author is Larry Allen, Systems Consultant, Gindoff & Swartz, CPAs, Los Angeles.

There are many makes and models of electronic computers and computer systems on the market today, no two of which are identical. Furthermore, each model may include various optional features, so it may be said that very few of the EDP systems now in use are similar.

Computer Systems

Semantics has become more of a problem in business than ever before. For example, the terms "electronics" and "computer" are uttered almost indiscriminately. Consequently there are many misconceptions as to what constitutes an electronic computer. Following are characteristics of a true electronic computer, as distinguished from other data processing equipment:

In digital computer systems, the term "configuration" is frequently used. Its meaning in this connection refers more specifically to the type, number, and arrangement of the units comprising a computer system, rather than to the relative disposition of parts, which is the usual meaning of the term. The configuration of the synthetic computer is the simplest possible assemblage of units that can be classified as a computer system.

Input unit. The function of an input unit is easy to understand: It is that of sensing the data which it is desired to process. An analogy can be drawn with the familiar funnel. Business problems are literally poured into this funnel. There are many forms of input units, but, whatever the form, the function remains the same.

Memory unit. The storage unit of a computer system may be most easily visualized as a compact arrangement of numbered pigeon-holes. Each numbered compartment may be called a memory cell, a storage location, or any one of a dozen names. The number which designates a memory cell is known as its address in memory or its location.

The function of the memory unit seems quite obvious—that is, it should be capable of "remembering" instructions and data in alphabetic and numerical form, within the machine. Memory may be either magnetic drum, disk, or core storage—external memory on punched cards or the use of mechanical card calculators do not fall within our definition. There are many types of memory: large, small, fast, and slow. But every computer system must have a memory.

Arithmetic and logical units. The "arithmetic" designation seems quite clear. Every computer system must be able to add and subtract, at the very least. Some can only add, subtract, and multiply. The largest units can perform only four arithmetic functions: adding, subtracting, multiplying and dividing. In the simpler units (add and subtract only), multiplication is performed by multiple addition just as on a comptometer, and division is accomplished by multiple subtraction.

The "logical" designation requires some explanation. A computer cannot perform any deductive or inferential reasoning. Its decisions are simply based upon "Yes/No" conditions established by the program in use at the time. Almost every computer can sense whether: (1) a specified number is plus, minus, or zero; (2) a number is greater, equal to, or less than another number. Using these simple comparisons, a skilled programmer can almost make it appear as if the computer had a brain of its own. There are many forms of arithmetic and logical units, but the functions are similar and differ only in scope.

Console. A console is provided so that the operator of a computer system can have a means of checking the performance of the system, determining the source of trouble when testing out a new problem solution, making corrections, and, in general, supervising the operation. The usual console has various signal lights which tell the operator what the system is doing at the moment; lights which will identify such conditions as "input unit empty," "output unit not ready," "unacceptable input record." Some consoles have literally hundreds of lights and switches, but in principle they are all alike. Sometimes the console is attached to the main frame of the system; sometimes it is remotely located.

Output unit. The only remaining essential of a computer system is some form of output. The output unit may take any of a number of forms, and the output itself may be produced simultaneously in several forms.

Comparison with EAM

With electric accounting machines, every machine function has its counterpart in manually operated office equipment. By the same token, every function of a computer system is paralleled both in EAM and manual equipment. The real difference lies in the elimination of the human link in a chain of operations.

In a manual system a clerk makes the decisions. In EAM, the sorter, collator, accounting machine, and calculating punch all make logical decisions. Each punched card machine has its own individual input and output. Several units, such as the accounting machine and calculating punch, have excellent arithmetic units. The real difference then between EAM and computer systems is that punched card equipment consists of a group of separate, single-purpose machines, while a computer system consists of a group of integrated and interconnected units capable of communicating with each other in machine language. One enters the complete problem and obtains the complete solution without human intervention, and at the speed of light. Care should be exercised, however, lest a substantial oversimplification be inferred of what is really involved in the preceding statement.

Computer Program

What is a "program"? A program is a series of instructions which tell the system what to do under any and all conditions. A good illustration would be to compare the mechanical program of an automatic record player with that of an electronic computer.

Figure 4

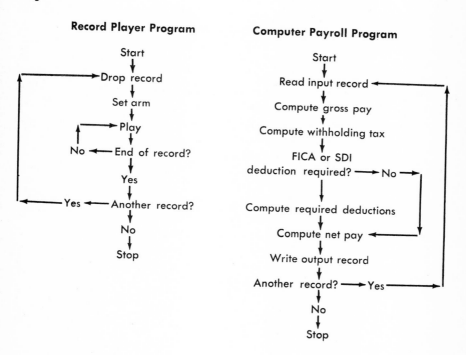

The two diagrams in Figure 4, above, illustrate the type of program initially written for any computer problem or application to define the elements of the problem. Each element is studied to determine the best method to use, and then, detailed instructions are written.

Programming

Since electronic computers do a number of steps in sequence, the machine must be instructed in advance as to these steps. This is called "programming." There are various methods—in some cases wiring a second control panel is all that is required; in others, instructions are cut into cards; in still others, they are coded on a tape, all depending on the type of machine.

Programming involves three steps:

1. The job must be laid out step by step. This usually involves steps not normally considered separately. As a simple example, assume a payroll job in which no check can exceed $100. In a manual operation, the clerk would watch for items over $100, without realizing that every time he writes, say $88.35, he subconsciously decides that the amount is under $100.01. In a computer, the program must provide for testing each net amount for this comparison.

2. The steps just outlined must be coded in the form of instructions that the particular machine accepts.

3. The coded instructions must be set up in the form used by the calculator (control panel, punched cards, tape, or other form, as used by the particular machine).

The time required for programming depends upon several factors, but primarily on the complexity of the job. If the work is relatively simple and some illustrative applications (as issued by most companies) are available, programming might be a matter of two or three hours. A normal payroll job without such assistance might take as much as a day. An elaborate job involving basic method changes might take a month or more to study, plan, and program, or even longer, if it involves combining several routines into one big job.

Two actual cases, based on a big, stored-program type of machine combining all functions, will serve as illustrations. A typical industrial wage payroll (including provisions for all possible irregulars) required 1,102 program steps, while an industrial plant cost distribution, with all the cost allocations involved, required 734 steps.

It may well take longer to set up a job than to run it. With repetitive jobs, programming need be done only once, and even in special runs the combined programming and running time may represent a substantial time saving. While it requires a good deal of training to develop a competent programmer, it has proved quite practical to do so.

The question of records in connection with electronic accounting machines deserves careful consideration. The attitude of a representative of one of the companies prepared to develop machines to order seemed to be: "Records! Are you going to be old-fashioned and want records?" With punched card electronic machines, there is usually no change in the basic system, and the same type of records now obtained from non-electronic machines may be expected.

A different situation exists in the case of machines using tapes for output purposes. Anything on a tape may be printed and a record obtained. But a tape will hold a lot of information, and there may be a temptation to store tapes, particularly underlying tapes, instead of printing records. Whether the auditor will be satisfied to have certain specified tapes run for his use, or whether he will require everything printed out, will probably be a matter of development and experience. The machines can produce any records required.

A *typical computer*

The name CRAZIAC originated at California Research to identify their Automatic Zealously Immediate Audible Computer. The name, but not the design, has been borrowed to illustrate the inner workings of a typical computer. All technical details have been omitted.

Here is a list of twelve operations which can be used to complete a one-man weekly payroll:

00 Read and store input record
01 Clear and add into accumulator
02 Add to accumulator
03 Subtract from accumulator
04 Multiply
05 Divide (not used in this problem)
06 Store in memory from accumulator
07 Compare (not used in this problem)
08 Branch if accumulator is not minus
09 Add from accumulator to memory
10 Unconditional branch
11 Write output record

A computer instruction in its simplest form consists of two parts: (1) the operating part, which tells the computer what to do; and (2) the address part, which tells the computer where to find the operation or where to put the result.

Having written a suitable program and recorded it in machine language on some medium acceptable to the CRAZIAC, the first step is to load the program. By this step, we have:

1. Reserved space in memory for the input record (locations 1 to 10)
2. Introduced the program constants required by the problem
3. Reserved space for the results of the computations
4. Stored the program in locations 51 to 90 (see Table 2, page 278).

The program is now started by obeying the first instruction. This is found in memory address 51 and reads:

Operation   00 (Read and store input record)
Address   01 to 10 (Locations 01 to 10)

With this data in place, the computer will proceed to compute gross pay (steps 52 to 59). The computer is then instructed to compute withholding tax (steps 60 to 66), up-dating the year-to-date tax (step 67). Then it makes tests to determine the need for FICA and SDI deductions, and in this case it computes both (steps 68 to 81). The final computing steps (82 to 88) make a series of subtractions to arrive at net pay. The completed pay record is written out in step 89. The computer will branch back to step 51 and read in the next record until the payroll is complete.

Table 2

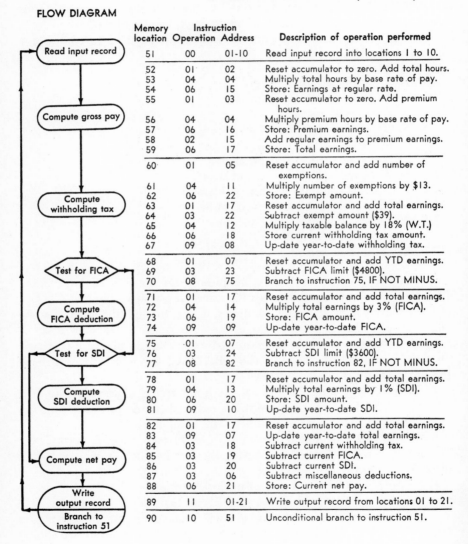

FLOW DIAGRAM

Memory location	Instruction Operation	Instruction Address	Description of operation performed
51	00	01-10	Read input record into locations 1 to 10.
52	01	02	Reset accumulator to zero. Add total hours.
53	04	04	Multiply total hours by base rate of pay.
54	06	15	Store: Earnings at regular rate.
55	01	03	Reset accumulator to zero. Add premium hours.
56	04	04	Multiply premium hours by base rate of pay.
57	06	16	Store: Premium earnings.
58	02	15	Add regular earnings to premium earnings.
59	06	17	Store: Total earnings.
60	01	05	Reset accumulator and add number of exemptions.
61	04	11	Multiply number of exemptions by $13.
62	06	22	Store: Exempt amount.
63	01	17	Reset accumulator and add total earnings.
64	03	22	Subtract exempt amount ($39).
65	04	12	Multiply taxable balance by 18% (W.T.).
66	06	18	Store current withholding tax amount.
67	09	08	Up-date year-to-date withholding tax.
68	01	07	Reset accumulator and add YTD earnings.
69	03	23	Subtract FICA limit ($4800).
70	08	75	Branch to instruction 75, IF NOT MINUS.
71	01	17	Reset accumulator and add total earnings.
72	04	14	Multiply total earnings by 3% (FICA).
73	06	19	Store: FICA amount.
74	09	09	Up-date year-to-date FICA.
75	01	07	Reset accumulator and add YTD earnings.
76	03	24	Subtract SDI limit ($3600).
77	08	82	Branch to instruction 82, IF NOT MINUS.
78	01	17	Reset accumulator and add total earnings.
79	04	13	Multiply total earnings by 1% (SDI).
80	06	20	Store: SDI amount.
81	09	10	Up-date year-to-date SDI.
82	01	17	Reset accumulator and add total earnings.
83	09	07	Up-date year-to-date total earnings.
84	03	18	Subtract current withholding tax.
85	03	19	Subtract current FICA.
86	03	20	Subtract current SDI.
87	03	06	Subtract miscellaneous deductions.
88	06	21	Store: Current net pay.
89	11	01-21	Write output record from locations 01 to 21.
90	10	51	Unconditional branch to instruction 51.

Flow diagram labels: Read input record; Compute gross pay; Compute withholding tax; Test for FICA; Compute FICA deduction; Test for SDI; Compute SDI deduction; Compute net pay; Write output record; Branch to instruction 51.

Administration and Control
of EDP Projects[5]

THE INSTALLATION OF advanced data processing systems can provide more operating information on a more timely basis, can improve efficiency and reduce costs, and can open the door to more advanced and effective management tools to meet the challenge of tomorrow's increasing volumes and complexities. Or it can generate a tangle of error and confusion at a high cost in money, employee misery, and management embarrassment.

Which will be the result depends on how well the program is thought out and executed. Making sure that qualified personnel carry out the basic steps required is management's prime responsibility. If this responsibility is met, there is no need to fear the approach of automation.

Planning and implementation

No matter how carefully and thoroughly the preliminary studies for a typical EDP project may have been performed, the plans which emerge hardly qualify as blueprints. They are bound to be more in the nature of preliminary sketches with most of the details still to be worked out. In most cases, the staff assembled to carry out the planning, programming, and conversion work is facing these problems for the first time. The fact that they are paid for their work will not divest them immediately of their amateur status.

Under these circumstances, detailed advance planning and close day-to-day control over progress, which are so important to the construction superintendent, are next to impossible for the typical EDP manager. Lacking these administrative tools, at least in the beginning, the people responsible for a major EDP project must to a large extent play by ear, making detailed plans as they go along and controlling progress less closely than they would like to. The many uncertainties which seem to be characteristic of EDP projects make the administrative job unusually difficult and at the same time critically important.

Before considering what might be called the implementation side of an EDP job (which has to do with organizing, directing, and controlling the day-to-day work of a sizable staff), some mention must be made of the planning side of EDP management which leads up to the implementation program and provides a foundation for it. How solid this founda-

[5]Pages 279-84 first appeared as an article in the Summer 1961 issue of *The Virginia Accountant*. The author is Duane E. Watts, Principal, Management Advisory Services Division, Price Waterhouse & Co., New York.

tion is determines, to a very large extent, what can be built on it. It is fair to say that no amount of good management during the implementation phase can bring off the project as planned and achieve the objectives expected unless these plans and objectives were realistic in the first place.

In most companies the persons who are assigned major responsibility for the implementation phase will have participated in and probably had some responsibility for the studies which led to a decision to proceed. In EDP, as in most things, the man who suggests that something be done is very likely to wind up with the job of doing it. One would expect this to ensure a high degree of realism and conservatism in the proposals and estimates issuing from feasibility studies. However, experience demonstrates that this is not always the case, even though the over-optimism is often quite unintentional and, in fact, was often thought to have been restrained.

Cost reduction or increase?

An administrative vice-president of one company stated that one of their several EDP applications had turned out to be a serious disappointment despite the fact that, in his opinion, an excellent job had been done in developing the system and making it operative. The only trouble was that when the new system was in and running smoothly, it was costing about 20 per cent more than the old system. He had to admit that the new system was a lot better in many ways than the old one; but even so, the principal objective had been to reduce costs, and this simply had not been achieved. It was clear in retrospect that the preliminary studies had been superficial and oversimplified and that there should have been a reappraisal of the situation during the implementation phase, when more accurate predictions could have been made.

Since cost reduction is often the principal reason for installing a computer, it is extremely important that the cost and savings estimates be realistic. Some good indications of cost reduction can be obtained through objective answers to three key questions.

1. In conducting the feasibility study, have the details of the data processing work to be fed to the computer really been understood? If not, there is more than a slight chance that the final result will fall short of expectations. The net effect of not completely understanding what the system must do has ranged from slight to serious.

2. Was the proposed computer system, including the associated manual and punched card procedures, worked out in sufficient detail to permit valid estimates of the equipment needed, machine times, and personnel requirements? Even when the proposed system has been designed in considerable detail, the tendency is to underestimate these important cost elements.

3. Were the estimates of present costs to be replaced by the computer

developed in detail, with a clear understanding of what work the computer system will take over and what will continue to be performed by other methods? Did the operating people now responsible for these operations participate in making these estimates, or at least concur in them? Actual savings realized have frequently fallen short of original estimates, and in most cases where this has happened, the trouble can be in part traced to superficial estimates made without assistance from operating people.

Unless each of these three questions can be answered with a confident "Yes," there is a strong possibility that cost reduction objectives may not be fully achieved. If cost reduction is a principal goal, then it is a good idea, as part of an engagement, to re-examine the original estimates and reappraise the economics of the proposed systems, as details are worked out. Minor variations from the original estimates are to be expected. If major differences show up, it may become necessary to redesign the system, change its scope, or possibly drop the application altogether. While none of these alternatives is pleasant to contemplate, it is better to recognize the need for them early, before conversion, when it is still relatively easy to take corrective action.

Importance of timetable

Assuming that the operating cost and savings estimates on which the go-ahead decision was based will stand up under a critical reappraisal, the next important concern of the EDP engagement is whether or not the project timetable can be met. A number of companies which have finally succeeded in reaching the first of their original objectives, have done so only after a considerably longer time than was originally anticipated. The engagements that have come closest to meeting the schedules set up at the outset have been those that phased in the easiest projects first, working up gradually to the full system.

The wish is always strong to step directly from the present system to one that is totally integrated; and, given ideal conditions and enthusiastic assistance from the affected operating departments concerned, a giant stride of this kind might be possible. In the usual situation, though, it is more practical to think in terms of a more modest step-by-step approach.

One manufacturing company, for example, decided as a result of considerable study that its ultimate objective would be an integrated computer system of broad scope to handle billing, inventory control, production scheduling, payroll, and cost accounting. The data flow between these various functions suggested many integration possibilities and it would have been easy to tackle the whole problem at once. After some deliberation, however, they decided to concentrate on the easiest parts first. The only practical way to attain an integrated system is to start small and build on.

Deciding what the scope of the first applications should be is largely a question of good judgment. It is a matter of balancing conflicting objectives and arriving at a reasonable compromise. On the one hand, there is the desire to keep the application simple so that a largely inexperienced staff will not be overwhelmed. On the other hand, there usually is a requirement that the first applications pay the computer's keep. If these are pared down too much, they may not.

The larger companies are at a distinct advantage in dealing with this problem since, in their case, even pared-down applications are more likely to provide a worth-while computer work load. The smaller companies are more likely to feel compelled to go after more or bigger applications all at once, only to discover later that their plan was too ambitious.

Realizing achievable goals

One can never be certain that the applications chosen as first steps represent realistic, achievable goals. Until the work is actually in progress, it is hard to say just how difficult it is going to be in relation to the skills and abilities of the staff that can be assembled. Some companies have made fast and worth-while progress in the use of computers by selecting as first applications work which was either already mechanized on punched cards, or was simple enough to have been so mechanized; work that was already done at a central location; and work which was under the control of a single department. They have found that, by so limiting their first applications, they have been able to concentrate for the first couple of years on developing an experienced staff and learning exactly what is involved in developing and installing computer systems. Companies that have taken this approach believe that they are then in a much better position to tackle more difficult applications, involving work which was not previously mechanized and which may have been scattered among a number of departments and locations. However, this point of view is by no means widespread.

To summarize, whatever initial applications may have been chosen, it is part of the administrative and managerial job to make sure, as the work progresses, that the goals are and continue to be realistic and achievable. Nothing is more frustrating to the members of an EDP staff and more harmful to a company's entire EDP program than to have goals and objectives which cannot reasonably be met. Most companies have found it necessary at one time or another to lower their sights or lengthen their schedule. Knowing when and how to do this requires good administrative control and frequent reappraisals as the work progresses. Daily reappraisals are certainly not necessary; but in EDP projects where funds are usually limited, every few months is not too often for a hard, searching look at how the project stands in relation to the timetable.

Organization of EDP staff

How best to organize a company's EDP staff is a problem that has been solved in a variety of ways. There is no one best way, since each company has special conditions favoring or requiring a particular kind of organization.

The easiest situation, from an organizational standpoint, is the one in which all or most of the work to be done by the computer is within the jurisdiction of one department. Here there is little point in having the top EDP man report to anyone but the department manager. In fact, most EDP installations so far have this kind of reporting relationship, usually to the controller. When the proposed applications affect a number of operating departments, the usual practice is to have the EDP manager report either to an administrative vice-president or to a high-level steering committee, composed of senior officers and heads of the departments concerned. Whatever the reporting relationship of the EDP manager may be, it should be designed to promote a good working relationship between the EDP staff and the operating groups whose work will be affected. This is most easily achieved if both the EDP manager and the operating groups in question report directly to the same man. The need for developing and maintaining good working relationships with the affected operating department cannot be overemphasized.

It is absolutely essential that the operating people, whose work is to be taken over by the computer, participate actively in developing the new system and that they feel a sense of responsibility for the over-all result. Passive acquiescence is clearly not enough. Active assistance from the operating people is particularly important during the conversion from the old system to the new. Obtaining the necessary help and support is usually much easier if the EDP group and the operating groups are organizationally close. Otherwise there is a clear need for a steering committee, a carefully planned public relations program, and a great deal of statesmanship on the part of the EDP manager.

The internal organization of an EDP group can take many forms, nearly all of which have been proven workable in practice. The most frequent practice is to set up a systems design and programming staff under one director and a computer operations staff under another, both reporting to the EDP manager, who may have any one of a dozen titles. The organization within these groups varies rather widely from company to company, both as to structure and formality. No noticeable correlation has been found between a particular style of organization and the over-all rate of progress in getting work onto the computer.

Highly formalized organizations are more appropriate in situations where the over-all job to be done is regular, recurring, and completely understood. In EDP projects this is generally not the case. The nature of the work to be done changes considerably from phase to phase. The organization should therefore be flexible enough to change with the work.

The manufacturer's representative

Throughout an EDP project, the role of the manufacturer's representative should be: (1) to supply the technical knowledge which may be lacking in the customer's staff; (2) to make sure the customer's staff understands all the jobs to be done; and (3) to serve in an advisory capacity at all levels. It is not realistic to expect the manufacturer to assume a responsibility for actually designing or programming any substantial part of the system.

It is generally recognized by now that even after an installation is running smoothly, accurate assessment of its value to the company is very difficult. Costs associated with the computer are usually easy enough to determine; the difficulty lies in deciding what the operations would cost without the computer. Changes in volume, in company practices, in organization, and in wage and salary structure, all tend to cloud the picture to make valid comparisons complex and difficult. It is only a rare and fortunate EDP manager who is spared the necessity of making some kind of accounting to management from time to time.

Changing Concepts in
EDP Feasibility Studies

IT IS IMPORTANT IN any EDP project that a consultant also conduct a feasibility study. The underlying concepts of the feasibility study have changed in recent years almost as much as the equipment has.

A computer feasibility study should develop answers to two major questions: What is the best way of utilizing EDP? Which computer, if any, best meets the company's requirements?

The factors that govern the development of the answers to these questions are subject to continuous refinement and change. Technological improvements are being developed continuously by the computer manufacturers. Equally important developments are being made in application concepts. Gradually, users are learning that full utilization of EDP requires extension beyond routine bread-and-butter applications. Broad, company-wide applications are beginning to materialize. These cross departmental lines and mechanize decision processes that previously were performed more or less intuitively by human beings.

As a result of these improvements, feasibility studies today are apt to develop positive conclusions that could not have been developed a few years ago. Many companies that initially were merely bystanders now find they can profitably apply electronic data processing to their business needs. It is therefore imperative to review current trends in the two factors just mentioned—technological developments and changing application concepts—for these factors weigh heavily in any consideration of computer feasibility.

Technological Developments

The most significant recent development has been the introduction of solid-state computers, the so-called "second generation" of machines. This breakthrough served as a needed stimulant to the industry, and the computer manufacturers and their customers were quick to respond. Several hundred machines have already been delivered, and several thousand more are on order, counting the smaller systems that do not use magnetic tape.

The over-all contribution of the new family of machines is obvious— the customer gets more processing capacity for his dollar. More specifically, the machines offer:

1. Faster processing
2. Greater reliability
3. Lower programming costs
4. Lower installation costs (less floor space, lighter weight, less air conditioning)
5. Lower operating costs (less power, floor space, and air conditioning)

The transistor, of course, has made most of the improvements possible. The tiny new device quickly outmoded the vacuum tube, just as magnetic cores outmoded the cathode ray tube a few years earlier. The result was miniaturization, improved performance, and lower costs.

The introduction of the transistor, however, was only partly responsible for the success of the new computers. Equally important was the development of new processing concepts, which, in turn, led to the development of new ways of assembling basic components into more flexible systems overall. The new processing concepts included the following:

1. Parallel processing of multiple programs
2. Consolidation of the capacities of scientific computers and business data processors into dual-purpose machines
3. Expansion of the building-block principle to permit easier transition to EDP
4. Simplification of the programming task

Parallel processing

From the very beginning, the designers of business data processing machines have concentrated on techniques of performing more than one processing function at a time. First, buffer storage devices were developed which enabled the machines to read one magnetic tape record while another was being written out on a second tape. This concept led to:

1. Simultaneous writing of one tape record, processing of a second, and reading of a third
2. Simultaneous operation of any two functions, such as:
   (a) Printing a line of report while reading a tape
   (b) Punching a card while writing a tape
   (c) Reading a card while computing

These developments greatly reduced the time required to process a given computer program. The next step, then, was to design the machines to permit processing of more than one program at a time. The first computer with this feature provided the ability to overlap the processing of one main program with any two of the following so-called peripheral operations: (1) card-to-tape, (2) tape-to-printer, and (3) tape-to-card. This was a significant breakthrough. It meant, for example, that a lengthy stock status report stored on magnetic tape could be printed during the same time a payroll was being processed and written on another tape.

This concept has since been expanded. One computer now has the power to run up to eight programs on a parallel basis, adding significantly to the machine's capacity for work.

Initially it was thought that scientific and engineering problems required a special family of computers. These problems usually involved little in the way of input and output, but required considerable high-speed computing. Perhaps because few companies could afford both types of machines, certain machines are now designed to accommodate both requirements.

Machines of this type provide large (or variable) word sizes, floating-point arithmetic, and binary mode arithmetic primarily for processing the engineering and scientific problems. The same machines provide the following features primarily for commercial applications: fast input and output, overlapping of processing functions and programs, and rapid sorting, file maintenance, and related operations peculiar to business applications. Many other features have been developed which facilitate both the scientific and the business applications. These include larger memories, index registers, and microsecond processing speeds.

The building-block principle

The building-block principle in computers enables a user to acquire a "stripped down" machine for initial requirements. Then, as the business grows or as additional applications are developed, additional machine capacity can be acquired. From a cost viewpoint this makes the whole idea of converting to EDP much more attractive.

There are several ways of expanding the initial capacity of a system:

1. By acquiring additional internal storage

2. By acquiring additional card readers, tape units, and printers

3. By exchanging the initial card readers and tape units for faster models

4. By acquiring buffer storage to permit simultaneous operations, such as the overlapping of printing with internal processing

5. By acquiring an additional machine of a compatible model (Here, compatibility means that the tapes prepared by one machine can be processed on the other, and, to a limited extent, the programs for one machine can be processed on the other.)

Simplifying the programming task

Significant steps have been taken by the manufacturers to simplify the programming task and thus reduce the costs of converting to EDP. The principal developments of this type are:

1. Development of more effective automatic programming methods. Under so-called "English language" programming, the program is written in English, following precise rules. The program is then translated automatically into the language of the computer, using a special program furnished by the computer manufacturer.

2. Development of extensive libraries of programmed routines. The manufacturers now furnish programs for commonly needed routines, such as tape label checking and other input-output functions, sorting, merging, and the preparation of output reports.

3. Development of complete program packages for specific industries. A public utility, for example, can now copy appropriate portions of a generalized program furnished by the computer manufacturer. This approach minimizes the amount of original programming required on the part of the customer.

Changing Application Concepts

It is becoming increasingly clear that extensive planning by qualified systems analysts is needed if the full potential of electronic data processing is to be realized. Such planning has led to a new approach to application development, which is sometimes referred to as the "total system" approach or "systems engineering."

The new concept

The total system approach introduces a new outlook or attitude toward data processing. The analyst begins by viewing a business as a single enterprise composed of related parts. He approaches his task as he would a jigsaw puzzle. First, he studies the picture on the box cover, the end product. Then, he examines each interlocking piece and determines where it fits into the over-all picture and how it relates to other pieces. He does not attempt to work the puzzle merely by examining the shape of each piece. Instead, he observes the flow of color patterns from one piece to another and purposefully builds these patterns into the over-all picture that was preconceived and established in his mind at the outset.

The systems analyst, therefore, endeavors to determine how the component parts of a business relate to one another and how they fit together to form a total entity. The interlocking parts he deals with are the various corporate functions. These include research, engineering, sales, production, finance and accounting, and the many subfunctions within each of these. And just as color flows link the puzzle pieces, information flows link the corporate functions. The analyst knows that the information needed for one purpose is often needed for several other purposes. His initial objective is to spot the common information and determine who uses it, when it is needed, and why it is needed.

Earlier concepts

This point of view stands in sharp contrast to most of the earlier attitudes toward EDP application development. Here are a few cases in point:

1. Our initial objective should be to gain firsthand experience with the new equipment. The advocates of this approach have always started with a simple, well-understood application, such as payroll. Experience now indicates that this approach seldom produces significant results. Since there is no longer any doubt about machine performance or any fear of programming pitfalls, analysts can now tackle the more complex areas with complete confidence.

2. Let's learn to walk before we try to run. This thinking has merit, of course, but it has often been overemphasized. It led to the once-popular belief that an application should be converted to punched card processing as an interim step toward electronic data processing. The danger here is that if an area can be mechanized in its entirety on punched card machines, the subsequent substitution of EDP equipment may again produce no real benefit to the company.

3. Let's move into EDP gradually, application by application. This is still the favored approach. But most analysts now say that a master plan of the ultimate total system should be developed first. Then, as each successive application is developed, the parts will fit together properly and the final goal will be achieved with a minimum amount of reprogramming.

4. Let's mechanize our existing tabulating applications and manual

procedures. This goes right to the heart of the problem. The opposite approach is to view the computer as a means of introducing new control techniques and an excuse for starting fresh to build a new and better system.

It is apparent that so far most computer application concepts and practices have not kept pace with technological changes in the machines and devices. But now that many companies have acquired considerable experience with computers, the situation is beginning to change. Computer hardware is being taken for granted, and the systems analysts are realizing that application planning need not be inhibited by hardware. Attention is being focused on the design of ultimate or "ideal" systems. The "total system concept" is one label that is used to describe the new high-order approach to EDP system design.

There is nothing really new about the total system concept. The true "pros" in systems work have always approached problems on a broad basis in order to uncover the interrelationships that exist with respect to a particular area. The thing that is new is simply this: electronic data processing permits application of the sophisticated systems at a reasonable cost.

An example of total system

The total system approach can be applied to any company. It is particularly appropriate, however, to manufacturing concerns. The approach in this area varies from company to company, of course, but there is a main flow of information that is basic to many of them.

The system begins with the receipt of customer orders. The orders are first edited and coded manually, then converted to computer input media. Usually the media are punched cards. Paper tape is also used, especially when it is feasible to prepare the tape as a by-product of the order-typing operation.

A computer-controlled chain reaction then takes place. Working with magnetic tape files of master information, the computer summarizes the orders by promised delivery dates and prints a report for sales management purposes. The computer then determines all manufacturing requirements: The production schedule is adjusted; requirements for manufactured parts and subassemblies are redetermined; loading schedules are adjusted for the individual manufacturing and assembly centers; production papers are prepared, including process sheets, tool requirements, material requisitions, labor tickets, and production move orders; and the purchasing department is automatically notified of raw material needs.

As materials and purchased parts are received, the computer updates the inventory records and prepares stock status notices for items needing human action. As manufacturing proceeds, labor time tickets, material requisitions, and production move orders are fed back to the computer. It reviews the factory work load and reports on jobs that have fallen behind schedule and jobs that are costing more hours or material than scheduled.

The employee time tickets are automatically costed for account distribution purposes and the data is held for the subsequent preparation of payrolls. Completed production counts lead to the automatic preparation of shipping documents, which in turn lead to the billing and accounts receivable operations, all performed on the computer. Finally, at the end of the month, the accounting information is rounded up on magnetic tape ledgers, and the computer completes the cycle by printing budget comparison reports and other financial statements for review by management.

In operation, such a system works smoothly and efficiently, with a minimum of human assistance. Each transaction is recorded on input media only once; thereafter it may be processed against several different tape files. Accuracy is assured, since transcription from record to record is eliminated. Basic tape files provide a single source for all requirements, which again insures accuracy.

The daily operation may include fifteen to twenty computer runs, each requiring its own program. The programs, however, are stored sequentially on a single reel of tape. This enables the computer to proceed from one run to the next without pausing for manual selection of program tapes. The only interruption in the processing occurs when the computer notifies the console operator to change a certain reel of tape, to set up a printer, or to perform some other physical task.

Systems such as this require planning and design of the highest order. In designing the inventory control portion of the total system, for example, the analyst must first consider broad objectives and policies before getting into the specifics. He should consider the following points, among others:

1. The company's policy regarding over-all inventory levels
2. Means of balancing the costs of carrying excess inventories with the economies of continuous production
3. The consequences of being out of stock and of being overstocked

Conclusion. The stream of technological improvements, which has been characteristic of the industry from the start, is continuing today at a steady pace. Application concepts are becoming more sophisticated, pointing out more effective ways of tapping the potential of the machines. Both factors affect the outcome of feasibility studies. In a growing number of cases, the outcome is a positive indication that a computer can be applied effectively and economically to a company's data processing requirements.

EDP Control Problems[6]

RANDOM SURVEYS HAVE REVEALED that electronic data processing managers are a bruised group. The more fortunate manage to last through a turbulent conversion period. Others, hopefully a small minority, find that their programs fall short of expectations. There are a variety of conditions that can account for this problem. A significant but subtle one is error-detection and error-correction controls.

Error problems

Electronic data processing installations have been troubled extensively by error problems. These are most prominent in the conversion phase and, to some degree, shortly thereafter. In some cases error problems exist indefinitely. This is an ironic circumstance—control problems exist and thrive in the midst of immense control capability. Why? The answer is found in the characteristics of the electronic data processing error environment.

There appear to be—or really may be—more errors in a system of which electronic data processing is a central element. This phenomenon can go on for some time.

Computer systems are superior devices for the detection of "quiet" errors. Quiet errors existed in previous systems but went undetected for indefinite periods—and if detected were not discovered dramatically.

The tendency of manual and semimanual systems is to diffuse the detection of errors. Computer systems concentrate detection as to time and place.

Computer systems require formalization of error processes to a far greater degree than heretofore experienced.

Every system has a subsystem for detecting errors, making corrections, and handling other disturbances. This subsystem requires data processing operations that do not follow routine channels. Generally it is true that error procedures are not as formal as regular procedures. Often they tend to reflect the instantaneous adaptation of affected individuals. To the extent that error processes behave this way, they are "quiet" in present systems. Accordingly, the magnitude of error occurrences may not be appreciated because they are handled unobtrusively.

[6]Pages 291-95 appeared in *Financial Executive* (then known as *The Controller*), July 1962, and in the *Lybrand Journal,* vol. 43, no. 2, 1962. The author is Felix Kaufman, partner, Lybrand, Ross Bros. & Montgomery, New York.

Increase in the number of errors. The number of errors occurring in data processing seems to increase when electronic data processing is employed. There may in fact be new errors of a type not encountered before, or there may be errors which previously went undetected. Finally, they may have been discovered inconspicuously in the previous system, to the point of appearing not to exist. Whichever the category, the effect is the same—initially, the computer system seems to increase the number of errors.

Transfer errors. Since many new machine applications require a transfer of source information to machine-sensible form, the transfer inevitably creates an error-producing problem. This is particularly true when input operators are in the "learning" phase. In addition, there is a tendency to lower cost by skirting verification operations until an intolerable error rate requires the adoption of verifying operations.

Although the maintenance of perpetual inventory records to achieve better inventory management is enhanced by the use of EDP, developing a new set of records sets up the possibility for discrepancy between the actual count of stocks and the book records. In perpetual inventory systems, based on electronic data processing, the number of errors revealed by comparisons of book and physical on-hand quantities is initially large.

The creation of records where none previously existed—and the consequent error condition—is not an electronic data processing phenomenon. To the extent, however, that computers have acted as catalysts, a careful distinction as to blame is not likely to be made.

The problem is compounded if the system, as initially designed, is only a posting system to which is added fairly frequent print out of status by stock-keeping units. Such a system cannot readily—if ever—attest to its managerial capabilities. Its errors are conspicuous. Its control features may not exist until some decision rules are incorporated into its program with attendant exception reporting.

Detection of quiet errors. Unquestionably every data processing system commits errors which go undetected. We know that outside parties—particularly customers—provide a voluntary detection source by reporting errors which are against them. Is it unfair to assume that there are other errors as well which are not reported, namely those in favor of the customer?

Through the use of EDP there is probably no increase in errors as such, but the number of detected errors is greater. The consequences of this condition depend upon the psychological effects of the error and its impact on error-correction processes.

Clearly the detection of errors which favor the customer cannot be considered detrimental by the user of electronic data processing. Nevertheless, if this among other conditions has disturbed the user's over-all error-correction apparatus, it will play some role in creating a chaotic and turbulent data processing environment.

The detection of such errors, or their avoidance entirely, occurs because of higher reliability in extending prices and amounts, footing totals, applying prices, and the like. It is also the consequence of the application of better logic to the relationships of a transaction.

Concentrating error detection. Electronic data processing systems concentrate the error-finding process in time and space. Their design permits them to find errors early in the data processing stream. Accordingly, they speed up the error-finding process and at the same time concentrate what was formerly a diffused error-finding method.

The powerful error-detection logic that can be incorporated into programs is best applied where error detection is really concentrated in machine-sensible form. Established files contain converted information (from predecessor files) and the information deposited as a result of processing transactions. In an EDP system, the old manual processing files should be purified during the transition period.

Many examples of the change in the timing and location of error detection can be cited. One will suffice at this time. In brokerage activity, it is common to assign an origin code to the trade to identify, among other things, the market involved. Via programming, the computer can relate security numbers to a security glossary and in so doing check the validity of the market digit in the origin code. Where they disagree, the trades so affected are rejected immediately for correction. In the manual system, the incorrect origin code resulted in the listing of an affected trade on the wrong blotter. The routine reconciliation of this blotter with the other side of the trade—as reported by the other broker—would detect the error. In general, detection took place about four days after execution of the trade.

While the change in the time and place of error detection has its continuing effect on source data, there is also an important transient condition affecting files when they are transferred from their pre-electronic data processing form. During this period, many conditions will be detected that otherwise might never have been found or may have been dormant for long periods of time. They are detected through comparisons and through the application of reasonable criteria. Comparisons occur when two or more files are to be consolidated and common items of information can be tested for agreement.

In general, the conspicuous effect on the error environment occurs in connection with these editing processes. Therefore, a smooth transition to electronic data processing depends upon the preparation made to deal with the consequences of this powerful and accelerated error-finding technique.

Formalizing error procedures

An elusive and not widely appreciated quality of manual processing is the informal adaptation of processes to errors. Mistakes occur. People confer about them. They decide on a course of remedial action and then act. Such processes are inconspicuous and may leave no trail. In many cases corrections to files are made at the instant of detection without a document that formally describes the error, indicates remedial action, and serves as a record of action.

Electronic systems have specified error-generating paths. Subsystems must exist to handle the errors flowing down these paths. These sub-systems must provide for the reinsertion of rejected data into machine processes. They must also provide for the insertion of appropriate adjustments of machine records when errors are discovered in operations outside the machine system. These needs are a burden to systems designers in several ways because (1) they do not anticipate the volume or procedural implications of certain types of errors and as a result fail to provide the resources to handle them; and (2) they do not anticipate the psychological consequences of finding certain types of errors.

In general, we are not adapted initially for the change from informal to formal processes of error correction. Indeed, one of the most disturbing consequences of this problem is the fact that informal methods may continue unco-ordinated with the necessary formal processes. In any customer relationship, for example, complaints may be investigated and a course of action indicated to the customer. If the course of action is not transmitted to machine-maintained files, the same erroneous information will be transmitted to the customer again.

In less automatic systems, notably where punched card calculations were employed, some of the detection processes available in electronic data processing also existed. These systems, however, lacked comparable facility to list and identify their findings. Systems people tend to use them in less disciplined ways in the treatment of rejected events.

Overcontrol. Overcontrol in error-finding processes exists when: (1) error finding, or the means for error finding, produces costs which are in excess of the values obtained by detection; (2) a discipline results which is not compatible with the customs of the effected part of the business (useless information is provided).

There is some tendency toward overcontrol when computer systems are used. This is the consequence of the ease with which screening programs can be developed, and the extreme difficulty in measuring the point at which overcontrol occurs. It may only be a matter of timing. Detection processes that cannot be appreciated today may be in order tomorrow. It is unfortunate, however, to worsen the complex error environment created by legitimate detection processes with other processes that cannot be used effectively.

Conclusions

Electronic data processing systems have powerful control features. *What are they?* A listing follows. (The points overlap because the classification was not intended to be rigorous, nor does it need to be for these purposes.)

Computer systems provide unprecedented reliability.

The logical (programmed) processes of a computer expose the input data to an unprecedented validity-testing trial.

Control in a computer system is simultaneous with the processing action and does not depend upon "policing" by a retrospective evaluation of data processing acts.

An integrated application comprehends the interactions and ramifications of a data processing event, thereby insuring that all affected records are altered and the effects recognized.

The employment of these features can produce serious, but hopefully transient, incompatibilities between error-detection and error-correction capabilities. To deal with this problem, those responsible for the design and implementation of electronic data processing systems must: (1) design and implement subsystems which anticipate the consequences of error detection; (2) assess the compatibility of new error-detection capabilities and the available error-correction capability; and (3) recognize the possibility and desirability of tightening or relaxing the error-detection capability.

Controls associated directly with an EDP system can and should be integrated with operations. The acts of control and the performance of the operations being controlled can be simultaneous in electronic data processing.

Accordingly, we might advance this postulate: Control is a pre-eminent condition to data processing effectiveness. A properly controlled system will operate effectively with less than optimal design and equipment. The converse is not true.

It is true, however, that a comprehensive definition of system design includes the formulation of the structure of the control apparatus. The insertion of control, therefore, pervades all phases of electronic data processing activity. The intertwining of control does not affect the validity of previous observations.

What is needed, however, to deal with these problems is a sense of humility in the beginning about the consequences of these programs. Control should be the result of after-the-fact humbleness by those who find that what can happen usually does.

Rental Versus Purchase
of Data Processing Equipment[7]

In deciding whether a client should rent or buy data processing equipment, a CPA has a wide range of elements to consider, from the purely financial to the purely technological. The importance given to these elements may vary with the particular interests of the man who makes the final decision; his chief concern may be with finances, taxes, or systems.

There is, nevertheless, a middle ground on which a reasonable and intelligent comparison of rental and purchasing can be made. The comparison does not have to be complicated with involved technical terminology, nor does it have to be so naïve as to be meaningless.

The problem discussed here is not how to justify equipment in terms of clerical savings, as might be done in a feasibility study. Rather it is how to determine whether a piece of equipment whose installation has already been decided upon should be rented or owned.

Some of the elements that must be considered eventually, for example, the company's cash position, its fixed asset policy, and its income tax position, will be established by business conditions and corporate policy. They are, however, more directly related to questions of over-all financial policy than to the problem of equipment purchasing.

The foundation for the rent-or-buy decision should be a careful analysis by the company's data processing staff. Unless this analysis is valid and realistic, the application of financial theories will be nothing more than academic exercises. A sound analysis requires the intelligent use of basic information about the company's needs and equipment. It also requires a forecast of the company's data processing activities for a reasonable period of time in the future.

Factors for comparison

The factors needed to build a comparison for any piece of equipment are:

1. The annual rental cost and attendant taxes
2. The purchase cost and attendant taxes
3. The system life of the machine
4. The annual maintenance cost
5. The salvage value of the machine when the company no longer has use for it
6. The rate of interest that the company has to pay for money it borrows or that it expects to earn on money it has

[7]Adapted, with permission, from an article by Edwin D. Wolf in the February 1962 issue of *Management Controls*. Copyrighted 1962 by Peat, Marwick, Mitchell & Co.

Little time need be devoted to explanation of the first two items, rental cost and purchase cost. It should be mentioned, however, that for a machine already in operation, the purchase cost means the price that would have to be paid for the machine now, not its original price. Taxes include Federal excise taxes and, in some states, sales taxes.

System life. Determination of the system life of the piece of equipment is probably the most important single factor in the analysis. One of the most abused terms used in connection with rental-versus-purchase decisions is the word "obsolescence." Too often it is used as an excuse for not making any real effort to analyze a situation objectively. It is much easier simply to state flatly that there is no reason to consider purchase now because the equipment will be obsolete in no time.

Anyone will grant that no piece of equipment in use today is going to stand for any great length of time as the ideal tool for its job. Punched cards some day will be replaced by more advanced methods of data processing. Transistorized computers have already replaced tube machines; eventually character recognition may replace key punching. But this is not the real test of obsolescence.

The real test lies in the company's own situation. Where does it stand in its development of data processing? What will it be doing three years from now? Five or ten years from now? What will the applications be? What will the volume be? What pieces of equipment on hand today will be used tomorrow?

In the last analysis, the carefully thought-out answer to this question of system life is the primary element in any purchase evaluation. It can mean real dollar savings for the organization. The question must be answered separately for each type of equipment. An entire configuration cannot be appraised intelligently as one ball of wax, for each type of equipment has a specific job to do. That job can disappear, continue, or grow as the company's activities and techniques change. So each piece of equipment and its relation to the whole data processing picture should be considered individually.

How can the company's data processing future be appraised? It is necessary to know today's system and the areas it encompasses, the peak load volumes, and the schedules of input and output that largely dictated the present installation. It is also necessary to forecast what the future holds. Of course, no one will go out on a limb and predict all developments for the next twenty years. But every organization must plan—and is planning. Goals are being set for next year's sales, production, and purchases; trends and relationships are being established; someone is charting the company's course.

An intelligent estimate is better than a wild guess. So the first task is to prepare an estimate of the company's business activities for the next few years. The next step is to round up plans for additional areas to be mechanized and changes, if any, in the data processing concept itself, with allowance for the time required within the organization for surveys, estimating costs, winning approvals, planning, and installing.

No matter what the main data processing configuration will look like eventually, some of the present equipment will still be required. For example, so long as cards make up some part of the basic information media, some kind of card handling equipment will be used.

It is not necessary that all these projections be pinpointed specifically before the analysis can move ahead. This forecasting is designed simply to provide a realistic idea of the system life of the individual components of the existing installation. The items reviewed above are major considerations in determining the system life of each piece of equipment.

Once its system life has been determined, each piece of equipment should be written off over that life. Sometimes the so-called productive life of the equipment, as estimated by the manufacturer, is used as the depreciation period. In a system life analysis, productive life ordinarily is not a major factor; it should, however, be as long as or longer than the estimate of system life.

Maintenance cost. The next problem is to estimate the maintenance cost. Rental costs include maintenance; purchase usually does not. Any company whose prime business is not the manufacture and repair of electro-mechanical equipment is probably better off, at least from the cost viewpoint, to consider purchasing maintenance on a contract basis. The contracts usually provide for preventive and repair maintenance on a standard shift, including the cost of replaced parts. With second-shift or weekend maintenance, costs are somewhat higher.

It is also possible to plan for maintenance on a time and materials basis rather than under a contract. Cost schedules, available from the manufacturers, vary with the type and age of equipment. Time and materials rates are fixed, but determination of annual costs requires forecasting the frequency and seriousness of breakdowns.

Salvage value. The salvage value of the equipment at the end of its system life should not be ignored. If plans call for the removal of a piece of equipment well before the end of its productive life, the company will have an asset of some real worth. If the system and productive lives are identical, salvage value can be ignored in the analysis.

The manufacturers publish lists of trade-in values by equipment type and age. Relating these values to the expected age of the equipment at the end of its system life gives a fair idea of the approximate value of the equipment at that time. One manufacturer considers its equipment to be fully depreciated at the end of seven years, even though the productive life is quoted at nine or ten years. So the established salvage values may be considered to be fairly conservative.

Exhibit 1

PURCHASE VERSUS LEASE COMPARISON—1

Machine:	082 Sorter		
Age:	7½ years		
Current purchase cost:	$672		
System life:	4 years		
Cost of money:	6%		
Salvage value:	Nil		

Annual rental costs:

Rental (@ $55 month)		$660	
Federal excise tax (10%)		66	
Sales tax (Pa. @ 4%)		26	
			$752

Annual purchase costs:

Maintenance (@ $30 month)		$360	
Amortization:			
Purchase cost	$672		
Federal excise tax (10%)	67		
Sales tax (Pa. @ 4%)	27		
Present value of cost to be amortized	$766		
Payment @ 6% for 4 years		$221	$581
Annual savings of purchase over rental			$171

A point that is not directly involved in the calculation of purchase costs, but that should be considered in the over-all evaluation, is the freedom of movement the owner of purchased equipment is likely to have when the time comes to collect its salvage value. Trade-in value rather than potential cash realization probably should be the test. Although there are no restrictions against selling data processing equipment in the open market, no market of consequence has developed to date.

Often manufacturers place some restrictions on the proportion of the cost of new equipment that can be absorbed by a trade-in. Furthermore, the necessity for trading in rather than selling can tend to bind the buyer to a single manufacturer; otherwise, the salvage value will be lost.

Interest rate. The last factor that must be considered is the rate of interest the company pays for borrowed money or the rate it expects to earn on an investment. All money, whether used in the business or placed in the bank, is a potential interest earner. Therefore, no valid comparison of purchase versus rental can be made without considering interest rates. The appropriate rate for use in the analysis may vary depending on the organization and on the type of activity being considered.

Making the analysis

Once all this information has been assembled for each piece of equipment under consideration, the analysis can be made. The mechanics of the analysis are fairly straightforward, once the problem of applying the interest rate is resolved.

This is the basic principle involved: To buy something for $100 today and to pay for it over a period of time, interest on the unpaid balance must be paid. The problem then is to determine equal annual installments that, at the end of the system life or write-off period, will equal the $100 borrowed plus the cost of interest. For example, payment of $100 over ten years at 6 per cent interest would equal a total of $135.80, or an annual payment of $13.58

The determination of these interest factors has been a problem for many persons for a long time. As a result, standard tables showing the factors needed have been developed. Once the correct table is selected, the calculations are simple. Exhibit I (page 299) illustrates a comparison for a 7½-year-old machine with no salvage value. To buy it today would cost $672. We estimate that it will be useful for four years and that the money will cost 6 per cent a year.

The comparison starts with the annual rentals to be paid. Against this annual purchase costs are applied. The first item in purchase costs is the maintenance for the year. This rate is constant because of the age of the machine; so the calculation is simple.

The purchase price of the machine, including taxes, totals $766. This amount should be spread over the four-year system life at a 6 per cent interest rate. The CPA can then refer to a standard table called "Present Value of an Ordinary Annuity of 1 per Annum." Under the 6 per cent interest column for four years, the table shows a factor of 3.465. Dividing $766 by that factor gives an annual payment of $221. The annual payment plus the maintenance costs approximates the annual cost of purchasing the equipment. This figure, when netted against the rental cost of $752, shows a saving of purchase over lease of about $171 a year.

Example with salvage value. Exhibit 2 (page 301) includes some elements that were omitted from the first example. In this example, a new machine costing $2,600 with a salvage value at the end of its five-year system life of $390 is considered. While the rental costs are the same, the calculation of annual purchase costs becomes a little more involved. The maintenance contract over the five-year period will not be consistent: For the first three years, it will cost $16 a month; after that, it will cost $21 a month. So the figure used is the weighted average of these two contract prices, or $18 a month.

The machine will be worth $390 five years from today. With the present cost of money, though, that $390 is worth less today. To determine its present value, a factor of .747 from the standard table is used. Multiplying $390 by that factor gives a present value for the salvage of $291. The net purchase cost to be paid off in installments is therefore $2,673.

Exhibit 2

PURCHASE VERSUS LEASE COMPARISON—2

Machine:	082 Sorter		
Age:	New		
Current purchase cost:	$2,600		
System life:	5 years		
Cost of money:	6%		
Salvage value:	$390		

Annual rental costs:

Rental (@ $55 month)		$660	
Federal excise tax (10%)		66	
Sales tax (Pa. @ 4%)		26	
			$752

Annual purchase costs:

Maintenance (@ weighted average of $18 month)		$216	
Amortization:			
Purchase cost	$2,600		
Federal excise tax (10%)	260		
Sales tax (Pa. @ 4%)	104		
	$2,964		
Less: Present value of salvage @ 6% for 5 years	291		
Present value of cost to be amortized	$2,673		
Payment @ 6% for 5 years		$635	$851
Annual cost of purchase over rental			$ 99

Following the same method used in the first case, we find that the annual payment is $635. When this payment is added to the maintenance costs, it would cost about $100 more a year to own the equipment than to lease it.

Conclusion. If the analysis shows a saving through rental, that normally settles the question. It is important, however, to be sure that the system life is realistic. It is easy to show savings simply by lengthening the write-off time, but unless the equipment actually will be useful to the company for that entire period of time, management is simply deluding itself.

If the comparisons reflect an appreciable saving through purchase, the decision is less clear. Ultimately it must be made in the light of the company's financial position and policies. At least, however, the decision will rest on a sound comparative cost foundation.

CHAPTER SIX

Cost Reduction

Introduction [1]

THE FIRST STEP in a cost reduction program is to select a particular department and make a detailed survey of present procedures. In the course of this survey, a breakdown of each employee's time by operation must be obtained. The volume of each transaction handled must be determined and each piece of paper followed from its origin to final destination. Detailed flow charts should be prepared to illustrate instances in which papers are shuffled back and forth between departments. Interviews to determine such facts should start with the departmental supervisors. The information obtained from the supervisors should then be checked by interviewing the employees.

All volume statistics obtained should be independently verified. In many instances, accurate statistics are not maintained and estimates need verification. This in itself is a good reason for including the CPA in this program. Many of the statistics are already in his working papers; moreover, he probably has a fairly good understanding of the present system.

The CPA's Role

During the course of the interviews, the need for every report, form, and the method of operation itself must be constantly questioned. The CPA must determine what is actually needed in the way of reports and controls. In many cases, unnecessary control records are maintained. For example, in many companies documents are logged in and out of departments, usually because a document has been lost in the past. In some cases logging is essential, but often such tight control is superfluous.

[1]Pages 303-306 were excerpted, with permission, from an article by Harry E. Littler in the June 1959 issue of *Management Controls*. Copyrighted 1959 by Peat, Marwick, Mitchell & Co.

Here again, the CPA's experience will prove valuable because he will know what to eliminate and what to retain for good internal control. It is of the utmost importance that the CPA maintain a questioning attitude during the interviews. So many operations continue to be performed merely because they have always been performed, even though the need for them has disappeared. Yet every operation eliminated can result in clerical cost reduction. Even more important, an operation must be reduced to its essentials before any improvements through mechanization are considered. Mechanization of unessential information and reports can be extremely costly.

After the CPA has completed his interview, gathered volume statistics, prepared flow charts, and questioned the necessity of each operation, report, and form, he must evaluate the findings of the survey. When evaluating the survey information, the first thing to be determined is whether the volume of work performed seems reasonable. Current data must therefore be compared with the amount of work turned out by average employees in the past. Standard data, methods time measurement, or some other method of employee time study may be used.

During the course of his interviews, the CPA will have observed the pace of the work in the various departments. He will also have noticed the quality of the supervision given the employees. In his previous experience as auditor, he will have undoubtedly come in contact with these departments and is probably aware of such things before the present survey.

Planning a system of operations

After he has eliminated all the unessential reports, forms, controls, and operations, the CPA must then map out the system for performance of the remaining operations. This is a key step in the cost reduction program because the improved system constitutes the basis for all future decisions. The system must be as streamlined as possible and personnel requirements must be based on the work output that can be expected from average, well-supervised employees. A comparison between present and proposed methods should show some savings. The amount will depend upon the efficiency of present procedures, the caliber of supervision, and the ability of employees.

At this point, the CPA should let his imagination roam. He should examine other methods of performing the various jobs, with the assurance that he can now determine the amount of cost reduction, if any, which can be attributed to the new method of work performance.

The CPA must examine *all* existing methods of performing a given operation; and the alternatives are often numerous. For example, spirit, offset, or vellum masters can be used for order invoicing, bill of material and process sheet, labor ticket, or purchase order preparations. Various kinds of copying equipment can be utilized in different places. Key sort cards can be used for labor tickets and sales and expense analysis. Many types of billing equipment and bookkeeping machines of varying capacities are available.

Tabulating equipment can be obtained in all sizes for diverse business needs. Some of the machines and methods can be eliminated immediately by simply considering the size of the company. Machines in the appropriate size range, however, present a problem because each system must be mapped out separately so that its special cost advantage can be determined. Flaws must be uncovered through critical examination. Will forecasted changes in volume or methods of doing business affect the various systems? Once the unsuitable systems have been eliminated, installation costs will have to be estimated for the remainder. The period of time needed to recover the costs must also be established.

Evaluating direct and indirect benefits

The next step will be to consider what benefits other than direct cost reduction may accrue from the installation. Such benefits will be mainly intangible, but they should be considered when the installation of data processing equipment is contemplated for cost reduction purposes. The equipment may be used primarily for inventory control and production scheduling to realize inventory reduction and possibly to speed up the processing of orders. A corollary benefit might be a reduction in the amount of equipment necessary to handle the volume of work in the shop because of an ability to sequence-schedule and avoid bottlenecks. The sales analysis and market research information produced by mechanical and electronic systems may lead to increased sales and a more effective selling force.

The preceding benefits are real enough, but they are intangible in the sense that no monetary value can be assigned to them. The sponsor of a program based on intangibles is more likely to be held accountable in the future and have a harder time justifying himself than is the sponsor of a program based on cost reduction. A solid though small foundation of cost reduction can go a long way to help sell management on a superstructure of intangible benefits.

Getting a program under way

A thorough selling job is necessary to start the program rolling. In fact, selling should begin with interviewing. Top and middle management, supervisors, and clerical personnel will all have to be convinced that the new proposals will benefit the company as a whole without hurting individuals involved. Management should give the clerical people in particular a guarantee that there will be no layoffs and that normal turnover will absorb the cost reductions.

Selling up the line, however, will probably be more difficult. Supervisors may resist a reduction in the clerical force; they may feel, for reasons of prestige, that a larger force will improve their own positions. They must be convinced that they will be more appreciated if they do a good job and make money for the company than if they simply run a large, inefficient operation.

Ideas must be advanced for discussion. Undoubtedly a number of good ideas will come from the workers themselves. One cannot fail to learn all about a particular operation if one is engaged in it daily. Moreover, an individual is more likely to resist a change if he did not originate or contribute to the idea himself. Good salesmanship means emphasizing that workers' ideas can be very good and explaining that the CPA's main role is simply to sell these ideas and make them operative.

Developing a timetable

A timetable of anticipated goals should be developed in order to avoid discouragement over what may appear to be slow progress. It should be recognized at the outset that the time needed to effect an adequate control system depends largely on how much control already exists in the business. If a business can build on good records, and perhaps on some basic budgeting by way of simple performance standards, results should appear quickly. But if there is little or no control at the start, much more time will be required.

A business cannot work effectively on all of its cost elements and areas at the same time. One element or area should be selected in which savings are most likely to result; this will serve to stimulate the program. Two elements, time and materials, should bear the brunt of the attack on costs. Experience indicates that the best results are obtained in this way.

Business activity should be reduced to control areas and a plan of priority should be developed. The following guideposts have been found useful:

1. Look for a bottleneck area. When employees constantly mill around an organization and expedite everything in sight, waste is apt to set in.
2. If no such area can be found in the small business, look for an area in which things have been done in the same way for a long time. Methods and procedures which have been taken for granted for a number of years are often in dire need of change.
3. The first area to be controlled should generate enough savings to

justify its selection. But, in addition, a project should be important enough to ensure wholesale participation and co-operation.

Once the list of priorities has been drawn up, these steps should be taken: (1) Tell the employees what is going on. (2) Determine to what extent the area selected is presently being controlled. (3) Decide, on the basis of the data collected, what procedures can best be utilized for reducing and controlling costs. (For example, what control methods will contribute to increased productivity or control of material usage?) (4) Establish the instruments for analysis and control.

Whether the business is large or small, there just is no magic formula available to devise a control procedure that can be used in all areas or situations. Nor will the answer be found to lie altogether in the review of an accounting system or report. Labor cost control, for example, may require the introduction of time standards and an improved control procedure over employee selection and training. Manpower control requires a continuous review of what is being done and how, as well as who is doing it. In summary, it is only by collecting and analyzing all the facts that appropriate control procedures can be established.

The basic technique of cost control in any business entails a comparison of actual operations with standards by means of cost reports. This does not necessarily require the installation of a cost accounting system following the setting of standards resulting from time studies conducted by engineering experts. If a small company can afford such cost control elements, the outcome will be a more competent job; but they are by no means absolutely necessary in every company.

Setting standards. The reporting aspect of the control procedure should pose no problem for the CPA. It is rather the establishment of standards or other measures of performance that may give rise to certain questions. This is often believed to be the engineer's exclusive province. However, the CPA is capable of, and is becoming more adept at, formulating standards.

Standards can be effectively established in any division of a business on the basis of scientific observation, through use of historical records, or simply with the help of informed judgment. Standards may at first be useful only as an over-all method of measurement to evaluate variations in a month's operations in one activity area. Then, as the standards are refined and expanded to include other areas, the reports can begin to disclose the effects of efficiency or changes in prices or volume. Ultimately they may form the basis of a complete standard cost accounting system.

Every business must have basic standards of *measurement*. Where a business is managed by default, the employee sets the work standards himself. The setting of formal standards in some companies may therefore call for changes in employee work habits. Employees, being human, will naturally resent the idea of being controlled. Consequently, any changes made in the first activity area should be as simple as possible. Additional changes and tighter standards can always be instituted later on.

Keep a close watch over, and think in terms of improving, the various activity areas; this is the final step in cost control. Neither the stockholders nor the officers of a business have any direct control over its activity areas. The foreman or supervisor is in the first line of responsibility. The reporting process must therefore be geared to his needs; the reports themselves should be kept simple in both content and design. The foreman's own ideas as to presentation should be explored and, wherever possible, accepted. Since the internal cost report is such a valuable control instrument, it is essential that it be both informative and understandable to the individuals responsible for the costs to be reported.

When planning new or revising old reports for each activity area, it is also important to consider the accounting procedures and records from which the reports are to be prepared. The system used to obtain basic operational data may require revision. Report preparation and data recording in the general records should not require two distinct analyses of the operating data. The reports should be a function of the general records. In short, all functions may have to be reviewed.

In conclusion, if the certified public accountant fails to advise his business clients through the steps just outlined and to get them started on a formal cost reduction and control program, there is reason to fear that the project will fail.

Following up. There is a natural tendency, after cost reductions have been achieved, to congratulate oneself and sit back and relax or get immersed in day-to-day operations. No company can really afford to allow this. It may be possible to survey all clerical areas the first time around, but there will *always* be room for improvement in at least a few areas. New equipment and techniques are constantly being developed which may make additional savings possible. The size and character of a business may be changing so that today's impractical method may be tomorrow's suitable one. It is precisely because he is continuously reviewing a company, that the CPA can constantly be on the lookout for cost reduction opportunities.

The program outlined above may appear to be very drawn out and time-consuming. A CPA may wonder where he would ever find the time to participate in it, and at the same time discharge his responsibilities as an independent auditor. The CPA should feel the need to satisfy himself, as part of his annual examination, as to the adequacy and efficiency of the internal control system and of the systems and procedures themselves. This responsibility is important and one that will grow in the years to come.

Cost Reduction and Control Programs

Most large companies have established cost reduction and cost control programs on a formal basis. In the typical large company, the planning and administration of a cost reduction program is often assigned as a full-time responsibility to a top executive. The larger businesses have learned from experience that successful cost reduction and control efforts must be applied continuously if full benefits are to be obtained. Experience also proves that programmed cost reduction in any business, large or small, must have one basic element if it is to succeed, namely aggressive and imaginative leadership.

In large organizations responsibility for cost reduction and control usually rests with a financial man. In the largest businesses the financial man may be a controller who functions as a specialist in this sphere. However, whether the business is large or small, the CPA is becoming the experienced adviser in cost reduction and control programs. He has an intimate knowledge of business operations and is able to install the necessary standards, reports, and controls. His independent status provides other signal advantages: (1) He can often spot potential cost-saving areas or operations that management itself has taken for granted. (2) He can exert independent pressure on management for action which people within the organization would hesitate to apply. He can discuss a trouble area critically and so build client relations. Employees will often refrain from suggesting changes that may involve co-workers. (3) Because of his wide experience in serving businesses, the certified public accountant can apply the experience acquired in one business to another.

The CPA cannot do the job alone, any more than a program leader in the biggest business can. Cost reduction must become a team job. The CPA can work with business management in the role of adviser. The creation of a favorable company atmosphere, development of cost consciousness, and program implementation are the prerogatives of management. The CPA may advise and guide business management in cost reduction; but moving too fast in this area can prove disastrous. The CPA should therefore set the pace for management.

Recognizing the Obstacles

Many businesses pay little attention to a formal cost reduction program. Some of the reasons are:

1. It takes time to establish a program and even longer to achieve planned results. The control and reduction of costs, development of a favorable company climate, and gradual inculcation of cost consciousness throughout the organization cannot be accomplished overnight. Interest has often been lost before reduction programs have had an opportunity to yield tangible benefits. This undoubtedly occurs in small business programs because there is no leader to keep the atmosphere and program alive.

2. Current operations are satisfactory and complacency sets in. Cost reduction is seldom taken seriously in small as well as in large organizations until sales or profit margins slip. Yet costs cannot be trimmed any faster in periods of declining business than at other times. The lag in adjusting costs to lowered sales or margins is less serious in the business that has formally and continuously practiced cost reduction.

3. Continual cost reduction strains the business organization. It adds another burden to management, which already has too much to do, and exerts pressure on the employees. It involves more work for everyone; and cost investigation or operational change can sometimes result in disruption. Some managements are apparently reluctant to face up to these facts.

4. Tradition is often the biggest obstacle to cost reduction programs in the small business. Management generally accepts the fact that employees do not like change, but management itself may not be as aggressive and dynamic as it thinks it is. Maintenance of the *status quo* gives management a feeling of security. Business managers who have been operating by force of habit generally overlook ways to save money. There is *always* a *better* way of doing things. Tradition should be cherished, but not allowed to dominate business progress.

5. It costs too much to cut costs. The engagement of a consultant and the addition of control reports, staff, or supervision logically appear to be additional expenses, not reductions. The certified public accountant must demonstrate that it takes money to save money. Successful management recognizes that capital additions will often contribute to cost reduction.

6. Potential disruption of relations is another reason for not adopting cost-saving techniques. The strain on employee relations has already been mentioned; but union and customer relations are also regarded as uncontrollable areas because of possible relationship problems. However, experience suggests that changes in factory methods and procedures will not *always* violate the mechanical improvement or automation clause in

a union contract. Customers are not likely to be distressed because the billing procedure is revised.

7. Cost-saving operations are rarely apparent in the small business. A big business has expert cost accountants and industrial engineers on its staff who, in spite of the operation's complexity, can detect high cost areas and do something about them. But a small business operation is rarely so complex. A small business management must be convinced that expensive cost reports and industrial engineering departments are not needed to locate and correct out-of-line costs. The introduction or expansion of a simple accounting system, establishment of even informal standards of performance, and development of a few basic reports drawn from the system are often all that is required to unearth high cost operations, reduce them, and then keep them in line.

The CPA can help business management recognize barriers to cost reduction. None are insurmountable, particularly if management is aware of their existence. Many are the result of inertia, but management itself is responsible for some. Too often management lacks the time or financial information necessary to launch an attack on costs. The CPA should therefore seize the initiative in advising on cost reduction and control programs.

What the CPA can do. In many instances, the CPA has played much too limited a role in advising on cost reduction and control programs. Actually, very few people in an organization are in a better position to perform the four essential steps required in a successful cost reduction program:

1. Determining the areas with a good potential for cost reduction
2. Establishing the changes to be made
3. Installing these changes
4. Following up to make certain that the cost reductions are achieved

Since the CPA has contacts throughout the company, he is particularly well situated to perform steps 1 and 4. With some training and experience, the CPA can advise and help to install the changes.

Limiting factors. Before describing how the CPA can accomplish cost reduction, let us consider some of the factors which may tend to limit the CPA in this area: (1) The present work load may preclude additional work without additional staff. (2) There may be a lack of training and experience in the systems field and lack of opportunity to obtain it. (3) There may be a strong systems and procedures department, which resents outside activity in this area as an encroachment upon their duties. In this case, the certified public accountant can certainly assist in the determination of potentially good areas and follow up to see that cost reduction is achieved.

Principles of Successful Cost Reduction

CERTAIN BASIC PRINCIPLES to be followed in a successful reduction and control program have already been touched upon, but owing to the importance of avoiding pitfalls in undertaking cost reduction, some discussion of the major principles of programmed cost reduction is necessary.

Cost reduction and control is a team job. The first step in developing a cost reduction program is to get top management behind the program. Management is often defined as the art of getting things done through other people. The area of cost reduction and control is no exception. Cost reductions can only succeed through the co-ordinated efforts of employers as well as all employees. While one individual must provide the leadership in activating the program and keeping it alive, the ideas, activities, and participation of the employees will prove to be of greatest benefit in cost reduction. In a small business, particularly, possible reductions in one area must be weighed against the possibility of increased cost in other areas. The combined thinking of several people will furnish the best answer.

All employees, from office boy to president, must join the cost reduction team. The foremen or supervisors are most important. These are the people whose enthusiasm can help instill the proper cost-conscious climate throughout a business. In a small business, a few foremen and the office manager represent the first line of responsibility for the great majority of operating costs. They work directly with the people who make the product, waste the forms, break the tools . . . and who come up with ideas for reducing the costs they generate. First-line supervisors must be sold on cost reduction and control, and they, in turn, must sell other employees on the importance of continual cost reduction. Employees at this level are really in the best position to follow up ideas and changes to ensure that cost reduction is actually carried out.

Selling cost consciousness is not easy. The keys to success are (1) enthusiasm for cost reduction in the supervisory ranks, and (2) ability of supervisors and management to motivate other employees with their own enthusiasm and enlist their co-operation through financial and nonfinancial rewards.

This chapter cannot delve into the techniques of employee motivation, but it is so important to win employees over to the cost reduction and control program that a few basic facts should be mentioned. The CPA need not be an expert on employee relations to determine if the personnel practices of his client foster sound employee attitudes. He is generally aware of such attitudes. But if these appear to discourage employee participation in cost reduction, he should alert management to the situation and perhaps suggest corrective action. If the majority of employees of a small business do not identify themselves with management's objectives, the company will have lost its most valuable allies in the effort to reduce and control costs.

The basic causes of this lack of identification should not be difficult to uncover. They usually stem from a want of financial incentives. Experience indicates that an underpaid worker will often cost the company more than the going rate as a result of his peevish attitude and lack of initiative. If low salaries have created an excessive turnover rate, the cost of continual rehiring and retraining may well amount to more than the few cents per hour across the board needed to correct the situation.

Furthermore, management should evaluate jobs objectively, even if informally, so that higher wages are paid for the more difficult and demanding jobs. Time has often resulted in salary favoritism based solely on seniority. If jobs are reviewed, employees should understand the process and know that they will be evaluated again if their jobs change.

Financial incentives should extend beyond base pay. Any group of employees, each of whom is capable of producing a different quantity of output, is likely to maintain a common level of production in the absence of individual incentive. The quality of work performed by the better worker will tend to approximate that of the inefficient producer. A wage incentive system will provide the better employee with the opportunity he needs to relate his superior abilities to a larger pay check.

Financial incentives should specifically promote cost reduction. A suggestion program or other formal means of rewarding active participation in cost reduction should be established. Most large businesses have set up systems that satisfy this need, and an overwhelming majority have profited by doing so.

While it is well established that people are motivated quite effectively by money, this is never all that is required. Many nonfinancial factors seriously influence employee attitudes and are necessary to satisfy their emotional needs. A lengthy discussion of such factors would only serve to stress the point that the small business must develop a positive attitude on the part of its employees. As an adviser on cost reduction to business management, the CPA can help to exemplify the basic function of management, the art of getting things done through other people.

Three approaches to cost reduction

There are three typical approaches to cost reduction:
1. One of the most common is the "meat-ax" approach. The boss calls in the supervisory personnel and flatly states that all costs must be cut 10 per cent without regard for the facts involved. In some situations this approach seems to get results and may be necessary at times. It

usually prevails where some particular crisis such as an operating loss situation, a shortage of cash, or some other almost cataclysmic event causes the company to need to reduce its costs drastically and rapidly. This often results in an arbitrary slash in expenditures.

2. Another approach is an intermittent interest on the part of management as a result of spasmodic cost consciousness, depending upon current competitive economic and profit conditions. This cannot be very effective on a long-range basis and has an unfavorable influence on the general morale of the personnel involved. Many executives feel that after the business has run along for some time it inevitably needs a housecleaning. The business undoubtedly must have taken on some unnecessary frills, supervision has become lax, and employees are not working as hard as they should. Accordingly, the company is launched on a program of cost reduction.

3. The most effective approach to planned cost reduction is one that is continuous and established on a sound basis. It is a carefully planned and programmed operation that can be carried out in two ways: on a special-project basis, as, for example, in reducing the cost of manufacturing or transportation; or on a continuing basis, where a permanent cost reduction group is established and given the job of continuously undertaking cost reduction studies and moving from one segment of the organization to another.

The folly of a crash program. Cost reduction cannot be crash programmed. The crash program initiated by management on the spur of the moment is rarely effective in the long run. More often than not, a crash program will fail as soon as management relaxes the pressure. Cost reductions attributable to across-the-board cuts are likely to be short-lived and costs will tend to creep up again.

Good results can be achieved only if cost reduction and control are practiced continuously. Cost consciousness must become a state of mind with both employer and employee, an integral part of the daily operations of a business. Individual cost-reducing efforts must be consolidated with an over-all system of cost control. Management must be convinced that the best way to obtain continuing cost reduction is not through across-the-board slashing, but through persistent efforts to eliminate, simplify, and think of better ways of doing the job. In his role as adviser, the CPA should be in a position to benefit management greatly in this matter.

Availability of information. Costs can be effectively reduced and controlled only if adequate cost information is available. Effective reporting is a vital principle of cost reduction. A profit and loss statement with the usual schedules of expenses is seldom sufficient, though in some businesses it can be a starting point. It is in this area that the CPA can make his largest single contribution to management. By virtue of his knowledge of the client's operations and his understanding of the attitudes, strengths, weaknesses, and needs of management, he is in the best position to supply this necessary element of cost control. The client's needs and the accounting and reporting methods to be used will vary according to circumstances. The CPA must evaluate each case separately to ensure that management receives adequate information about its costs. The reports of cost activity must be oriented to the requirements of the individual directly responsible for costs. This calls for a change of thinking on the part of business managers who often prepare reports with only directors and stockholders in mind.

Reports for Action[2]

The term "management reports" conjures up many types and styles of reports, from the conventional income statement to analyses of product cost. However, management reports should basically report on the performance of managers. This group of men in every business enterprise is responsible for making a profit. They have the responsibility for making the decisions that direct the business, regardless of their titles, the size of the business, or the formality of the organization. They produce sales and they incur expenses. Although they work collectively, they act as individuals, and these actions should be measured.

Purpose of reports

Successful management has frequently been described as one that has made the right decisions 51 per cent of the time. Regardless of the validity of this statement, it is indicative of the difficulty of decision making. It may also be indicative of the inability of management to localize the responsibility for action and to initiate steps to take advantage of the circumstances, whether it be to increase sales activity or to reduce costs. Decisions generally have their origins in historical facts or in plans for the future. Where they are applicable, accounting reports to management should strive to provide comprehensive knowledge of what has happened that can be applied to predictions of what will happen. This can frequently be accomplished by identifying the problem in terms of specific responsibilities for action, thus enabling management to concentrate on the decisions at hand.

The growth of business in both size and complexity has increased the

[2]Pages 315-323 appeared as a paper in Haskins & Sells' *Selected Papers,* 1959. The author, William W. Gerecke, is a manager with Haskins & Sells.

chief executive's need for a reporting system that recognizes the accomplishments of each manager. He is at the point of action, where sales are produced and expenses incurred. The reporting system should focus on the efforts of the individual manager by indicating his profit contribution, for profits are created through the efforts of people to control expenses as well as to maintain sales at profitable levels. The manager also needs this information as a measure of the effectiveness of his decisions. It is the efforts of these crucially situated men that the chief executive must praise or challenge if he is to assure the continuity of profits.

The problem with reports

Unfortunately, few business executives receive management reports that describe the results of management. Instead, they generally receive a functional statement of operations that describes the general health of the business. Nowhere in such a financial statement can the chief executive or the owner of the business determine the contribution each of his managers has made to the net profit. These facts are usually buried and can only be resurrected by special analyses. Management reports traditionally suffer from the fact that they are historical even when timely, but when they must be supplemented by special analyses their value is further diminished.

Likewise, the managers, whether they are foremen, sales managers, or accounting supervisors, rarely have a good comprehension of the effect of their operations on the profits of the business. How frequently one hears these men speculating on the cost of operating their departments, and yet how rarely is this curiosity satisfied by departmental operating reports prepared at regular intervals. These men are at the points of action in every organization. Their jobs require them to make decisions frequently. They should be assured a means of measuring the effectiveness of their decisions.

Attacking the problem

Management needs an integrated system of reports on the quality of decision making, a means of maintaining management control. This need is usually most evident in programs for controlling expenses where effectiveness of control can be appraised only by measuring the efforts of the individuals responsible for control, rather than by measuring the business as a whole. The first requirement of the system is that it report on the execution of responsibilities by department heads, foremen, and general managers; the second requirement is that the accounting for the system be simple and straightforward; and the third is that the reporting be timely.

Responsibility accounting provides the means of satisfying the first requirement, for it associates the daily transactions of the business with the managers responsible for the execution of these transactions. Thus, it has the potential to direct to specific areas of control the stream of facts that pass through the accounting department. The buried transaction becomes a thing of the past, for managers as well as accountants become interested in the correctness of each distribution. Managers are suddenly profit-conscious.

Accounting simplicity can be achieved through the use of natural account descriptions identified by a logical sequence of account numbers. Natural accounts provide for the accumulation of income or expenses by their basic elements rather than by job or functional categories. Salaries and wages, for example, might be classified by type of employee as to base wage, such as salesmen, clerical, or supervision, and by premium pay and fringe benefits. Thus, basic analysis of what each manager has done is accomplished in the initial accounting distribution of each transaction. The use of natural accounts will also facilitate the consolidation of transactions for financial statements, for there will be a common definition of the elements of income or expense, irrespective of the area of responsibility.

Timely reporting of accomplishment is the third requisite of a successful system of management reports. The reporting system must be organized to record information promptly if management is to act on facts rather than on intuition. Much can be done in this respect by reviewing the sources of information required to prepare periodic operating reports and by assigning a completion date to each source. If journal entries are the source records for the accounting system, the chief accountant should assign a due date to each standard entry and should indicate the accountant who is to prepare the entry. A number of entries, such as depreciation, insurance, and taxes, can usually be prepared and posted before month-end. Methods of handling entries, which can only be prepared at month-end, should be streamlined to facilitate a prompt closing. Accounts payable, for example, can usually be closed by the fifth working day if accruals are made from purchase orders or receiving documents for significant items and the remainder of the nominal, recurring expenses are allowed to fall in the following period.

The business machine manufacturers have also come to the aid of the accountant in solving the problem of timeliness by introducing a wide variety of machines and devices committed to the task of coping with business data processing problems. Their application will be discussed later.

The reporting system

The scope of the reporting system is a function of executive management's recognition of the problem of control. As a practical matter, nearly every business organization, regardless of size, delegates authority to act quite far down in the organization, but there is frequently a reluctance to tell the men at the lowest management level how they are doing. Familiarity with the requirements of the job does not necessarily mean comprehension of the cost of doing it. This is a fact many businessmen overlook when they create their reporting systems. Yet these same businessmen expect their first-line supervisors to exercise good judgment when making decisions about the use of men and materials.

The objective of the reporting system should be to report to the first line of supervision—the point of action. This level may vary with the size of the organization, but it can be identified most effectively by preparing an organization chart to portray the line-reporting relationship of the various managers. The reports should pyramid from the point of control to the executive head of the organization and they should summarize details at each successively higher level of management. The broader the manager's responsibilities, the lesser are his interests in a myriad of details. A summary of divisional expenses is usually more meaningful to a division director than the details of expenses of departmental segments. This latter information is important to the department manager, however, for it keeps him apprised of the cost of his plan of action (see Figure 1, opposite).

Summary reports of income or expenses to the next higher levels of supervision should describe what was done and by whom. This is accomplished by reconciling the performance report of each subordinate manager in total with the total of the income or expense transactions reported by their natural descriptions in the summary reports. In this manner it is possible to relate the responsibility for performance from the top to the bottom of the organization and to direct inquiries to specific managers rather than search through every department in quest of answers. The profit contribution of each manager is clearly identified, yet the traditional presentation of income or expenses by natural types is preserved.

Performance measurement

Reports on management performance are valuable records of action by the men who make the day-to-day operating decisions, but, by themselves, reports on current activities lack any measure of quality. They are purely measurements of quantity describing how much was done, rather than how well it was done. As long as a business is profitable, businessmen are prone to gauge their proficiency by history. "I'm doing as well or better than this time last year," is a fairly common expression of this state of mind. This comparison can rarely direct the efforts of a group to attain its potential or identify the causes of problems. It merely com-

PRO FORMA RESPONSIBILITY REPORTS

Figure I

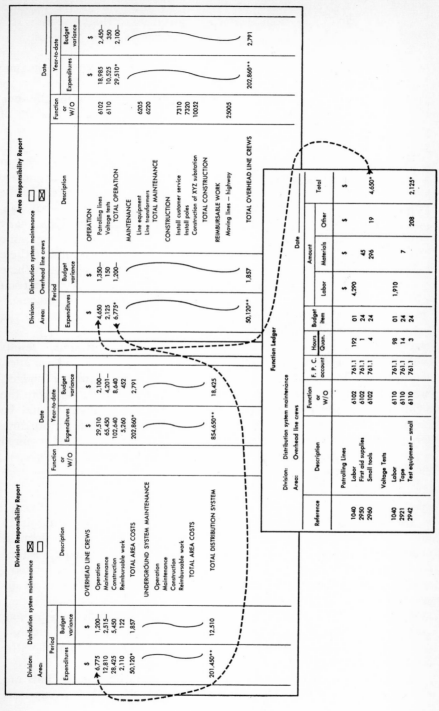

SOURCE: *Responsibility Reporting*, p. 140. Copyrighted 1961 by Peat, Marwick, Mitchell & Co.

pounds the errors and the windfalls from the inception of the business, for there is rarely any method of flagging the unusual transactions as a means of preserving "true performance" for comparative purposes.

Reports for action need a second dimension that can act as a guide or standard of quality for the manager and his superior to use in judging his performance. Operating budgets and standard cost allowances are two examples of the yardsticks commonly used in business for this purpose. Each serves to provide the manager with a goal or a standard of conduct established in advance by mutual agreement between the manager and his superior.

When these measurement tools are used, they should be included in the system of management reports so that a comparison of performance and goals is made concurrently. Results can then be interpreted in the proper frame of reference—what was anticipated, rather than what happened in entirely different circumstances a year ago. In 1958 many businesses were affected by a recession; in 1959 many of these same businesses set new earnings records. A comparison of the results of these two years would not do justice to either year, for in neither case is there a valid basis for determining what might have been done. A comparison with potential, on the other hand, should provide a balanced judgment, since the potential would be derived by considering historical facts in the light of anticipated conditions.

Modern management reporting in systems comparing actual results with standard generally limits the presentation to actual and variance, omitting the budget or standard allowance. The standards or budgets are usually available to the managers, and thus will only detract from the significance of the performance reports, where the emphasis should be on accomplishment. It is not unreasonable to conceive of performance reports stated only in terms of variances when managers have acquired a thorough comprehension of their responsibilities expressed in dollars.

Identifying areas of responsibility

The first step in a program to create responsibility reporting is to identify the areas of management responsibility and to portray them in an organization chart. A numerical accounting code should be assigned to each of the areas on the chart. A three-digit code will suffice for most organizations, automatically recognizing three levels of management responsibility. For example, assume that the number 213 identifies a specific sales district; 210 will identify the district with a specific sales region; and 200 will identify the region with the sales division. Each digit indicates a level of management reporting and the individual to whom the report is directed.

Next, the responsibilities of each manager should be defined. This can be accomplished at meetings with department heads and their superiors by identifying the personnel on a current payroll with the manager who has primary responsibility for their employment. The other elements of income and expense of the business can also be covered at these meetings. This review will help to define the scope of the manager's responsibilities and will clarify his understanding of his job. At the same time it will provide the accountants with an accounting description of each manager's responsibilities.

The second step in the program is to prepare departmental accounting manuals based on the review of responsibilities. The manual is the basic means of communicating to managers and accountants the content and intent of accounts, and it assures the continuity of accounting treatment through changes in both managers and accountants. Verbal instructions and assorted memoranda are no substitute for a manual that presents basic company accounting policy as well as insight into the scope of each manager's responsibilities. A departmental manual common to several managers would suffice where the nature of their jobs is alike. The first preparation of the accounting manuals will require considerable effort, but thereafter revisions resulting from changes in organization structure or in accounting policy will be relatively easy to handle.

The account numbers can also perform an important function in the preparation of information for management by arranging the accounting data in a logical sequence and by providing for the automatic summarization of information for the different levels of management. The first step in the assignment of account numbers is to decide which elements of income or expense can logically be summarized together. For example, four primary classes of expenses may be present in dealing with operating expenses: salaries and wages, production materials, operating supplies and expenses, and facility expenses. The next lower level of detail in salaries and wages might identify the general types of employees, such as clerical, supervisory, and general and professional; and the third level might identify specific types of employees, such as secretaries, bookkeeping machine operators, and accounting clerks. A sample account number for one of these elements of expense will illustrate the point. If 5134 identifies all employees classified as secretaries, it is possible to match each digit with one of the levels of information just described. The "3" identifies clerical salaries, the "1" salaries and wages, and the "5" operating expenses. Thus, each of the three high-order digits, 5-1-3, indicates a point of summarization that will correspond to a specific level of management responsibility.

At this point all of the elements of responsibility accounting and reporting are present. There is one important consideration that must be recognized before pressing the start button. The accounting system is prepared to recognize two separate sets of facts concurrently. First, it is geared to account for responsibilities; hence each accounting distribution must designate a manager. Second, it will accumulate transactions by types; therefore, each accounting distribution must also designate an account. Thus, the system is accounting in two separate dimensions, by responsibility and by account. The codes that identify each are separate although constructed by the same principle of automatic summarization through the logical use of numbers.

Preparing responsibility reports

Accounting for responsibility will usually increase the size of the accounting records over those maintained when accounting only for company or geographical operations. There are several methods of solving this problem without materially increasing the size of the accounting department to cope with the preparation of reports at month-end. The two principal criteria to be considered in choosing the appropriate method of data processing are the number of areas of responsibility to be recognized in the system and the amount of detail required by the chart of accounts.

When manual methods are used, the income and expense ledgers should be organized by responsibility codes with the detail by accounts maintained within these controls. This is the primary means of using the information for internal management and thus will satisfy the most frequent needs for reference. The accumulation of income or expenses for the business as a whole can be obtained readily by preparing departmental trial balances on preprinted peg strips and by cross-footing the amounts. As a rule of thumb, one ledger clerk can generally handle the posting and report preparation on a timely basis for approximately twenty-five areas of responsibility.

When there are more than twenty-five areas of responsibility, the potential for bookkeeping or tabulating equipment should be evaluated for this and other suitable machine applications. A single bookkeeping machine will function effectively in handling the accounting and reporting of twenty-five to seventy-five areas, while tabulating equipment can handle up to several hundred areas on a timely basis. Service bureaus offer any business the opportunity to use tabulating equipment at nominal cost. When a system of responsibility reporting is used in conjunction with a profit-planning system, tabulating equipment is the most satisfactory data processing method because of its ability to make comparisons between plan and actual while preparing performance reports.

General considerations. Decision making is management's toughest job; it is tougher when managers must make decisions with only limited facts. Reports to management from a system of responsibility accounting enable management to focus on decision making at the first level of supervision —the point of action—and to judge the accomplishments of individual managers. These men also benefit, for they have a record of what has happened to help them decide what should happen.

Responsibility accounting is a dynamic form of management accounting that is relatively easy to install, for it merely requires that each transaction be identified with a manager as well as an account. It is the logical prelude to any program of cost reduction. It is applicable in businesses of any size, for almost every owner delegates some responsibilities for action. If his business is to grow and prosper, the owner must consider this problem, but he should also be assured that each manager will be held accountable for the execution of his responsibilities.

Guide for preparing internal financial and operating reports[3]

Very often, during the survey of a reporting procedure, one finds oneself actually, or at least mentally, developing a check list as a guide to insure consideration of all the salient features of the operation. The following check list was used in a recent engagement and appears to have general applicability to any survey of internal financial and operating reports.

Reporting level

1. Make results identifiable with responsible executive.
2. Prepare for each executive a statement reflecting only results for which he is responsible.
3. Integrate individual statements in a pattern that clearly follows the organization chart—so that, for example, net profit can be "exploded" like a bill of materials.
4. Ignore subsidiary corporate entities for management reports when such corporate structure does not coincide with the management organization.
5. Design report structure so that statements for lower management levels can be added without altering existing statements.

Content

1. Present only one set of results—avoid estimates that are subsequently connected to actual.
2. Compare results with expected performance.
3. Present results on an exception basis that only emphasizes good and bad performance.
4. Segregate controllable from noncontrollable expense.
5. Establish predetermined amounts for allocated expenses over which the charged department has no control.

[3]This check list is reprinted from the January 1959 issue of *Management Controls*. Copyrighted 1959 by Peat, Marwick, Mitchell & Co.

6. Use standards for transferring costs that "flow" with production between departments.

Timing

1. Issue statements immediately after end of month—preferably within five working days.
    (a) Use control totals. Do not wait for detail distributions.
    (b) Accumulate "totals to date" as month progresses.
    (c) Do not cut off before end of month any item significantly affecting profits.
    (d) Decrease monthly report load by issuing daily and weekly reports on items like sales, production, and the like.
2. Stagger release of statements where necessary to ease digestion of contents.

Form

1. Present information in the same manner that executives plan and think about their operations.
2. Let statements highlight results; do not try to present all the answers; leave exhausting details in the books to be used only for special statements and analyses when required.
3. Express results in one figure at the bottom of the statements; make the figure easily traceable to a single figure on the next "higher" statement.
4. Make statements easy to read.
    (a) Use 8½ in. by 11 in. paper.
    (b) Limit columns of figures to not more than three columns in a group.
    (c) Leave plenty of white space on page.
    (d) Omit all cents; omit thousands of dollars where possible.
    (e) Segregate only significant expenses; group remainder.
    (f) Use operating terminology, but make items understandable to uninformed third party.
    (g) Clearly caption each statement and use informative headings.
    (h) Show "year-to-date" figures to the left of account description.
5. Provide sufficient space on each statement for statistics and interpretive comments.

Cost-saving Potentials

A number of different approaches to cost reduction have been outlined and the importance of good reporting in particular has been stressed. Let us now recall the principle introduced on page 312, namely that cost reduction and control is a team job in which *all* employees must participate. This principle is closely related to the recognition that cost-saving possibilities are available throughout a business. In businesses where failures stem mainly from management deficiencies this principle is particularly significant. Both cost control and efforts at cost reduction should encompass the entire operation. Economies may not be achieved immediately, but sooner or later costs generated in any area can be reduced if that area is covered in the cost control program.

Management must be convinced that the CPA can make an important contribution to the cost reduction program. And the best way to convince management that the CPA is the man for the job is for the latter to keep presenting worth-while and practical suggestions that will lead to cost reduction. A selection should then be made of the most appropriate areas in which to begin the program.

Causes of excessive costs[4]

A cost reduction program calls for systematic planning and execution. It demands top management's active leadership and support. It requires that causes of excessive costs be identified and that effective measures be adopted to eliminate them.

It is appropriate, therefore, to examine some of the more common causes of excessive costs. The following discussion identifies some of them and weighs their impact.

Policies. Management policies may create unnecessary expense. They may be inherently unsound, may have been erroneously interpreted, or may have become outmoded with the passage of time. For example, let us assume that management sets a formula for deciding the annual limit of capital expenditures. If it is excessive, wasteful expenditures may result; if it is inadequate, operating costs may rise unduly because of the failure to modernize, replace, or purchase equipment.

Lack of management effort. A constant drive is needed to seek out and eliminate unnecessary or excessive expense. Management failure—at any level—is a common cause for perpetuating inefficiency in this respect. Thus, if standard unit costs are used for appraising operating performance, they may not reflect recent method improvements. Operating inefficiencies may be hidden under a cloak of false standards.

[4]Pages 325-329 were excerpted with minor revisions from an article, "The Cost Reduction Program," in *The New York Certified Public Accountant,* October 1960. The author is Maurice B. T. Davies, CPA, partner with Lybrand, Ross Bros. & Montgomery.

Inadequate planning. Each change in operations and business conditions calls for plans to be re-evaluated. Changes in plans are sometimes overlooked; at other times they develop through a subconscious adherence to precedent. Unnecessary expense is a common result. A business, for example, may introduce a second-line product to supplement its original line. It paints, finishes, and packages its new line according to existing specifications. However, lower and less costly standards might be appropriate for its second-line products.

Empire building. Officials sometimes add to their subordinate work force and functions in an effort to increase their personal stature. This tendency may escape detection when business conditions are satisfactory and activity is on the increase. Consider, as an illustration, a home office industrial relations division which has staff counterparts at each plant. Their work is similar, it overlaps, and active communications take place between the home office and plant staffs. Economies could be achieved by centralizing the staff.

Lack of imagination. Continuous exposure to a specific condition may cause a person to accept it and fail to observe opportunities for improvement. The imagination becomes dulled, and potential savings are not realized. For example, the manufacturing process requires a flow of semifinished products from one type of machine to another. Machines are physically grouped by type for ease in supervision. Through a change in plant layout and supervisory philosophy, it would be possible to group machines according to production flow rather than by type. This would eliminate excessive products movement within the plant and permit better control of quantities of semifinished products.

Outmoded techniques and equipment. Busy attention to its daily problems and tasks often prevents management from devoting sufficient time to the study of new developments and trends. Facilities for improving methods, techniques, and equipment are constantly becoming available, yet their potentialities may not be fully explored. Take the case of a large payroll department which compiles data from time cards and job cards, calculates payrolls, distributes payroll expense and prepares pay checks—all by hand. Its work may be performed more accurately, speedily, and economically through the adoption of punched card techniques.

Corporate fictions. Many businesses are engaged in a multitude of operations, particularly when there has been a conscious move to diversify. Some operations are performed by corporations acquired through merger; others by separately created subsidiaries. There is a tendency for a multiplicity of organizations and methods to result. This may be overlooked because separate corporate entities are involved. In a group of associated corporations, for example, there may be a separate purchasing department in each corporation. By combining these departments it may be possible to reduce administrative expenses, obtain important advantages through added purchasing power and larger orders, and stimulate intercorporate transactions.

Absence of incentives to save. The business activity responsible for the production function is in general constantly aware of the need for controlling costs. Overhead departments, on the other hand, tend to emphasize the value of the services they provide and become less conscious of the need for controlling costs. After he has waged his "annual battle of the budget," the manager of an overhead department is frequently satisfied simply to operate within his budget; exceptional savings might prejudice his budget in the following year. This may be illustrated by reference to a company having a number of regional offices which process customer orders. By developing and publishing unit processing costs, it may instill a spirit of competition among the regional offices, provide an inducement to cut these costs, and establish keener standards for future budgets.

Lack of supervisory perspective. The pressure of daily routine and inertia caused by adherence to accepted practice tend to reduce a manager's ability to review his operation objectively. Chances to produce fundamental improvements are consequently overlooked. The superior is often similarly placed, and unable to compensate for the loss of perspective. Assume that excessive scrap and rework expense is caused by the adoption of unreasonable inspection standards. The situation may come to light through inspection by a home office team that provides an entirely fresh and independent viewpoint.

Inadequate information. Effective information is the springboard to productive action. Sometimes that information is not developed; at other times, though available, it is not presented to the people who could use it to stimulate action. An illustration of this would be a multiple-plant company which ships products on a nation-wide basis at uniform prices, F.O.B. destination, and absorbs transportation expense. Each plant develops statistics on the effective selling prices for each destination after providing for freight costs. The company traffic manager may be able to arrange for switches of delivery points among plants and thus reduce freight costs.

Luxuries. Certain expenses add to the comfort of working conditions and improve the morale of employees, customers, and others. While not wholly necessary, they have a public relations value and may be justifiable in favorable times. However, they call for re-evaluation in a period of adverse business conditions. To illustrate: Regional salesmen's conferences are held annually at resort country clubs. The programs are spread over a period adequate to provide for relaxation and entertainment. As a result of reduced sales, it may be desirable to hold the meetings in company premises or nearby hotels, condense the programs, and let the salesmen know that country club meetings will be resumed when sales improve.

Unprofitable time. Employees' time is generally fully occupied in a period of intense activity, and the work force grows to absorb the excess of work to be done over available working capacity. With a downturn in business, a lag generally occurs before the work force is reduced. The extent of unprofitable time, particularly in overhead activities, is not readily discernible because work tends to be done more slowly and idle time is otherwise camouflaged. Assume, for example, that invoices are prepared at decentralized sales offices. By keeping statistics of the relationship of invoice volume to paid man-hours, the company can compare present with past productivity and appraise the performance of one office against another. As minutes per invoice become excessive, the company should order staff reductions.

Slack buying practices. Under the pressure of active business conditions, a purchasing department may be compelled to adopt short cuts, buy inappropriate quantities, devote inadequate care in securing bids, and spend insufficient energy in exploring markets and consulting with suppliers. Thus, a company may buy parts for its manufacturing operations according to standards defined by its engineers. The purchasing agent may invite suppliers to visit the plant, observe operations, and meet the plant management. He may explain the urgent need for reducing costs and call for the suppliers to make a contribution. By careful examination of specifications and discussion of alternatives, the suppliers may be able to produce a less costly product by fabricating it to less exacting or less expensive standards.

Overstocking. The hazards of excessive or unbalanced inventories are less apparent when sales are rising, when an atmosphere of optimism prevails, and when the principal aim is to be prepared to meet every sales opportunity. An unfavorable business trend often develops with dramatic suddenness. Inventories reach disproportionate levels; slow-moving stocks, obsolescence, and spoilage become matters of greater concern; and a drive is instituted to reduce inventory. Changes in inventory policy should then be explored. Consider the case in which inventories are carried in ample quantities at decentralized warehouses, supplied from a centrally located plant. It may be desirable to reduce decentralized inventory levels and make greater use of central storage facilities. The total inventory investment could then be reduced and production schedules geared to a level where greater protection is afforded against excessive inventories in the face of a falling market.

Inefficient routines. The methods of performing repetitive tasks, though individually insignificant, may have an important collective influence on costs. When methods are first installed, it may not be possible to visualize the ultimate volume and, as the activity expands, the basic methods may be insufficiently questioned. Potential savings may be achieved through work simplification, elimination of routines, combination of tasks, or discovery of duplicated effort. However, the necessity for the over-all activity should be studied before attention is given to the methods involved. A good illustration would be the procedure whereby a shipping order, bill of lading, and invoice are prepared for every outgoing shipment. When items are not immediately available, a back order requisition is also initiated. It may be possible to originate a single all-purpose document to meet all these needs by using a reproducible "master" to record the essential data. This should reduce clerical time and eliminate transcription errors.

Watered budgets. The budget is sometimes an illusory standard for controlling expense. Budget requests frequently include margins for contingencies which are not entirely eliminated in the budget reviews. The budget provides an adequate measuring device only when it is linked up with a factor based on volume. Consider this example: A drafting department has successfully requested an increased budget. However, its costs may be evaluated when expressed in terms of cost per authorized drawing produced. If this factor is introduced, department expense may be subjected to a dual type of budgetary control, one expressed in terms of absolute dollars and the other based on productivity.

The preceding are some of the major causes which should be explored in an endeavor to reduce costs. But the process of seeking them out will generally be burdensome and may not develop at the pace necessary to produce substantial savings rapidly. A co-ordinated and systematic approach is therefore essential.

We will now approach the problem of cost reduction by means of an analysis of a cost system review.

Lowering Costs Through an Objective Cost System Review[5]

The classical definition of profits describes them as the excess of revenues, proceeds, or selling prices over related costs. Stated in another

[5]Pages 329-335 appeared as a paper in Haskins & Sells' *Selected Papers*, 1961. The author is John E. Kolesar, partner.

way, they are the monetary benefits arising from commercial operations or transactions. Although technically correct, these definitions imply that profits are residues or excesses left over from business transactions; that profits are passive rather than active; and that they are more in the nature of by-products than the principal product of the business organization. This is a mistaken impression held by many business managers and accountants. Subconsciously, these attitudes influence their business judgment and decisions, which in turn are often reflected as losses in the financial statements or as inadequate returns on investment. More properly, however, profits are the principal product of management. They are dynamic and can be influenced through the skillful use of management tools.

For purposes of illustration and in support of the latter definition we can compare the activities required of management to generate a profit with those required to manufacture a product. Academic knowledge suggests that five basic management functions or activities are required in any successful business organization. They are planning, organization, motivation, co-ordination, and control. Each of these five activities must be applied in some form, at proper stages of completion, to manufacture a product that will be accepted by the ultimate consumer. In the planning stages the product is designed; detailed drawings, blueprints, and bills of material are prepared; and specifications and tolerance are precisely engineered. Organization is furnished when route sheets are prepared, materials are ordered, and the manpower and machines are scheduled. Through the functions of production control, timing and co-ordination are introduced into the manufacturing processes. Wages, incentives, and fringe benefits provide the motivation for skilled labor to produce a quality product, in a reasonable period of time. And finally, through a program of inspection, measurement, and comparison with product specifications, management provides quality control over the finished product.

If we agree that a reasonable return on investment is the product the manager has been hired to produce for the owners of a business, then it is reasonable to assume that he should apply all the available management skills, to the fullest extent possible, to produce this return for the owners. Modern management methods are frequently referred to as management sciences. Their application requires proper management tools, used with the touch and imagination of the skilled craftsman. Ironically, however, many managers, who would not think of producing even the simplest product without detailed drawings and specifications, begin each new fiscal year without adequate sales and profit objectives, without budgets, forecasts, standard costs, or even a reasonable breakdown of fixed and variable expenses. Many managers who insist on the finest equipment and technology for their products will undertake to build profits with inadequate or antiquated management tools.

The cost system

Business managers have numerous management tools available with which to plan, form, build, and develop profits. Cost accounting, the related cost system, and their principal output, management reports, can be management's greatest servant if designed and administered properly. This is particularly true in an industrial enterprise. Costs and cost systems refer principally to product costs and costs of sales. However, the same basic principles also apply in most cases to distribution costs, administration costs, and all other costs not directly related to the product.

Design. A properly designed cost system can furnish data with which to plan, forecast, set standards, develop budgets, set sales prices, and form policies. Control over materials, manpower, and machines can be provided by comparison with standards or norms. By incorporating the principles of responsibility accounting, management reports can motivate action, if properly designed to highlight problem areas. To serve its masters well, cost accounting and the related cost system, like any machine or tool, must be well designed for the purposes intended. A cost system is dynamic. It requires periodic maintenance and lubrication to keep it running smoothly, generating timely data. It must be replaced when obsolete, and modified if changes in products and processes occur. Like any tool, the cost system or its output will only continue to be used by management as long as it can generate desired results. Cost accounting in many businesses has degenerated to, or has never risen above, a historical record of costs incurred, thereby serving little or no useful management purpose.

The responsibility for an effective and smooth-running cost system rests jointly on management, which uses the data generated, and on the cost accountant, who generates it. The business manager should tell the accountant what information he needs, and when he needs it, to do his job most effectively. He should keep the accountant adequately informed on projected changes in products, processes, or policies that might affect costs. On the other hand, the business manager must rely on the accountant to keep him up to date on what management data is available or can be made available from the system. In some cases the accountant may find it necessary to educate members of management to the proper interpretation and use of this data.

Modifications. The responsibility for initiating modifications in the cost system rests primarily with the cost accountant because of his technical knowledge and experience and the fact that his close contact with the system should disclose needed changes. Accordingly, the cost accountant should periodically emerge from the mass of details and objectively appraise the effectiveness of the system and management reports being generated. This, quite often, is easier said than done. As a result, needed changes never get made and, in time, weaknesses in the system pyramid, producing inadequate or incorrect data on which management is basing its profit-planning decisions. As auditors and as management services specialists, CPAs frequently must make an objective appraisal of the effectiveness of certain cost controls or data, without making a detailed survey of the cost accounting system. In so doing, they must be constantly on the alert for "flags" or "smoke signals," which are symptoms of weaknesses in the system, related controls, and management reports. Like many physical symptoms discovered by a family doctor, they are not conclusive evidence that a serious problem or disease exists. Like most physical symptoms, the flags require further investigation to isolate any serious problems that may exist. Solving cost system problems generally is not simple; but the recognition of their existence often is a giant step toward their cure.

Review of the cost system

As a guide in making a cost system review, we will now discuss some of these flags and cite some examples of how costly management problems are uncovered. Probably the most common flag is the abnormal inventory adjustment or variance. Frequently serious management problems are covered up by stereotyped explanations of inventory adjustments and variances. In one case, a company manufactured and assembled fabricated metal products. The annual physical inventory disclosed a very significant adjustment of the in-process and finished goods inventories. The size of the adjustment was unreasonable in consideration of the highly controlled and sophisticated engineered standard cost system in use in the plant. The adjustment was at first explained as probably due to a poor cutoff at the time of the last physical inventory. Top management was not satisfied and demanded a full investigation. It was established that proper cutoffs had been made. A new physical inventory was taken six weeks later, which disclosed a further downward adjustment in the in-process and finished goods inventories. By combing the production reports prepared during the six-week period between physical inventories, it was discovered that more scrap was being sold than was being reported. Investigation disclosed that the night-shift employees were dumping generated scrap into railroad cars on a siding within the plant without properly reporting it, thus overstating production. Further evidences of overreported production were discovered, which in turn disclosed the real problem. Over a year prior to the physical inventory, the plant made certain changes in its production incentive system without reviewing its control over production reporting, thus making it very lucrative for production employees to devise means of overstating their production. By isolating the real problem, management was able swiftly to initiate proper controls and pave the way to possible cost reduction.

Discovering weaknesses. Indications from employees, or by other means, of a lack of confidence in data prepared by the cost accounting department is generally a sign of serious weaknesses in the cost data or system. An unusual case in point was discovered in connection with a cost study made under a cost-plus agreement for certain outside conversion work. In assembling basic data for the study, the accountant noticed that a certain product carried a different code on each of three reports examined. Inquiry disclosed that the reports were prepared by the cost department, the sales department, and the mill office. Investigation disclosed that the sales department and the mill office developed product codes to assemble their own cost information, because they lacked confidence in the data prepared by the cost department or because the cost department's data was inadequate for their management needs. Top management was aware of these three codes, but was unaware of the degree to which useless duplication of effort had progressed because of a lack of confidence in the data generated by the cost department.

Cost system controls. The absence of many of the usual cost system controls reflect unfavorably on the effectiveness of the system and the reliability of the cost data generated for management's use. Examples of the controls most frequently missing in cost systems are the absence of standards or norms against which performance can be measured, the absence of cost-center responsibility accounting, the use of general overhead rates in preference to easily determinable cost-center rates, or the use of a memorandum cost system which cannot be tied into the general ledger. As for the latter, one management services consultant who specializes in cost-system problems summarized his experience with memorandum cost records as follows: "A cost system which isn't good enough to tie into the general ledger, generally produces reports which aren't good enough for management needs."

Counteracting the status quo. A feeling of contentedness with the *status quo* in a cost system should raise a flag for possible weaknesses. For instance, indications that the standards are not periodically reviewed and updated, or that a system is so perfect it has not needed any revision in years, often require a careful look, because chances are there is plenty of room for modification and improvement. One sheet metal manufacturer, going through a very serious economic period, began to look into ways of reducing costs. When the question was raised as to why the company operated entirely on a job order system, the old-timers in management responded: "We've always operated on a job order basis; it's the practice in the industry." They explained that their customers, who are principally machine manufacturers, insist on a great variety of metallurgical compositions and sizes with varying tolerances. After the smoke cleared, it was decided to look into the matter. Considerable similarity was discovered in a great percentage of the orders. In co-operation with the customers, the range of sizes and metallurgical requirements were narrowed down substantially. From this the customers also learned that their engineers lacked co-ordination in developing their materials specifications; this was costing them money. These changes resulted in the processing of larger quantities of certain products, to be stocked in intermediate sizes. As orders were received, these semifinished products were transferred into job orders for final processing and finishing. The end result to the company was more economical purchasing, reduced quantities of mill overruns, improved scheduling, and generally reduced processing costs.

Another example of the *status quo* mentality is presented by a company that did not believe in updating standards when technological or processing changes occurred. The company had a very substantial punch press operation. A rather simple stacking device was developed and added to the presses which automated, to some degree, the previous manual operation. New standards were not developed on the machines. Production increased approximately 10 per cent, which reflected a favorable variance for the department. Management was satisfied. Over a year later, during a general revision of standards, it was discovered that reasonable production capacities for the punch presses were 10 to 15 per cent greater than actual performances to date. Old standards in this case had covered up substandard performance and lulled management into a costly complacency.

Review of management policies

Unusual ratios, if noticed and investigated, quite often point to serious management problems. An unusual case of this nature arose in a manufacturing company that operated quite an extensive network of field sales stores. It came to management's attention that, on the average, 1½ sales invoices were being prepared by the stores for each purchase invoice. This was abnormally low, considering the thousands of small-priced items that were stocked and handled through the stores. This fact initiated a review of what appeared to be very costly purchasing and store sales policies and practices. In this case it was not the usual practice to make this comparison, but an alertness on the part of one individual to somewhat unrelated data raised the flag for action.

Service department budgets that do not take into consideration the level of operations should raise a flag to the reviewer. In such situations budgets quite often are set too high, encourage padding, and result in costly waste. In maintenance departments, for instance, the level of operations is often measured by production hours or number of work orders completed. The level of operations in the billing department can be measured by the number of invoices prepared, in the drafting department by the number of drawings produced, and in the storeroom by the number of requisitions filled. Average cost per invoice is particularly useful to management in establishing sales policies on small orders. With increasing clerical costs and decreasing profit margins, management must know the breakeven points.

The cost system without adequate perpetual inventory records and without a plan for periodic review of inventories for obsolete, damaged, or slow-moving stock should point to system improvements and cost-saving possibilities. In practically every company there are individuals who, probably with good intentions, keep hoarding supplies or machine parts on the premise that some day they just may need these items. This can be costly from the standpoint both of record keeping and of idle investment. If the cost accounting system does not provide for easy identification of inactive stocks, then a periodic review should be provided. This nibbling can be minimized by a demonstration of what it costs to maintain these stocks and what cash would be freed if idle stocks were promptly used or disposed of. Periodically identifying slow-moving finished goods for management is necessary to stimulate sales pressure on these items.

Other warning signals. Other flags or smoke signals can lead to fires in the system which are burning away profits. Excessive or recurring overtime or unemployed time in productive or service departments and recurring bottlenecks in the processing of product or paper work may be signs of more serious problems. The use of "fudge factors" and reserves in arriving at the monthly cost of sales or to cushion adjustments tends to create misleading management reports. These are also devices used by accountants who are too lazy to isolate and correct the basic problems. Signs of poor housekeeping in clerical and tabulating departments may also be clues to attitudes and carelessness in record keeping, which in turn filter into management decision reports.

In conclusion, the following three principal points should be kept in mind: (1) Profits are the principal product of top management; (2) profits can be influenced by the skillful use of management tools; and (3) cost accounting and the related cost system as a principal tool of management must be maintained and operated at maximum efficiency in order to be used effectively.

An attempt will now be made to list certain specific areas in an organization which are susceptible of cost reduction.

Cost Reduction Areas[6]

Following are some potential areas for lowering costs which the CPA can discuss briefly with his client.

Purchasing. The cost of raw materials, parts, components, supplies, packaging and shipping materials, and all of the thousands of items purchased by the average manufacturing company represent a significant percentage of total costs, perhaps 40 to 60 per cent. Managements realize this in a general way, but in many instances this area is not given the attention it warrants in connection with cost reduction. In many companies, the sales dollar proportionately being spent through purchasing has been gradually increasing.

In too many companies, the purchasing department is taken for granted; the attention of management is focused upon sales and production. This does not mean that purchasing agents as a group are not doing their job and are inefficient. Often their opportunities are limited because managements do not expect enough and do not attach sufficient importance to the function.

Cost reduction programs in purchasing, with the active interest and support of managements, have accomplished significant results in some cases. Several questions might be asked:

1. Does the item being requisitioned best serve the purpose for which it is being bought?
2. Are specifications included that are not necessary?
3. Are new and better materials and products available?
4. Could better delivery be obtained on an alternative item?
5. Are services and operations being asked for that could be eliminated?
6. Is proper balance being maintained between quantities and price?
7. Does the purchasing department have the necessary lead time?
8. Are standard items being used wherever possible?
9. Are the best values being obtained?

The fact that these questions are asked does not mean that the purchasing agent is substituting his judgment for that of a design engineer or production superintendent. However, the purchasing agent, in dealing with suppliers in competition with others, hears of many ways to reduce costs. He should be alert to such possibilities and pass them on to the proper people for consideration. In some companies, the purchasing department through lack of authority or initiative seldom questions the item to be procured or considers alternatives and thus becomes merely an order-placing function.

[6]Pages 336-340 were excerpted from an article in *The Arthur Andersen Chronicle,* October 1959. The author is George R. Catlett, partner.

Purchasing does have a big impact on profits and can affect them accordingly.

Inventory control. Inventory control and the related field of production control are broad subjects which have been discussed in detail in an earlier chapter. However, this represents one of the greatest potential areas of cost reduction in manufacturing companies, both large and small. The possibilities are so great because of the significance of (1) production inefficiencies resulting from unbalanced materials and parts; (2) constant expediting and special efforts to avoid crises; (3) late deliveries of finished products; (4) obsolescence of excess stocks; (5) extra costs from not procuring economical order quantities; and (6) interest cost on excess inventories.

If the inventory control system will permit cycle counting during the year and eliminate the need of shutting down the plant for inventories, this benefit may also be substantial.

The managements of many successful manufacturing companies are beginning to realize more fully the importance of inventory control.

Materials handling. Materials handling covers the movement of raw materials, purchased parts, supplies, and finished goods to or from trucks and railroad cars and within factories and warehouses. A great deal more time is spent moving things around than is realized. The costs are frequently not known.

Great progress has been made in reducing costs of this type in recent years. The development of special shipping facilities, the more effective utilization of space, and the use of mechanical handling equipment have made significant cost reductions possible. New types of conveyors, automatic lifts, gravity chutes, pallets, racks, lift trucks, and other new equipment offer a wide variety of possibilities.

In approaching this problem, the places to investigate are the receiving department, the warehouse and storage areas, the production department, and the shipping department. The following items should be examined: (1) excessive movement as to distance and possibilities of rearrangement; (2) elimination of handling, if possible; (3) inefficient utilization of space; (4) extra manual work; (5) too much time in performing various functions; and (6) poor loading, stacking, and the like.

A great deal can be accomplished by standard equipment and simple methods. There generally is no need for elaborate equipment.

Material usage. Material costs are influenced by design, production methods, and standardization of parts. This general subject was mentioned in connection with purchasing, but the primary responsibility rests with the design and production departments. The effect of the product specifications on costs must be constantly emphasized. Also, the possibility of substitutions must be considered continually because of new developments.

Standardization is obviously important, but the design engineer is frequently thinking along other lines. Many companies do not know what parts are standard, so they are handicapped in capitalizing on standardization. The savings from standardization and interchangeability of parts are much greater than sometimes realized. If a company has thousands of parts, the time saved in purchasing, receiving, storing, controlling, accounting, and so on, can be significant.

The men in the shop are close to the actual production problems and are in a position to suggest many ways of reducing costs if they want to do so.

Maintenance. With the increase in mechanization and automation throughout industry, maintenance is becoming a major operating cost. With the emphasis on larger and better production, the advances in maintenance have not always kept pace.

Maintenance has two aspects: breakdown maintenance and preventive maintenance. Many companies do not have an efficient or economical maintenance program. In some cases, the management does not fully support such a program.

Preventive maintenance programs are advantageous in many ways. They reduce not only production costs through fewer breakdowns, but also maintenance labor costs, including overtime. Through planning and scheduling maintenance work, the personnel can be used more effectively and economically. Such a program also should include good records of maintenance work, which can be used for the determination of trends and the measurement of performance. Excessive maintenance may indicate that certain facilities should be replaced.

Savings can sometimes be achieved by subcontracting maintenance and overhauling of equipment rather than using company maintenance personnel.

Transportation. Transportation costs have increased substantially along with everything else. This function is frequently limited to the more mechanical aspects of routing, checking rates, approving freight, and so on. Most companies would benefit by broadening their concept of the traffic function and assigning a more important place to it in the companies' operations.

In choosing routes and type of transportation, rates are only one factor. Consideration must also be given to other factors, such as additional handling, lapsed time in transit, and the physical aspects of packaging and loading.

A company gains to the extent that claims can be prevented or minimized. If ways can be found to improve the protection of the product during shipment at a reasonable cost, a net savings may well result.

Some companies have found it advisable to engage outside agencies to check freight bills, and this procedure may be worth investigation for small- and medium-sized companies.

Clerical work. Most companies over a period of years tend to get loaded down with clerical and paper work. This is not limited to the accounting department; it occurs in all departments. Existing procedures generally have accumulated over a period of many years, with different forms, records, and reports being added by numerous people in different departments, at various times and for many reasons. When someone has a new idea, a new form or procedure is added, but few are abandoned.

Unless the management organizes a co-ordinated work simplification program and emphasizes its importance, there is a strong tendency to favor the *status quo* in the whole field of paper work. Most employees are too busy to make changes. A few companies have attempted to develop standards for clerical work, but this is a relatively new field.

Some of the areas where simplification may pay good dividends are order handling, billing, receivables, inventory control, and cost accounting. Efficiency in such areas may accomplish much better results as well as reduce costs.

It is not uncommon to find three or four duplicate perpetual inventory records in the accounting, purchasing, and production control departments, and in the storeroom; or to find the credit manager keeping his own accounts receivable ledger for credit purposes. These are merely examples of situations that develop over a period of years.

The use of open invoice systems, elimination of monthly accounts receivable statements, use of a check copy for cash disbursements records, elimination of accounts payable ledgers, and many other relatively simple changes all add up to a savings in time.

The possibility of filming permanent and semipermanent records has been publicized frequently, but most companies have done little in this regard. With the cost of space and file cabinets and other storage containers going up, this may be worth considering.

Reproducing equipment is being used considerably more for a variety of purposes. Many companies are reproducing reports in pencil on preprinted forms rather than typing them. Some companies are now printing all of their own forms.

Rapid strides are being made in office equipment of all types. One of the problems of controllers and office managers is to keep up with all of these developments and determine which equipment will best meet their needs.

Miscellaneous ideas. A few other ideas that may have application in some instances follow:

1. An organization study may reveal that departments, divisions, or subsidiaries may be effectively merged with other parts of the company.
2. With higher interest rates, many companies are consolidating bank accounts and investing any temporary excess funds in short-term government securities.
3. Carry-over of obsolete and surplus inventory items creates additional costs for storage, handling, and working capital. "String saving" can be expensive, and obsolete items very seldom improve with age.
4. The segregation of scrap by type, size, and so on, may result in greater recovery.
5. The over-all insurance program can often be reviewed on a competitive basis with advantageous results.
6. Leasing of equipment has been increasing in recent years and is worth investigation in some instances.
7. Indirect labor and overtime are two areas where excessive costs may exist.
8. The reclamation of cutting oils through the use of equipment designed for that purpose not only saves most of the oil but reduces drum handling and other related activities.
9. In larger companies, secretarial pools and centralized filing departments are sometimes found to offer advantages.

Conclusion. The right kind of a cost reduction program can accomplish effective results if properly organized and consistently followed. Constructive management support and encouragement are necessary.

The saying that "a dollar saved is a dollar earned" may sound dated, but even depreciated dollars are worth saving. In terms of net profits, a cost saving of $10,000 may be equivalent to additional sales of $100,000. Profits are the basis of our free enterprise system, and they depend on keeping costs a reasonable distance below sales income.

CHAPTER SEVEN

Office Management

Introduction

Statistics show that, on the average, one-half of every dollar spent in office functions in the United States is wasted.

Some businesses face up to this office problem and take effective steps to meet it. Others at least recognize it by making common-sense attempts to promote productivity on the part of their office personnel. However, the sound practice of up-to-date office administration involves the use of a technical body of knowledge which extends beyond common sense. The office management function can no longer simply be delegated to a senior clerk or head bookkeeper. Today's office manager must have a knowledge of the theories of scientific office management.

Companies able to afford office analysts, systems and procedures experts, and forms design men in addition to competent office executives, have made tremendous strides in increasing the productivity of their clerical operations. Some companies have engaged CPAs to survey and correct office practices. Their work may encompass specialized studies in office automation or the setting of time standards for clerical workers. Most large business offices today bear the earmarks of scientific management; constant effort and expenditure have enabled these companies to realize far more than the average rate of productivity.

The smaller business on the other hand, can rarely justify the engagement of a full-time systems and procedures expert or the installation of expensive tabulating equipment. It is easy to pretend that serious office management problems exist only in big companies where the employer cannot see what is going on. But, regardless of its size, the office is in fact the nerve center of any business. It supplies most of the data upon which operating or policy decisions are made.

Small businesses will generally agree that their greatest advantage over larger competitors is flexibility: their ability to change directions more quickly to gain competitive advantage. With big business offices now able to gather, sort, and report facts by means of tabulators or computers in a matter of minutes, the day may not be far off when big businesses will be able to make informed decisions long before small businesses know what is going on. The small business that continues to neglect its nerve center is therefore asking for trouble.

Increasing Office Efficiency

What can business do to increase office efficiency and productivity? It can follow the lead of the more progressive concerns: identically, in the case of functions such as personnel selection, testing and training, and office organization; and similarly, with respect to mechanization. For example, a company can increase efficiency by 25 per cent by putting the payroll on tab equipment. The smaller business may not be able to afford this, but a simple pegboard system of payroll preparation could increase productivity in this department more than 25 per cent. Businesses, both large and small, can thus experience similar gains simply by utilizing what might appear to be radically different instruments of mechanization.

Obstacles to watch for

Two obstacles can impair the ability to increase office productivity:

1. Business management does not take its offices or its office managers seriously. Sales-oriented managers shun paper work; production-minded managers are dedicated only to raising plant efficiency. A study showing that the office is 40 per cent productive, for example, might open the minds of some managers to the need for improvement.

2. The office supervisor can rarely turn to someone who is in a position to evaluate his ideas or assist him in some of the more technical aspects of office administration. He may, for example, be pretty sure that the purchase of a $3,000 bookkeeping machine will pay for itself in a year and provide the input mechanism to produce the punched tapes he has read about, but he is not really positive it will work. He needs advice and support.

The CPA's role

The CPA can help in several ways. He can alert a negligent management to the significance of office operations and then recommend where and how to improve them. He can sell improvements more convincingly than the office supervisor because he can support his suggestions with evidence gathered in the course of an independent observation of the client's office operations. Indeed, the CPA is often the only one available to provide the necessary technical advice and assistance.

The CPA, like today's trained office manager, must know the techniques and theories underlying modern office management. In this chapter, we will attempt to outline a few of these techniques.

There are two main resources from which a business can achieve more output: personnel and office methods. These are at the heart of every office operation. The following pages will review how employees are hired; whether they are basically competent; whether they have been well trained for their jobs; whether they have the best tools to perform their tasks; and whether their jobs are properly organized, simplified, and supervised.

Greater Productivity Through Personnel

It is generally conceded that the ultimate fate of a business depends on its employees. The competence of management is obviously the chief determinant; but the abilities of people right down the line will contribute significantly to a company's success or failure.

Nevertheless, it is startling to see how many offices are staffed with people who are distinctly not up to par. Some managements attribute the low quality of their office staffs to the fact that competent help is hard to find. But the better-informed managements point to their offices with pride. The great majority of companies in this category come from the ranks of progressive business.

Small versus large companies. The larger business may appear to have great advantages over the smaller one because of its ability to employ its own or outside personnel experts and invest heavily in screening, selecting, and training office staffs. However, many smaller companies have turned their attention to this problem and established formal, up-to-date personnel programs. Successful business managers have proved that the return on their investment, which need not be substantial, fully justifies the expenditure involved.

How can a smaller business adopt big-business techniques in selecting and training its office personnel? Isn't this a highly complex process involving social and psychological considerations and requiring the skills of an industrial relations expert? The answer is *no*. To be sure, a personnel expert can assist a business in establishing and operating a program, but he is not essential to improved selection and training, particularly at the clerical level.

The CPA can be of considerable assistance to business in its personnel selection, provided he has a working knowledge of up-to-date hiring methods, including screening, interviewing, clerical testing, orientation, and training. Though mastery of these functions may require a little further study, none of them should prove particularly difficult.

343

Finding and hiring office personnel

Unless a business develops sources which can provide a reasonable number of job candidates, it will be hampered in the rest of its selection program. The first step in the selection process is therefore the stimulation of an adequate supply of candidates.

Advertisements. Two principal sources of applicants are newspaper advertisements and employment agencies. It is wise to prepare a newspaper advertisement with care. As with any form of advertising, the advertiser is trying to sell something. In this case, a company is trying to sell itself. It may stress short working hours, good salaries, liberal vacations, opportunity for advancement, insurance benefits, sick leave, a training program —or perhaps a congenial working climate. Such advantages when stated in an ad will enhance its effectiveness. On the other hand, disadvantages such as a difficult location or irregular working hours should also be mentioned. In short, an advertisement should "sell" and at the same time enable an applicant to determine whether the company will be interested in him.

Agencies. Employment agencies can be valuable sources of clerical help. The employer must naturally satisfy himself that the agency he selects is both ethical and competent. An agency can do a better screening job for a small employer if it is allowed to become thoroughly acquainted with its management, policies, and environment. For example, an agency representative could be invited to visit the company so as to establish a closer working relationship. Employment agencies which specialize in specific types of personnel should be consulted where appropriate.

Referrals. A source of candidates which is growing in importance is employee referrals. Some business managers object to it on the grounds that an employee may be offended if his friend is rejected. Others argue that the rules of internal control may be violated if, for example, a bookkeeper's sister is hired as a typist. Nevertheless, some companies encourage the practice of employee referrals by offering bonuses to employees. Such companies, often located in areas where labor is scarce, feel they might as well boost the morale of a present employee as pay an employment agency fee.

Schools. Schools are another source of candidates. Large companies probably have an advantage in their relationship with schools, in that they contact the schools more frequently, have fairly standard requirements, and are almost always in the market for employees. The small company, on the other hand, needs personnel only sporadically and lacks the staff necessary to maintain contact with and precisely define its needs to the schools. The success of small business firms that have utilized schools effectively as a source of employees is due to the schools' genuine interest in the employer's reputation, the nature of his policies, and the working environment he can provide.

Many businesses have representatives visit local schools and participate in school projects such as career days and guidance programs. Some companies will invite commercial teachers to their offices when a new business machine is installed, for example. Other companies enhance their reputation by giving away used office machines or shop equipment to local schools. This allows a company to obtain a tax deduction for the market value of depreciated assets and promote goodwill at the same time.

Application, interview, and references

These three elements are extremely important in the hiring of office staffs. A properly designed or selected application form is a valuable aid to evaluation. Unless complete information is obtained, it is extremely difficult even to begin the appraisal process. Larger organizations can afford skilled interviewers and abbreviated application forms. In the absence of expert interviewers, however, a full application form which includes questions on interests, health record, and financial responsibilities ought to be required. This will insure that all pertinent information is placed in front of less experienced interviewers, thus reducing the chances of error in selection simply because the interviewer forgot to ask a pertinent question. Not all businesses have trained interviewers on their staffs. Yet few utilize the application form to best advantage and, surprisingly, some ignore it entirely.

An interview, of course, is a universal practice in the selection of office help. But if the function is left to a poorly qualified interviewer, a valuable selection device will be wasted. Good interviewing is a technique in itself, and a small business can profit by having some of its supervisors or managers learn more about the subject by looking up the literature or enrolling in special training courses.

The examination of references, for some reason, seems so anticlimactic that it is often neglected. A personnel expert, with all his ability and experience in using selection devices, will rarely fail to check an applicant's references. But companies which do not have a qualified personnel man who might pass an expert judgment on applicants often ignore this important factor.

Proper selection of competent office employees depends, at least in part, on obtaining a proper application form, conducting a worth-while interview, and checking references. The CPA who is advising his client in this basic area of staff selection should recommend correction of deficiencies.

Clerical testing programs

Selection of the right office worker for the right job can insure the fullest utilization of human capacities in increasing office output. Testing is at the heart of this process. Certain disagreements exist among experts as to the value of personality tests, T groups, temperament schedules, and other controversial tests, but there is virtual unanimity in recognizing the value of clerical tests.

A clerical testing program, properly established and used, is in itself sufficient to improve substantially the selection process. Office employment is one of the few occupational areas in which the value of testing is well established through research and experience. In the majority of clerical jobs, strengths in personal characteristics can never overcome weaknesses in aptitude, basic skills, or learning ability. These can be detected through a simple testing program.

Yet the adoption of clerical testing programs in business is retarded by the misconception that a personnel specialist is required to install, conduct, or evaluate the tests. As long as the requirements of a job are primarily of a physical nature—involving, for example, typing speed, shorthand ability, or speed and accuracy in checking—the testing process is not complicated. The value of even the simplest testing process, however, depends on a number of factors. The following principles are involved in the successful use of clerical testing:

1. *Tests must be carefully selected or developed and must be valid.* Tests that measure the wrong abilities, that are too easy or too difficult, or that place a premium on special types of experience or training will generally give poor results. Furthermore, unless the validity of the tests used has been proven, there is absolutely no sense in administering them in the first place. Many excellent clerical tests are available from reputable organizations. A CPA assisting a small business client in the selection of those tests should, if in doubt, either consult a personnel specialist or thoroughly investigate the source and background of the tests. A valuable source of guidance or comparison might be a larger client who uses a testing program, or another CPA who has had experience in this area or who could investigate the tests used by his larger clients.

2. *The testing program must be well administered.* While a clerical testing program is basically simple, an adequate program cannot merely be purchased, installed by anyone, and left to run itself. The standard tests of reputable publishers all contain standard instructions, which must be conscientiously followed. The program must be carefully planned by competent persons, and everyone connected with it must thoroughly understand its mechanics and purpose. The people who administer the tests need not be highly trained in personnel matters, but must know how and under what conditions the tests are to be given. Executives and first-line supervisors must be instructed in the program so that they can in-

telligently participate in evaluating test scores. Most important, perhaps, is the need of administrative follow-up and review. If the testing program is allowed to degenerate—for example, if the tests are given in slipshod fashion, or if minimum acceptable score standards are not maintained— its benefits will be lost and it will become just another burden. Testing must be taken seriously and applied consistently in a manner which will assure that each applicant's performance will be typical of his abilities and that interpretation of results will always be based on similar standards.

3. *Clerical testing is not infallible.* Tests can be the principle, but should not be the final determinant of employment. Not every applicant who scores high in tested ability has good work habits and attitudes. This statement may sound odd in view of the fact that clerical testing has been well established. But test scores can only supplement the findings of personal interviews, references, and the like. They must be weighed in consideration of the whole person, including the defects and strengths of the applicant and the effectiveness of the supervisor. In short, clerical tests can be a valuable tool only when integrated into the entire selection process.

Types of tests in use. In general, four types of tests are used in clerical testing programs:

1. *Tests designed for the purpose of measuring an applicant's learning ability.* Why is this important on the clerical level? If the applicant knows how to type well, isn't this enough? This attitude is likely to be a costly one, particularly in an office where constancy of function is not patterned. If an applicant is unable to learn the immediate job quickly—as well as future jobs—much is lost. For example, assume the learning period on a clerical job—that is, the period of time required, on the average, to attain full efficiency—has been six weeks. Applicants of superior learning ability will reach top productivity sooner than six weeks; others will take longer. The effect on costs is obvious, but consider Figure 1 on page 348.

The shaded area is profit if employee A is selected instead of employee B, with further profits accruing from less supervisory time. Furthermore, this relationship will exist each time changes occur in the job or the employee is asked to learn something new. The potential savings in the office through selection of people with average or better-than-average learning ability become even more dramatic when the high rate of turn-over ordinarily found in clerical personnel is considered. Since the tenure of a new clerical worker is likely to be limited, it is even more important that maximum effectiveness be reached quickly.

The tests of learning ability will have identified the promotable applicants—and the office staffed with promotable people can generally help to keep salary costs down by permitting the employment of new people on lower levels, while at the same time keeping employee morale high by advancing people from within the organization to more responsible positions. A word of caution is in order here. It would be a bad error to hire geniuses for file clerk jobs. The learning ability test should help to identify these potential turnover cases, for applicants with very high scores may become bored if the requirements of the job are too simple. Test norms ordinarily enable the user to identify applicants that fall within certain ranges of ability. Those with too little or too much ability for a particular job are quickly spotted.

Tests of learning ability vary. Some are rather specialized; others are more general. The selection of the best type of test, particularly where office work is not highly specialized, is a delicate matter. Care and expert counsel are in order if doubt exists.

2. *The clerical battery is rarely complete without a test of speed and accuracy, generally a "name and number checking test."* This type of test has become standard in almost every company using clerical testing

Figure I

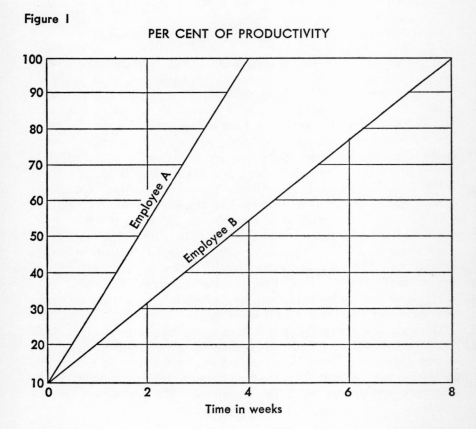

PER CENT OF PRODUCTIVITY

programs. It is one of the best predictors of the probability of satisfactory performance on the job. The tremendous values of speed and accuracy in clerical work probably need not be dramatized. If one employee works 10 per cent faster, with equal accuracy, than another, the former's contribution to office productivity is obviously greater. This will also promote economies, in the small as well as in the large office, since fewer employees will be required because of increased productivity with the same degree of accuracy.

3. *The third type of clerical test measures specific skills required for a particular job.* Included in this group are performance tests of typing and stenography, spelling, arithmetic computations, coding, reading ability and grammar, alphabetizing, and others. Obviously a typist should know how to type and a bookkeeper should be able to quickly and accurately add, subtract, multiply, and divide. This is the purpose of such tests. Many time-proven tests are available which eliminate the need for businesses to develop their own. Some businesses are reluctant to use standard tests on the grounds that special terminology, vocabulary, or office machine problems are encountered in their particular organizations. It is well to keep in mind that the applicant with the required basic skills and adequate learning ability will generally be able to master the special requirements quickly. The latter should not therefore be allowed to serve as an excuse for omitting the testing of basic skills.

4. *Other types of tests, less often included in the clerical battery, are personality or temperament tests and interest inventories.* A personality test and an interest test are not the same thing. An examination of an applicant's interest, simply stated, is intended to provide a basis for evaluating his probable interest in his job. Used by trained testers, interest inventories can be of value.

Personality tests differ to the extent that they attempt to offer some insight into the temperament of the applicant. For example, they may measure the dominance of his personality and the level of his ambition or aggressiveness. Used by an experienced psychologist, these tests may have some value, but there is considerable debate on this point, even among psychologists. Personality tests, used by the inexperienced, can be dangerous. The amateur psychologist will reach wrong conclusions more often than not. The inclusion of personality and interest tests in the clerical battery requires that the strictest consideration be given to (1) who will evaluate them, and (2) if they are used, what emphasis will be given to them in the over-all score. It may be that companies which do not employ industrial psychologists ought to ignore this type of testing, at least until better evidence of its value is forthcoming.

Such companies can adopt a more obvious method of gaining some insight into an applicant's temperament and personality. Interviewers should simply *observe* the applicant during the interview, and particularly during the testing process. What attitudes does the candidate reflect while taking the tests? Is he or she co-operative, willing, critical, nervous, conscientious, relaxed, sincere? The individual administering the tests, if competent and conscientious, can learn a good deal about attitudes and temperament. There is the danger that the overzealous tester or interviewer may read into the situation attitudes or characteristics that are irrelevant. Moreover, if the person giving the tests is trying to do another job at the same time or otherwise fails to devote full attention to the testing, all the benefits of the observation process cannot be realized.

The latter type of test might be administered to employees by one of many reputable testing centers. Some CPA firms are staffed to render employee testing services. It is rarely necessary to use an agency for general clerical testing; but perhaps a smaller concern would be well advised to have one of these agencies give the entire clerical battery, at least until some experience with the testing processes has been acquired.

Four types of tests have just been described. The inference should not be drawn that a clerical testing battery must include all of them. Some concerns may find that one alone is helpful in the selection process. A recent study of orders placed by businesses for the purchase of clerical tests indicated that 78 per cent were for one test, 13 per cent for two, and 9 per cent for three or more. Estimating a rough adjustment for separate orders placed by the same firm, it was still concluded that at least one-half of the firms using any tests at all were using just one test. Another third were using two tests, and not more than one firm in six was using three or more. This sampling included a large proportion of rather small businesses. Intelligence tests and clerical aptitude tests make up a little better than half of those ordered in this sample. Mechanical aptitude tests were ordered almost as frequently as clerical aptitude tests. Interest inventories and personality or temperament tests trailed far behind the others.

The establishment of a testing program for office workers is not reserved to personnel experts. After a little careful study, the CPA can assist business management to install a profit-building selection program. If, after further study, he has doubts about his competence to proceed, he should seek the guidance of a reputable personnel specialist during the development of the proposed program. It will then be the CPA's responsibility to follow up the program continuously to assure that its potential is fully realized. Once he is familiar with the basic techniques, the CPA should be able to conduct the follow-up process competently and develop similar programs for other businesses.

Orientation and training

The finding and hiring of the right office worker does not insure that maximum productivity will automatically follow. Proper selection must be followed up with proper orientation and training of the new employee.

Many companies neglect this important step. They may have an effective testing program; but once an applicant has been selected, he is too often given a desk and a few hurried instructions and then left to his own devices. Even if his own devices appear adequate, this practice may entail a big loss of productivity. Moreover, the employee's morale is likely to decline in the absence of a systematic program to acquaint him with the company and to train him in his new position.

A far larger percentage of big businesses have orientation and training programs than do small businesses. From the point of view of need, this seems paradoxical. In the larger office, with its higher forms of mechanization, automation, and employee specialization, it might be expected that the new employee would be shown a typewriter, briefly instructed on the job, and left alone to concentrate on a single function. Yet in most large companies the new employee is usually asked to participate in a formal orientation and training program.

In the small office, on the other hand, where the new employee will generally have a host of jobs to perform, there is rarely a formal effort to provide thorough instruction. Education in the demands of the job is too often left to chance. Admittedly, trial and error will eventually implant the functions in the employee's mind. But by then a considerable number of hours may have been lost, and mistakes may have alienated customers and created more work for co-workers. Moreover, the employee will have developed his own habits and changed the job the way he thinks best. When the employee leaves and is replaced by another carefully selected employee, the same routine of self-development is repeated, with its attendant loss of productivity and rearrangement of the job. By this time, the procedures originally established for the job have probably been so transformed that the work is performed by private arrangement of the office staff. Consequently, in the small office, where flexibility of office staff is very important, an orientation and training period is more necessary than in the large office.

The orientation process is relatively simple. If a little time is devoted to helping a new employee get a good start, the investment will pay dividends. It must be remembered that a new job or a first job is a major adventure in anyone's life. The first weeks in a new office will produce apprehension and other adjustment problems in varying degrees, depending upon the character of the individual. The new employee's reactions to co-workers, superiors, and many seemingly insignificant matters will influence his attitude and determine the quality as well as the quantity of his work for a long time to come. Companies which are generally intimate units should have little difficulty in quickly making the new employee a part of the family. But a welcoming attitude is not all that is required. Company policies, history, products, office rules, employee benefits—all these should be thoroughly explained more than once, because the information imparted during the first interview may have been forgotten. This may prevent later costly misunderstandings. The new employee should be taken on a short tour of the plant; and some of the other office staff might be invited to join. People often do a better job if they are in touch with what goes on in other areas of the company.

Employee handbook. An employee handbook is an invaluable tool in the orientation process. A mimeographed copy of a personal letter from the owner or president in which all pertinent matters are explained is often a good start. Such a letter might also be presented to prospective employees as a recruiting tool. The preparation of an employee handbook is easy, once all sources of information, such as administrative memos, personnel announcements, insurance pamphlets, and general notices are gathered together. Following is the table of contents of a typical employee handbook. It should prove a useful guide in determining which matters can valuably be included in such a book.

CONTENTS OF EMPLOYEE HANDBOOK
Working Together
at
Ashworth Manufacturing Company

Conclusion. An office training program cannot be entirely standardized. Each business must study its own needs and decide in which area its staff can most profitably be trained. Methods of training will vary, depending largely on the number of people to be trained. Continuous training and review of general office procedures is beneficial. For example, the use of reproducing equipment or copying machines, or the make-up of letters, can be reviewed periodically in groups. For the smaller office staff, most other training will be on an individual basis.

The small organization does not always have a person of competence or experience to teach those who want to improve. It would be well advised, therefore, to encourage employees to attend business schools or colleges at night. An evening or two a week, with all expenses paid, for training in job-related subjects cannot fail to make employees more productive. This is a common practice in business today. It has paid dividends in spite of the high turnover rate of clerical workers. An argument often advanced against such training is that clerical workers are not interested in devoting their leisure time to furthering their own knowledge or acquiring new abilities. This is often true, but if the right people have been engaged in the first place, they will recognize that improving their performance on the job often is the best route to more responsible positions and higher salaries.

In order to determine whether a client is realizing the fullest productivity from his first basic office resource, namely people, the CPA should begin by examining and evaluating the client's selection and training procedures. These important functions are generally performed by the office managers and controllers of the larger companies. The managers of smaller companies, unable to enjoy the benefits of such full-time talent, are likely to rely on the CPA for advice. Indeed, many CPAs now offer personnel selection services for all types of employees, supervisors, and even executives. The experience acquired in selecting clerical help is often valuable in executive recruitment.

Some of the problems encountered in executive selection and placement will be outlined in the following pages.

Executive Selection and Placement[1]

Successful selection and placement of executive personnel is undoubtedly one of top management's most difficult tasks. Lack of careful, thoroughly considered action in filling an executive position may cost a company thousands of dollars and have serious effects upon morale. For good management, it is essential to follow sound precepts in choosing and placing executives.

[1]Reprinted with permission from the April 1962 issue of *The Canadian Chartered Accountant*. The author, Robert D. Elhart, is manager in the Toronto office of Peat, Marwick, Mitchell & Co.

Basic considerations

Whenever an executive vacancy occurs, or a company decides to create a new position, there is always the basic choice of filling the place from within the company or going outside the organization into the executive labor market. Any valid approach to executive selection demands either that company personnel be carefully considered for the position before outside applicants are sought or should be screened along with them.

To do this successfully, top management must engage in a little soul searching. It must lay aside its prejudices and carefully study the requirements of the position in relation to the skills of the existing management group. There are those who argue that all senior positions should be filled through promotions within an organization, because of the beneficial effects on management morale and the lower risk involved when management knows more about the candidate's qualifications for the job. Others insist that any company needs fresh blood and ideas from time to time and that internal promotion can be overstressed.

If an organization consistently resorts to outside selection, weaknesses in organization planning and executive evaluation and development obviously exist. By and large, an organization should be able to set down its managerial requirements for the future as part of its long-term planning program. Furthermore, whether an organization is large or small, top management should have methods of assessing the capabilities of younger executives and carefully assigning them to tasks that will develop their experience in the desired direction for future requirements. If this is done, it should be possible to find most candidates for executive selection or placement programs within the organization.

Screening data

Many a screening program for an executive position is carried out largely on the basis of a few rough notes about the job or a mental image of the ideal man as visualized by the executive who is responsible. Under such circumstances, screening is difficult and essential details of experience, background, or personal qualifications may be omitted. Adequate and reliable screening requires three basic types of information:
1. A precise definition of the position's responsibilities and its relationship to the rest of the organization
2. A detailed outline of the necessary experience, education, and professional qualifications for the position
3. A summary of the personal qualities required of a man to do the job successfully in the specific organization

When these three guides for screening are well defined, the process becomes much more selective, and certainly less time-consuming, than when more informal methods are used.

Careful selection of the screening team is also important. Those chosen to carry out the screening process, whether company personnel or outside advisers, should be thoroughly familiar with the general organizational situation, the particular unit, and the personalities involved. Before interviews actually begin, interviewers should have an opportunity to study any material designed to assist in the selection process.

Position descriptions. There are many ways of compiling position statements. However they are organized or captioned, it is essential that the following information be included:
1. A summary of the purpose or function of the position
2. A reasonably detailed list of all the important responsibilities of the position
3. A precise description of reporting and supervisory relationships
4. A statement of specific authorities involved, such as employment powers, expenditure limits, and the like.
5. In many cases, a summary of the criteria to be used by top management in evaluating performance in the position

Position descriptions and/or responsibility statements are necessary in thorough executive selection, particularly when the position is a new one, so that there will be no argument over the responsibilities of the man when the position is actually created by his appointment. To attempt selection through outside agencies without such material is extremely hazardous.

Experience requirements. Defining essential experience for an executive position is not easy. Frequently an executive with a lifetime of experience in one industry can make a successful career in another, yet he may not be successful when making a change within the same industry. Experience should be considered in relation to the duties of the position, industry conditions and problems, and certain management or organizational environments. All of these areas must be kept in mind in defining the experience requirement.

The first stage of screening candidates for executive positions always involves verifying their experience and its relation to the new requirements. It is general practice to look for experience that is in some way parallel to that demanded by the new position statement. The farther up the management ladder the job is, however, the harder it is to define this experience parallel.

It is important, therefore, that the experience requirement be carefully drawn up. It is better to show what is believed to be the minimum experience necessary in terms of position skill, industry, or environment than to call for the maximum or ideal experience; the latter practice tends to make the screening process overselective. The experience specification should outline the basic types of duties, situations, and the like with which a well-qualified applicant should be familiar. It also would normally define the essential educational and professional qualifications.

Personal profiles. The screening process for executive selection seems to divide naturally into two stages: those steps concerned with verifying experience and selecting an initial group of suitable candidates and those involving the evaluation of these candidates in depth.

In the first stage, applicants are sorted by experience in relation to the requirements of the proposed position. Attention is focused upon locating men with the skills and background appropriate to the position. Once this stage has been completed and the field has been narrowed to three or four suitably qualified or experienced executives, the second and more intangible process of evaluation begins.

The final selection process tends to be dominated by considerations of personality, general behavior, communication skills, interests, and attitude. In effect, it is usually a question of whether the man X, who has all the experience required, will fit in with the existing management group.

At this juncture, personal interests or prejudices can have a dangerous effect. Consequently, in order to make this stage of the screening process as reliable and useful as possible and to counteract possible prejudices, it is important that those responsible for final screening have a firm idea of the personal profile acceptable for the position. This personal profile should be determined before the selection process begins so as to avoid its being reshaped or biased by the available candidates at the final selection stage.

Because management positions usually involve placement in an organization in such a way that a number of relationships with other people are affected, the personal profile is indispensable. The fact that a position calls for strong personal leadership, decisiveness, caution, or some other quality is often material in the successful accomplishment of a job. The personal profile is therefore based upon the nature of the job to be done, the circumstances in which it will have to be done, the people with whom the executive must work, and those whom he must control and lead. Consideration of these factors should permit the formulation of a reasonably definite picture of the personal characteristics conducive to success in a position.

Selection program

Once the position requirements and screening data have been collected and the interviewing team or agency designated, the screening program can begin with the evaluation of applicants' employment histories or written applications. Thorough examination of written applications and related data can save a great deal of time. In studying responses to an advertisement, it is advantageous to look for indications that the applicant has studied the advertisement carefully and given some thought to his qualifications in relation to the position. Evidence of keen interest in the position and reasonable facility in the presentation of personal background should be sought. There is little point in wasting time reviewing applications that are poorly constructed or hastily compiled or that reflect a merely casual interest when soundly conceived applications are available for consideration.

Interviewing. Once the interview list has been determined, the interviewing program can proceed. In executive selection, three to five interviews are normally required. They consist of the following steps.

The initial interview is usually fairly brief, designed to determine whether the individual applying has to any significant degree the elements of experience required for the position, interest in the position and the company, and acceptable personal characteristics.

With the results of the basic screening available, the interviewing team is now familiar with the type of men available for a specific position. Candidates' experience and qualifications now can be examined in detail to determine which candidates belong on a short list of those who seem to have the basic necessary background.

After the preparation of this short list, the third interview permits application of opinions as to the suitability of candidates for the organization. Discussion with the candidates is of a more general nature, it concerns attitudes, habits, beliefs, ideas, and the like. On the basis of this interview, it should be possible to rank candidates in order of desirability, depending on over-all suitability for the position. Often this third screening or interview will produce the employment or placement decision; otherwise, outside aid may be sought.

Outside appraisal. In some cases, because of difficulty in evaluating experience or background or because of doubt as to the acceptability of certain personal characteristics, an organization that has arrived at the final candidate or candidates will engage the services of a business adviser or psychologist for an independent appraisal. This appraisal may include psychological testing if the man responsible for the final hiring decision considers it necessary. The outside appraisal should be properly evaluated in relation to the basic information developed during the company's own screening process. Obviously, an outsider will not know as much about the position or situation as the company does. His remarks should therefore be interpreted carefully, with due regard for his professional background.

The group or multiple interview. In some employment situations, after the interviewing team has reached a basic decision as to the suitable candidate for the vacant position, this person is interviewed informally by a number of persons in the organization with whom he might be associated in the future. Such a process can have a beneficial effect upon morale and upon acceptance by colleagues of the new man if he is employed, provided the interview situation is carefully organized and controlled.

Members of the company invited to interview the applicant should be given reasonably detailed information about him and about the results of the prior screening processes. It is probably advisable for a member of the interview team to sit in on all the informal chats. The results of these interviews can be quite valuable where the placement situation involves difficult organizational relationships.

A standard form should be developed for recording, summarizing, and evaluating impressions gained in the course of interviews. Although the format cannot be precise for executive positions, a standard method of recording impressions as to experience, suitability, and personal characteristics is an invaluable aid in making comparisons.

Interviewing techniques. Personnel assuming screening duties should always be of rank equal to or higher than that of the person being considered. It is certainly unwise to delegate initial stages of the screening program to a junior executive. In most instances, screening should involve a minimum of two or three executives whose combined judgments, based upon the results of the series of interviews, should be one of the best selection indicators possible.

Psychological testing may be a valuable tool for erasing question marks as to basic abilities and personal characteristics. It is most often used in evaluating the final group of candidates. Those engaged in the screening process must realize that the psychologist's report is primarily a personal opinion developed on the basis of the information given him by the testing media used. To be most valuable, a psychologist should spend adequate time with a candidate and be well equipped with information about the position and its general requirements.

Interviewing skill is not a major determinant of success in executive selection. If the men who make the choice have responsibilities that will be directly affected by successful performance in the position, and if the necessary groundwork—position description, experience requirement, and personal profile—has been laid, the interviewing process will be satisfactory.

Summary. If an organization devotes sufficient time to anticipating and planning its future organization requirements and develops a sound program for providing the necessary experience to potential future managers, its selection problems should be limited.

When circumstances give rise to difficult executive selection or placement situations, problems can best be minimized by means of a carefully organized and well-planned approach to filling the positions.

Initially, it is important that all possible sources of candidates be considered carefully, including personnel already in the organization. It is essential that the selection program proceed upon the basis of adequate knowledge of position requirements, experience and background needed, and an appropriate personal profile. Care and thought in screening and interviewing, along with an organized method for recording impressions, can insure that final candidates will be well qualified.

However, careful selection alone is not enough to insure success. There are inherent risks in combining a job and a man in an organization that may be strange to him. Management must follow through on the executive selection process. It should make certain that the incumbent is properly introduced to the persons with whom he will be working, that he thoroughly understands the nature of his position and the criteria on which his performance will be measured, and that he is given a suitable period of time to acclimatize himself to his new environment.

We will now proceed to the second major resource in which a business can seek improvement in order to increase output, namely, office operation methods or techniques.

Greater Productivity Through Methods Analysis[2]

Simply stated, the office is an operating department charged with the prime responsibility of operating the information system of the business. It records, processes, and stores this information. Unfortunately, the office today frequently performs these functions in an unintegrated and unco-ordinated manner. It is not uncommon, for example, to find several sets of comparable perpetual inventory records maintained at different locations within a company, or to find sales statistics accumulated in both the sales and accounting departments.

This problem of lack of integration and co-ordination has its roots in at least two causes: the accelerated growth of business in the last fifteen years, and the need to obtain information faster as a basis for management decisions. Consequently, many clerical functions have been decentralized to put them closer to the points of decision. Although the logic of this has been difficult to dispute, it has led to the haphazard growth of office staffs and the duplication of services and facilities. Increased competition, improved communications, and data processing technology have attracted the attention of executive management to continually increasing office costs. Computers may well have provided the greatest single stimulus to management in recent years to determine the cost and efficiency of office operations, for the speed and capabilities of

[2]Pages 360-362 and 363-365 were excerpted from a paper in Haskins & Sells' *Selected Papers*, 1960. The author, William W. Gerecke, is a manager in the Los Angeles office of Haskins & Sells.

computers have captured the imagination of businessmen. For companies which have conducted feasibility studies, a principal benefit is the knowledge of what is being done currently, by whom, and how well. For many this is the first time that the unit cost of performing office functions has been established. Rather suddenly, management has begun to express a strong interest in techniques that have long been applied in factories to control the cost of clerical work and increase the productivity of clerical workers.

When examining the techniques that have been successfully applied to this problem, it should be remembered that productivity is the result of methods *and* motivation. Each by itself can accomplish only part of the work task; together they constitute a formidable team in achieving a high level of productivity and obviate the need to resort to the psychology of fear or uncertainty. No method by itself will accomplish a given end in the absence of adequate motivation on the part of the worker; conversely, motivation by itself will not successfully lead the worker through the requirements of his job in the absence of a satisfactory method.

Techniques for improvement

As pointed out earlier in this chapter, proper selection and training of employees is essential to the increase of office productivity. Four techniques are also fundamental in achieving this goal, and offer the greatest potential for improvement. Based on observations and experiences in working with clients, they are (1) work simplification, (2) work measurement, (3) job rotation, and (4) job enlargement. These techniques are listed in order of general importance, although it is difficult to recommend one over another. Actually they tend to complement one another and so merge into a single technique. (Mechanization has been purposely omitted.)

Work simplification

Work simplification is an organized effort to find the easiest way of doing a job and thereby increase productivity by eliminating waste time, energy, and space. The objectives of a work simplification program should be:

1. To reduce the nonproductive elements in each job to a minimum. An example is the feeding of continuous forms into a typewriter by pin-feed sprockets, thus eliminating the need to reach for forms individually, position them for typing, and remove them when typing is completed.

2. To balance the work flow from operation to operation and so eliminate peaks and valleys to the extent practicable. For example, the

cycle billing procedure used by department stores and public utilities has done much to level out the peaks in the billing function.

3. To design procedures that are as simple as possible. An example is the use of multicopy forms combining the requirements of several departments or users, thus permitting one writing of the vital information and eliminating the need for a separate transcription in each department.

4. To stimulate interest, initiative, and imagination through understanding of the program's objectives. An illustration of this would be interviews with employees during a procedures study to solicit their ideas on how forms or procedures can be improved and so provide them with a sense of participation in the study.

The individual or group assigned to the project should have the authority to review a job from the point of origin to the last step in the work process in order to develop an improved work flow. The study should be guided or reviewed by an individual skilled in methods and procedures work to ensure that the proposed procedures will make appropriate use of people, paper, and machines.

A new or improved procedure will not usually sell itself to the employees who must apply it. Therefore, heavy emphasis should be placed on the fourth objective of work simplification—personal interest and motivation. The individual employee must be convinced that he has a personal stake in eliminating unnecessary procedural steps if he is to accept the fact that the improvements really are better. Frequently this can be accomplished by inviting his participation and suggestions.

Clerical cost control. Daily work volume statistics often are not maintained in an office because management is not as interested in details as it is in results. When details are maintained, they are usually a weekly statistic and quite often unused or misleading. For example, an order entry department supervisor proudly pointed out that his department was handling 25 per cent more work than it had the previous year, without any additional people. He based this on a weekly record of the dollar volume of orders processed. An objective analysis disclosed that although the dollar volume was up 25 per cent, the actual number of orders processed had increased only 4 per cent.

Work volume in many clerical operations is fairly consistent from week to week. However, on a daily basis it may vary by as much as 200 per cent or more. To determine why, attention must be focused on the individual clerks. Lost time because of late starts, early stops, and long coffee breaks and lunch periods is quite obvious, but this can be observed on the large volume days as well as the small. How can it be explained? Clerks pace themselves: during one hour they will produce a reasonable amount of work, the next hour a less than reasonable amount, the next a more than reasonable amount, and so on. However, when their total output for the day is measured, it can often be described as less than reasonable to much less than reasonable.

Self-pacing is the result of uncontrolled work flows and a lack of individual output requirements. Work usually flows through clerical operations in lumps. At one time, a clerk will have a large pool of work from which to draw. At another time, he will have little or no work. As the work runs out, his pace slows down. Seldom does he know what is expected of him in terms of output. When he does know, the lumpy characteristic of the work flow prevents him from achieving it.

Work is divided into small specialized steps causing circuitous work flow and increased processing time. The sequence of work may be improperly planned, causing the return of work to the same work station more than once. Figure 2, page 364, illustrates this situation. Streamlining the flow of work reduces the number of stops and the number of returns to the same station, thus reducing processing and handling time.

Duplication and unnecessary work creep into an operation because supervisors are too busy with their own clerical responsibilities to be systems-minded. Individual clerks are often permitted to formulate their own method of introducing a new procedure. Frequently one clerk will keep the same records as another clerk because the first is too impatient to wait for the second to provide him with the data. Unreliability of another person's information also causes an individual to compile data independently. It is also common for clerks to make innovations in existing procedures to keep themselves busy or guarantee accuracy of information which may be guaranteed further on down the line.

Still further duplication may exist without anyone's knowledge owing to the organizational structure and unco-ordinated efforts of various departments.

In brief, low individual productivity, duplication of effort, and unnecessary work are the major contributors to industry's ever-increasing high cost of clerical labor.

Work measurement

Work measurement is both a method and a form of motivation. It is a method in that its objective as applied to office work is to establish what a fair day's work should be. It is a form of motivation in that it provides both the employee and his supervisor with a factual basis for appraising performance and furnishes the employee with a yardstick by which he can determine what is expected of him. The value of this technique is that it permits management to determine what its personnel requirements should be to operate present office routines.

Work measurement can be applied to office routines that contain a large volume of highly repetitive operations, such as billing, payroll ac-

Figure 2

ACTUAL FLOW OF WORK—27 STOPS

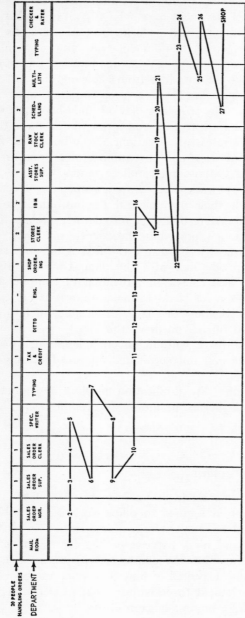

PROPOSED SIMPLIFIED FLOW OF WORK—16 STOPS

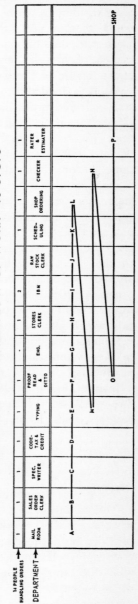

STREAMLINING REDUCES THE WORK PROCESS AND HANDLING TIME.

counting, or check writing. Standards can be set if the work is done in a repetitive manner, is similar in content from one time period to another, can be counted, and occurs in sufficient volume to justify counting and maintaining records of production. Standards should not be applied where the work is essentially creative, or where a person is employed regardless of work volume, such as a personal secretary. The development of performance standards and the determination of clerical work loads involve measurement of *time* required to perform a task and measurement of *units of work* produced during a reporting period.

The standards can be developed in several ways. The simplest and least expensive methods are through estimates based on past experience, work sampling, or time records of work performed. More accurate and sophisticated standards can be obtained by micromotion studies, predetermined time systems, or time and motion studies. The first group of methods of estimating and sampling will have the broadest applicability for those interested in initiating work measurement programs. None of them is expensive to initiate or administer, and any one of them should give an indication of the potential of this measurement and control tool.

A technique for measuring clerical productivity. The technique used is a form of statistical sampling with which many practitioners are generally familiar, and which is applied to the details of clerical operations. It requires that production data in terms of units of work be recorded by each clerk. To apply the technique effectively, one should become motion-economy-conscious. This is as easy as becoming electricity-, hot-water-, or gas-economy-conscious. Once acquired, such an awareness is never lost. The auditor will never enter an office without automatically appraising the extent of the waste of human energy and the cost of this waste to the client. Because clerical waste is of great material significance, auditors perform a valuable service by reporting it.

To be able to observe waste of human energy in an office, one must take an interest in symptoms of waste. Obvious symptoms are walking, talking, telephoning, and absence from the work area. It is also advisable to develop a sensitivity to other activities which are symptomatic of waste but not as obvious. Traffic through or within sight of a clerical area, for example, creates waste by causing interruptions in the work group.

Poor housekeeping results in waste of human energy because it causes extra work whenever anyone must find something. The man-hours spent in running down items and searching for records are incalculable. Poor work-station layouts cause waste by making extra motions necessary in order to perform a task. Faulty equipment, such as broken or hard-to-open file drawers, requires extra energy. Crowded or inadequately indexed files create additional searching time. Rough desk tops cause errors and errors cause erasures or corrections.

Such examples could be extended for pages. The point to be stressed is that one must learn to become conscious of motions which do not contribute directly to producing the essential work of the group.

In an office where human energy is obviously being wasted, one may gauge the extent of the waste quite easily by applying a technique which has been used in production and distribution areas to obtain approximate work/waste productivity evaluations without going through time-reporting analysis and comparison with work standards. This technique has by some been called "ratio delay" observation. To illustrate:

Draw a line down the middle of a piece of paper. Head the left-hand column "work" and the right-hand "no work." Glance around the room once an hour. Note in the left-hand column how many people are working and in the right-hand column the balance of the total number of people who are supposed to be in the room. Continue this until the totals of both columns add up to at least one hundred, as in the example shown below:

Cost Department—Ten Clerks

Work	No Work
4	6
5	5
8	2
3	7
8	2
6	4
5	5
3	7
6	4
7	3
55	45

The important thing in making the observations is to decide whether each person is working or not on the basis of the first look. What the person was just doing or is about to do next is of no significance. If he is in the midst of posting a record, but is actually lighting a cigarette at the moment of observation, count him as not working. If a girl is typing a letter, but happens to be bent over the machine erasing an error, count her as not working, and so on. Also, do not look up every hour on the hour, but at random times within each hour. Use random numbers from a statistical sampling book to select the minutes within each hour, for a more scientific approach.

After one hundred observations have been recorded, the percentages of the total "work" and "no work" times should be accurate to within plus or minus 10 per cent. In the example above, the true amount of time spent not working lies somewhere between 35 per cent and 55 per cent of the total time worked. Four hundred observations should increase the absolute reliability to plus or minus 5 per cent.

All human beings require a certain amount of time for personal needs and fatigue. There is no fixed rule as to how much should be allowed. Estimates range from 5 per cent to 20 per cent. Whenever one finds that the time spent not working exceeds 20 per cent, one has something a client should know about because all of the "no work" time being paid for over 20 per cent of the total work time is a 100 per cent loss of time and money. In many offices the total "no work" time may run between 30 per cent and 45 per cent.

It must be remembered that with this technique one can analyze only the more obvious nonproductive activities. The technique is not designed to measure less obvious matters such as poor forms design or unnecessary transcriptions. In discussing the result of your test with a client, be sure to point out that a great deal more waste undoubtedly exists than was discovered from this simple test.

In discussing with the client the installation of a system designed to reduce clerical waste and control clerical costs, it is important to emphasize that a properly installed system improves rather than hurts morale, that it definitely is not a "speed-up," and that measurement should be used to establish reasonable goals and identify waste motion and nonproductive activity which will then be reduced or eliminated through methods work. It is a matter of working more effectively with the same effort, not working harder with greater effort.

It is not always necessary to install a system to control clerical time waste. Merely advising the responsible persons that a waste condition exists and publicizing the results of the simple observation test very often produces improvement, so long as specific individuals in the clerical force are not identified in the data generally shown. In organizations that have more than one office or separated office sections, the publication of comparative test results may develop a competitive "team" attitude toward the work, if handled properly.

Job rotation

Job rotation is certainly not a new technique, but one that is often forgotten by many organizations. Job rotation should be an inherent part of every organization plan, for it accomplishes a multiplicity of purposes. First, it is a part of the training program of both employees and supervisors, providing them with the opportunity to learn the intricacies of the business first hand. Second, changes of responsibilities at regular intervals are stimulating and help the individual keep an open mind to cope with changes in the business and its procedures. The individual may also initiate changes or suggestions for changes based on previous experience. Third, it prevents the possibility that individuals will develop a proprietary interest in a particular job and never share the knowledge of how the job is done before death or retirement. Fourth, it protects the company's interest in the continuity of operations.

Job rotation need not require that an individual always move vertically in terms of the change in his rank or responsibilities. Lateral moves are desirable until the individual has demonstrated his capacity and ability to become a supervisor. His responsibilities should also change at regular intervals at this level for another reason besides those mentioned previously. His subordinates should be exposed to the management methods of several supervisors as part of their grooming for future promotions. No single department should be under the supervision of one supervisor for too long. The period of time spent in each job will vary with its complexity, but in general the length of the assignment will grow, the higher one advances in the scale of rankings. However, every job should have a time limit on it so that the energy of a department is not dissipated by lethargy. Job rotation is the force that maintains the vigor and vitality of every organization.

Job enlargement

Job enlargement is more a form of motivation than of method. It probably originates in the work in recent years of industrial psychologists and social scientists. It represents a reversal in the trend of training employees to perform single functions, such as the account distribution of payables, the vouchering of payables, and the disbursement of payables. The purpose of job enlargement is to give an employee a stronger sense of identification with a complete job, rather than with a single function which cannot be readily identified in the finished product. It also has the advantage of broadening his skills and understanding of the area in which he works. This technique has also been applied in some factories to machine tool operations, with a noticeable increase in employee morale and productivity.

Control of forms, reports, and paper work

A chapter on office management cannot ignore the control of forms, reports, and paper work. Many authorities on office management believe this is the most neglected area in the average office today—and the one requiring the most attention.

Statistics have dramatized the effort being spent—and wasted—in paper work. It is fair to assume that CPAs will be the first to testify to the magnitude of the paper-work problem.

The controller or systems specialist in a big company is engaged in a continual effort to minimize paper work for forms. The typical controller in a company without a systems specialist will conduct a periodic drive during which he will review all internal reports, forms, and paper-work procedures. Each drive generally discloses superfluous reports or obsolete forms which can be eliminated, combined, or otherwise improved. As a result, office employees become more conscious of the forms they use and the reports they are asked to prepare. This creates an atmosphere wherein paper-work simplification and the control of forms and reports is given a state of continuity not usually found in small companies.

A paper-work survey can produce astonishingly productive results for a small business. Simplification can be achieved in at least two ways: (1) through the elimination of paper work, reports, and forms, following a thorough appraisal and willingness to take a calculated risk in discarding marginal records; (2) through the adoption of more efficient procedures and methods of performing the work. This step will normally include the establishment of a method by which the use, design, and re-design of forms is continually controlled.

Improvement of the paper-work structure of a small office is not difficult. The process involves nothing more than an appraisal of the paper-work and reporting methods which may have become entrenched through habit. A few basic questions will suggest certain areas that might be inspected and yield clues as to how small business management can receive more and better information from its nerve center at the same or less cost. For example:

1. Are expensive forms being purchased when similar but less elaborate forms could be prepared on many of the economical reproducing machines available today?

2. Are all of the internal reports typed? How much paper and time might be saved, with no loss of value in the reports, if this function were eliminated?

3. Are separate reports compiled from the informational work sheets, requiring more paper and expenditure of time? Could copies of the work sheets themselves, reproduced by photographic equipment, serve equally as well as informal, internal reports to management?

4. Are all of the internal reports really necessary? Can they be combined? Does every executive in the small business really need a copy of all the other executives' reports as frequently as they are now being distributed? Do office employees have their private stocks, that is, are they accumulating data rarely asked for, but kept "just in case"?

Forms control will now be examined in greater detail.

Forms control[3]

With an estimated eleven million Americans handling the numerous forms used in business, the potential for reducing office costs through vigorous forms control is almost limitless.

Forms are the basic tools underlying every business transaction and pro-

[3]Based upon a talk given by Linden C. Speers, partner, Peat, Marwick, Mitchell & Co., Phoenix, Arizona, at a National Association of Accountants regional meeting in San Mateo, California. Reprinted with permission from the March 1961 issue of *Management Controls*. Copyrighted 1961 by Peat, Marwick, Mitchell & Co.

cedure. Efforts made to improve them should meet with the same success the factory achieves by refining production tools. More efficient tool design is accepted as a major step toward reducing manufacturing costs, and more effective forms design is a fundamental move toward lowering office costs.

Forms control is really a phase of work simplification; it is the organized use of common sense in searching for better ways of doing things. All forms, reports, and records indicate clerical activity. Unnecessary or poorly designed forms and reports create extra work. Clerical costs are not at economic levels unless forms are logically and firmly controlled. Work flow will then be smoother, more accurate, and more efficient.

Impact on the organization. To accomplish its task, forms control should start at the top and be conducted on a broad basis. Management must believe in it, and every employee must be given a chance to participate. Within a narrow range, forms control might be limited to good forms design, economical forms procurement, and effective forms inventory management; but, in a broader sense, it cannot be divorced from related procedures and the total work flow. Satisfactory results from design, procurement, and inventory control may still produce many extraneous forms and not the over-all cost reduction one might expect from an integrated program, imaginatively conceived as a systems approach. Once it is firmly entrenched as a basic part of office cost reduction, the program should not be treated as a sporadic activity to be emphasized when "the heat is on," but rather as a continuing management function.

Development of a positive attitude by management from top to bottom is mandatory. Management sets the pace and example by being enthusiastic about change. A receptive attitude on the part of everyone is best encouraged by making change the expected or normal situation. A do-it-yourself atmosphere needs to be developed among all employees in a work simplification program. People should be asked for their ideas and suggestions, whether they concern form, writing method, or procedure. It is the one sure way to transform opposition into enthusiasm.

Objectives. All thorough forms control programs have a threefold purpose:
1. Elimination of superfluous forms
2. Improvement of essential forms
3. Control of new and reordered forms through analysis of:
    (a) procurement and storage
    (b) design (layout, specification, construction)
    (c) processing
    (d) filing

Ideally, forms control is conceived in an atmosphere of planning, and not on a sudden, crash-basis, economy-wave approach resulting from a profit-squeeze directive. The shortsighted program usually fails to produce desired results. Other problems are likely to emerge from the narrow approach. For example, the volume of paper may be misjudged; although revenue or activity is down, volume may stay up or even increase because customers place small orders which may require as much processing time as the large ones. Or there may be imbalances in the work effort among departments; one may be doing a much more efficient job than another and consequently may suffer in subsequent reductions.

Organization. Where the size of a company warrants it, forms control should be considered a full-time activity. To maintain proper control over the procurement, design, and inventory of forms, a larger company will require a permanent forms control staff of one or more persons, preferably with procedures experience. All forms would come under the surveillance of this section, where approval of requisitions would ensure continual review with each reorder. The files of this section would contain all the vital forms data: who prepares them, how they are prepared, and who uses them. Follow-up would include such steps as the following:

1. Is each form properly designed?
2. Will another already on hand serve just as well? (Functional files will detect overlap.)
3. Will a change in construction reduce costs or improve efficiency?
4. Should forms be purchased or duplicated internally?
5. Are reorder points and quantities correct?

When a forms control program is being initiated, it may be desirable to begin with a pilot project. Select a situation where an extremely poor form is in use and the potential benefits are great. Document the entire procedure of tackling the problem by exhibiting the forms on a panel. A flow chart, of major importance to every study, is then prepared to demonstrate operation in the environment of the clerical system. This provides a convenient way of reviewing the problem and formulating a solution. The same procedure is followed for the recommended proposal to compare results and point out tangible ways to achieve savings in this area.

Flow charting has other advantages. It will spot multiple responsibility as well as the lack of it. It is surprising how frequently one department duplicates the work of another or, in some instances, how neither assumes responsibility.

Do not become too immersed in the form itself. Eighty-five per cent of the cost of running an office is in labor, and, while forms are important, the clerical costs involved may be twelve times as high. One way to reduce labor in the office is to cut down the motions required in the performance of work. This may be achieved partly through elimination of unnecessary forms, reports, methods, and procedures, and partly through simplification of the remaining ones.

Where forms design is a full-time operation, it is best left to a qualified specialist working with a methods and procedures analyst. The person who conceives the need may not be an expert on forms construction and design and may not appreciate its effect on other operations in the department as can the trained forms specialist.

When a new form is needed, design becomes very important and the principles of good forms development come into play. The specialist will consider the following:

1. Logical sequence and arrangement of items
2. Continuous execution
3. Minimum of writing
4. Adaptability to machines
5. Method of reproduction
6. Economy of space and quantity
7. Size for filing
8. Ease of reading or posting
9. Ease of identification
10. Understandability

Functional forms design is often treated as secondary to the physical specifications relating to size, type of paper, and so on; nonetheless, the cost of labor can hardly be overlooked.

Potential savings. Dramatic individual savings are not the entire objective of forms design, but they serve to emphasize the point. Relatively small improvements add up, and a small saving on a job of high frequency may be as important as the elimination of a big job. For example, if an average key stroke takes 0.0036 minutes, dropping 275 key strokes from typing a certain form would save the average typist less than a minute. On 10,000 forms, however, this adds up to more than 20 man-days. Other typical examples of savings are as follows:

1. One company reported the elimination of 100 out of 415 forms in a year's time.
2. Another reported that, of 3,000 forms reviewed during the first year of its control program, 480 were thrown out and 100 added, producing a net reduction of 380.
3. A third showed a reduction from 67 to 6 in the number of pieces of paper handled to process a customer's repair order.

Substantial economies can thus be realized through effective forms redesign or elimination, procurement control, and regulation of inventories. It brings to mind the story of the mail order house manager who called his work force together and showed them an incoming order. "I want you," he said, holding up the order, "to visualize this order as being coated with a thin sheet of gold leaf. That gold leaf is the profit on the order. Every time it is touched, a little of the gold rubs off and that much profit is lost to the business." It should be noted that continuous cost reduction resulting from forms control will really show where there is (1) sound organization, (2) total personnel participation, (3) planned and measured progress, and (4) recognition of results.

The preceding material on work simplification, work measurement, and forms control is intended to relate the subject matter of earlier chapters to the subject of office management. We will now briefly examine techniques of microanalysis.

Microanalysis[4]

The construction and analysis of organization charts, procedural flow charts, and log sheets frequently suggest the need for additional data for methods improvement and work simplification.

For example, complex handling or large expenditures of time in the processing of a document suggest the use of a process chart. Numerous or extended transportations may indicate the need for a layout flow chart. These are two examples of detailed analysis procedures known as microanalysis techniques. A brief discussion of each and some principles of utilization will follow.

Process flow chart. A process flow chart can be defined as "a graphic representation of the sequence of all operations, transportations, inspections, and storages occurring during a process or procedure." It also includes other pertinent information, such as time required and distance moved. This chart is used when work volumes and personal loads are complex, heavy, or repetitive, and provides a step-by-step detailed description of what actually happens in a given situation to a given document. Such a detailed description provides for the comprehensive analysis of the elements of work, thereby affording a means for the determination of a better method.

Care should be exercised in the use of the process flow chart. It requires expenditure of a relatively large amount of time; it should not be used to analyze simple operations that consume only a small amount of time or manpower.

An example of possible application of a process flow chart would be the following. Assume a procedural flow chart has been made which indicates that a particular business document flows through many departments. In one of these departments the document is extensively handled and processed, but the procedural flow chart shows only that the form is filled in while in that department. At this point, a process flow chart may be used to define and analyze the detailed steps in-

[4]Pages 373-374 were excerpted from the *Office Control Staff Training Manual* of Lybrand, Ross Bros. & Montgomery, New York.

volved within the department, so that operational improvements can be made.

A brochure is available from Remington Rand, entitled *Instructions for the Effective Utilization of the Process Analysis Work Sheet in Office Work Simplification Procedures*. It is an effective guide to the use, construction, and analysis of process flow charts.

Layout flow chart. A layout flow chart is a scale drawing of the physical area in which the activity being studied occurs. The flow of this activity is indicated by lines and arrows connecting the locations of the work areas involved.

This chart is used when the flow of work is characterized by frequent transportations and possible backtracking. It is often used in conjunction with process flow charts, since it permits visualization of the process.

An office layout template and relative booklet of instruction are available from Remington Rand. The booklet contains recommended scale, description of symbols, and a guide to the construction of a layout chart. The template illustrated in Figure 3, page 375, contains certain standards for office layout work, such as aisle space, space between desks, and so on. Utilization of this material by the CPA for office layout work is recommended.

Two examples of layout charts utilizing the template symbols are shown in Figures 4 and 5, pages 377-378. Figure 4 depicts the original layout of a process, whereas Figure 5 depicts the "re-layout" following analysis and improvement. Note that the distances and transportations are greatly reduced in the revised layout, with inherent efficiency as a fringe benefit.

Another important area for possible savings is the matter of site selection.

Advising Clients on Site Selection

The choice of a location for plant or office is one of the most important which any business has to make. Yet there is evidence to indicate that in a high percentage of cases, some major factors are overlooked when such a choice is made.

Over a few years' time, most independent accountants have one or more clients who decide to change their location. A few may move to another state or region, but most merely move to another site in the same town or locality. When this happens, the accountant can save his client money and headaches if he is aware of some of the problems

Figure 3

OFFICE PLANNING AND LAYOUT TEMPLATE

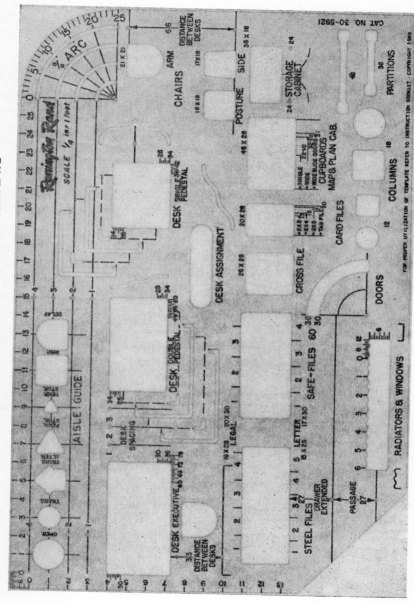

Reproduced with permission from the Remington Rand Office Systems Division of Sperry Rand Corporation.

which may arise. Despite the headlines that big company location changes receive, the great majority of moves are made by small businesses.

When advising on site selection, the most important principle to keep in mind is the need for extreme care in assembling and evaluating information. The extra time it takes to check all the available facts and to assemble additional information as needed, is well worth the effort in terms of future headaches avoided.

There is strong evidence that over half the new locations selected show one or more serious defects within one year of the move. Mr. Leonard C. Yasseen, senior partner of the Fantus Factory Locating Service, reported in the March 1957 issue of *Dun's Review* the results of over one thousand interviews with managements of relocated firms during a three-year period. Nearly 60 per cent of these managements expressed disappointment with the new location on the basis of one or more major miscalculations in making the move. The choice of a new site is one which the firm's management is often not prepared to make on an objective basis. This is where the accountant can offer assistance.

Community factors. With the general area of operations already determined, the selection of a specific location means choosing both a community and a site within that community. Differentiating among cities and towns often requires complex comparisons. Taxes, for example, are a common basis for comparing costs of operating in two or more communities. Many businessmen have made the serious mistake of comparing tax rates alone. However, the total tax burden in dollars depends on both the tax rate (or mill rate) and the assessment base. A town with a low tax rate may still have a relatively heavy tax burden if assessments are high.

In addition, more than one level of government frequently levies taxes on property. It is not enough to investigate municipal tax rates and assessment policy; counties, townships, school districts, and special taxing districts should all be checked.

The tax burden is only one side of the community coin, however. Taxes are levied to pay for municipal services. Low taxes may not represent a saving at all, but simply a lack of publicly provided services. A large machine shop that recently moved from a large city to a suburban community discovered that there was a municipal water and sewer system, but no line came within a mile of the new shop. The expense of hooking into the public systems was prohibitive, so the firm had to provide its own facilities on the site. Many a firm has located near a gas pipeline only to discover that it was not possible to tap into the line.

It should be remembered, too, that the community is a place in which to live as well as work. Executives in particular must find attractions in living there, or at least the place must be easy to reach from their homes.

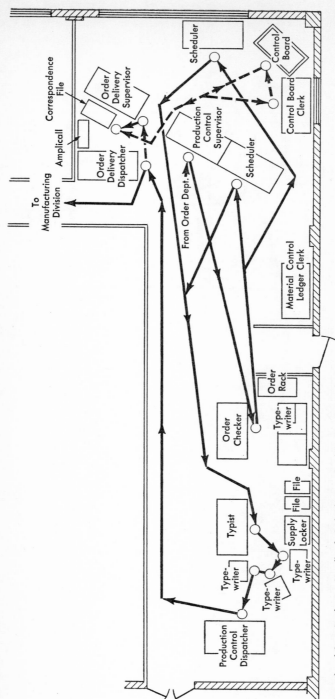

Figure 4

ORIGINAL LAYOUT

Figure 5

REVISED LAYOUT

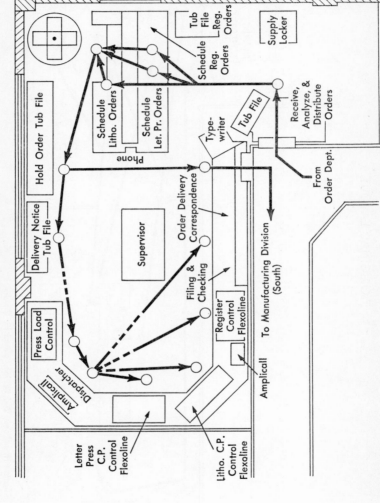

Reproduced from *Production Handbook*, 2nd Edition, edited by Gordon B. Carson. Copyright 1958. The Ronald Press Company. *Original source:* The Standard Register Co.

Otherwise, the possible economic advantages of a town may be more than offset by personal disadvantages for the management.

Special inducements. The attractions of a community may often be enhanced by offers of assistance, tax concessions, and the like. Experience has shown that a special inducement should not be the primary reason for selecting a community. Professionals in the business of plant location point out that the concession, which may very well prove to be temporary, cannot counterbalance a serious economic defect. Then, too, the firm should consider what offers will be made to other firms in subsequent years, and how much of the cost of attracting them it will have to bear. Of course, small businesses do not usually receive dramatic offers from communities. But large firms do, and the small concern may very well find itself paying a share in attracting the large ones if it locates in a community with a history of special inducements.

The management should investigate the business population of the community very carefully. There may be many firms moving into town, giving superficial evidence of a strong, healthy community. But how many firms have moved out in recent years and what kinds of firms were they? It may well be that the particular industry or the size of business in question is finding the municipality unhealthy for continued operations. This illustrates again the importance of detailed investigation before a move is made.

Site factors. Within the community, a specific site must be chosen. A frequent and major stumbling block at this point is zoning. This is a local governmental control. The uses permitted or excluded in commercial or industrial zones vary considerably from town to town, so particular care is required in checking on zoning. In one recent instance, a firm selling mill work was ready to sign a five-year lease on a very desirable store when the appraiser hired to evaluate the lease arrangement uncovered a very disquieting regulation. The store was in a commercial zone, and the sale of lumber and related products was permitted in commercial zones, except that such activity was specifically prohibited on Main Street in this particular town. Since the store in question was on Main Street, the firm was nearly stuck with a five-year lease on unusable property. Attention to the fine print avoided an embarrassing and costly error.

This case also points out the desirability of turning to trained professional specialists to obtain assistance in evaluating alternative sites. Professional appraisers, in particular, can save the accountant and his client time, effort, and possible grief. Those designated M.A.I. (Member, American Institute of Real Estate Appraisers), S.R.A. (Senior Member, Society of Residential Appraisers), or A.S.A. (Senior Member, American Society of Appraisers) have met the requirements of their respective associations in terms of experience, training, and demonstrated ability.

They can offer professional and impartial advice on many important aspects of plant location.

Physical characteristics. If the proposed use is permitted on the site or sites being considered, then their physical characteristics deserve consideration. Size and shape are important determinants of the future, as well as the present, usability of the site. The management of a metals firm that moved to a small town bought what they thought was plenty of land for a new plant, an expected subsequent addition, a parking lot, and landscaping. Three years later, when they wanted to expand, they were forced to move again. They neglected to plan for the additional parking space needed because more of their employees now drove to work. The old plant had been served by a bus line; the new one was not. This is not an isolated case. Some 10 to 12 per cent of firms newly located in the United States reportedly fail to provide adequately for expansion in the new site.

Other physical attributes such as topography, subsoil, and ground water should be studied. A professional engineer is usually called in to handle these investigations. His fee will be money well spent in avoiding serious losses. The owners of a small foundry recently discovered that piles had to be put down to keep their footings from buckling. A printing firm was forced into slab construction because the cellar hole filled from a subterranean spring. Many firms have utilized slab construction because they hit ledge just a few feet below the surface. Expensive correction of poor surface drainage or of flooding adds to the list of avoidable mistakes. In some instances, the firm might very well have gone ahead even with the knowledge of the physical site problems. But with this knowledge they would have been able to calculate probable costs and decide on the basis of all the facts.

Utility considerations. Utilities have already been mentioned as a community service. It bears repeating that it is not enough to ask at City Hall whether the town has sewer, water, and gas service. The exact location of lines to serve the particular site should be ascertained, along with the size of those lines, the plans for the future, and the rates. The cost of connecting is also important. One electric appliance manufacturer purchased a site only a few hundred feet from a municipal water main. When he found out the cost of a connection of the required size, and that he would have to bear the entire cost, he drilled two wells instead. His original calculations were upset because he did not check until after he had signed to buy the land.

Transportation facilities are still an important consideration, particularly for getting employees to and from work. Firms moving to suburban locations have discovered some very interesting facts about commutation. More workers drive their own cars as both they and the firm move to the suburbs. Yet a substantial number do not wish to drive to work. A major metals fabricating concern in an industrial city shelved plans to move to a suburban location when a commutation survey revealed that nearly 20 per cent of the employees walked to work and another 35 per cent depended on buses. Nearly 30 per cent did not even own a car!

Establishments with a large proportion of female employees have a special problem because experience shows that women do not drive to work to the extent that men do. Therefore textile firms, large office concerns, retail establishments, and assembly (rather than fabricating) plants must be either within easy walking distance of the population center from which they draw workers or on relatively inexpensive public transportation lines.

At the end of the list, there is the matter of cost of site. The price usually reflects the absence or presence of desirable features. The "bargain" often proves to have no facilities, poor transportation service, serious drainage problems, or some other major defect. If it did not, competition and demand would soon force up its price. There is the case of the brewery which located in a metropolitan city on a site that cost five times as much as an alternative lot in a "highly desirable" suburb. Detailed analysis by the firm's management and the consultants it hired revealed that substantial long-range economies would probably be realized in the central location. It is not only the immediate outlay that counts. Instead, the long-run advantages or disadvantages determine the effectiveness of the location choice.

Summary. The accountant, then, can be quite helpful to his small clients if he keeps the following considerations in mind:

Consult published references for check lists of factors to be considered in making a location decision. Two useful lists are those issued annually by *Industrial Development and Manufacturers Record* and *Factory Management* magazines. There are also excellent summaries in *Plant Location in Theory and Practice,* by Melvin L. Greenhut (University of North Carolina Press, 1956) and in *Plant Location,* by Leonard C. Yasseen.

Analyze the specific requirements of the individual firm very carefully, because each problem is a special case. The check lists can serve only as a starting point.

Consider the retention of specialists, particularly appraisers and engineers. The client may object to the cost, but professional advice may well prevent a serious error.

Emphasize to the client the importance of taking nothing for granted. The investigation must be so thorough and methodical that no detail is overlooked.

CHAPTER EIGHT

Operations Research

IF A FACTORY making a simple product requiring only two sequential production steps were to find that the same number of men and machines were concentrated at Step 1 and Step 2, but that Step 1 took only half as long as Step 2, so that there was a continual backlog of work at the second work station and total production for any given time period was only half that of production at the first work station, the problem would be pretty obvious and the solution fairly simple.

Double production capacity at Step 2.

No one would dream of dignifying such an obvious solution as an example of operations research at work. Yet in essence the answer to the problem is found by the same methods that are employed in operations research. Elaborate mathematical techniques were not required in the above example, because the answer is apparent to the mind of the observer. The mathematics of the solution take place in the subconscious, but it is there; mathematics forms the basis of the logical solution.

Increasing the Variables

Take the same situation, but alter the circumstances so they are far more complicated. For example, assume we now have a multistep production process in which many parallel processing lines are working on assemblies which eventually are joined on a final production line to make the finished product. In noting the flow of production, dozens of little bottlenecks of varying degrees of seriousness are found. Work Station B on line 1 can only produce two-thirds as many semifinished units as Work Station A which supplies it; Work Station F on line 3 has idle man and machine time at intervals throughout the day because production at Work Station E is limited. Finally Work Station G on the final assembly line has a backlog of units from Production Line 1 because lines 2 and 3 are not producing at the same volume as Production Line 1.

The same basic problem faced in the two-step production cycle found in the first example is also found in the second example except that the number of variables has increased tremendously. There are now two ways of solving the problem:

1. Arbitrarily increase man and machine capacity at every point where there is a backlog of work until the production system is roughly in balance.

2. Alternatively, a mathematical model of the entire production system could be constructed to determine what the desired total output of finished products should be. Then by controlling the variables (men and machines) at each work station in the entire production cycle an "optimum" situation in terms of labor and machine costs could be found.

The "management sciences" approach

The second solution is pure operations research, even though it merely represents a refinement and/or a formal statement of the solution reached by mental shortcut or trial and error in the original situation.

Mathematical models which allow the user to make precise adjustments of the variables which are within his control to arrive at an optimum solution—these are the essence of operations research.

Actually, this is the feature that distinguishes operations research from the services offered by many management consultants. The management consultant and the operations research specialist are attacking the same types of problems. The difference therefore is not one of approach, but one of technique. The operations research specialist usually has had a more scientific background, and he employs the theorems of science to attack business problems.

Besides his attribute of framing problems and arriving at their solution in quantitative terms, he also has the primary characteristics found in every good management consultant. These primary characteristics are objectivity and the refusal to take anything for granted. In his particular case, he is distinguished from many management consultants—sometimes to the advantage of the operations research specialist, sometimes to the advantage of the consultant. That is because many management problems do not lend themselves to mathematical solution. The operations research man is apt to force a problem into a mathematical mold whether or not it is appropriate.

For example, in the situation cited above where the production lines have varying production rates at sequential work stations, and consequent backlogs at points along the production lines, a management consultant might approach the solution by flowcharting all production lines, marking in the production rates per hour at each station, and then working out a balanced production cycle by trial and error. The operations research man, however, would probably arrive at a solution through the use of a mathematical model. Both would have employed models; a flow chart is a model of an existing situation just as much as the equation is. The difference is solely one of technique.

The potential of OR

The illustration used illustrates the approach and the methods of operations research rather than an actual example of it. Obviously, the problem has been oversimplified. It is a rare factory that has a set of machine tools that can be shifted easily from one work station to another, even though it might have a work force that could be re-assigned easily enough.

In a perfectly fluid situation, where the significant variables (in this case, men and tools) can be controlled, operations research techniques can be extremely powerful aids to management. The techniques do not consist simply of an exhaustive examination of alternatives. If they did, the majority of real problems would be almost impossible to attack, even with the aid of powerful computers. Rather, operations research devotes its efforts to the creation and use of analytical techniques which make exhaustive examination unnecessary.

Operations research has become increasingly important since the war (where it had its origins in a British-government sponsored program to make the most effective use of R.A.F. planes in defending the island against German bombing raids) because of the development of computers. Computers make possible for the first time the quick solutions of thousands of mathematical problems. None of the problems is complicated in itself; but it is necessary to solve each of an enormous series of similar problems in order to get the best possible answer. Operations research techniques, in other words, are no longer impracticable.

Linear programming

It cannot be emphasized too strongly that OR is not any one technique or group of techniques. It is an approach which has evolved many different techniques and which, hopefully, will in the future create more. The important thing for the consultant to understand is that the approach is useful in solving many business problems; he does not himself have to know the details of any given OR method, but he should understand the type of problem susceptible to OR so that he can call on the services of a specialist for his client whenever the situation falls in a category where the OR approach seems to promise the best results. With that qualification, let's see how one of the most commonly used OR techniques might be applied to a common business problem: finding the best way to distribute a product manufactured at several different factories to widely scattered sales outlets.

The scientific approach would require a consultant to take into account at least the following:

1. The standard of service it is desirable to render the various scattered sales outlets and, indirectly, the ultimate consumer
2. Production costs
3. Transportation costs
4. Inventory carry costs
5. Data handling costs

To simplify matters this example considers only the second and third of these. The pertinent data are shown in Exhibit 1 below. The problem is to determine (1) how much each plant should produce and (2) which sales outlets should be supplied from which factory in order to minimize the sum of production costs and transportation costs. This is a simple version of how this problem would appear in most business situations because it was intentionally made to be so. Nevertheless, the problem stated is not an easy one. If an attempt to solve the problem by merely using business judgment were made, quite a few conflicts would be encountered. In attempting to take advantage of the best

Exhibit 1

		TRANSPORTATION COSTS FROM PLANTS				
Warehouse	Market (10# Units)	1	2	3	4	5
A	50M	$.250	$.375	$.375	$.500	$.175
B	250	.175	.250	.325	.450	.140
C	75	.100	.225	.275	.425	.175
D	25	.140	.220	.225	.425	.190
E	30	.195	.190	.150	.400	.220
F	40	.325	.210	.175	.235	.315
G	50	.350	.190	.150	.210	.325
H	200	.290	.190	.220	.125	.240
I	60	.295	.175	.190	.110	.250
J	40	.220	.090	.210	.150	.215
K	20	.450	.200	.175	.175	.340
L	150	.175	.350	.275	.325	.175
M	70	.200	.350	.300	.325	.200
N	10	.225	.375	.325	.350	.225
	1,070M					
Productive capacity	1,300M	250M	300M	250M	300M	200M
Unit production cost (10# Units)		$10.80	$10.75	$10.65	$10.80	$10.75

freight rates it might be found that some of the factories' available capacity is not being utilized sufficiently to take advantage of a lower cost of production. When an attempt is made to take advantage of the full capacity of the lowest cost plant, it may be found that the freight costs will be maximized. Further, in an attempt to minimize allocation costs there is no specific knowledge of whether an optimum solution was actually achieved.

The mathematical solution

In a situation of this nature when the consultant is caught between Scylla and Charybdis, mathematical methods become valuable in selecting the best or optimum course of action.

Exhibit 2, page 387, shows the formula used in a solution to this problem. The development of this formula does not appear too formidable when it is broken down into its elements and the relationships of the various factors are explained in words normally used in everyday conversation. However, they are frightening to the nonmathematician when merely presented as a body of symbols. But, through the use of these formulas and with the aid of a large-scale computer, it is possible to solve these rather intricate formulas in less than five minutes, of which fewer than five seconds are required for the actual computing. The answer to the problem is shown in Exhibit 3, page 388.

This problem may be easily solved by arithmetic; however, when two or more alternatives are involved, the limitations increase and the amount of arithmetic required in order to work out all the possible combinations makes its use very impractical. In the most unsophisticated cases a graphic presentation may also be used to explain linear programming. However, a graphic presentation cannot be used beyond three dimensions because of a spatial relationship limitation. The optimum solution to this problem was secured through the use of one of the mathematical techniques known as linear programming. This is a method used to produce the best solution to a problem where the relationships fall into a straight line; that is, they are linear and the total cost varies directly with volume.

In the foregoing problem cost was assumed to vary directly with volume. It was a problem merely of selecting the best out of a number of courses of action. This relationship doesn't always hold true. In real life it would almost surely not be true even in this case. So linear programming doesn't solve all problems.

Other advantages of linear programming

Of particular significance in this problem is the fact that the linear programming solution provides two additional optimum programs, i.e., three solutions were obtained, each of which yields a minimum cost schedule. This information could be very useful to management since a particular one of the three solutions might be preferable on some basis

Exhibit 2

FORMAL MATHEMATICAL STATEMENT OF PROBLEM

Let

X_{ij} = no. of units of product manufactured in plant $i (i = 1,2....5)$ and shipped to market $j (j = 1,2....14)$

C_{ij} = unit cost of manufacturing product at plant i and shipping to market j

then

$C_{ij}X_{ij}$ = cost of manufacturing X_{ij} units of product at plant i and shipping this quantity to market j

so that the total manufacturing plus shipping cost to be minimized is given by

$$C = \sum_{i=1}^{5} \sum_{j=1}^{14} C_{ij}X_{ij}$$

Since the market requirements are limited and the plant capacities are likewise limited, it is necessary to include these restrictions in the solution. Thus, let

R_j = no. of units required by market $j (j = 1,2....14)$

and

A_i = no. of units capable of being produced at plant i $(i = 1,2....5)$ then the X_{ij} which minimize the above cost function must satisfy the following restrictions:

$$\sum_{i=1}^{5} X_{ij} = R_j \ (j = 1,2....14)$$

$$\sum_{j=1}^{14} X_{ij} \leq A_i \ (i = 1,2....5)$$

and finally since negative shipments are not meaningful here we must have that

$$X_{ij} \geq 0 \text{ for all } i \text{ and } j$$

For the benefit of those who may have forgotten the meaning of some of the mathematical symbols used above:

Σ is a *summation sign*, the limits of the summation indicated by the numbers written above and below the sign. Thus $\sum_{i=1}^{5} X_i$ denotes the sum X_1, X_2, X_3, X_4, X_5, the *index* ranging from 1 to 5.

Finally, the symbol $\leq$ indicates that the left hand side is smaller than or equal to the right hand side; the symbol $\geq$ that the left hand side is greater than or equal to the right hand side.

other than minimum cost. Perhaps some more or less intangible factors relating to the personalities of the plant managers, for example, might suggest the desirability of choosing one alternate best solution over the others.

An interesting and perhaps not self-evident fact is that one of the major benefits to be obtained from this approach is the determination of the best course of action to be followed when things go wrong—i.e., in a time of crisis. Some companies which have made investigations of what actually happened when a plant, part of a plant, or something else

Exhibit 3

OPTIMUM (MINIMUM COST) SOLUTION

WAREHOUSE	Require-ments	Plants 1	2	3	4	5
Alternative I:						
A	50,000					50,000
B	250,000	30,000	70,000			150,000
C	75,000	75,000				
D	25,000			25,000		
E	30,000			30,000		
F	40,000			40,000		
G	50,000			50,000		
H	200,000				200,000	
I	60,000				60,000	
J	40,000		40,000			
K	20,000			20,000		
L	150,000	145,000		5,000		
M	70,000			70,000		
N	10,000			10,000		
Plant capacities		250,000	300,000	250,000	300,000	200,000
Unused plant capacity		0	190,000	0	40,000	0
Alternative II:						
L		(70,000)		70,000		
M		70,000		(70,000)		
Alternative III:						
L		(10,000)		10,000		
N		10,000		(10,000)		

Total production cost = $11,503,000
Total transportation cost = 174,325
Total cost = $ 1,677,325

became inoperable have concluded quite definitely that they make their big mistakes—and their expensive ones, too—when the unexpected happened. The advantages of the combination of mathematical formulas and computer are that alternative methods can be ascertained rather quickly in an unemotional manner, with a high degree of assurance that the suggested solution is a good one in light of the new conditions.

In some cases different types of forms of mathematics are needed.

Statistical sampling

The use of statistics and probability theory are extremely important tools of decision making. In the illustration of how products were to be allocated among factories, certain figures were used for expected sales, productive capacity, transportation costs, etc. For purposes of the illustration they were considered to represent the future. We must confess that we are not certain whether they would or not. To admit uncertainty at the start unfortunately is of very little help, for the degree of certainty or uncertainty varies in different ways and in different degrees concerning these items.

Utilizing the figures for productive capacity as an example, a probability model is explained. The determination must be made of the likelihood of productive capacity reaching 1,300,000 units. Barring strikes and major catastrophes, one may feel fairly certain that this capacity could be reached; however, there is a chance that it would not. Through searching questioning utilizing historical data as well as future projections, a probable frequency of occurrence might have been developed.

Estimated Productive Capacity	Probable Frequency of Occurrence
1,450,000 — 1,600,000	1%
1,350,000 — 1,450,000	3
1,250,000 — 1,350,000	90
1,150,000 — 1,250,000	3
1,050,000 — 1,150,000	2
Less than 1,050,000	1
	100%

In most situations, however, hardly anyone would be willing to rate the ability to estimate total sales with anything like that degree of precision. This is particularly true in rating sales by individual areas. Because of the unwillingness to estimate total sales ability the following table may result.

Estimated Error	Probable Frequency of Occurrence
Over by + 30 to + 50%	5%
+ 10 to + 30%	10
− 10 to + 10%	50
− 30 to − 10%	25
− 50 to − 30%	10
	100%

These are probabilities related to our ideas of future events of a somewhat general type. Other probabilities can be developed which are more specific.

1. What is the probable traffic pattern over the George Washington Bridge throughout a day?
2. What is the probable number of customers desiring service in a bank during a Friday peak?
3. What is the probable number of mechanics' requests for tools at a tool crib during various periods of the day?
4. What is the chance that an item will be out of stock if a given minimum quantity of a particular item of inventory is carried?
5. What is the probable number of buses which will be out of service on a given day because of mechanical breakdowns, etc.?

The significance of probability data is this: It helps the businessman to take specific cognizance of the degree to which uncertainty exists and thus to plot alternative strategies or a single strategy taking these facts into consideration.

A businessman in the illustration previously cited would be quite likely to consider that a capacity of 1,300,000 units would be available in the next period since this will be true 94 times out of 100 and because in 97 times out of 100 available capacity would equal or exceed 90 per cent of 1,300,000—and could presumably, therefore, be brought up to 100 per cent either by depleting inventories or working overtime, etc. He would, therefore, in the absence of specific information to the contrary, be inclined to make his plans on the assumption that the capacity would be available.

Sales estimates are quite a different matter. In 35 per cent of the cases, sales would fall below expectations by from 10 to 50 per cent. Much less "certainty." This would probably lead the businessman to adopt a more cautious policy in producing and stocking items and also lead him to incur the expense of constantly revising his forward sales estimates. More cautious, yes; but how much more cautious? It would depend on the potential loss from overstocking, the potential loss of sales resulting from understocking, the increased or marginal costs of producing additional quantities on an accelerated or emergency basis, etc.

Once again, within the limits of our ability to obtain data, all this can be expressed mathematically and thus an optimum strategy can be developed taking cognizance of the probability that a given set of conditions will occur a given number of times. Statistics thus can help to cope with the risks of uncertainty.

There is one additional fact about statistics which might be mentioned before we leave this unsophisticated and definitely incomplete discussion of them. Many forms of statistics are fairly cold-blooded; they search for normal and abnormal patterns of behavior and often attempt to ascribe them to causes without, you might say, getting excited about it. Statistics is full of words like "random," "stratification," "confidence level," "standard deviation," etc. The way you use statistics may be very warm-blooded indeed, but basically the process itself is not.

Game theory

This last statement is in fairly sharp contrast with the next subject—game theory—which also involves mathematical statistics. It is a "theory" which states the quite obvious fact that in a situation in which two or more forces are competing for the same goal, the strategy employed by the opposing forces is itself of vital importance in selecting the best strategy to follow. This is just as true whether it be in a game of tennis or in war where each force directly opposes the other as it is when the opponents compete for some third party—such as the customer and his money. Game theory is at the base of the management game.

Theory applied intuitively

Business management has often applied a good deal of the game theory intuitively. It has taken certain facts and added its hunches about what competitors might do in the process of attempting to guess how they may decide a particular situation. If management had the game stated in a formula and had the necessary computing capacity available, it could actually compute what the best course of action would be if the competition were to take certain action (or actions within certain ranges). If management then also applied its estimate of the probability that its competitors would take certain actions, it could work out what would be the ultimate move which would most often be the most profitable in accordance with its concept of the situation. Likewise management could work out the probable consequences (both favorable and unfavorable) of taking another course of action. There would thus be available a valuable device to sharpen management planning and to reduce the uncertainty on business plans.

The theory of games is, as yet, used relatively infrequently—primarily because the mathematics of such complex situations cannot be satisfactorily handled. Undoubtedly, however, this difficulty will be overcome sometime so that one may expect this theory to play an increasingly important role in business life.

Other common techniques

The theory of games is only one of a number of theories or models which are being applied to practical business problems. Among the more well-known theories being put to work on practical problems which might be mentioned are:
1. Mathematical programming (which includes linear programming and transportation type models as special cases)
2. Queuing or waiting line analysis
3. Search theory (which is concerned with the development of a pattern of most profitable opportunities)
4. Automatic control theory, which includes the formal considerations related to the "feedback" principle
5. Information theory as it pertains to the gathering, processing, and disseminating of data
6. Failure theory as applied to problems involving preventive maintenance policies

Of course, in addition to the above specific types of models, one utilizes directly some very basic mathematical disciplines, such as :
1. Matrices (useful for input-output analyses)
2. Probability and statistics (as noted earlier)
3. Higher algebra (including the theory of equations)
4. Differential and integral calculus
5. Concepts taken directly from geometry

and many more, limited only by the nature of the problem and the ingenuity of those responsible for its formulation and solution.

Areas of application

The problems which are now being solved by the mathematical techniques of OR (for this is what for the most part has been discussed) are certainly not new problems. They have bedeviled the businessman for many years and he has rather successfully coped with them through the application of good judgment. He has produced sound, logical answers to these problems. However, with the assistance of these mathematical techniques, he can normally improve these answers. Generally, if the problem has been carefully studied and the best possible judgment answer supplied, that improvement is not great—often only 5 to 15 per cent, but at times it is less and at times substantially more. This additional improvement, however, can place a company in a far better competitive position and often means the difference between a moderately successful and a highly successful operation, for most of this 5 to 15 per cent is added straight to net profits (or at least to net profits before taxes).

At the present time not all of the potential uses for these OR techniques are known. However, a good many uses are known. Stressing once again that we are trying to find the best way to equate a number of interrelated factors, we can cite the following:

Inventory control:
Variations in lead period
Variations in item demand rate
Marginal cost of carrying stock
Marginal cost of "ordering" or producing lots of various sizes
Penalty for being out of stock
Exposure to obsolescence
(Inventories can include such things as repair parts, production materials, saleable items, airline hostesses, etc.)

Production scheduling and control:
Capacities of machines
Length of production cycle
Cost, etc., of carrying buffer stocks
Influence of lot size on production costs
Breakdown probabilities
Characteristics of demand for product
Cost of emergency production
(Scheduling and control apply not only to factories but also to such "nonfactory" activities as train movements, etc.)

Facility location—production allocation:
Standard of service
Production costs
Transportation costs
Inventory costs
Data handling costs
(The illustration previously discussed at some length is typical of these problems.)

Service facility (men—equipment):
Standard of service—cost of delay
Cost of facilities
(Service facilities include the men and equipment provided for such things as toll booths, teller cages, check-out counters, tool cribs, etc.)

Breakdown protection:
Probability—frequency of occurrence and duration

Standard of excellence
Cost of standby facilities
Cost of maintenance
   (Applies to such diverse areas as buses broken down, employees absent, machine tools out of service, etc.)

Effort allocation:
   As—Sales effort
   As—Product mix
   As—Quality control

This is obviously not intended to be a catalog—only an indication of types of areas in which the techniques can be used.

Simulation, the use of models as an aid to more precise decision making, is so obvious an aid to management that its comparatively recent emergence in business would be surprising, except for one factor. Although the mathematics of decision making is relatively simple, the number of computations that must be made in even a fairly uncomplicated business situation is so intolerable that many of the most valuable techniques could never have been used without the development of electronic computers, which can make hundreds of thousands of simple computations in a second.

Need for computers

What is the relationship between mathematical management—this term may be used to describe the general process of management assisted by mathematics—and high-speed data handling?

The grand concept of business is that business consists of a large number of complicated interrelationships capable of being expressed in terms of mathematical formulas. Business data processing under this concept consists of two parts: (1) the housekeeping part, i.e., paying employees, paying vendors, billing customers, collecting cash, etc., and (2) the data producing part, i.e., providing the information necessary for the decision-making control cycle. The second part of this job (the production of data for decision making and control) can be thought of as providing the raw material which these formulas need to work. One can easily visualize pouring into a computer a large amount of data about sales, costs, expenses, etc.—factual data taken from the company's records—plus a lot of additional data—about company plans, market conditions, price trends, competitor actions, general economics, and some factors for the probability that certain events will occur and certain actions will take place. Once within the computer, these data would be operated upon in accordance with the rules laid down by the mathematical formulas developed to represent reality. The result would provide a basis for reviewing the past, or taking action in the present, or planning for the future.

To do this in anything like its complete form would require, even in smaller companies, a fantastic amount of computing capacity. It has not been and, in all probability, never will be done in anything like its ultimate detail.

Nevertheless, as a concept, the grand concept is absolutely valid. Express the business relationships as mathematical formulas; feed in data about past or future facts and probabilities; calculate results and choose a course of action; determine actual results and recalculate course of action. So far, this concept has been applied only to a limited area of a business—to inventories, to sales effort allocation, to determining work force needs, etc.

How computers are used

Leaving aside the grand concept, then, how is a high-speed computer system used? It is used in four ways:

1. To solve the formulas when the time required for their solution by other means is excessive
2. To develop some of the data required to be put into the formulas in the first place
3. To routinize some lower-level decisions
4. To facilitate the process of control

The problem of allocating production to plants, warehouses, and customers, previously cited, produced a fairly awesome number of complex calculations even with the relatively few facts and relationships being considered. Quite obviously, in a real-life situation, the number of calculations could be extended tremendously by the addition of plants, customers, or other factors.

In an oil refinery, for example, 350 formulas with 500 unknowns are to be used to determine how the refinery should be scheduled to turn what quantity of what crudes into what quantity of what finished products to obtain the maximum dollar profit from the operations. This computation will take, it is estimated, a couple of hours on a very large, very fast computer. This, we hasten to add, is considered to be a relatively simple refinery with many of the more sophisticated time-consuming calculations intentionally omitted. Obviously, then, electronic machines can be useful in solving the formulas.

They can also be useful in producing or processing the data necessary for the formulas—by providing the following opportunities which might otherwise not be available:

1. To break down the data in a more detailed fashion than was previously economical
2. To produce the data more quickly and/or more frequently

3. To explore the data to determine the kinds of relationships which actually do exist

The availability of high-speed electronic equipment can make it possible to analyze data in a more detailed manner. It is obviously more practical to think of manipulating figures into more detailed patterns when the cost of doing so decreases. A more detailed analysis of transportation movements, or of the manner in which materials are used, or of the sources and causes of scrap, for example, can provide valuable data for the mathematical models.

That high-speed equipment can make data available more quickly and/or frequently can also be accepted as a general rule even though numerous exceptions can be cited.

Determining significant relationships

An example falling outside business will perhaps be more explicit concerning the final use. A scientist trying to find out how and why something works often conducts a large number of experiments. These experiments produce results to which a consultant will tag the term "data." To find out what this data means, the scientist will try to arrange them according to all sorts of different patterns to see what kinds and degrees of relationships exist. When the correlation is low or nonexistent, the scientist will probably be unimpressed, unless he is trying to eliminate factors. But when the correlation is high, the scientist will know he has found a significant factor. This process of developing important relationships is partly intuitive and partly mathematical. As the quantity of data increases, the proportion which is mathematical increases tremendously. That is why so much use is made of high-speed computational facilities in our scientific and research world.

The same situation exists with business data although, admittedly, we often do not think of it in this manner. It is true that the consultant can seek out relationships and degrees of correlation in much the same manner that the scientist does and that even though the answers may be less exact and as hard or harder to find, what he does find can provide an important competitive edge. In this respect, the high-speed computer holds an important potential. Important work has been and is being done, for example, to determine the value obtained from varying the amounts of sales effort—or from various amounts and types of advertising, just to cite two examples.

Simplifying operating decisions

Computers can make it eminently practical to routinize a large number of operating decisions.

It can easily be demonstrated that many business actions which are dignified by the use of the term "decisions" amount to very little more than the application of a set of carefully prescribed rules to individual business events. Checking to see (1) that a credit limit has not been exceeded, (2) that the time has come to follow up a delinquent debtor, (3) that the inventory on hand has fallen below the reorder point, are well known illustrations of this point.

Many of the rules that are applied are capable of expression in mathematical terms—dollars of credit, number of days' supply on hand, number of units, percentage of change from last or normal, etc. A computer, tackling the decision-making problem, could compare these mathematically stated rules with the facts of the case. It could, using its skill and facility, accept or reject the customer's order on the basis of its acceptability from a credit standpoint, decide which customers to follow up, decide when and how much to order, etc., or write out for human intervention the relatively small proportion of the situations in which really high-grade human judgment is needed.

A computer could, therefore, apply the rules of mathematical management in a virtually automatic manner to many lower-level operating decisions.

Computers likewise have a contribution to make to the process of control. Perhaps this contribution can be expressed most succinctly by expanding that well-known "catch phrase"—"if you can't measure it, you can't control it"—into—"If you can't measure and compare it, you can't control it."

The essence of control is comparison—comparison with past performance, or with a standard, or with a norm, or with a statistical deviation from a norm—to cite a few examples. Once again, this means that if the events can be stated in numerical terms, and if they can be measured, and if the standards of comparison can likewise be stated in numerical terms, a real opportunity exists to use computing equipment to make these comparisons, i.e., to exercise control.

Easing management's burden

This generally means two things which should be fairly obvious: (1) that the machine can pass over those items falling within acceptable limits, and (2) that the comparisons made can be somewhere between moderately and highly sophisticated in their nature. What may not be quite as obvious is that in the process one can also free a lot of the time of managers which is now spent by them in merely identifying problems and their causes for the more productive work of curing the problems and reducing the chance of their recurrence in the future.

However, to leave the impression that high-speed computing equipment is essential in even a majority of cases would be wrong. Very useful results can be obtained in a large proportion of the cases either without it or with only its occasional use. These results are useful because:

1. Valuable intuitive ideas will result merely from having some smart people look at a situation or a problem area.
2. Often the calculations are not so extensive that they cannot be made by less powerful equipment.
3. It is often practical to omit certain refinements, and thereby to simplify the calculations, without sacrificing too much of the value which could be obtained from the ultimate solution.
4. Many times it is feasible to solve the problem by the occasional use of high-speed equipment and to portray the results in tables, charts, or graphs which can be used in day-to-day operations.

Thus, to employ some terms already used, the correlation between mathematical management and high-speed electronic equipment varies all the way from unnecessary to nice to essential.

Limitations of OR

All of this is not, of course, quite as simple as it may possibly have been made to sound. Limitations on the usefulness of these methods do exist. A deliberate choice was made not to clutter up the consideration of the basic ideas with a lot of qualifications but instead to treat these limitations en masse.

Some of the limitations represent just as severe limitations on the application of intuitive judgment. These should be mentioned briefly because of the apparently unavoidable human characteristic of imputing a high degree of precision to almost everything which is expressed in mathematical terms—whether this is deserved or not.

The limitations are these:

1. The inability of people and machines to ferret out of the mass of business data which is available a precise statement of the relationships and interrelationships which exist. This problem, it might be added, is in no way helped by the fact that many of these relationships conflict in such a way as to obscure rather than to clarify real causes and effects.

2. The great difficulty of predicting with a high degree of accuracy the impact of some new event—military, economic or technological, or even a hit TV show—on a business or its competitor's position.

3. The absence of a great deal of important information about past actions and events—information which was not kept because it was considered of only transient significance. We can often tell, for example, what happened but not the conditions which existed nor the reason for the action, and not the consequences of taking the action or of not taking it. To choose a very simple, yet key bit of information, which is rarely available—how often were we out of stock and what were the consequences of this?

4. The basic absence of information about the past, present, and future acts of competitors and of the business world in general.

5. The fact that in many instances we are concerned with marginal or incremental values and costs—with the net marginal gain from stocking more or less inventory, with the net marginal gain from changing the staffing of a toolroom, with the net marginal gain from changing the maintenance policy, etc. This information is not normally available at present—or at least without many approximations and/or a great deal of digging. As a matter of fact, many thoughtful accountants believe that a new or at least drastically modified concept of accounting and record keeping may be necessary before this information does become readily available on a reliable and routine basis.

6. The difficulty in placing a concrete value on some of the intangibles —customer goodwill, good employee morale, community reputation, etc.— which form an important consideration in many business decisions.

7. The need to develop additional mathematical techniques which are capable of coping with some of the problems and relationships of business. A number of mathematical methods now in use, strange as it may seem, did not exist ten to twenty years ago but were created to fill the need. Still more are waiting to be developed.

8. The fact that computers themselves with all their power and abilities can be and often are physically and economically outstripped by the size and complexity of business problems and relationships.

This sounds like a fairly imposing set of limitations, and it is. But imposing as they are, they do not offset the present and potential power of OR as a valuable aid to management.

"How do we use these methods?"

One question which is often asked by business executives is "How do we organize to use these methods?" From the previously cited list of problems, you can undoubtedly recognize many problems which would be susceptible to solution by OR techniques. The question, therefore, of what to undertake seems to be the simple one. The problem of how to undertake it is not quite so easy.

First, a competent technician must be available. These people are not easy to find. The degree of success in OR technique will, however, depend upon the quality of the personnel employed in the effort. The operations researcher to be effective requires a rather broad knowledge of many different scientific techniques. He must know probability statistics, differential equations, calculus, etc., as well as many of the concepts which have been developed in the physical sciences. He must know when he cannot use a mathematical expression for a normal distribution or a Poisson distribution, when to use certain mathematical theorems, when to use linear programming, when to use game theory, as well as all of the other various tools which have become available.

Once a technician is employed, it is necessary to supplement his efforts with those of people who know and understand business operations. This may be contradictory to the statement of many of the well-known operations researchers, but it has been found that solutions to problems are obtained far more quickly and in a far more practical manner if the team studying the problem contains someone who is thoroughly acquainted with the operation under study. No benefit can be obtained from any technique unless a practical, usable solution is derived. Therefore, it is necessary to avoid a completely ivory tower approach, and put emphasis upon the practicability of results. On the other hand, one should not completely discourage a certain amount of research beyond the requirements of the immediate problem, for in the longer view one can expect a payoff for such freedom as a result of the basic stimulation which an OR man receives under such conditions.

No one can provide a nonmathematician with sufficient knowledge of the techniques in a short time to enable him to carry out the technical parts of the studies. The important thing for the nontechnician is to know that mathematical techniques are available for stating some of the complex relationships which exist in business today. It is important for the nontechnician also to know that with some study and effort he can generally check the logic expressed in these mathematical relationships so that he is able to provide the technician with the benefit of his knowledge of the intricacies of business relationships and to apply common sense checks to the results.

Business is just on the threshold in the development and use of these techniques. However, we have learned enough even at this point to know that, despite their limitations, they can be highly beneficial and often lead into relatively new concepts in the solutions to problems. We do not know enough about applications at the present time to fully define all types of problems which may be susceptible to solution through use of these methods. We do know that the area of applicability is very broad.

We do know that the methods and techniques of science can contribute to the art of business management.

Index

elements, 232
film and terms, 231-232
synthetic time formula, 232
Total Annual Variable Cost formula, 162-163, 175, 180
Total system, 287-290
Trade associations, 45-50
lines, 46-49
Trade statistics, 44-50
Transportation and transportation costs, 338-339, 385
TVC
See Total Annual Variable Cost

Underwriters, 118
Uniform Commercial Code, 113
Uniform Warehouse Receipts Act, 113

Unit time standards, 227-229, 230
United States Federal Trade Commission, 46

Wage incentive systems, 6
Warehouse management, 170-171
slot system, 171
Waste in office expenditures, 341, 365-373
Weaknesses
See Internal weaknesses
Work backlog
See Operations research
Work distribution charts, 216-217
Work flow and work flow charts, 216-217, 364
Work measurement, 235-236, 363-367
Work simplification, 361-364